INTERNATIONAL COURTS
AND TRIBUNALS SERIES

General Editors

RUTH MACKENZIE
CESARE P. R. ROMANO
MIKAEL RASK MADSEN

Subsidiarity, Legitimacy, and the European Court of Human Rights

INTERNATIONAL COURTS AND TRIBUNALS SERIES

A distinctive feature of modern international society is the increase in the number of international judicial bodies and dispute settlement and implementation control bodies; in their case-loads; and in the range and importance of the issues that they are called upon to address. These factors reflect a new stage in the delivery of international justice. The International Courts and Tribunals series has been established to encourage the publication of independent and scholarly works which address, in critical and analytical fashion, the legal and policy aspects of the functioning of international courts and tribunals, including their institutional, substantive, and procedural aspects.

Subsidiarity, Legitimacy, and the European Court of Human Rights

RETO WALTHER
Legal expert, Federal Administration, Bern, Switzerland

OXFORD
UNIVERSITY PRESS

OXFORD
UNIVERSITY PRESS

Great Clarendon Street, Oxford, OX2 6DP,
United Kingdom

Oxford University Press is a department of the University of Oxford. It furthers the University's objective of excellence in research, scholarship, and education by publishing worldwide. Oxford is a registered trade mark of Oxford University Press in the UK and in certain other countries.

Published in the United States of America by Oxford University Press
198 Madison Avenue, New York, NY 10016, United States of America.

British Library Cataloguing in Publication Data
Data available

Library of Congress Control Number is on file at the Library of Congress

ISBN 9780198921424

DOI: 10.1093/9780198921455.001.0001

Printed and bound by
CPI Group (UK) Ltd., Croydon, CR0 4YY

The manufacturer's authorized representative in the EU for product safety is Oxford University Press España S.A. of Parque Empresarial San Fernando de Henares, Avenida de Castilla, 2 – 28830 Madrid (www.oup.es/en or product.safety@oup.com). OUP España S.A. also acts as importer into Spain of products made by the manufacturer.

MIX
Paper | Supporting responsible forestry
FSC® C013604
FSC www.fsc.org

Series Editors' Preface

Protocol 15 to the European Convention on Human Rights and Fundamental Freedoms, which entered into force in August 2021, introduced express reference to the principle of subsidiarity into the Preamble of the Convention. As is well known, the Contracting Parties to the Convention adopted this amendment against a background of significant criticisms and controversy over the perceived 'activism' of the Court, its legitimacy, and its proper role vis-à-vis national authorities in the protection of the rights and freedoms defined in the Convention.

In essence, the amendment affirms the primary responsibility of the Contracting Parties to secure the rights and freedoms established in the Convention and its Protocols, subject to the supervisory jurisdiction of the European Court of Human Rights. In this sense, it clarifies the subsidiary role for the Court vis-à-vis domestic political authorities of the Contracting Parties: as the Explanatory Report to Protocol 15 (paragraph 9) explained, '[t]his reflects that the Convention system is subsidiary to the safeguarding of human rights at national level and that national authorities are in principle better placed than an international court to evaluate local needs and conditions'. While Contracting Parties have the obligation to secure the rights and freedoms set out in the Convention to those within their jurisdiction, and to provide an effective remedy before a national authority where those rights and freedoms are violated, the Court provides a safeguard for individuals whose rights and freedoms are not secured at the national level.

In this book, Reto Walther offers an in-depth examination of the role of subsidiarity in the system established in the European Convention on Human Rights and its Protocols. The book provides far more than an evaluation of subsidiarity in the practice and case law of the European Court of Human Rights. Instead, it develops a comprehensive, wide-ranging, and original analysis of the principle of subsidiarity in the context of the functioning of the Court, as a broad principle underpinning the democratic legitimacy of the entire system of human rights protection established under the Convention. The book traces in detail the wider development and rationale of the principle of subsidiarity and provides a theoretical justification for the principle, using this as lens through which to reflect upon what subsidiarity means for the Court's role in interpreting the Convention and in reviewing the acts and omissions of national authorities. At the same time, the book emphasizes the responsibilities that subsidiarity places upon States as the primary guardians of human rights within the European system.

Reto Walther's book is a timely and ambitious contribution to the academic literature on subsidiarity, on the role and functioning of the European Court of Human Rights, and more broadly on the interaction between supranational courts and domestic political authorities.

Preface

This book is about the principle of subsidiarity in the European Convention on Human Rights system. Although scholars have published a vast literature on the subsidiarity principle, among many other things, there are hardly any monographs on subsidiarity *per se*.

This study does not represent yet another attempt to conceptualize the margin of appreciation—which dozens of books, journal articles, chapters, and other contributions present as *the* doctrinal instrument of the European Court of Human Rights for implementing the principle of subsidiarity. This enterprise would be doomed to fail anyways: those who know the Strasbourg-based Court best know only too well that 'theorising' is neither a strength nor an aspiration of the Court, that the Court would 'rather avoid' the concept of legal doctrine *qua* set of case-law-deduced maxims that predictably apply to future cases, constituting a consistent whole, and, more specifically, that the notion of a margin-of-appreciation doctrine is itself doubtful.

The present work takes quite a different tack, seeing subsidiarity as a principle that underpins the entire Convention system and seeking to understand it, as well as its implications, through an investigation into its (recent) history, its *raison d'être*, and its theoretical justification. The study suggests that the Court's subsidiarity can actually explain and justify the relative lack of principled Strasbourg jurisprudence to a considerable degree. Simply put, the argument is that the subsidiarity principle takes its justification from its purpose of bringing democratic politics into the Convention system. Situated at the international level, that system would otherwise operate in a 'democratic vacuum'. On this account, the democratic legitimation of the largely judge-made Convention law occurs through the bottom-up convergence of the States' democratic human rights practices at the hands of the Court, and the more or less smooth domestic reception of the Court's corresponding jurisprudential practice: only a casuistic (ie flexible, varied, case-based) praxis allows for the continuous operation of this inter-institutional, dialogic development of the Convention law.

***

The Court's case law is available online at HUDOC, along with other documents of the Court referenced in this book: visit <https://echr.coe.int>. Documents from other bodies of the Council of Europe, namely the Committee of Ministers and the Parliamentary Assembly, are available online under <https://coe.int>.

Acknowledgements

I wrote this book on the basis of the research that I conducted for my PhD, which I obtained from the Faculty of Law at the University of Zurich in Spring 2022. I am especially grateful to Professor Helen Keller, who served as a judge at the European Court of Human Rights from 2011 to 2020, for her support. My work with her provided me with a deeper understanding of the system established under the European Convention on Human Rights than I could ever have achieved otherwise. I would also like to thank Professors Andreas Føllesdal and Geir Ulfstein for their support at the PluriCourts Centre at the University of Oslo, as well as Professor Armin von Bogdandy for his support and for his invitation to the Max Planck Institute for Comparative Public Law and International Law in Heidelberg. On my way to completing this book, I had the chance to meet countless other researchers—thank you all for your valuable feedback and our helpful discussions!

For his excellent help in polishing my non-native English in the early stages of my work on this book, I thank Chad Jorgenson, as well as the Faculty of Law at the University of Zurich for its financial support in this regard. In later stages, I received outstanding support from Oxford University Press. I am especially grateful to Robert Cavooris for his belief in my project, to Rizwaan Ahmad for seeing it through to the production stage, and to all those involved in the review, editorial, and production process for their insightful reviews, professional editorial assistance, and meticulous revisions.

I acknowledge the generous support I received from the Swiss National Science Foundation, which financed my research (2018–2021) and the open-access publication of this book (2025/26).

Reto Walther, January 2026

Contents

Cases of the European Court of Human Rights

Cases of the European Court of Human Rights and its predecessor institutions are cited in accordance with the Court's own rules, as set out in its 'Note explaining the mode of citation ofthe case-law of the Court and the Commission' and applied by the Registry in its 'Case-law references of judgments, advisory opinions and key case decisions'.

1

International Authority

Legitimacy Through Subsidiarity? The Case of the Strasbourg Court

A) Introduction

Since the turn of the millennium, international law has increasingly been shaken by unforeseen resistance. Many regional and global systems and organizations of international law have met unpredicted backlash. In some areas, such as global trade, critics of the economic globalization highlight issues related to inequalities, social injustice, and environmental degradation. In domains devoted to democracy, the rule of law, and human rights, the trust many of us have put in the global success of the liberal-democratic credo has seen a setback due to authoritarian regimes that challenge the liberal-democratic value system more and more openly. Cosmopolitan ideas, namely, in fields concerning various forms of migration, have experienced defiance in the form of renewed and heavier border protection. Voices critical of transnational power elites, expertocracy, and technocratic governance have become louder. As a result of all of this, international organizations have been dismantled, crippled, restrained, or left by its member states and compliance with once well-established rules and principles of international law has decreased. This development raises the question about the past, present, and future role of international law and organizations and, in particular, about their role in a world still dominated by national belonging and state-level politics.[1]

There are many and diverse examples of the described development, including, in random order:[2] the World Trade Organization has struggled with maintaining the functionality of its dispute settlement mechanism since the end of 2019 when its Appellate Body became inoperative due to a lack of members caused by the United States on the grounds of discontents about the Appellate Body's jurisprudence; the European Union lost a prominent member when the United Kingdom's withdrawal became effective in 2020; the Southern African Development Community dissolved its SADC Tribunal in 2012; between 2016 and 2019, the International Criminal Court saw withdrawals from two of its members, two further states

[1] Recently, eg Carmen Pavel, *Law Beyond the State* (OUP 2021).

[2] See also Karen J Alter and Mikael R Madsen (eds), *The International Adjudication of Mega-Politics* (2022) 84(4) LCP 1.

Subsidiarity, Legitimacy, and the European Court of Human Rights. Reto Walther, Oxford University Press.
 DOI: 10.1093/9780198921455.003.0001

threatened to do so, and the United States imposed sanctions on members of that court; Russia and China partnered to issue a Declaration on the Promotion of International Law (2016) in which they explain their preferred reading of international law, which assigns great value to state sovereignty, non-intervention, and immunity, but not to democracy, human rights, and (quasi-)judicial dispute resolution; Europe's migration policy has become increasingly discredited because of illegal, but politically tolerated pushbacks; Russia's war against Ukraine paralyses the UN Security Council as the world's major peacekeeper to an unparalleled degree; and the Council of Europe—Europe's prime guardian of democracy, the rule of law, and human rights—was for many years curbed in its activities with a budgetary policy of zero growth, its spending power decreased over many years, while its best-known institution, the Strasbourg-based European Court of Human Rights (the Court, ECtHR), has faced a backlash from its member states.

That Court, its members (the States) and, in particular, their relationship are the subject of this book. A common thread running through the developments just mentioned is the return of a certain nationalism[3] and, perhaps less worryingly, of attention to the state as the political forum where the individual still has the strongest feeling of belonging and the most of a say in communal affairs. As we will see in the course of this book, the state *qua* polity where democratic politics functions vastly better than at any *inter*-national level has important contributions to make to systems of international law committed to liberal democracy. In fact, both the national and the international level are important and valuable, which brings the difficult task of arranging their interaction to the fore.

The developments described above demonstrate the need, driven by a corresponding political desire, to rethink, and possibly recalibrate the relationship between international regimes, on the one hand, and the states as the still predominant political communities, on the other. In the system set up under the European Convention on Human Rights (the Convention, ECHR),[4] this sentiment most importantly and formally culminated in an amendment to the Preamble of the Convention. Article 1 of amending Protocol No 15 of 2013 (in force since August 2021) makes clear that the role of the Court is 'subsidiary' to that of the States.[5] Thus, in Europe's architecture for the protection of human rights, the States are intended to be the primary guardians of human rights, while the Court should merely provide support to them.

The principle of subsidiarity offers guidance when public authority must be allocated and exercised in multi-level governance systems, as we will see in the second

[3] See Karen J Alter and Mikael R Madsen, 'The International Adjudication of Mega-Politics' (2022) 84(4) LCP 1, 2.

[4] Convention for the Protection of Human Rights and Fundamental Freedoms, as amended, of 4 November 1950, in force since 3 September 1953, 213 UNTS 221, CETS No 005.

[5] Protocol No 15 amending the Convention for the Protection of Human Rights and Fundamental Freedoms of 24 June 2013, in force since 1 August 2021, CETS No 213.

chapter. At its core is a rebuttable preference for keeping authority at the primary ('lower') governance level in order to protect values related to autonomy and pluralism. The idea of structuring authority according to this rationale is far from new. In the Convention system, we can trace the subsidiarity principle back to at least 1968,[6] but it has a much older history in Europe's political thought. However, in recent years it gained new attention due to the recognition that the international juridification of many policy fields, which massively increased, has perhaps exceeded what is socially and politically acceptable to large swathes of people.

The principle of subsidiarity may offer normative guidance wherever and whenever there is a need to mediate between, or reconcile, demands for 'sovereignty' voiced by constituent units on the one hand and claims of 'supremacy' alleged by a central unit on the other. It appears in different forms in federal states, systems of *inter*national law, and in the arguably *supra*national European Union.[7] And even in systems where it does not explicitly appear, subsidiarity may be of help in explaining, understanding, and critiquing the multi-level governance order.

Seen from this broad perspective, the present book appears as a mere case study, but one that will be just as instructive for European Union and constitutional law specialists as for general international lawyers. To European human rights lawyers, by contrast, it offers more than a case study. It provides them fundamental insights into the theory and practice of the Convention system by transferring perennial debates of constitutional law to the Convention's *trans*national, quasi-constitutional human rights regime. Most importantly, its Chapter 9 shows that the Court enters into an interpretative dialogue with the national law-makers just like constitutional courts have been shown to do, while its Chapter 10 shows how restrictions of rights that proportionately pursue politically chosen public interests serve to bring about the implementation of separation-of-powers thinking in the domain of rights. It thus explains how the Court, when it shows appropriate deference and restraint in the course of its proportionality assessment, contributes to respect for a balanced allocation of authority between its States' (notably political) authorities and itself.

The principle of subsidiarity can govern different types of authority, as Chapter 2 shows. For example, EU subsidiarity structures legislative authority and in international criminal law the so-called principle of complementarity of the Rome Statute sequences jurisdictional competences. In the Convention system, the subsidiarity principle is mainly concerned with the Court's judicial and the States' political authority, as just suggested. Thus, this book's underlying and essentially *constitutional* theme is the democratic legitimacy of the Court's rights-based quasi-constitutional review of domestic-political choices.

[6] *Case 'relating to certain aspects of the laws on the use of languages in education in Belgium'* (merits), 23 July 1968, para 10 (p 31), Series A no 6.

[7] See Andreas Føllesdal, *Subsidiarity* (CUP 2025).

The provision of legitimacy is an important purpose of the subsidiarity principle in every multi-level system in which it appears. On the one hand, the principle of subsidiarity can ensure that public responsibility is allocated to the level that is most efficient and effective. On the other hand, the subsidiarity principle may secure local level governance and, hence, guarantee due respect for value pluralism and proximate political participation. Both reasons for leaving authority with the primary level or, exceptionally, for transmitting it to a central unit, may provide legitimacy and both reasons will receive their attention in this book, although the focus will be on the latter, more fundamental and interesting one.

Addressing the question about the Court's democratic legitimacy in a similar manner as constitutional scholars address the question of how democratically legitimate constitutional courts are may seem controversial. Of course, we cannot just apply standards of democratic legitimacy known from constitutional law to public international law. However, scholars broadly agree that the Convention system bears many similarities to supranational and even constitutional systems. The undeniable fact that the Court exercises major review powers vis-à-vis the States' political authorities and over their policy choices not only makes it a sort of constitutional court but also explains why the worries about the democratic legitimacy of constitutional review known from domestic constitutional courts apply in a comparable way to the Strasbourg Court. Thus, arguments about the democratic legitimacy of constitutional review known from domestic constitutional debates may well inform our analysis of the Court's democratic legitimacy, although we must not ignore the remaining differences between the Court's and national courts' rights-based review. The present book seeks to bypass this methodological trap by paying special attention to the particulars of the Convention system. For example, when we come back to the problem of how judicial review may challenge democratic politics in Chapter 4, we rehearse important arguments common to this debate in light of some of the Convention systems' institutional and procedural peculiarities. Similarly, in Chapter 6, we put the Court's expansive judicial law-making into the context of its position at the European level, which is distinct for the Court's lack of direct political counterparts.

B) The Strasbourg 'counter-majoritarian difficulty'

Europe's principal human rights system has not been excluded from the recent upsurge of criticism against international law and institutions. This cannot surprise, since the Strasbourg Court is intrusive by design, as it were:[8] it essentially functions like a *supra*national constitutional court when it admits applications by

[8] Alter and Madsen, 'International Adjudication of Mega-Politics' (n 3) 2.

individuals who allege violations of their human rights and renders binding judgments, which may oblige States that were found in breach of the Convention not only to pay damages but also to implement potentially far-reaching changes in their domestic laws and policies. Considering these—measured by standards of international law—extraordinary judicial powers, complaints about a lack of understanding of domestic procedures, national value choices, local sensitivities, and the like must be expected. All of this came together, for example, in the Court's *Hirst (no 2)* judgment on the British prisoner disenfranchisement policy: the United Kingdom felt that the Court disrespected the parliamentary decision-making procedure, ignored traditional value choices, and transgressed into a sensitive domain of internal affairs.[9]

International human rights law has indeed been the prime example of the verticalization of international law. Nowhere is the demise of absolute state sovereignty as palpable as in systems where international human rights courts command states to change their (presumably) democratically made laws at the request of single individual applicants. The need to strike the right balance between due respect for a state's self-government and justified international oversight, mentioned above in terms of national sovereignty and international supremacy, for which the subsidiarity principle is frequently called up, is therefore especially imperative in the context of international human rights courts.

Beware of hasty conclusions, however, since, in principle at least, constraining the States is precisely what the Court has been set up for. Some sixty years ago, European countries established the Court as a bulwark against totalitarianism. It was built to protect Europe's liberal democracies against their relapse into aggressive, fascist regimes. Important arguments *in favour* of the Court's powers of review follow: the Court may support the States' democratic processes by securing individual freedoms without which no democracy can function, and it can, in particular, protect individual liberties of members of (political) minorities and other vulnerable groups. To effectively carry out this mandate, Europe's international human rights court *has* to be powerful.

Historians of the Court leave no doubt that the Court, since it became operative and practically effective, has in fact exercised a tremendous influence on the domestic institutional arrangements of the States and, much more so, on their substantive laws and policies (see Chapters 3 and 6). Doing so, the Court has helped the States to develop into more just polities; to claim the opposite would appear untenable given the overall impact its case law has had in areas such as the war on terror[10], the growing inclusiveness of our societies,[11] or transitional justice in Central and Eastern Europe.[12]

[9] *Hirst v the United Kingdom (no 2)* [GC], no 74025/01, ECHR 2005-IX.
[10] See e.g. *El-Masri v the former Yugoslav Republic of Macedonia* [GC], 39630/09, ECHR 2012.
[11] See eg *Dudgeon v the United Kingdom*, 22 October 1981, Series A no 45.
[12] See eg *Marguš v Croatia* [GC], 4455/10, ECHR 2014 (extracts).

Having said that, this book starts from the well-founded assumption that opinions can and do reasonably diverge when it comes to many of the changes that the Court has contributed to realizing. Were it otherwise—if there was broad consensus about the substantive decisions that must be reached in the Court system—a study of the principle of subsidiarity *qua* procedural (institutional, organizational) principle for the allocation of decision-making authority would seem a rather futile exercise: the question 'who decides?' usually becomes controversial only when there is substantial disagreement. This book is thus not about the Court's substantive jurisprudence, but about the distribution of decision-making authority in the Convention system, between the Court and the States individually and collectively, when there is disagreement. In more precise terms, it is about the role that the Court does and should play within today's Convention system, given that it is *de lege lata,* by virtue of the Convention's Preamble, subsidiary to the States.

On the account we develop here, the Court system's subsidiary role is justified by the value of (political) equality and, by extension, the legitimacy flowing from the political democracy that genuinely exists only within the States. In short, we argue that the principle of subsidiarity in the Convention system serves to defuse the 'counter-majoritarian difficulty' that the Court's international review poses to the States' political democracies. As we will see throughout the book, while rights-based judicial review may protect democratic processes, it simultaneously challenges the democratic principle to a considerable degree.

That said, we should make two points to avoid misunderstandings. First, it bears emphasis that we are at most marginally concerned with another problem that has plagued the Convention system and that has also sometimes been addressed with reference to the subsidiarity principle: the Court's heavily overloaded docket which is due to repetitive and systemic human rights problems in only a handful of States. The systemic and repetitive human rights problems that threaten to suffocate the Court are due less to reasonable disagreements about rights than to the concerned States' insufficient institutional capacities and willingness to comply with well-established standards.

As we will see in the course of the book, the normative justification and implications of the Court's subsidiarity do not depend on its caseload—quite to the contrary: whereas in order to solve the Court's caseload problem, it might be thought that it should move away from its casuistic and flexible jurisprudential approach, so as to make it easier for the States to 'mechanically' implement the Convention law as specified by the Court, the problem that the principle of subsidiarity is intended to defuse requires precisely the jurisprudential approach pursued by the Court. That is, the Court's subsidiarity can not only explain, but also justify and defend, its casuistry and variable jurisprudential authority: only a flexible approach to adjudication can enable the Court to develop Convention law through such a collaborative dialogue with the States that guarantees the Convention law's democratic legitimacy. This insight is important, since it makes it possible to kill two birds with one stone, as it were, viz the Court's alleged weaknesses in terms of both democratic legitimacy *and* judicial methodology: the Court's flexible jurisprudential approach, often criticized for inconsistencies, is justified with arguments from democratic legitimacy, while the Court's democratic legitimacy benefits from (and can also be affirmed on the basis of) its flexible jurisprudential approach.

Note, though, that this book does not attempt to explain the Court's subsidiary role by way of induction, by construing a theory of the Court's proper role from its case law. This would be contrary to the fact that the Convention's subsidiarity principle has recently become important not due to the Court's having resort to it, but—originally at least—because the States forcefully invoked subsidiarity to claim a greater role for their political choices and to put the Court in its place (see Chapter 3). Thus, our discussion begins by understanding the States' *qua* treaty-law-makers' call for greater subsidiarity on the part of the Court, along with the justification for that call, and it ends by looking at the Court's practice through this prism. Since the States, when they enshrined the Court's subsidiary role in the Convention text, did not intend to completely overhaul the Convention system, but rather aimed for a nuanced rebalancing, the last part of the book (Chapters 9 and 10) will also serve as a sort of plausibility control of the previous argument.

The second point we should emphasize to avoid wrong expectations of this book is the following: given this book's focus on procedural and institutional questions resulting from persistent, reasonable disagreements about rights, it does not and could not seek to justify the Court system's role vis-à-vis the States by appealing to the substantive results Strasbourg produces. This claim aligns with the observation that the democratic believer will be constrained to accept democratic choices that she considers thoroughly unjust, because they were arrived at by means of a procedure that respects political equality, whereas the unflinching liberal rights theorist may be forced to oppose democratically legitimate choices in favour of what he considers the substantively just outcome. In short, inconsistencies between a theory about what ought to be done and a theory about how decisions ought to be made are unavoidable when there is reasonable disagreement about what ought to be done.[13] Not only is an all-encompassing political theory combining a procedural theory of authority with a substantive theory of rights and justice beyond the scope of what is possible here, but it is also not possible for us to discuss the many things—both positive and negative—that one might say about democracy in Europe, although this book relies heavily on arguments related to political equality and democracy;[14] the lack of attention paid to the democratic problems that plague many States is perhaps the major flaw of this book. However, for reasons of scope

[13] Richard Wollheim, 'A Paradox in the Theory of Democracy' in P Laslett and W Runciman (eds), *Philosophy, Politics and Society* (Blackwell 1964).

[14] Instead, see Rory O'Connell, *Law, Democracy and the European Court of Human Rights* (CUP 2020) ch 1.

and stringency, we must limit ourselves to the Court and its role vis-à-vis democratic decision-makers, with the result that we can make no more than a handful of remarks about how the Council of Europe's political actors could contribute to strengthening the Court in the legitimate exercise of its role, as specified by the principle of subsidiarity.

Adopting a limited approach to the procedural question concerning the Court's role in deciding rights issues is preferable to scattering around largely unexplained and under-theorized substantive claims about what constitutes a right and just decision throughout the book. To be clear, it is beyond doubt that persuasive arguments of the latter type—that is, theories about what ought to be done, about the rightness and justice of the Court's decisions about rights—have equal importance to, and are in no way rendered moot by, the approach adopted here. At the same time, voluntarist (democratic) concerns are just as important as non-voluntarist considerations: both are fundamental matters of justice. In other words, choosing to study the principle of subsidiarity means choosing to study a procedural principle of authority. Once this choice has been made, reasonable modesty then demands that arguments about substantive justice be left aside. This is also why the reader will not find here any explicit or detailed assessments of the Court's substantive jurisprudence. Even when we discuss the Court's interpretative and review practice in Chapters 9 and 10, our focus lies on judicial methodology and doctrine instead of the Court's substantive decisions.

C) Approach and framing of the study

Having said what this book is about, there are some important points about its approach and framing. As this book is concerned with Strasbourg's subsidiarity, ardent defenders of a strong Court—whatever this means precisely—will presumably take issue with at least part of our argument. However, to borrow a caveat from David Robertson, what may appear to some commentators as wrong, insufficiently nuanced, or reckless may, in some cases, amount to nothing more than a choice of emphasis in the exposition of normative arguments or of the Court's doctrine. These differences may, in turn, simply be the result of how the study is framed and, in certain instances at least, be compensated for elsewhere in the book.[15] That said, it is worth elucidating at the very outset the approach and framing of the book, in addition to explaining why it proposes what some will take as an excessively restrained approach to the role of the Court. We shall summarize our position in three points, albeit spelled out in some detail, so as also to explain the resulting methodological choices.

[15] David Robertson, *The Judge as Political Theorist* (Princeton University Press 2010) x.

a) Subsidiarity *qua* legal fact

A first, 'legal-historical' reason for our approach is straightforward, namely that this book takes as its starting point the call for a more subsidiary Court expressed in the Brighton Declaration, which resulted in the addition of an explicit reference to the Court's subsidiarity to the Convention Preamble that has entered into force per August 2021.[16] One ought to beware of dismissing this amendment as 'merely' preambular—in fact, it is nothing short of momentous. 'What better indication of the importance of the Convention's Preamble is there than its amendment with the addition of a paragraph in accordance with Protocol No. 15?', asks William Schabas rhetorically, only to respond that '[i]t is an exceedingly unusual development for the preamble of a treaty to be amended in this manner. That the Committee of Ministers deemed it useful and important to modify the Preamble attests to its significance'.[17]

For the very first time, the Convention was amended with the effect not of expanding the Court's powers, but of constraining them. Moreover, it is fair to say that the principle of subsidiarity has shaped the Convention system and the Court's jurisprudence like no other preambular provision, that is, anticipatorily and distinctively.[18] It is clear, therefore, that the concerns behind the (at times) vociferous calls for 'more subsidiarity' that led to this amendment deserve to be taken very seriously, as we will do in this book. By contrast, we will not mount the most forceful possible counterargument, which anyway would have little hope of convincing many of those calling for a more subsidiary Court. Thus, when we sometimes pay more attention to the challenges that the Court's review poses to political democracy than to the contribution that rights-based judicial review may make to democratic processes, this is due to the drafting history and telos behind the decision to enshrine the Court's merely subsidiary role in the Convention Preamble. If we want to understand the *legal* principle of the Court's subsidiary role, we must not put the focus on why the Convention system might do—and perhaps even fare better—without it, but on why it might be explicable and justifiable.

b) Political equality and democracy

A second, 'normative' reason for our approach is that some of the arguments cautioning against an overly strong Court *are* sound. One major worry underpinning the Convention amendment mentioned above concerns, if not the rebalancing,[19]

[16] Article 1 Protocol No 15.

[17] William A Schabas, *The European Convention on Human Rights* (OUP 2015) 54.

[18] Ed Bates, 'Activism and Self-Restraint: the Margin of Appreciation's Strasbourg Career... Its 'Coming of Age'?' (2016) 36(7–12) HRLJ 261, 272.

[19] Mikael R Madsen, 'Rebalancing European Human Rights: Has the Brighton Declaration Engendered a New Deal on Human Rights in Europe?' (2018) 9(2) JIDS 199.

then certainly the stabilizing[20] of the equilibrium between international-judicial and domestic-political decision-making. On our account, the argument against an overly strong Court derived from political equality is paramount. It holds that matters concerning all ought to be decided by all—that is, through a process equally open to all. The judicial process generally fares worse in this regard than democratic politics. This disbalance points to the problem that lies at the heart of this book: the tensions between the States' domestic democratic politics and the Court's international rights-based judicial review. These tensions are, of course, well known from domestic constitutional orders and have been the subject of intensive and extensive debates among, in particular, theoretically minded legal, political, and philosophical scholars whose works we draw on, crossing disciplinary boundaries not in the naive belief that this book can contribute to other fields, but in the hope of enriching legal discourse with insights from other disciplines. Given the Court system's constitutional role and significance, there is no reason not to take this issue seriously, mutatis mutandis, at the level of the Convention system as well. The fact that Convention scholarship has only infrequently looked at how the Court system poses a challenge to democratic politics does not distract from, but rather adds to, the value and justification of doing so.

It follows that our focus lies on the relationship between the Court and domestic-political authorities. By contrast, we are at best tangentially interested in the—no doubt important—relationship between the Court and domestic judiciaries, which judges and scholars have extensively discussed, both in relation to specific themes such as 'judicial dialogue' and more generally. This choice of focus cannot be emphasized strongly enough, since it may seem to run counter to the fact that the domestic courts are, in practice, always 'interposed' between the Court and the domestic legislative, executive, and administrative authorities, due to the obligation imposed on applicants to exhaust all domestic remedies before turning to Strasbourg.[21] However, this procedural reality does not belie the fact that the Court de facto often does either explicitly review political choices—which were merely applied to an individual case by the 'interposed' domestic courts, albeit with greater or lesser discretion—or, at a minimum, implicitly call into question domestic policies.

Moreover, freedoms, such as those protected in the Convention, instead of marking out apolitical and pre-legal private spheres, cannot but be the result of a system of legal rules, the product of society and its politico-legal arrangements.[22] The triadic nature and public dimension of rights, as well as the assumption of persistent reasonable disagreement about rights, suggests that rights fall into the 'circumstances of politics'—the domain where common decisions and concerted

[20] Angelika Nußberger, *The European Court of Human Rights* (OUP 2020) 95.
[21] Article 35(1) ECHR.
[22] Philip Pettit, *Republicanism* (OUP 1999) 66–67.

action are indispensable, even if there is no deep theoretical agreement about the nature of justice.[23] This is not to say that law and the courts play no important role. The point is merely that rights are also, and crucially, a subject of politics.

Notwithstanding the domestic judicial hierarchies operating upstream of the Court, the Court system cannot but impinge on democratic choices made within the States, as just explained. One must also not forget that the States' political bodies play central roles before the Court, in the implementation of its judgments, as well as in critiquing the Court system. Studying the relationship between the Convention system and the States' democratic politics is thus of sufficient importance to justify the choice to largely ignore the interposed domestic judiciaries.

This choice is unavoidable due to constraints of space and time, as well as a preference for deep, rather than broad, analysis. However, it also chimes with the argument ultimately developed here, namely that the Court is subsidiary, because its system for the protection of legal equality in rights cannot account as well for political equality as States' domestic orders can. In other words, the argument that only the States in which legal *and* political equality are in place are adequate primary sites for the democratically legitimate protection of human rights naturally entails a focus on the Court's role vis-à-vis the States' political authorities.

It should be noted here that we understand 'democratic' in its primary, standard sense. In this understanding, 'democratic' refers to institutions and institutionalized decision-making that follow the principles of public deliberation, competition, and majority rule, institutions that are generally held to be of great value.[24] That is, we do not understand a 'democratic' system to be one that complies with certain substantive, key values, which would allow for the argument that, due to its adherence to these values, a system is justifiable even if the individuals subject to it have little or no control over the system in the standard sense of democracy—the political egalitarianism of the identity of the rulers and the ruled is central to democracy, after all.[25] So when we speak of democratic institutions, on the one hand, and the Court, on the other, we do not mean to suggest that the Court system is undemocratic in this latter, more substantive, sense of democracy. Given the understanding of democracy adopted here, we do not argue for the actual democratization of the Court system or suggest that subsidiarity demands this. Instead, we argue that the equal moral status of all individuals requires equal legal rights, but also political equality, that is, democracy, which, while not requiring the democratization of the Court system, demands adequate institutional interaction between (domestic) democratic political and (European) judicial institutions within the Convention system.

[23] Richard Bellamy, *Political Constitutionalism* (CUP 2007) 20–26.

[24] See Andreas Føllesdal, 'Constitutionalization, Not Democratization: How to Assess the Legitimacy of International Courts' in N Grossman and others (eds), *Legitimacy and International Courts* (CUP 2018) 318–325, 335.

[25] Vividly, Michael Walzer, *Spheres of Justice* (Basic Books 1983) xii–xiii.

c) Viability and effectiveness

The third reason for the approach adopted here provides a link between the first two. Precisely because there are undeniably strong arguments for a subsidiary Court, mounting a defence of a highly activist Court that does not take seriously the strong arguments against such a court model would not convince those individuals—and they are numerous—who are neither against human rights per se nor opposed to their European-level judicial protection as matter of principle, but who simply consider it important to anchor Strasbourg's human rights practice in the States' democratic polities. The third, 'prudential' reason for the present approach, then, is the following: if one reasonably believes that the Court's protection of human rights can only be successful to the extent that it is widely and firmly backed by political will—which predominantly forms within the States—the long-term success of the Convention system depends on its being backed by domestic politics. Thus, if there is robust political backing *only* for a subsidiary Court—and how this ought to be understood properly is the main theme of this book—then subsidiary the Court should be.[26]

However, the argument put forward in what follows is not merely pragmatic, in this sense, but, for the most part, actually even normative, since it develops a conception of the Convention's subsidiarity principle that is, arguably, normatively justifiable. This is not to claim that no other, better, or more morally appealing theories about the Court's role could be conceived—at least, if it were not for the principle of subsidiarity *qua* legally binding principle of Convention law and the political sentiments that underpin this international law-making decision. The argument that subsidiarity in the Convention system is concerned with, and that it has been emphasized due to the perceived need to strengthen, the Convention system's democratic legitimacy is thus not to be confused with an argument about enhancing the Convention system's legitimacy more broadly conceived. In this sense, the politico-legal 'is' informs the 'ought' elaborated here. It is in this spirit that the proposed understanding of the Court's (subsidiary) role is formulated, in light of concerns about the Convention system's viability, rather on the realistic, non-ideal side of the spectrum of possible theories.[27]

The commonplace that less is sometimes more deserves to be emphasized, not least in order to (hopefully) appease all those fervent human rights lawyers who are highly sceptical of the idea of a markedly subsidiary Court system. In short, we argue in this book that neither legally protected liberal moral rights nor democratic voluntarist politics is more fundamental than the other—a claim that rests on both the belief that, in order for the Convention system to be viable and effective in the

[26] See Allen Buchanan, *The Heart of Human Rights* (OUP 2013) 112.

[27] Similarly, Roni Mann, 'Non-Ideal Theory of Constitutional Adjudication' (2018) 7(1) GlobCon 14, 21, 24.

long run, it needs widespread political support and the normative proposition that those who call for a subsidiary Court have a point, insofar as the principle of political equality requires the Court's subsidiarity properly understood.[28] In this sense, this book offers an argument *for* Convention subsidiarity. This means that it spills a good deal more ink discussing why and how the Court system's subsidiarity is justifiable than justifying the Convention system as such. The focus of this book is not on the question why the Court must be powerful, but on the question why it must not be *too* powerful as the States have recently insisted. It further follows that we are not concerned with developing an ideal Court system, but with the question of why the actual Convention system's subsidiarity, as envisaged in the Convention Preamble since its amendment by Protocol No 15, is justified and contributes to legitimizing that system, and how this can explain some of its important, though controversial, features. The conception of the Convention's subsidiarity principle we will ultimately develop thus claims to 'fit and justify' the Court system as stipulated by the treaty-law-makers in broad lines, that is, with some critical potential.

Those who oppose the Court's subsidiarity, including those who 'embrace' it by reconceiving it as, above all, 'positive' (ie enabling or empowering) subsidiarity, will perhaps read this book as critical of the Court system. While it may present a critique, it is not intended to be a criticism, in the sense of an attempt to undermine or weaken the Convention system. The final Chapters 9 and 10 suggest that the Court system, as it operates today, is justified on the treaty-law-based account offered there. In this sense, our account of the Convention's subsidiarity principle is in agreement with former Vice-President of the Court Angelika Nußberger's observation that the recent addition of the principle of subsidiarity to the Convention Preamble 'is in no way revolutionary, but rather confirms the Court's generally well-entrenched approach'[29]—although one may have to further specify this approach, as Ed Bates does, as representing a more explicit and contemporary version of it.[30]

Some will reject this account of the Court system as overly restrained, on the grounds that it heavily qualifies the idea of the Court's supranational judicial supremacy. In response, we could simply call our account 'sober'. When studying subsidiarity in the Convention system as human rights lawyers, there is a risk of complacency. Tackling this danger requires ruling out any simple rejection of the principle of subsidiarity, because this would neglect the concerns that led to the insertion of this principle into the Convention Preamble in the first place. The arguments underpinning these concerns merit serious consideration, however; after all, they prevailed, prompting the first-ever amendment to the Convention to curtail the Court, at least on a formal and symbolic level.

[28] See Chapter 8.
[29] Nußberger (n 20) 95.
[30] Bates, 'Activism' (n 18) 274.

Those on the other side of the debate, by contrast, may take issue with our account of the Court, claiming that it is specious, because it would still effectively give the Court too much of a say. In response to this objection, we could answer that we account for a Court that is 'non-void': when reflecting on the Convention's principle of subsidiarity—given the risk of pushing back too strongly against the Court based on concerns supporting its subsidiary role—it is important not to lose sight of the purpose of the Court system, which has always been to yield effective authority, that is, authority that actually makes a difference.[31]

Interestingly, both sides of the debate by and large assume that the Court exercises a form of supranational judicial supremacy, albeit for different reasons—either as model and ideal to defend or as foil and target of criticism. Although our discussion, too, proceeds based on this assumption, in the end, we will in effect argue against the Court's supranational judicial supremacy, on the grounds that it is descriptively inaccurate, normatively unjustified and, on the whole, an insincere and disadvantageous claim: it promises too much, offers too easy a target for critics with hostile intentions, and makes it possible to abuse the Court system as a 'bogeyman' for unpopular decisions. It is not only normatively better justified, but also descriptively more accurate to describe the Court's oversight as a combination of legally weak-form, but practically strong-form rights-based judicial review, or so we will argue. To speak plainly, I sincerely believe that the strongest, most convincing defence of the Court system lies not in an aspirational, utopian vision, but in a sober argument pointing out that Strasbourg *is* subsidiary in law and practice, and that it therefore conforms in a democratically legitimate manner to the mandate given to it.

Hence, it would be wrong to understand this book as being directed against the Court system. Rather, it is intended as a nuanced defence of a conception of this system that not only conforms to Convention law and practice, but that is also politically viable and normatively justifiable. By contrast, this book is critical both of extremely ambitious visions for the Court and of surreptitious attempts to dismantle the existing Court system. We aim to offer a defence of a *robust* theory of the Convention system, one that stands between those fragile visions for the Court that appear either overly ambitious, to the extent of becoming unviable due to weak democratic legitimacy and lack of political support, or excessively critical, to the extent of undermining the Court system's legitimacy based on normatively appalling arguments and/or factually inaccurate grounds.

To highlight one further—and essentially methodological—point, the perspective offered here fills a gap. European human rights scholarship provides far more defences of the Convention system against arguments for its subsidiarity than

[31] *Marckx v Belgium*, 13 June 1979, para 31, Series A no 31; *Airey v Ireland*, 9 October 1979, para 24, Series A no 32; *Artico v Italy*, 13 May 1980, para 33, Series A no 37.

attempts to develop a charitable, defensible account of the—admittedly, sometimes misleading and overly hostile—calls for its subsidiarity. The imbalance between, on the one hand, a wealth of scholarship that argues for a rather activist Court and/or whose doctrinal analyses of the Court's jurisprudence leave the Court's legitimate role either untouched or beyond question and, on the other hand, a relative paucity of scholarship that squarely faces the Court's democratically legitimate role also explains and justifies the approach taken here. Even scholars who extensively discuss the Court's influence on domestic democracy never pose the question about the Court's legitimacy to do so.[32] Once again, this consideration relates to the idea that less is sometimes more: arguably less academic adoration of the Court would, in some cases, give a more impartial and credible impression,[33] and could therefore be more effective at convincing sceptics of the Court's value than ongoing scholarly veneration.

The account of the Convention system offered and defended here suggests that the Court is actually much more 'politically bounded'[34] than its most fervent adherents would admit or like it to be. However, this is as good a thing when it comes to its democratic legitimacy, as it is a—to an extent worrying—reminder that one should not rely on the Court as a judicial institution and the Convention law, while forgetting that, at the end of the day, freedom and equality are fought for, rights defended, and the Strasbourg institutions maintained by convincing one's fellow citizens of all of their benefits by *political* argument. 'Strasbourg' has not, cannot, and will not bear the majority of the work of preserving Europe as a relative island of democracy, rights and, the rule of law. Politics must do the job instead.[35]

This leads us to a final consideration. The recent backsliding of certain States in terms of liberalism and democracy was—perhaps due to a widespread and overly naive belief in a teleological narrative of progress—not foreseen.[36] Just as the Convention's subsidiarity principle per se is little concerned with the Court's case overload, so too is it, *qua* principle for the allocation of responsibility within the Convention system, poorly prepared to deal with States whose domestic constitutional orders are fundamentally at odds with the foundational values proclaimed in the Convention and the Statute of the Council of Europe.[37] Protocol No 15's

[32] See eg O'Connell (n 14) 280.

[33] See Shai Dothan, 'Judicial Deference Allows European Consensus to Emerge' (2018) 18(2) Chi J Intl L 393, 396.

[34] Tom Ginsburg, 'Bounded Discretion in International Judicial Lawmaking' (2004) 45(3) Va J Intl L 631, 668.

[35] See Tom G Daly, *The Alchemists* (CUP 2017) 293.

[36] Armen Harutyunyan, 'The Future of the European Court of Human Rights in the Era of Radical Democracy' (2021) 2(1) ECHR L Rev 20, 20.

[37] Statute of the Council of Europe of 5 May 1949, in force since 3 August 1949, 87 UNTS 103, CETS No 001.

emphasis on the principle of subsidiarity was not the result of an awareness that it produces a gap ('variable geometry'[38]) between States that fulfil their obligations as primary defenders of human rights—while reasonably disagreeing on certain questions concerning the development of the Convention law—and States whose domestic institutions make them neither willing nor able to do so. This is not to say that a theory of subsidiarity in the Convention system has nothing to say about the question of the Court's role in cases of deficient domestic decision-making. Yet, it certainly cannot offer a silver bullet: it does not suggest that, much less so how, the Court could prevent trends of liberal-democratic backsliding. Rather, as is evident from the historical process of establishing its predecessor institutions, the Court was conceived as, and can reasonably be relied on to be,[39] not much more than the sounder of the 'alarm'.[40] The backsliding seen in some States is, in the first instance, a political problem to be dealt with by political institutions. Thus, given that the subsidiarity principle is concerned with the interaction between political and international-legal institutions, it emphasizes the primarity of the States' collective political responsibility in this context over the Court's important, but modest role in sounding the 'alarm'. The same goes for the not entirely unrelated problems emerging from situations of war between the States. These conflicts, too, must ultimately be politically settled.[41] The Court system is scarcely prepared to deal with this type of issue: it was not set up to handle mass claims processes resulting from the collapse of a State's rule-of-law institutions with the effect that no domestic remedies are available.[42] Thus, a study of subsidiarity in the Convention system such as this one must, in relation to the Court, focus on identifying the mechanisms it can employ to sound the alarm and, in relation to the States, highlight their collective responsibility to come to the defence of the system's foundational values. By contrast, it cannot come up with solutions enabling the Court to bridge the gap between functioning and dysfunctional domestic rule-of-law systems. The latter constitute an unforeseen anomaly[43] that requires political answers and perhaps even institutional changes,[44] which the Court can, at best, elicit, but not directly bring about.

[38] Başak Çali, 'Coping with Crisis: Whither the Variable Geometry in the Jurisprudence of the European Court of Human Rights' (2018) 35(2) Wis Intl L J 237.

[39] Daly (n 35) 293.

[40] Ed Bates, *The Evolution of the European Convention on Human Rights* (OUP 2010) *passim*.

[41] See *Greece v the United Kingdom*, no 299/57, Commission report of 8 July 1959, p 22; Philip Leach, 'On Inter-State Litigation and Armed Conflict Cases in Strasbourg' (2021) 2(1) ECHR L Rev 27, 37.

[42] See *France, Norway, Denmark, Sweden, Netherlands v Turkey*, nos 9940/82 and others, Commission decision of 6 December 1983, Decisions and Reports 35, p 143; Leach (n 41) 39.

[43] Harutyunyan (n 36) 25.

[44] cf Parliamentary Assembly, 'Resolution "Complementary Joint Procedure Between the Committee of Ministers and the Parliamentary Assembly in Response to a Serious Violation by a Member State of Its Statutory Obligations"' (29 January 2020, 6th Sitting, Res 2319 (2020)).

D) Outline

a) Subsidiarity: its meaning and implications in the Convention system

The question addressed in this book is that of the meaning and implications of the Convention's principle of subsidiarity, and, in particular, of the Court's subsidiary role (see, especially, Chapter 8). Importantly, the principle of subsidiarity is understood here as a broad principle, underpinning the entire Convention system *qua* system for the democratically legitimate protection of equal legal human rights, as proclaimed in the 4th recital of the Convention Preamble, and applying to all stages of an application to the Court. What is being sought is a conception of subsidiarity that corresponds to the *ratio legis* behind the Convention Preamble and can explain the Court's procedural subsidiarity, as expressed in its admissibility rules, its subsidiarity in deciding questions of facts and law, as manifested, among other things, by doctrines of deference and restraint, and its subsidiarity in the implementation of its judgments under the primary and ultimate control of the Committee of Ministers. Conversely, if it is to be useful, a conception of the Convention's subsidiarity principle should also inform the question of what responsibility the States, individually as well as collectively, must bear in order to ensure that the Court can fulfil its role, as specified by the subsidiarity principle, within a Convention system that is democratically legitimate on the whole. That said, the focus of the present work is on, in descending order: what animates and justifies the principle of subsidiarity in the Convention system, what subsidiarity implies for the Court's judicial role, especially as regards its interpretative and review practice, and what the States individually and collectively *qua* political authorities ought to do in order to enable the Court to play its role as well as possible in the Convention system *qua* system for the democratically legitimate protection of human rights. This last point will be treated in a rather succinct, fragmented, and exemplary manner: a central consequence of the States' 'primarity' is, after all, that they enjoy discretion in fulfilling their Convention obligations, such that, given their diverse domestic systems, traditions, and cultures, there cannot be a single right answer. To be clear, this book, in dealing with subsidiarity as a principle of Convention law, operates at the level of Convention law and does not look into the States' domestic orders in any detail.

b) Subsidiarity: the Court's most important practices

In the first sections of this chapter, we have said quite a bit about the political (Protocol No 15) and theoretical (democratic legitimacy) background of the subsidiary role that the Convention allocates to the Court. We have also noted that the recent emphasis put on the subsidiarity principle by the States *qua* masters of the treaty is not revolutionary, but rather corresponds to the Court's long-standing jurisprudence. However, we have not yet said much about this judicial practice itself. The following paragraphs make up for that, at least partly. They give a very brief account of the most important practices of the Court—namely its interpretative and review practices—and explain in a cursory manner how they validate the plausibility of our argument about the Court's subsidiary role.

In this context, we should recall that this book does not intend to start from the Court's practice to inductively develop a theory of the Court's subsidiary role. It is not primarily aimed at explaining and justifying the Court's practice as the Court might prefer to understand it, but at developing a normatively justified account of the Court's subsidiary role as foreseen by the Convention's treaty-makers. Pithily put, the Court should follow the law, not the treaty-law-makers codify what the Court does. This means that, when Chapters 9 and 10 discuss the Court's practice against the background of the book's previous chapters, this is rather a plausibility control than the final step in an attempt to develop a theory of the Court's subsidiary role that perfectly matches the Court's practice. As we noted above, the conception of the Convention's subsidiarity principle we will ultimately develop aims to 'fit and justify' the Court's role as envisaged by the treaty-law-makers, with some critical potential.

So let us say a couple of words about how the Court interprets the Convention and how this relates to its subsidiary role. The distinctive elements of the Court's interpretative practice are its 'casuistry' (ie its highly case-based, hence difficult to predict and sometimes little principled jurisprudence) and abdication of a strict principle of precedence, its abstention from claiming *erga omnes inter partes* effect, supremacy or direct effect for the Convention law, and its flexible European consensus doctrine (ie its practice of, as a rule, developing the Convention law at the earliest when similar developments occurred with a certain degree of robustness at the domestic level). While these doctrines give the Court great flexibility as to how it develops and reads the Convention rights when deciding a certain case before it, even so the Court generally tends to procrastinate on taking a robust stance on contentious interpretative questions: it tends to follow a strategy of interpretative incrementalism. Thus, apart from the distinct interpretative practices mentioned first, the Court also uses methods known from domestic constitutional courts to develop the Convention law only gradually, step by step, and when the time is ripe, namely variations of the *Ashwander* principles, different variants of judicial minimalism, and the firing of judicial 'warning shots' directed at the law-makers.

To be sure, the Court's wayward interpretative practice raises methodological concerns and has—understandably—attracted doctrinal criticism. However, generally and *pace* methodological critics, we can explain why, and justify that, the Court has adhered to this interpretative modus operandi. In short, for the Court, these practices are indispensable means to heed its proper role in the Convention system. As we will see in the following—early—chapters of the book, the subsidiarity principle has become important in the Convention system because the States have, after a long period marked by the ever-increasing judicialization of the Convention system, called for a greater say for themselves about how the Convention develops. Indeed, unless one took the rather extreme *qua* undemocratic position that the internationally situated Court is mandated to develop the Convention law without rooting these developments in the States' democratic polities at all, the Court must interpret the Convention bottom up, in dialogue with the States. This requires that it leaves some room for each State to develop its view on the meaning of a Convention right about which contentious interpretative questions persist. In sum, the Court's interpretative practices allow it to support the States in the task of achieving convergence with respect to a shared understanding of the Convention guarantees that the Court can then reimpose on the States in a democratically legitimate way. As we will see, this is an important mechanism to implement the principle of the Court's subsidiary role and, along with it, to bring democratic legitimacy from the State level into the Court system.

Let us turn to the Court's review practice, where the Court's normatively flexible interpretation of the Convention rights also becomes apparent: after all, the Court's adjudication on questions of Convention compliance by means of proportionality reasoning is possible only insofar as the prior interpretation of the Convention rights leaves room for the case-based weighing of competing interests. As, generally speaking, each of the judgments that the Court so generates feeds back into the interpretative specification of the Convention law, the Court's interpretation and application of the Convention law are often hardly separable.

Therefore, the explanation of, and justification for, the Court's interpretative practice that we have just given elucidates also the Court's review practice. Important and, seen from a comparative legal perspective, relatively distinctive elements of it are that the Court applies a very lenient control to the legitimacy of the public aim in the pursuit of which a State limits Convention rights, its usual abstinence from conducting a least-restrictive-means test, and the principle that it requires strong reasons to substitute its view for that of the domestic authorities if the latter duly assessed and carefully weighed all competing interests of a case.

As regards a democratic polity's public interests, this choice ultimately concerns the purposes of that community and is, therefore, an inherently political question falling within the scope of the polity's political institutions, unless an allegedly legitimate aim falls manifestly outside of those broad interests that the States *qua demoi*-cratic makers of the international Convention law laid down as legitimate grounds for rights restrictions. The Court's usual abstention from conducting a least-restrictive-means test relates to this. Were the Court to apply a strict least-restrictive-means test, it would intrude far into the domain of a State's policy choice: it would, on the basis of its own interpretation of the State's public interest, quite specifically determine the means that the State must adopt in order to pursue that end, namely *the* least restrictive but still sufficiently effective means. Finally, if a democratically determined legitimate aim is pursued with what can—due to a reliable domestic assessment—be assumed to be the least restrictive means, there remain few grounds to justify the Court's second-guessing of a careful domestic balancing exercise, given the imponderability of proportionality balancing. It is thus important that the Court requires strong reasons to substitute its view for that of the domestic authorities if the latter duly assessed and carefully weighed all competing interests of a case.

Clearly, for the Court to heed its subsidiary role, it does not suffice to interpret the Convention rights with some normative flexibility. It must, as a rule, leave the resulting decisional leeway to the domestic authorities, lest its normatively flexible interpretation of the Convention rights in dialogue with the States remains a mere fig leaf. Just like the Court's casuistic and incremental interpretation of the Convention law, its (conditionally) deferential and restrained review is crucial to implement its subsidiarity and, concomitantly, to carry the States' democratic legitimacy over to the Convention system. We will thus see in the course of the book that important, though neither uncontroversial nor consistently applied practices of the Court correspond to the subsidiary role that the democratic principle demands and the Convention Preamble indeed assigns to it.

c) Chapter-by-chapter overview

This book deals with the Convention's principle of subsidiarity *qua* legally binding notion of Convention law. It would not make sense, therefore, to start from the Court's jurisprudence, that is, from what the Court does. Rather, we must start our study with an enquiry into the notion of the subsidiarity principle so as to begin with developing an understanding of what the Convention law-makers meant to say when they enshrined the principle of the Court's subsidiary role in the Convention Preamble.

Our natural starting point is what we might call the 'basics' of subsidiarity in the Convention system, which we identify in Chapter 2. It offers a first, very rough, sketch of the principle of subsidiarity so as, on the one hand, to provide initial reference points for a further inquiry into the substantive meaning of the Convention's subsidiarity principle and, on the other hand, to clarify its conceptual structure. As regards the first aspect, although subsidiarity is a principle with a rich history and diverse practical applications in many different contexts, some widely shared ideas may be identified, namely, concerns about pluralism and diversity, as well as local autonomy and self-government. Similar ideas resurface when one looks into the Convention system, in order to situate subsidiarity within and to delimit this principle from other related notions used in the political and legal discourse bearing on the Convention system. As regards the second aspect, we will see that, in the Convention system, subsidiarity is essentially about the ordering of responsibilities of the Court and the States, individually and collectively, *qua* Committee of Ministers, in different domains of the Convention system.

The following chapters verify whether these initial intuitions also make sense in light of the (recent) history of the Convention system. Chapter 3 confirms that the principle of subsidiarity owes its contemporary prominence in the Convention system to the recent contestation of the balance between the Court and the Convention system's political actors: voices critical of the progressive judicialization of the Convention system have become louder and steered attention towards the principle of subsidiarity. Although disagreement about the proper role of the Court seems to persist, this retrospective makes clear that the emphasis on the Court's subsidiarity has crucially been driven by arguments underlining the role played by the States, as self-governed political communities, in the Convention system.

Since this corresponds to the previous chapter's findings, it opens up an analytical path to be pursued. Chapter 4 sheds more light on the concerns both of those who emphasize the Court's subsidiarity and of those who oppose it. These opposing sets of concerns touch on state sovereignty and international control, respect for due national leeway and the need for common standards, and political democracy and rights-based judicial review. The last pair is arguably the principal source of tension animating the subsidiarity principle, since state sovereignty and room for national diversity can themselves be justified in relation to political democracy, while international control and common standards are linked to the Court's rights-based judicial review.

Once again, this conclusion agrees with previous findings, to the effect that subsidiarity is about due respect for local self-governance and pluralism and serves to order responsibility. Moreover, the dispute between adherents of political democracy, who are sceptical of 'strong' judicial review, and proponents of judicial review, who are sceptical of 'unconstrained' democracy, resonates with the Convention system, in which the Court's prolific judicial law-making may be seen not only to challenge the States' domestic-political law-making, but to do so from the position of a relative 'democratic vacuum',[45] which refers to the observation that the Court largely lacks direct counterparts which could ensure that its jurisprudence is situated within the context of political democracy. All of this suggests that the imbalance between judicial rights protection and democratic politics lies at the heart of the justification of arguments for a subsidiary Court.

Chapter 5, discussing the difficult relationship between liberal rights and democracy, puts this idea on a theoretical foundation. The predicament of systems

[45] Christoph Möllers, *The Three Branches* (OUP 2013) 213.

committed to liberalism and democracy consists in the incompatibility of certain democratic and liberal demands: democratic legitimacy requires that competing individual claims of interests and freedoms be delineated in a process that treats everyone as an equal source of rights claims, but the very idea behind liberal rights is that these rights must not depend on the democratic majority's will, not least because democracy builds on the wills of free individuals. It is hardly possible to resolve this dilemma satisfactorily without the risk of excessive counter-democratic constraints or insufficient liberal rights protection. Whoever assumes the role of the 'constitutional guardian' inevitably occupies a position at the crossroads of the legal responsibility of protecting established individual rights and of the political responsibility of making choices concerning the delineation of competing claims of rights and interests.

Chapter 6 shows how this problem appears in the Convention system. On the one hand, it gives an account of the Court's judicial practice that emphasizes the characteristically political task of delineating competing spheres of interests and freedoms, with effects that are not only prospective and general, but also more or less comprehensive, that is, potentially extending over virtually all areas of societal life, with the effect of bringing potentially any exercise of public authority under the Court's control. On the other hand, it explains why the Court's position on the international level matters for this debate. Because the Court is not embedded in a fully-fledged democratic polity, its judicial law-making is much less anchored in the democratic life of a self-governed political community than that of constitutional courts. The Court's situation in a democratic vacuum may make the Convention's counter-democratic constraints appear even more like uncomfortable, top-down impositions than domestic constitutional constraints.

Therefore, the question of how the Court's situation in a democratic vacuum is assessed is of particular interest. This is, after all, what makes it distinct from constitutional courts. Chapter 7, shows, first, that, if one puts much trust in the Court and its members' judicial reason and worries little about its interference in the States' political democracies, the Court's location outside any political democracy may appear most welcome. However, upon closer inspection, this view is unconvincing. Second, Chapter 7 thus makes plain that rights are far from apolitical, but are, on the contrary, tightly linked to the process of political democracy. This does not mean that there is no legitimate role for rights and rights-based judicial review to play, but rather that democratic politics too must play a role in the delineation and protection of individual freedoms.

The discussion in Chapter 7 reinforces the idea that the Court's democratic vacuum justifies its subsidiarity. Noting that the two views discussed in these chapters take as foundational the equal moral status of every individual and their equality in terms of rights and of having political say, Chapter 8 argues that the Court's subsidiarity is justified by the value of political equality. If everyone has equal moral value, then it is not sufficient that everyone enjoys equal rights. It is also necessary that these rights, when reasonably contested, are specified in a process wherein everyone has an equal say. Since it hardly seems possible to do justice to this requirement outside political democracy and given that democratic politics occurs, by and large, only at the State level, the States must play a primary role in a practice of democratically legitimate equal legal rights. The principle of political equality could not be satisfactorily respected, if the Court system were to figure as the primary site of the Convention rights' protection and, more specifically and importantly, concretization. Thus, the Court is subsidiary because a legitimate human rights regime must heed everyone's political *and* legal equality and therefore develop from the bottom up, as indicated by accounts of subsidiarity that suggest that this principle allocates responsibility all the way down to the level of the individual. On the account developed here, the Court supports—and reinforces—the bottom-up development of Convention rights. First, entering into a dialogue with the States, it assists them with the specification of the equal legal rights that the equal moral status of all people demands. Second, it reinforces democratically legitimate human rights standards, developed in this way, by reimposing them on the States.

Finally, it is necessary to examine the more practical implications of this explanation and justification of the subsidiarity principle for the Court's and the States' responsibility in the Convention system. The focus is on the Court, as indicated above. Chapters 9 and 10 notably discuss how the Court's interpretative and review approach secures its subsidiary role, by fostering the kind of inter-institutional interaction with the domestic authorities that its subsidiarity commands. This can explain and justify some of the Court's more or less controversial practices, including the (procedural) margin of appreciation and the European consensus method. Some remarks are also made concerning how the States should interact with the Court, in order to enable the latter to heed its subsidiarity.

The Epilogue takes the form of an appeal to the States. It does no good to criticize the Court for judicial activism, if the States themselves stand back. If the Convention system is to retain its continuous democratic legitimacy and long-term effectiveness, the States, as its democratic constituents, must engage with it not in a reluctant, minimalist way, but seriously and in good faith. The States must stand up and face their political 'meta-responsibility' for the Convention system. The Convention system is, in the final instance, a moral project borne by political will. As such, the Court's human rights protection will only be as strong as the States' commitment to that project of liberal-democratic morality. That is, just as there is civil virtue in vigilant citizens who fight for their liberal-democratic commitments, the government of every liberal-democratic State ought to fight for its commitments with respect to political morality. Europe's human rights system stands and falls with the success of people (and peoples) convincing each other in political debates of the liberal-democratic morality underpinning this system.

2

An Approximation to Subsidiarity

A) Introduction

The principle of subsidiarity has gained much attention in the international law discourse that has been spurred by the shift of international law away from the Westphalian paradigm towards a system in which a vertical dimension stands alongside the traditional, horizontal one. In this vertical dimension of international law, international organizations and their laws may claim supremacy over states, threatening to erode national sovereignty. International human rights law, in particular, fundamentally challenges the traditional concept of state sovereignty, leading to difficult questions of 'who decides what?'[1]

Subsidiarity, as a principle that entails a preference for decision-making at the 'lower' or 'primary' level, but, importantly, a rebuttable one, has raised the hope of providing a solution to these difficulties: the idea is that it offers a sort of middle-position between the concepts of supranationality and state sovereignty.[2] As a principle for the allocation of authority, subsidiarity has traditionally been of special interest whenever situations of transformation lead to hard negotiations among equally sovereign units about the creation of and powers awarded to a central authority.[3] Given the current need to allocate, or specify, authority between national and international governance levels, subsidiarity may seem an obvious solution, since it lies between the extremes of unboundedly sovereign member units and a rigidly supreme central authority. In international human rights law, in particular, there would appear to be good reasons to give rebuttable preference to decision-making at the state level, if it is also clear that a state on its own may sometimes fail to meet the basic needs of its people.

However, there are also sceptical voices who doubt the potential of the subsidiarity principle.[4] Assessing its true potential is difficult, though, since various versions of the subsidiarity principle with different—sometimes incompatible—implications for the distribution of authority between governance levels coexist.[5]

[1] Tomer Broude and Yuval Shany, 'Introduction' in T Broude and Y Shany (eds), *The Shifting Allocation of Authority in International Law* (Hart 2008) 4–6.

[2] ibid 6.

[3] Andreas Føllesdal, 'Survey Article: Subsidiarity' (1998) 6(2) J Pol Phil 190, 191.

[4] Andreas Føllesdal, 'Competing Conceptions of Subsidiarity' in JE Fleming and JT Levy (eds), *Federalism and Subsidiarity* (NYU Press 2014) 215.

[5] ibid.

Subsidiarity, Legitimacy, and the European Court of Human Rights. Reto Walther, Oxford University Press.
 DOI: 10.1093/9780198921455.003.0002

While accounts of the variety of different 'competing conceptions' of the subsidiarity principle can be found in the literature, scholars generally assume that there is *a* principle of subsidiarity.[6] This suggests that *the* principle of subsidiarity can take many, but not any, form(s).[7]

Our enquiry into the principle of subsidiarity contained in the European Convention on Human Rights (the Convention, ECHR)[8] may gain some initial clarity from considering the history of political and legal thought lying behind the subsidiarity principle in general. That is, the traditions, interpretations, and usages made of the subsidiarity principle may offer first reference points for further enquiry, even if no ready-made understanding of what subsidiarity means in the Convention system will emerge. Let us therefore start by examining the intellectual history behind the subsidiarity principle. This allows us to acquire a preliminary notion of what subsidiarity is about and to identify further questions that we must address when attempting to make sense of the principle of subsidiarity in the Convention system.

B) Roots, history, and traditions

Subsidiarity looks back over a rich and varied history, spanning a wide range of contexts. This section attempts to find some common ground within these varied intellectual riches. In short, this enquiry suggests that the Convention's subsidiarity principle, in order to be properly called a principle of subsidiarity, must broadly be about lower-level self-governance, diversity, and pluralism.

a) Major strands of thought

In general terms, subsidiarity is 'a principle which guides the allocation and exercise of public authority in systems of multi-level governance ... [with] a preference for the allocation and exercise of governmental functions at the lowest level',[9] unless it can be shown that allocating the respective functions to a more central unit results in gains in comparative efficiency or effectiveness.[10] While we may simply employ the principle of subsidiarity in this way, when seen in light

[6] Samantha Besson, 'Subsidiarity in International Human Rights Law—What Is Subsidiary About Human Rights?' (2016) 61(1) Am J Juris 69, 86.

[7] Nicholas W Barber, 'The Limited Modesty of Subsidiarity' (2005) 11(3) ELJ 308, 309.

[8] Convention for the Protection of Human Rights and Fundamental Freedoms, as amended, of 4 November 1950, in force since 3 September 1953, 213 UNTS 221, CETS No 005.

[9] Isabel Feichtner, 'Subsidiarity' in Rüdiger Wolfrum (ed), *Max Planck Encyclopedia of Public International Law* (October 2007, OUP) mn 1.

[10] Føllesdal, 'Subsidiarity' (n 3) 190.

of its historical roots, this understanding of the subsidiarity principle is oversimplified: subsidiarity is deeply rooted in the theology, philosophy, sociology, and politics of European civilization. Among the early scholars, Thomas Aquinas, in particular, 'seems to have anticipated the contemporary principle of subsidiarity in several respects',[11] when he argued that in a complex society each group and association has its proper role and function.[12]

However, the contemporary popularity of the principle originated much later, namely, with the emergence of social pluralism and, in particular, its manifestation in Catholic social thought.[13] Generally speaking, social pluralism seeks to uphold and defend the existence of social groups situated between the level of the individual and that of the state.[14] The idea of cultivating social communities lying between the individual and the state has inspired Christian social thought,[15] where the principle of subsidiarity received its canonical formulation[16] in Pope Pius XI's 'encyclical Quadragesimo Anno' (1931). In this view, subsidiarity expresses an unchangeable feature of the ontological social order, according to which it is wrong 'to assign to a greater and higher association what lesser and subordinate organizations can do'.[17] Subsidiarity protects groups and other societal units, giving expression to the idea that each group's social function should be protected for the benefit of the superordinated group and, ultimately, for that of society as a whole.[18] The Catholic understanding of subsidiarity thus structures plural societies '"all the way down" to the individual',[19] based on the idea that each part of society should assume those functions that it is best suited to accomplish.[20]

While this notion of subsidiarity is very different from the idea of delegating power or support from the top down,[21] it nevertheless comprises not only a negative aspect, which is concerned with restraining the larger unit from unduly interfering with the smaller units, but also a positive aspect that allows, or even

[11] Nicholas Aroney, 'Subsidiarity in the Writings of Aristotle and Aquinas' in M Evans and A Zimmermann (eds), *Global Perspectives on Subsidiarity* (Springer 2014) 25; John Finnis, *Aquinas* (OUP 1998) 237.

[12] Thomas Aquinas, *Summa Theologiae, Part II (Second Part)* (R & T Washbourne 1918) Q 47, Article 11.

[13] Jonathan Chaplin, 'Subsidiarity and Social Pluralism' in M Evans and A Zimmermann (eds), *Global Perspectives on Subsidiarity* (Springer 2014) 66.

[14] ibid 67.

[15] Russel Hittinger, 'The Coherence of the Four Basic Principles of Catholic Social Doctrine: An Interpretation' in MS Archer and P Donati (eds), *Pursuing the Common Good* (Pontifical Academy of the Social Sciences 2008) 106.

[16] Patrick M Brennan, 'Subsidiarity in the Tradition of Catholic Social Doctrine' in M Evans and A Zimmermann (eds), *Global Perspectives on Subsidiarity* (Springer 2014) 30.

[17] See Pope Pius XI, 'Quadragesimo Anno: Encyclical on Reconstruction of the Social Order' (15 May 1931) paras 79–80.

[18] Chaplin (n 13) 70–71.

[19] Føllesdal, 'Competing Conceptions' (n 4) 218.

[20] Chaplin (n 13) 72.

[21] Brennan (n 16) 34.

requires, the larger unit to provide aid or assistance.[22] This support allows the smaller units to fulfil their social functions, in order to enable these flourishing smaller units to contribute to the broader flourishing of society.[23] Support can take different shapes: it can be 'enabling', if it provides the smaller units with the necessary conditions for their proper functioning; 'remedial', if it remedies the smaller units' failure to fulfil their functions; or 'substituting', if the larger unit compensates for a smaller unit that is perpetually incapable of carrying out its functions.[24]

We may detect all these forms of support in the Convention system: the Convention system can operate in an 'enabling' manner, when it offers a forum for its member states (the States) to articulate their views and converge on common standards of human rights; in a 'remedial' manner, when it intervenes in reaction to the occasional failure of a State to respect these standards; and in a 'substituting' manner, when it essentially substitutes for broken domestic institutions, by providing individual remedies for innumerable cases of systemic and repeated human rights violations.

According to the Catholic understanding, subsidiarity distributes competences in such a way as is required by the realization of the common good in any given situation.[25] To that end, it works bi-directionally both on a vertical and a horizontal axis: in order to realize the common good, the smaller units mutually support each other, while depending on support from the larger unit and vice versa.[26] Thus, a unit's 'subsidiary function' does not denote a minimal role, but rather a limited one, which is restricted to those functions that the unit properly assumes.[27]

Again, this state of affairs is discernible in the Convention system. On the horizontal axis, peer pressure with respect to human rights is an important rationale for international human rights systems.[28] Furthermore, all States have an arguable duty of justice to support international human rights systems, even if these systems ultimately operate mainly for the benefit of individuals living in foreign States.[29] On the vertical axis, the Convention system depends on financial and other forms of support from the States, while it, in turn, provides support to the States in different (enabling, remedial, and substituting) ways, as seen.

The difficulty with the Catholic conception of subsidiarity is that important questions relating to its practical application—namely, the conditions of legitimate intervention on the part of the central unit—depend on a normative account,

[22] Pontifical Council for Justice and Peace, *Compendium of the Social Doctrine of the Church* (Libreria Editrice Vaticana 2004) para 186.

[23] Brennan (n 16) 35.

[24] Chaplin (n 13) 74.

[25] Brennan (n 16) 39–40; Pontifical Council for Justice and Peace (n 22) paras 187–188.

[26] Chaplin (n 13) 75.

[27] ibid 81.

[28] Beth Simmons, *Mobilizing for Human Rights* (CUP 2009) 13.

[29] Andreas Føllesdal, 'Much Ado About Nothing? International Judicial Review of Human Rights in Well-Functioning Democracies' in A Føllesdal, JK Schaffer, and G Ulfstein (eds), *The Legitimacy of International Human Rights Regimes* (CUP 2013) 281–282.

which is likely to be contested both between the subunits themselves and between the subunits and the central unit.[30] Such disagreement persists also about the proper account of human rights.

At this point, a liberal contractualist's take on the subsidiarity principle might be helpful. Liberal contractualism suggests that a normatively legitimate social order must be justifiable to everyone, despite social pluralism, which might explain the rationale behind the principle of subsidiarity's preference for lower-level governance in procedural terms: leaving self-government to groups of individuals who live in similar circumstances and hold similar worldviews may facilitate this requirement of a legitimate social order. This suggests that intervention in the affairs of local communities on the part of a centralized authority, such as the European Court of Human Rights (the Court, ECtHR), should be minimal, consisting at most of the prescription of guiding directives. However, a social order that can command general agreement must perhaps also fulfil more substantive requirements, such as everyone's satisfaction of basic needs and all purpose means for pursuing their personal conception of the good life.[31] Contrary to the argument of the previous thought, this line of thought would provide an argument for an interventionist Court, which ought to intervene whenever a State fails to take care of the Court's conception of the basic needs of the individuals under its jurisdiction. Yet, as we will see in Chapter 3, the principle of subsidiarity has not been intended to prepare the ground for an (even more) activist Court.

The States, to oppose their undesired perspective of an interventionist Court, could refer to Johannes Althusius, known as the father of federalism, and his conception of the subsidiarity principle, which is largely proscriptive, directed towards proscribing unwelcome central intervention, rather than requiring the central authority to somehow assist the subunits by interfering in their affairs.[32] Confederalists subscribe to a similar understanding of subsidiarity. For them, political authority is held by the local units and transferred to a central authority only to the extent to which each subunit agrees. The intention is to shield the local units and to protect individual liberty from the tyranny of the central authority.[33] Quite obviously, this thought underlies international treaty law. Contracting states bind themselves only to the extent that they give their consent, and they retain a right to withdraw.[34]

However, the Convention, like other international human rights treaties, differs from other international agreements in an important point: its very purpose is to penetrate the state level, in order to protect individuals from the 'tyranny' of the

[30] See Føllesdal, 'Competing Conceptions' (n 4) 218–219.

[31] Føllesdal, 'Subsidiarity' (n 3) 210–211.

[32] ibid 202.

[33] ibid 204.

[34] See Article 9 Vienna Convention on the Law of Treaties of 23 May 1969, in force since 27 January 1980, 1155 UNTS 331.

States. Seen from this perspective, a proscriptive conception of subsidiarity suffers from the problem that it condones tyranny against individuals (or groups) within a subunit.[35]

As a result, none of these major strands of thought behind the subsidiarity principle seems, as such, well suited to the Convention system. The Convention system is neither set up to respect the sovereign States' immunity nor has it been established to coercively implement a specific vision of human rights protection regardless of how the States feel about it, as Chapter 4 shows in more detail: while it was indeed set up to control the States, it has also been designed in such a way as to leave the States a say when it comes to the standards of control and discretion as to how to ensure respect for these standards. The Court's margin of appreciation doctrine, enshrined alongside the principle of subsidiarity in the Convention Preamble, most famously testifies to this latter aspect of the Convention system. We must therefore continue our enquiry and look at more specific international law conceptions of the subsidiarity principle.

b) Subsidiarity in international law

In systems of international legal governance, the principle of subsidiarity may address questions about the subject-matter of international regimes ('what') and the exercise of international public authority ('how').[36] The first question concerns the issue areas that are internationalized, the degree to which they are legalized at the international level, the effect of a treaty within the national legal orders and whether only international norms or also international institutions that exercise public authority have been established. For example, world trade has been legalized at the international level to a large extent, with a high degree of detail. A counterexample is the issue of cross-border migration, which, with the exception of some regional treaty regimes and refugee law, has largely remained within the exclusive competence of the states. The second question only becomes relevant once a treaty regime has been established and international public authority with legislative, adjudicative, or administrative functions created.

The principle of subsidiarity appears in treaty regimes governing a range of different subject matters. Apart from human rights, these include, most importantly perhaps, international criminal law and European Union law.

The Rome Statute, which establishes the International Criminal Court (ICC), offers an illustrative instance of the principle of subsidiarity ordering international public authority.[37] The relationship between the ICC and its member states'

[35] Føllesdal, 'Competing Conceptions' (n 4) 217.
[36] Feichtner (n 9) mn 18–27.
[37] Rome Statute of the International Criminal Court of 17 July 1998, in force since 1 July 2002, 2187 UNTS 3.

jurisdictions is governed by the ICC's complementarity, a specific manifestation of the principle of subsidiarity. The Rome Statute's so-called principle of complementarity allocates the exercise of competences in its multilevel system with a presumption in favour of the lower (primary) level.[38] According to the relevant Article 17(1), the ICC has merely 'complementary' jurisdiction: it must not exercise its jurisdiction unless the national legal system with primary jurisdiction 'is unwilling or unable genuinely to carry out the investigation or prosecution'.

The Rome Statute's principle of subsidiarity is tacitly underpinned by criteria of goal-effectiveness. This was not made explicit in the wording of Article 17 in order to avoid giving the impression that comparative effectiveness could be determinative of the ICC's jurisdiction. During the negotiation process, concerns over national sovereignty and a potentially intrusive international court cautioned that comparative effectiveness could allow the ICC to intervene too readily.[39] As a consequence, 'absolute' criteria of capability and willingness serve to implement the goal-based approach of Article 17. As Antonio Cassese explains, the ICC's complementarity and, as its flipside, the preference for domestic jurisdiction is justified for practical and procedural reasons. Domestic fora are best suited to realizing the goals of the Rome Statute, because they are in a better position to collect evidence and because only they dispose of the capacities necessary to try not merely the military and political leaders responsible for a crime, but also the executioners.[40]

The Rome Statute's drafting history provides a warning against understanding the Convention's subsidiarity principle as essentially operating with criteria of comparative effectiveness: given the extent to which Convention law is normatively vague, leaving room for discretion as regards the implementation of the Convention, concerns about national sovereignty and intrusive international judges are serious in the Convention system, as Chapters 3 and 4 will show in some detail. The Convention system might thus benefit from a conception of subsidiarity similar to that of the Rome Statute's principle of complementarity. This would require the Court to intervene only when a State, despite its primary responsibility to guarantee the Convention rights, is unwilling or unable to do so. The justification for the States' rebuttable primarity would be the same as in the Rome system: the domestic authorities are better placed for reasons both practical (including spatial and resource-related) and procedural (including temporal) to widely enforce the Convention guarantees.

However, apart from this insight, the Rome Statute's binary conception of unwillingness or inability is not helpful for the Convention system. While Article 17

[38] Simon Hentrei, 'Generalising the Principle of Complementarity: Framing International Judicial Authority' (2013) 4(3) TLT 419, 431–432.

[39] See John T Holmes, 'Complementarity: National Courts Versus the ICC' in A Cassese, P Gaeta, and JRWD Jones (eds), *The Rome Statute of the International Criminal Court* (OUP 2002) vol 1.

[40] Antonio Cassese, 'The Legitimacy of International Criminal Tribunals and the Current Prospects of International Criminal Justice' (2012) 25(2) LJIL 491, 499–500.

of the Rome Statute answers the question of who is able and willing to investigate and prosecute, subsidiarity in the Convention system allocates responsibility in a much broader sense, as we will see before long: each State has, first and foremost, the responsibility not to violate human rights in the first place, which requires a host of legal and political efforts, whereas the Court is charged with a multifarious ex post facto responsibility concerning (alleged) past human rights violations if a State has failed to do so, which includes legal, fact-related (evidential), interpretative, and remedial responsibilities.

When we thus look for another international legal system that could provide inspiration for a conception of the Convention's subsidiarity principle, it seems natural to turn to the European Union. Not only are there potentially many activities to be governed by the subsidiarity principle, but 'subsidiarity' has also been used in both major European treaty systems as a tranquilizer against destructive fears of a European 'mission creep'. In the European Union, subsidiarity has indeed been praised as the word that 'saved'[41] the organization's foundational Maastricht Treaty of 1992.[42] Since then, the principle, which guides the exercise of legislative competences by the EU and its member states, is prominently enshrined in the Treaty on European Union. The grounds upon which subsidiarity became a principle of EU law are similar to the rationales underpinning the emergence of subsidiarity as a principle in federal states and in other areas of international law: fears of the central units' 'mission creep' that lead to emphasize the importance of ordering competences and protecting the value of diversity among the member units.[43]

In practice, however, subsidiarity, despite the weighty reasons behind it, has not acquired great importance within the European Union, although it has been a principle of EU law for about thirty years now.[44] For various reasons, it has proven difficult to implement:[45] there are intricate interpretative choices to be made; the EU courts do not systematically and thoroughly base their decisions on questions of EU competence on the principle of subsidiarity; regulatory failures have resulted from the latitude left to the states; concerns about a lack of subsidiarity are not always justified or based on convincing grounds; and private actors tend to favour a shallow implementation of subsidiarity for reasons of efficiency and regulatory certainty. Moreover, contrary to what its history suggests, EU subsidiarity operates with effectiveness criteria that do not value decision-making at the state level: it is a 'neutral concept', in the sense that it is geared neither towards restricting nor

[41] See Deborah Z Cass, 'The Word that Saves Maastricht? The Principle of Subsidiarity and the Division of Powers within the European Community' (1992) 29(6) CM L Rev 1107, 1107.

[42] Treaty on European Union of 7 February 1992, in force since 1 November 1993, OJ C 191, 29 July 1992, p 1.

[43] Paul Craig, 'Subsidiarity: A Political and Legal Analysis' (2012) 50(S1) J Com Mkt Stud 72, 72–73.

[44] Robert Schütze, 'EU Competences: Existence and Exercise' in D Chalmers and A Arnull (eds), *The Oxford Handbook of European Union Law* (OUP 2015) 91.

[45] Craig, 'Subsidiarity' (n 43) 74–80; Paul Craig, 'Institutions, Power, and Institutional Balance' in P Craig and G de Búrca (eds), *The Evolution of EU Law* (2nd edn, OUP 2011) 59–60.

towards empowering the European Union or its member states.[46] Unsurprisingly, its implementation is weak, since it ultimately depends on the European Court of Justice and the legislative institutions of the European Union: charging the central unit with ensuring respect for a principle that is supposed to put central authority in its place vis-à-vis the member units is, as to be expected, not very effective.

The insight that the effectiveness of a principle intended to constrain the central authority may lack potency if it is controlled by that same central authority, is likely to apply also to the Convention system. Thus, if the subsidiarity principle is supposed to constrain the Court, we might have to think about whether there is any realistic hope that reliance on the Court's own application of that principle will effectively result in the judicial restraint that the subsidiarity principle is intended to secure. Alternatively, we must consider the instruments that the States have at their disposal to (re-)enforce the Court's subsidiary role.

A third instance of the subsidiarity principle in international law to consider is found in international human rights law. There, subsidiarity functions as a structural principle, according to Paolo Carozza. For Carozza, subsidiarity denotes the idea that each level of a society serves the freedom of the lower level, all the way down to the individual whose flourishing is the chief concern. Freedom here means negative and positive autonomy: it protects against undue interference and secures all conditions necessary for the free exercise of individual autonomy.[47] Carozza's account thus highlights two important features of international human rights law: the inseparability of negative and positive rights, and the value of pluralism.

The principle of subsidiarity as conceptualized in Carozza's work goes beyond description and explanation, assuming a normative (ie prescriptive) function insofar as it operates as a mediation device between the national and the international level, and as an ordering principle that allocates responsibility in multilevel human rights systems. In this function, subsidiarity requires that international human rights systems: first, allow the states some discretion in the interpretation and application of uniform human rights standards; second, integrate national and international practice through a dialogue about their shared values; and third, limit their monitoring bodies' intervention to assisting the states so as to prevent the usurpation of the states' freedom to pursue their legitimate aims.[48]

Carozza's work suggests a 'subsidiarity-oriented' approach to resolving the tension indicated at the beginning of this chapter: the tension between, on the one hand, the piercing of the veil of state sovereignty by human rights and, on the other hand, the discretionary latitude left to the states by the highly indeterminate norms of international human rights law and by practices of restraint and deference on the

[46] Federico Fabbrini, 'The Margin of Appreciation and the Principle of Subsidiarity: A Comparison' (2015) iCourts Working Paper Series 15/2015, 9–10.

[47] Paolo G Carozza, 'Subsidiarity as a Structural Principle of International Human Rights Law' (2003) 97(1) AJIL 38, 42–46.

[48] ibid 53–58.

part of the international human rights judiciary. Carozza's approach aims to solve the dilemma posed by the conflict between the universal demands of human rights and state discretion, by enquiring about 'whether the good that human rights aim at realizing can be accomplished at the local level, and if not, what assistance is necessary'.[49] According to Carozza, this approach explains and informs pertinent doctrines and principles, such as the margin of appreciation and the exhaustion of the domestic-remedies rule.[50] The principle of subsidiarity thus conceived concerns the 'politico-legal structure' of the international human rights system as a whole, whereas 'the various techniques for embedding diversity [such as the Court's margin of appreciation doctrine] might be thought of as limited and partial manifestations, relevant to specific contexts, of the principle of subsidiarity'.[51] In short, the principle of subsidiarity in international human rights law seeks to strike the right balance between the interference with domestic affairs by international review bodies, on the one hand, and the states' national discretion, on the other, in a quite comprehensive way.[52]

C) Who decides what, when, and how?

Although one can link, and gain insights from, many of the conceptions of subsidiarity discussed above to the Convention system, none of them offers a 'ready-made' notion of subsidiarity that could simply be taken as equivalent to the Convention's subsidiarity principle. This is true even of Carozza's notion of international human rights subsidiarity. It is in no way adapted to the particulars of the Convention system, whose judicial review shares perhaps more traits with supranational and constitutional judicial review than with more traditional forms of international human rights review, as practiced, most notably, by the various human rights treaty bodies set up under the auspices of the United Nations.[53] While this might suggest that it is better to look to conceptions of subsidiarity known from constitutional orders, such as those established by federal states or the European Union, the discussion above has shown that conceptions of subsidiarity used in these contexts are rather ill-suited to the Convention system.

What has become clear, however, is that our enquiry must build on the elements of limited lower-unit sovereignty—as well as conditional higher-unit intervention—pluralism, and local self-government. These concerns and values make up the core of any proper conception of subsidiarity. When we now situate the Convention's subsidiarity principle in its context, we will see that it indeed

[49] ibid 66.
[50] ibid 67.
[51] ibid 69.
[52] See ibid 79.
[53] See Cedric Marti, *Framing a Convention Community* (CUP 2021).

shares this common ground—concerns about lower-level sovereignty, pluralism, and self-governance—with other instances of the subsidiarity principle.

The decision to mould the sharing of responsibility between the Court and the States in the Convention system around the principle of the Court's subsidiary role was taken by the States' ministers at the 2012 Brighton Conference[54] and formalized in 2013 when the States adopted Protocol No 15, which enshrined the principle of the Court's subsidiary role in the Convention Preamble.[55] The Brighton Conference marked a climax in the debate about the Court's subsidiarity vis-à-vis the States which was driven by concerns about the Court's allegedly excessive intrusions into the States' democratic political orders. A background paper to the Brighton Conference issued by the Court succinctly summarized the idea behind the emphasis put on the Court's merely subsidiary role as follows: the principle of subsidiarity 'offers a way of accommodating' the 'perceived conflict between international human rights protection and democracy'.[56] As any principle of subsidiarity, the Convention's subsidiarity principle is intended to structure the sharing of responsibility for the Convention between the States and the Court based on a preference for, and presumption of the proper functionality of, the primary units. As the Court's conference background paper put it, the Court has 'a clear responsibility to draw appropriate conclusions from effective implementation [of the Convention guarantees] at national level',[57] its 'scrutiny should be correspondingly restrained', as long as the legislative, administrative, and judicial authorities of a State fulfil their role in the Convention system.[58]

Since the 2012 Brighton Conference, the principle of subsidiarity has emerged as the key normative concept in the debate about the proper roles of the Court and the States, viz in the debate about how the Court and the States share the responsibility for the Convention rights. A notion of 'shared responsibility' has thus often appeared close to references to the subsidiarity principle. This notion 'aims at achieving a balance between the national and European levels of the Convention system, and an improved protection of rights, with better prevention and effective remedies available at national level', as the 2018 Copenhagen Declaration notes.[59] With a little more substance, the Copenhagen Declaration goes on to explain that

[54] 'Brighton Declaration' (High Level Conference on the Future of the European Court of Human Rights (Brighton, 19–20 April 2012)) para 3.

[55] Protocol No 15 amending the Convention for the Protection of Human Rights and Fundamental Freedoms of 24 June 2013, in force since 1 August 2021, CETS No 213.

[56] European Court of Human Rights (Julia Laffranque and others), 'Background Paper: Subsidiarity: A Two-Sided Coin?' (Seminar to Mark the Official Opening of the Judicial Year (Strasbourg, 30 January 2015)) para 43.

[57] ibid para 23.

[58] ibid para 41.

[59] 'Copenhagen Declaration' (High Level Conference 'Continued Reform of the European Court of Human Rights Convention System—Better Balance, Improved Protection' (Copenhagen, 12–13 April 2018)) para 9.

> [f]or a system of shared responsibility to be effective, there must be good interaction between the national and European level. This implies, in keeping with the independence of the Court and the binding nature of its judgments, a constructive and continuous dialogue between the States Parties and the Court on their respective roles in the implementation and development of the Convention system, including the Court's development of the rights and obligations set out in the Convention. Civil society should be involved in this dialogue. Such interaction may anchor the development of human rights more solidly in European democracies.[60]

It appears from this passage that the notion of shared responsibility is used to express, first, that the effectiveness of the Convention system requires efforts by the Court and the States; second, that the development of common European human rights standards should be firmly rooted in the States' democracies; and, third, that this requires a dialogic engagement between the Court and the States about their roles in implementing and developing Convention rights.

The common understanding of subsidiarity as a principle that guides the allocation of authority in a multilevel governance system suggests that the principle of subsidiarity may inform the sharing of responsibility between national and European actors in the Convention system. The Court itself assigns such normative (ie prescriptive, authority-ordering) meaning to the principle of subsidiarity. In its first reference to the 'subsidiary nature' of the Convention system in the 1968 *'Belgian Linguistics' case*, it reasoned that the 'national authorities remain free to choose the measures which they consider appropriate .... Review by the Court concerns only the conformity of these measures with the [Convention]'.[61] In other cases it held, for example, that '[s]ubsidiarity is at the very basis of the Convention ... it is for the [domestic courts] to establish the facts'.[62]

Today, the normative force of the subsidiarity principle is beyond question. As the Jurisconsult, a very senior registrar, whose directorate we might describe as the institutionalized jurisprudential mastermind of the Court, explains in a Note, the principle of subsidiarity allocates a complementary role to the Court: 'the Court's powers of intervention are confined to those cases where the domestic institutions are incapable of ensuring effective protection of the rights guaranteed by the Convention'.[63] This is in line with what the Explanatory Report to Protocol No 15 notes on the enshrinement of the Court's subsidiary role in the Convention

[60] ibid para 33.
[61] *Case 'relating to certain aspects of the laws on the use of languages in education in Belgium'* (merits), 23 July 1968, para 10 (p 31), Series A no 6.
[62] *Austin and Others v the United Kingdom* [GC], nos 39692/09 and 2 others, para 61, ECHR 2012.
[63] Jurisconsult of the European Court of Human Rights, 'Interlaken Follow-Up: Principle of Subsidiarity' (Note, 8 July 2010) para 3.

Preamble.[64] That said, unless this conception of the principle of subsidiarity as 'complementary subsidiarity' is further specified, its normative force remains very limited, for this understanding of the principle says nothing about the most important issue, namely how to proceed in cases in which there is disagreement between the Court and the States about what 'effective protection of the Convention rights' means. And this is what is essentially at stake in every case that comes before the Court and when the execution of a judgment is debated in the Committee of Ministers' deputy meetings, which take care of the supervision of the domestic implementation of the Court's judgments.

Despite the residual uncertainty about the meaning of the principle of subsidiarity, subsidiarity is intended to function as the Convention system's overarching principle from which normative guidance should be derived concerning the question of how the Court and the States complement each other: it responds, first and foremost, to the question of who decides what, when, and how (especially, with how much scrutiny, deference, and restraint). That is, the principle of subsidiarity must be understood as the normative underpinning of (ie the guiding principle behind) important doctrines of Convention law and practice. Looked at it the other way around, numerous doctrines in the Convention system 'implement' its subsidiarity principle. The margin of appreciation, and more generally the Court's doctrines of deference and restraint, which we will discuss in Chapter 10, are certainly the most prominent among them.

This is not to claim that subsidiarity readily provides unequivocal answers to these important and intricate questions of who decides what, when, and how. Yet, as providing answers to these questions is the purpose of the principle of subsidiarity, we must interpret the Convention's subsidiarity principle in such a way as to discern these answers.

D) Subsidiarity in the Convention system: the basics

In the Convention system, subsidiarity roughly is about securing the States' pluralism and diversity, as well as their self-governance in the face of the Court's powers, by dividing responsibility between the Court and the States' authorities in an appropriate way. Yet, so far, this remains a very abstract idea. To give the Convention's principle of subsidiarity more shape, it is helpful to clarify its structure (ie its conceptual dimensions). Samantha Besson has unpacked the principle of subsidiarity in seven dimensions: first, the subjects (or units) involved in a relationship governed by the principle of subsidiarity; second, the object of this subsidiarity-governed relationship; third, the function subsidiarity plays; fourth,

[64] 'Explanatory Report to Protocol No 15 amending the Convention for the Protection of Human Rights and Fundamental Freedoms' (Strasbourg, 24 June 2013) para 8.

the justifications of, and the criteria following from and determining the implications of, subsidiarity; fifth, the tests applied to operationalizing subsidiarity; sixth, potential limits to the applications of the principle; and seventh, the possibility of review and contestation of the presumed implications of the principle.[65]

This section clarifies what we might call the basic dimensions of, which are the easy questions about, subsidiarity in the Convention system: the actors ('subjects') whose relationship the subsidiarity principle structures, the responsibilities that the subsidiarity principle divides up between these actors ('objects'), and the ordering or structuring of responsibility itself ('function'). In the following chapters, we will prepare the argument made in Chapter 8 that the Convention's subsidiarity principle is justified and, in its implications guided, by the principle of equal moral status, that is, everyone's legal *and* political equality. We address the final conceptual dimensions in Chapters 8 to 10, albeit less explicitly, in the following three ways: first, our discussion of the degree to which Convention law is well established and of the restraint and deference owed by the Court to State authorities, who have carefully applied Convention law, pertains to the criteria and tests that are used to implement the subsidiarity principle; second, when we suggest a response to the question of whether there are 'hard' limits to the permissible limitations of the Convention rights, this concerns potential limits to the application of the subsidiarity principle; third, our remarks about the role of the States individually and collectively as checking and balancing the Court show that there are ways in which the States can contest the Court's reading of its subsidiarity.

a) Who is subsidiarity about?

In the Convention system, subsidiarity is primarily about the States and the Court. However, apart from the States individually, the States collectively, united in the Committee of Ministers, also play an important role in the Convention system. The Committee of Ministers essentially is a permanent 'forum of multilateral diplomacy'[66] consisting of the States' permanent representatives to the Council of Europe, rather than of ministers, who only meet once or twice a year.[67] It is, among other things, responsible to supervise the execution, the domestic implementation, of the Court's judgments.[68] Thus, subsidiarity in the Convention system can apply to relations other than those between the Court and a State. In the context of the implementation and execution of a judgment, the relationships of, respectively,

[65] Besson, 'Subsidiarity' (n 6) 88–104.
[66] Simon Palmer, 'The Committee of Ministers' in M Breuer and S Schmahl (eds), *The Council of Europe* (OUP 2017) mn 6.03.
[67] In detail, ibid mn 6.12–6.57.
[68] Articles 39, 46–49 ECHR.

the Court and a respondent State with the Committee of Ministers *qua* diplomatic forum consisting of the States' representatives may also be subject to the subsidiarity principle.[69]

Not a part of the subjects whose relationship the Convention's subsidiarity principle governs are first and foremost individuals in general and, more specifically, individual applicants before the Court. Individual applicants to the Court neither bear obligations nor possess competences in virtue of the Convention apart from being bound, *qua* litigants, by the Convention's procedural law. Because the principle of subsidiarity is concerned with ordering competing obligations and competences within the multilevel Convention system, as the next sections explain, individuals do not therefore figure among the subjects or units whose relations are structured by subsidiarity. The same holds with regard to other private actors engaged before the Court, namely, civil society third-party interveners, who play, as amici curiae, important roles in the Convention system.

b) What is subsidiarity about?

Article 1 of the Convention obliges the States to 'secure everyone within their jurisdiction the rights and freedoms defined in Section I of [the] Convention'. The Court on its part is competent, within its jurisdiction *ratione temporis, loci, personae,* and *materiae*, to review whether the States have observed this obligation. While the Convention assigns the States a primary responsibility that takes the form of an indefinite and comprehensive obligation of result, it allocates to the Court a, say, enabling, remedial, and substitutive responsibility that consists of a jurisdictionally limited competence to review. Neither responsibility is per se the object of the subsidiarity principle, however.

The principle of subsidiarity does not pertain to the States' obligation under Article 1 of the Convention, as the Court is not competent to secure (ie take measures to respect, protect, and fulfil) Convention rights within the States' jurisdictions: 'human rights duties and responsibilities under the ECHR address states only, and it is states that have to determine the precise content of a human right and the exact modes of implementation of corresponding obligations at the domestic level, in light of local circumstances'.[70] Nor can the principle of subsidiarity concern the jurisdiction to determine international State responsibility for a breach of the Convention. This competence, along with the competences that necessarily follow from it, namely, the competence to authoritatively determine what the

[69] See *Burmych and Others v Ukraine* (striking out) [GC], nos 46852/13 et al, paras 119–123, 218, ECHR 2017 (extracts).

[70] Amrei Müller, 'Domestic Authorities' Obligations to Co-Develop the Rights of the European Convention on Human Rights' (2016) 20(8) IJHR 1058, 1059.

Convention would have required from a State in an individual case, are reserved to the Court.[71]

What the subsidiarity principle is concerned with is the 'overlap'[72] between the States' and the Court's responsibility, including also the blurred division of responsibility with the Committee of Ministers.[73] The overlap between the States' and the Court's responsibilities is due to the comprehensiveness of the States' obligation under Article 1 of the Convention. Consider an ideal world in which the Court was a mere paper tiger because the States comprehensively realized the human rights protection envisioned by the Convention—even if only, in certain cases, by providing access to an effective remedy for an (alleged) violation of a Convention-guaranteed right. This ideal is envisaged in Article 13 of the Convention, according to which human rights violations shall be remedied at the State level.[74] However, reality does not correspond to this ideal which is why the Court is needed, competent to review whether a State complied with its obligations, and, if necessary, to provide international remedies for violations of Convention rights.

A first overlap between the States' obligation and the Court's competence that the principle of subsidiarity may address is, therefore, *procedural*. Since part of the States' obligation consists in providing effective domestic remedies to everyone whose Convention rights have been violated, the States are, just like the Court, engaged in reviewing alleged violations of Convention rights. Domestic and European review merely have different purposes: while the Court's review serves to determine international State responsibility, the States' domestic review aims to preempt such responsibility.[75]

Article 35(1) of the Convention sequences the resulting consecutive domestic and international review. This provision manifests the procedural aspect of the subsidiarity principle. 'Procedural subsidiarity'[76] explains why an applicant must (only) exhaust *effective* domestic remedies and it may suggest answers to problems, such as the controversies about the Court's review of cases, in which the relevant circumstances have substantially changed since the final domestic decision, or the Court's applicant-friendly interpretation of some of the admissibility criteria in Article 35 of the Convention. As we will see in Chapter 9, the procedural primarity of the States is justified on the grounds that the Court would otherwise lack legitimizing input from the States' comprehensive politico-legal orders.

[71] Articles 19 and 32 ECHR.

[72] European Court of Human Rights (Julia Laffranque and others) (n 56) para 6.

[73] See Elisabeth Lambert-Abdelgawad, 'The Court as a Part of the Council of Europe: the Parliamentary Assembly and the Committee of Ministers' in A Føllesdal, B Peters, and G Ulfstein (eds), *Constituting Europe* (CUP 2013) 299.

[74] Laurence R Helfer, 'Redesigning the European Court of Human Rights: Embeddedness as a Deep Structural Principle of the European Human Rights Regime' (2008) 19(1) EJIL 125, 144–146.

[75] Sébastien Touzé, 'La complémentarité procédurale de la garantie conventionnelle' in F Sudre (ed), *Le principe de subsidiarité au sens du droit de la Convention européenne des droits de l'homme* (Anthemis 2014) 63–78.

[76] Besson, 'Subsidiarity' (n 6) 79–80.

A second overlap concerns the interpretation and application of *substantive* Convention law. As far as the textually explicit negative obligations of the Convention are concerned, they impose obligations of result on the States that require them not to cause certain harm. Different contexts give rise to different duties. Thus, the States, in order to determine their exact duties on a case-by-case basis may need to interpret the Convention, implicitly at least, before the Court has the opportunity to do so: domestic authorities must, whenever they exercise public authority, consider what result they are obliged to avoid in virtue of the negative Convention rights; in novel situations, where no well-established case law exists or when challenging a Strasbourg precedent may be justified, they must interpret the Convention themselves.[77] In the area of positive obligations, which are mostly obligations of means or conduct,[78] this aspect is even more marked because the Court, at least nominally, leaves the choice of means to the States—'within their margin of appreciation'[79]—prescribing the States' obligations only in vague terms, such as 'effective',[80] 'adequate',[81] or 'reasonable'.[82]

Because the resulting coexistence or overlap of domestic and international interpretations of the Convention touches on questions of substantive Convention law, namely, the scope of the Court's control, this is the object of 'substantive subsidiarity'.[83] This overlap is more complex than the consecutive national and European review, and the Convention text does not provide ready solutions. The only major exception is Article 53 which stipulates that the States' domestic human rights protection may exceed that required by the Convention.

Connected to the issue of the interpretation and application of the Convention, there is, in the context of an individual case, a third overlap of responsibilities which concerns the collection and assessment of evidence and facts. Both the Court and the States must rely on evidence, justified beliefs, to carry out their respective competence and obligation in a non-arbitrary manner. Without knowing and assessing the relevant facts, the Court cannot arrive at a judgment about a State's international responsibility. Likewise, a State cannot determine and adhere to its specific duties in an individual case without knowledge of the relevant circumstances.[84] For this reason, the subsidiarity principle also appears as what we might call 'fact subsidiarity'.[85]

[77] See eg *Januškevičienė v Lithuania*, no 69717/14, para 57, 3 September 2019; *Burden v the United Kingdom* [GC], no 13378/05, para 42, ECHR 2008.

[78] See eg *Lopes de Sousa Fernandes v Portugal* [GC], no 56080/13, para 216, 19 December 2017.

[79] See eg *Lambert and Others v France* [GC], no 46043/14, para 146, ECHR 2015 (extracts).

[80] See eg *O'Keeffe v Ireland* [GC], no 35810/09, para 144, ECHR 2014 (extracts).

[81] See eg *Fadeyeva v Russia*, no 55723/00, para 92, ECHR 2005-IV.

[82] See eg *E and Others v the United Kingdom*, no 33218/96, para 88, 26 November 2002.

[83] Besson, 'Subsidiarity' (n 6) 80–82.

[84] See eg *Kryvitska and Kryvitskyy v Ukraine*, no 30856/03, para 43, 2 December 2010.

[85] cf Besson, 'Subsidiarity' (n 6) 80.

Its most important manifestation is the so-called fourth-instance principle:[86] the Court does not question national authorities' findings concerning the facts of a case, including questions of domestic law, 'unless and in so far as they may have infringed rights and freedoms protected by the Convention'.[87] This fits the conception of the Convention's subsidiarity principle developed in this book (see, especially, Chapter 8), suggesting that it is not the role of the Court to better the States' legal orders in a general manner, but only to secure those legal human rights that the moral equality of all individuals demands.

Finally, there is overlap as regards the remediation of Convention violations.[88] Traditionally, remediation has been part of the States' obligation supervised by the Committee of Ministers. The Court—whose judgments are binding, though merely declaratory[89]—has had no remedial competences, except for affording just satisfaction under the narrow conditions set out in Article 41 of the Convention, viz if the domestic law 'allows only partial reparation' and just satisfaction is 'necessary'. The supervision of the execution of Court judgments still lies within the competence of the Committee of Ministers according to Article 46(2) of the Convention, which is responsible for ensuring that a State found in breach of the Convention takes all measures to remedy the effects of its Convention violation, to desist if it is still occurring, and to prevent its repetition.[90] However, more recently, the Court has been given some remedial competences as a measure intended to facilitate and support the Committee of Ministers' supervision of execution.[91] Furthermore, the Court has broadened its remedial competence autonomously,[92] through its practice of specifying measures that a State must adopt in order to abide by a judgment[93] and of finding Convention violations 'simply' because a respondent State has, in its view—and contrary to the Committee of Ministers' resolution—not satisfactorily remedied a prior violation judgment.[94]

In sum, the Court's subsidiary role is to provide a redundancy in the event of a State's failure to protect, or at least to remedy violations of, the human rights of those under its jurisdiction. Because such a failure is not a mechanical problem, this redundancy does not take the form of a simple fail-safe feature that kicks in,

[86] Dinah Shelton, 'Subsidiarity and Human Rights Law' (2006) 27(1–4) HRLJ 4, 8.

[87] Eg *Jalloh v Germany* [GC], no 54810/00, para 94, ECHR 2006-IX; *Schenk v Switzerland*, 12 July 1988, para 45, Series A no 140.

[88] Lambert-Abdelgawad (n 73) 276.

[89] *Marckx v Belgium*, 13 June 1979, para 58, Series A no 31.

[90] See eg *Xenides-Arestis v Turkey*, no 46347/99, para 39, 22 December 2005.

[91] Article 46(3)–(5) ECHR; Rule 61(3)–(4) Rules of Court of 28 March 2024, in force since 28 March 2024; Committee of Ministers, 'Resolution on Judgments Revealing an Underlying Systemic Problem' (12 May 2004, 114th Sess, Res(2004)3).

[92] Helen Keller and Cedric Marti, 'Reconceptualizing Implementation: The Judicialization of the Execution of the European Court of Human Rights' Judgments' (2016) 26(4) EJIL 829, 831.

[93] See eg *Assanidze v Georgia* [GC], no 71503/01, ECHR 2004-II.

[94] See eg *Verein gegen Tierfabriken Schweiz (VgT) v Switzerland (no 2)* [GC], no 32772/02, ECHR 2009.

defusing the danger. Quite to the contrary, State failures and their alleviation often pose intricate questions at the procedural, factual, substantive, and/or remedial levels. In all these partly overlapping areas, the Court may deal with issues that should be and/or have already been dealt with domestically.

The States' obligation under Article 1 of the Convention and the Court's 'redundancy jurisdiction'[95] require them to deal with the same questions. These areas of overlap between the States' and the Court's responsibility are the 'objects' of the subsidiarity principle: it essentially addresses the question of whether, when, and how the States and the Court exercise their respective responsibilities in the event of such an overlap. In order to do so, it provides answers to questions concerning, among others, procedural sequence, the dynamics involved in the interpretation of the Convention, standards of review and deference, fact-finding and other issues of evidence, and the cessation, remediation, and prevention of Convention violations.

c) What is subsidiarity to do?

In the Convention system, subsidiarity applies in areas where the States' obligation to implement the Convention, the Court's jurisdiction, and the Committee of Ministers' supervisory competence overlap. The very function of subsidiarity is to allocate, in a justified manner, the responsibilities of these actors where their competences overlap.

This allocation of responsibility is most evident in the case of *procedural subsidiarity* which sequences domestic and European rights-based review. Most importantly, procedural subsidiarity conditions when the Court may exercise its review competence. For the States, this means that procedural subsidiarity determines the conditions under which a State can put on hold or even avert the Court's external review of the merits of a case, and when it must accept the Court's review. For instance, if a State does not provide access to effective remedies in the sense of Article 13 of the Convention, an applicant can turn directly to the Court.[96]

Substantive subsidiarity addresses the question how the Court and the States interpret and apply the Convention. In particular, it indicates the degree of scrutiny applied by the Court; it determines the intensity of the Court's review and conditions the Court's interpretative activism. As Besson puts it, 'the Court may only embark into an interpretation exercise whose outcome could benefit from jurisprudential authority if certain conditions are fulfilled. Those conditions are

[95] I borrowed this term from Robert M Cover, 'The Uses of Jurisdictional Redundancy: Interest, Ideology, and Innovation' (1981) 22(4) Wm & Mary L Rev 639.

[96] *Van Oosterwijck v Belgium*, 6 November 1980, para 27, Series A no 40.

dictated by the principle of subsidiarity'.[97] Since the Court's interpretation of the Convention can be more or less concrete (ie leaving more or less discretion to the States) and more or less activist (ie developing the meaning of Convention rights more or less progressively, as compared to the States' domestic laws and policies), its interpretative approach, as a part of its powers of review, is also governed by the principle of its subsidiary role.

Thus, most importantly, substantive subsidiarity controls the Court's restraint and deference and its usage of its interpretative doctrines. This explains why it is sometimes said that the principle of subsidiarity 'encompasses the principle of proportionality':[98] if proportionality is understood as the test applied by the Court when reviewing the merits of a case, subsidiarity specifies the strictness and the scope of this test. That is, to be more precise, subsidiarity controls, rather than encompasses, the Court's application of its proportionality test. For the States, this means that substantive subsidiarity determines how closely they are supervised by the Court in various areas of Convention law and how much of a say they are given in the development of the Convention law.

Fact subsidiarity determines whether the Court may abstain from assessing questions of fact and domestic law. At the national level, this is an indispensable part of the States' obligation to secure the Convention rights in each individual case. Thus, fact subsidiarity conditions the Court's reassessment of questions of fact. By implication, it indicates the standards that a State must respect, so as to avoid a reassessment by the Court.

Finally, *remedial subsidiarity* mainly conditions the Court's involvement in the remediation of Convention violations. The Court's role vis-à-vis the States' in this regard derives from Articles 41 and 46(1) of the Convention. The former subjects the Court's allocation of just satisfaction to certain conditions relating to a respondent State's failure to remedy a Convention violation. The latter states that the Court's judgments are binding, but merely declaratory. In practice, the Court has pushed the boundaries of both provisions quite far with its specification of remedies. This has repercussions for its relationship with the Committee of Ministers and the latter's relationship with the States individually. As regards the supervision of the execution of its judgments, the Court's role vis-à-vis the Committee of Ministers' is defined in Article 46(3)–(5) of the Convention. The more specific and authoritative the Court formulates the operative part of a judgment, the easier it becomes for the Committee of Ministers to tell whether the respondent State complied with the judgment which, however, also means that the Committee of Ministers' discretionary space shrinks. As such, the Court's remedial practice

[97] Samantha Besson, 'The Erga Omnes Effect of Judgments of the European Court of Human Rights—What's in a Name?' in S Besson (ed), *The European Court of Human Rights After Protocol 14* (Schulthess 2011) 162.

[98] Feichtner (n 9) mn 4.

potentially shifts the division of competence not only between the Court and the Committee of Ministers but also between the Committee of Ministers and the States: it limits the 'bargaining space' of a State in an execution process before the Committee. Thus, the Court must respect the principle of its subsidiary role also in the remediation process where it must not without good justification preempt the States' decision-making competences.

E) Convention subsidiarity as requiring justification of the Court's authority

The upshot is that, in the Convention system, subsidiarity primarily appears to be unidirectional and negative in character: it conditions and, therefore, restricts the Court's review competence, as well as its review-related competences, with respect to time, scope, and degree. Since the Court only supplements the States' comprehensive obligation to secure the Convention guarantees, the subsidiarity principle requires justification of the Court's authority, rather than of the States' authority. Despite the existence of variations, the general function of the Convention's subsidiarity principle as such is to determine whether, when, and how the Court should exercise its competence in matters that were already considered at the State level or, in the case of remedial subsidiarity, that are in principle dealt with between the Committee of Ministers and the States. This could not be otherwise, given that European-level actors always only become active after the States and that, unlike the States, they merely dispose of limited competences, meaning that the principle of subsidiarity can condition only their role in the Convention system. Why this arrangement is normatively justified will be a central subject of much of the following discussion.

That said, in the Convention system, subsidiarity does have a flip side: the conditions under which European actors may intervene indicate when a State is considered to have failed to meet its obligations under Article 1 of the Convention. Again, this could not be otherwise, since, if a failure on the part of a State did not trigger the intervention of the Court, the Convention system would be devoid of purpose. The subsidiarity principle is therefore unidirectional only insofar as the States' responsibility is never conditioned or restrained, but always comprehensive, while the Court may be instructed to defer to a State, or to abstain from or adjourn its review of a certain issue. By contrast, subsidiarity is bidirectional in three senses. First, it conditions the States' 'right to be left alone' by setting out the conditions under which the States must accept Strasbourg's interference with their treatment of individuals under their jurisdiction. Second, by specifying the conditions of this interference, the subsidiarity principle clarifies the States' primary obligations. This is evident, for example, in the requirement that applicants must only exhaust 'effective' domestic remedies: the criterion of effectiveness simultaneously clarifies a State's primary obligation and the conditions of the Court's subsidiarity. Finally, a system involving an ontologically subsidiary actor, such as the one set up by the Convention, depends on the primary actors' maintenance of the subsidiary unit, a horizontal and reciprocal obligation owed to each other by the primary units, which depend on the subsidiary unit's support to various degrees. Thus, the States are the bearers not only of the primary human rights obligations, but also of obligations to maintain the functioning of the Convention system, including, for instance, 'attitudinal' obligations to cooperate in good faith, as we argue in the Epilogue, and financial duties.[99]

[99] See Stefanie Schmahl, 'Budget and Financing' in M Breuer and S Schmahl (eds), *The Council of Europe* (OUP 2017) mn 5.28–5.29.

3
The Rise of Subsidiarity in the Convention System

A) Introduction

The history of thought behind the subsidiarity principle, if applied to the European Convention on Human Rights (the Convention, ECHR),[1] *qua* system devoted to human rights and democracy, suggests that subsidiarity aims at preventing the member states (the States) from getting away with human rights violations, while preventing the European Court of Human Rights (the Court, ECtHR) from dominating them. To do so, the principle of subsidiarity aims to divide up responsibilities within the Convention system. It conditions the degree to which the subsidiary European level can interfere with the affairs of the primary national level, and thus clarifies the expectations that the system directs at its primary units, the States, including with respect to the maintenance of a functioning subsidiary level. This is what Chapter 2's preliminary approximation to the principle of subsidiarity revealed.

The present chapter, investigating the developments and sentiments lying behind the recent codification of the subsidiarity principle in the Convention Preamble, gives further substance to these preliminary insights. It traces how subsidiarity appeared as the key normative principle in the debate about the Convention system and its future development, asking how and why subsidiarity became a much-discussed principle of Convention law. Of particular interest is what role the concerns about diversity and pluralism, as well as local autonomy and self-government, common to many conceptions of subsidiarity play in this debate.

The chapter begins by sketching the Court's continuous accumulation of power relative to the other national and international legal and political actors within the Convention system. This account shows that the Court and its predecessor institutions (the 'Strasbourg institutions')[2] themselves contributed heavily to this development of judicialization and centralization at the international level. We then

[1] Convention for the Protection of Human Rights and Fundamental Freedoms, as amended, of 4 November 1950, in force since 3 September 1953, 213 UNTS 221, CETS No 005.

[2] Prior to 1998, the Convention's mechanism of control consisted of a non-permanent court and a commission, which operated as a sort of filtering body upstream of the Court.

Subsidiarity, Legitimacy, and the European Court of Human Rights. Reto Walther, Oxford University Press.
 DOI: 10.1093/9780198921455.003.0003

address the concerns about, and criticisms made against, the Court that led to the emphasis contemporarily put on the Court's merely subsidiary role.

This chapter shows that the Strasbourg institutions have been, and continue to be, the main driving force behind the centralization of the Convention system in the form of international judicialization. No wonder, one might say, that there are voices calling for a more subsidiary Court. This suggests that the Court's activist conduct (in this descriptive sense) has contributed to normatively loaded calls for more subsidiarity on its part and, conversely, for more of a say for the States.

B) The Court's transformation

It is not necessary to provide another detailed account of the development of the Convention system.[3] Rather, we focus on how the Strasbourg institutions expanded their judicial authority over time and how they further developed the purpose and function of the Convention system. This retrospective appraisal makes plausible the assertion that the Court's progressive and expansive practice has been one of the primary causes of the criticism it has faced in recent years, as well as of corresponding calls for a more subsidiary Court.

a) Self-assertion

Initially, the Court was not supposed to become a major actor in Europe's politico-legal value order. The Convention system was conceived by its founding fathers, and accepted by the States, as a 'politico-moral commitment',[4] a 'collective pact against totalitarianism' operating at the '"State versus State" level'.[5] The Preamble of the Convention still bears witness to this focus. If one looks at it, the protection of human rights appears, together with the maintenance of effective political democracy, only as a method to pursue the aim of the peaceful coexistence of European countries. The idea of the Convention as a genuine European bill of rights, by contrast, though present in the minds of some, was viewed sceptically in the Convention's founding time.[6]

Given that the Convention was founded as a project to oppose totalitarianism and promote peace, it is not surprising that the States' 'legal diplomacy' dominated the Convention system in its first years.[7] It took almost ten years from the adoption

[3] See eg Ed Bates, *The Evolution of the European Convention on Human Rights* (OUP 2010).

[4] Mikael R Madsen, '"Legal Diplomacy"—Law, Politics and the Genesis of Postwar European Human Rights' in S-L Hoffmann (ed), *Human Rights in the Twentieth Century* (CUP 2011) 62.

[5] Bates (n 3) 8, 75.

[6] ibid 75 and his chs 3–4.

[7] Madsen, 'Legal Diplomacy' (n 4).

of the Convention in 1950 until the Court was established in 1959, and national political actors were the dominant forces even within the fledgling Strasbourg institutions:[8] the first judges and commissioners to serve in Strasbourg were mostly candidates with diplomatic backgrounds. Moreover, the Strasbourg institutions' operation was severely impeded by Convention provisions that secured the primacy of the States *qua* political sovereigns: the right to individual petition (then Article 25, today Article 34) and the jurisdiction of the Court (then Article 46, today Article 32) remained optional, and the States, for many years, widely used the option to remain uncontrolled.[9]

However, once established, the Strasbourg institutions quite soon and against all odds succeeded in bringing about a gradual shift of power. Even though early Strasbourg case law remained very limited in quantity, a small number of early cases proved ground-breaking for the further development of the system. In 1960, the Commission—a sort of filtering body upstream of the Court, which has become defunct by now—found the very first Convention violation. *De Becker*, made clear upfront, so to speak, that the Strasbourg institutions may, de facto, review domestic legislation upon individual applications.[10] Later, in 1968, the *'Belgian linguistics' case* strongly presaged the future of the Court as a court with constitutional functions. Though the Court's judgment expressed—nota bene, for the first time—the idea that the Convention mechanism is of a 'subsidiary nature',[11] the case intruded heavily onto what Belgium perceived as its sovereign realm, making clear that there was no such thing as a *domaine réservé*.[12]

Starting from approximately 1975, the Court was repeatedly asked to decide cases in which it was compelled to make a choice between developing the Convention towards a transnational instrument of human rights and treating it as a common international treaty. It decidedly chose the former option, thus definitively developing into a progressive judicial authority at the cost of the predominance of the national political and legal domains. The resulting judgments clearly favoured the protection of the individual over respect for a classical understanding of state sovereignty. These judicial landmarks continue to be cited as leading cases today:[13]

Golder rejected a restrictive (ie state-sovereignty-friendly) reading of the Convention guarantees.[14] *Klass*, holding that exceptions to Convention

[8] Jonas Christoffersen and Mikael R Madsen, 'Postscript: Understanding the Past, Present, and Future of the European Court of Human Rights' in J Christoffersen and MR Madsen (eds), *The European Court of Human Rights Between Law and Politics* (paperback edn, OUP 2013) 236.

[9] Bates (n 3) 134–137, 175, 182.

[10] *De Becker v Belgium*, no 214/56, Commission report of 8 January 1960, Series B no 2.

[11] *Case 'relating to certain aspects of the laws on the use of languages in education in Belgium'* (merits), 23 July 1968, para 10 (p 31), Series A no 6.

[12] *Case 'relating to certain aspects of the laws on the use of languages in education in Belgium'* (preliminary objection), 9 February 1967, Series A no 5.

[13] See Bates (n 3) 15, 143.

[14] *Golder v the United Kingdom*, 21 February 1975, paras 28–36, Series A no 18.

guarantees are to be interpreted narrowly, turned this argument squarely on its head.[15] In *Engel*, the Court declared itself competent to interpret key terms of the Convention autonomously from their meaning in the States' legal systems.[16] *Sunday Times* and *Handyside* established the proportionality test and the margin of appreciation,[17] which allow for much judicial discretion. *Tyrer* developed the idea that the Convention is a 'living instrument which … must be interpreted in the light of present-day conditions' so as to enhance and expand the Convention's protection.[18] *Marckx* marked the starting point of positive obligations[19] and laid the foundation for the Court's subsequent blurring of the lines between civil and political guarantees, which are explicitly set forth in the Convention, and economic and social rights, which lack a basis in the treaty text.[20] Finally, the Court's *Airey* judgment famously held that the 'Convention is intended to guarantee not rights that are theoretical or illusory but rights that are practical and effective',[21] sanctioning judicial activism in the name of judicial effectiveness.

The methods and doctrines adopted in these cases still constitute the core of the Court's armament that secures its judicial power, and the subject matters of this case law leave no doubts about the Court's intentions concerning its own role and reach. The Court admitted, and found violations in, cases involving difficult conflicts between individual rights and public interests, as well as in cases dealing with policy issues that were traditionally thought to fall within the political realm or at least outside the specific material scope of the Convention. The Court thus appropriated a role that contrasts with the more system-than-individual-focused purpose that the Convention's founding fathers had in mind.[22]

To put it pithily, the Court imposed on the States its own vision for the Convention system, namely, a system strongly geared towards individual justice and the protection of individuals' rights through legal proceedings before an influential European judicial authority that interprets and enforces the Convention case by case. Today, the seminal choices made in the Strasbourg institutions' early leading cases count not only among the popular landmarks of the Court system, but also among the main targets of its critics.

[15] *Klass and Others v Germany*, 6 September 1978, para 42, Series A no 28.

[16] *Engel and Others v the Netherlands*, 8 June 1976, paras 80–81, Series A no 22.

[17] *The Sunday Times v the United Kingdom (no 1)*, 26 April 1979, para 62, Series A no 30; *Handyside v the United Kingdom*, 7 December 1976, para 48, Series A no 24.

[18] *Tyrer v the United Kingdom*, 25 April 1978, para 31, Series A no 26.

[19] *Marckx v Belgium*, 13 June 1979, para 31, Series A no 31.

[20] See *Airey v Ireland*, 9 October 1979, para 26, Series A no 32.

[21] ibid para 24.

[22] Steven Greer and Luzius Wildhaber, 'Revisiting the Debate About "Constitutionalising" the European Court of Human Rights' (2012) 12(4) HRLR 655, 664–665.

b) Empowerment

The evolution of the Convention system brought about by the Strasbourg institutions had a special appeal to central and eastern European States that, in the course of their post-Cold War democratization, were eager to join the Council of Europe and to submit to the Court's control despite full knowledge of its activist practice.[23] As Andrew Moravcsik argued, submitting to international control allowed them to 'lock-in' their still fledgling rule-of-law based democracies.[24]

In the 1990s, the Convention system witnessed an enormous increase not only in ratifications, but also in individual applications. The resulting case overload led to a number of reform measures, most notably the establishment of the permanent Court as we know it today. When the States ratified the reforms of amending Protocol No 11 in 1994,[25] they essentially embraced the legalization and judicialization of the Convention system that had occurred over the previous twenty years—an evolution shaped perhaps more by the Court's predecessor institutions than by the political decisions of the States themselves.

Four measures of the reform of 1994, in particular, emphasized and strengthened the international judicial character that the Convention system had assumed. First, the individual right to petition the Court became obligatory and the Court received mandatory jurisdiction in all matters concerning the interpretation and application of the Convention.[26] Second, the Court presumably became the sole authoritative interpreter of the Convention.[27] Third, the reform confirmed the Court's power to determine in its plenary meetings many organizational matters, which are only rudimentarily governed by treaty law;[28] if the States want to change the Convention system on the institutional, organizational, or procedural level, they must—in contrast to the situation in other international court systems with court statutes under the member states' control—agree to amend the Convention itself, which requires the cumbersome procedure of unanimous ratification of an amending protocol to the Convention. Unless they reach agreement, the Court may 'govern through'. The reinforcement of the Court system was made complete with the abolition of the decisional powers previously held by the Committee of Ministers (and thus the States' political

[23] Wojciech Sadurski, 'Partnering with Strasbourg: Constitutionalisation of the European Court of Human Rights, the Accession of Central and East European States to the Council of Europe, and the Idea of Pilot Judgments' (2009) 9(3) HRLR 397, 435.

[24] Andrew Moravcsik, 'The Origins of Human Rights Regimes: Democratic Delegation in Postwar Europe' (2000) 54(2) IO 217, 225–229.

[25] Protocol No 11 to the Convention for the Protection of Human Rights and Fundamental Freedoms, Restructuring the Control Machinery Established Thereby of 11 May 1994, in force since 1 November 1998, CETS No 155.

[26] Articles 32–34 ECHR.

[27] Article 32 ECHR.

[28] Section II of the Convention.

representatives). The Committee's role was reduced to supervising the States' duty to abide by the Court's judgments.[29]

c) Constitutionalization

The just discussed reform measures aimed at bringing the Court's caseload under control, which had surged upon the ratification of the Convention by the many central and eastern European States. However, the reform did not succeed. In 2004, the States, therefore, undertook another attempt to reform the Convention system with the goal of reducing the Court's heavily overloaded docket. This time, they seemed to emphasize the States' primary responsibility for guaranteeing the Convention rights and, thus, the Court's merely subsidiary role therein. However, this seeming shift of responsibility largely remained a matter of semantics:[30] the reform measures adopted with Protocol No 14[31] did not seek to solve the problem of the Court's case overload by shifting authority and responsibility in any significant way away from the Court to the national and political domains, but focused on improving the operative effectiveness of the Court system.[32]

More successful was the Court's strategy to take its reliably high caseload as a reason to further increase its power. To do so, it began to claim stronger authority for its judgments and interpretative decisions in relation to their domestic implementation and effectiveness.[33] In institutional terms, the Court started to understand its role more and more as that of a constitutional court and less as that of a subsidiary human rights guarantor.[34] The Court's development of its own role was successful: the largely judge-made Convention law saw a remarkable growth in relevance at the domestic level[35] and effectively came to govern European human rights issues at a transnational constitutional level. Ultimately, the Court developed into an extraordinarily powerful and influential European human rights court and essentially became a de facto constitutional court in the domain of human rights.[36]

[29] See Article 46 ECHR.

[30] 'Explanatory Report to Protocol No 14 to the Convention for the Protection of Human Rights and Fundamental Freedoms, Amending the Control System of the Convention' (Strasbourg, 13 May 2004) paras 12, 15, 82.

[31] Protocol No 14 to the Convention for the Protection of Human Rights and Fundamental Freedoms, Amending the Control System of the Convention of 13 May 2004, in force since 1 June 2010, CETS No 194.

[32] 'Explanatory Report to Protocol No 14' (n 30) para 2.

[33] Oreste Pollinico, 'Toward a Convergence Between the EU and ECHR Legal Systems? A Comparative Perspective' in G Repetto (ed), *The Constitutional Relevance of the ECHR in Domestic and Europen Law* (Intersentia 2013) 100–101.

[34] cf *Loizidou v Turkey* (preliminary objections), 23 March 1995, para 75, Series A no 310.

[35] See Helen Keller and Alec Stone Sweet (eds), *A Europe of Rights* (OUP 2008).

[36] Mikael R Madsen, 'The Challenging Authority of the European Court of Human Rights: From Cold War Legal Diplomacy to the Brighton Declaration and Backlash' (2016) 79(1) LCP 141, 166–167.

Looking back from this climax of the Court's evolution on the developments that led up to it, it is remarkable to observe that 'Strasbourg's' transition from mostly idle institutions to an extremely productive and influential quasi-constitutional court was, to a significant extent, brought about by today's permanent Court and its predecessor institutions themselves. First, they adopted as their model the individual justice paradigm, instead of opting for a more restrained judicial role. Second, they freely chose most of their (occasionally praised, often criticized) doctrines as their judicial methods. Third and related, they replaced the original systemic purpose of the Convention—namely, the maintenance of peacefully coexisting minimally democratic and human-rights-respecting States—by the objective of securing individual human rights in as many cases as possible through a legal process before a powerful transnational judicial authority. In short, the Strasbourg institutions themselves shaped the Convention system and their own role within it perhaps more than any other actor.

C) The States' backlash

The Court's major transformative power has, of course, only been possible due to the great discretion that it was granted by the drafters of the Convention and its amending protocols. However, in recent years, the States, after decades of accepting the Court's seemingly irreversible rise, have sought to have a greater say again. The most recent development of the Convention system has been shaped by concerns about what some perceive as the Court's overly dominant role within it. Since 2010, substantive criticism has become explicit in the declarations adopted at the State representatives' high-level conferences which have, from 2010 onwards, regularly taken place to discuss the Court system's future development. In 2013, these concerns led to the explicit enshrinement of the Court's merely subsidiary role in the Convention Preamble, which was the first time that the States formally decided to restrain the Court.

a) Criticisms

The Court's role within the Convention system has become a political focus around the year 2010. The Interlaken Conference of this year marked the beginning of a reform process concerning the Convention system's 'longer-term future',[37] or perhaps rather the *Court's* future role. In the Declaration concluding the Interlaken

[37] See Steering Committee for Human Rights, 'CDDH Report on the Longer-Term Future of the System of the European Convention on Human Rights' (11 December 2015, CDDH(2015)R84 Addendum I).

Conference, the States urged the Court not to intervene in certain matters,[38] suggesting the Court should 'take fully into account its subsidiary role in the interpretation and application of the Convention'.[39] With this, the States meant to say that the Court should be rigorous in its admissibility practice and abstain from reconsidering questions of fact and law that have previously been decided by national instances. This early pushback marked the beginning of the rise of subsidiarity to the level of an important structural principle within the Convention system.[40]

Subsidiarity indeed resurfaced in a sharper tone, when high representatives of the States gathered one year later at the 2011 Izmir Conference. This time the ministerial Declaration mentioned the principle of subsidiarity early and as 'a fundamental and transversal principle' of the Convention system.[41] The skilfully drafted diplomatic document was 'precise and firm',[42] emphasizing the Court's subsidiarity frequently and underlining that 'the authority and credibility of the Court constitute a constant focus and concern' of the States.[43] In fact, the States put the role of the Court quite generally into question: they called for nothing less than 'long-term strategic reflections' about its future role.[44]

These misgivings about the role that the Court plays within the Convention system grew louder and fiercer in the following years. On the one hand, criticism expressed from within the States—by scholars, senior judges, and high-level politicians—has taken the form of quite specific misgivings about the Court's doctrines, methods, and practices that are perceived as deficient, at odds with general international law, or otherwise unjustified. On the other hand, more general attacks have been made against the Court's power to authoritatively interpret the Convention and to issue binding judgments on this basis. In sum, many of the working methods established by the Court in the course of what we called the Court's self-assertion have become important and permanent targets of its critics.

The Court's critics make four main types of allegations. First, they claim that the Court lacks respect for the States' decision-making in matters of law and fact ('lack of international deference and restraint'). Second, they reproach the Court for its judicial law-making ('undemocratic legislative activism'). Third, they accuse the Court of overstepping its jurisdiction and competences ('activist expansion of judicial domain'). The fourth and last cluster of criticisms concerns the

[38] Jon P Rui, 'The Interlaken, Izmir and Brighton Declarations: Towards a Paradigm Shift in the Strasbourg Court's Interpretation of the European Convention on Human Rights' (2013) 31 Nord J Hum Rts 28, 39.

[39] 'Interlaken Declaration' (High Level Conference on the Future of the European Court of Human Rights (Interlaken, 19 February 2010)) para 9 (Action Plan).

[40] See Jurisconsult of the European Court of Human Rights, 'Interlaken Follow-Up: Principle of Subsidiarity' (Note, 8 July 2010).

[41] 'Izmir Declaration' (High Level Conference on the Future of the European Court of Human Rights (Izmir, 26–27 April 2011)) para 5.

[42] Rui (n 38) 34.

[43] 'Izmir Declaration' (n 41) para 2 (Follow-up Plan, section F).

[44] ibid para 15.

Court's allegedly excessively discretionary, casuistic, and unpredictable practice in the areas of admissibility decisions, law interpretation and application, as well as remedies ('judicial arbitrariness'). As we will argue in detail later in the book, the Court's casuistry is, generally speaking, positively related to its subsidiary role vis-à-vis the States: it is a precondition for a functioning dialogue between the Court and the States without which the States would have even less of a say in the Convention system. What matters more for the moment are these three first categories of criticism that are better suited to ground calls for more subsidiarity on the part of the Court, that is, for more national discretion and for more State control over the Convention system in terms of substantive Convention law as well as in terms of procedural and institutional matters. These criticisms against the Court, to the extent that they are more than mere polemical attacks on 'evil' international judges, form the basis for in principle justifiable demands for a Convention-law principle of subsidiarity that puts the Court in its place: they target practices of the Court through which the Strasbourg judges have, at times, fundamentally challenged the States' proper role in the Convention system.

Lack of international deference and restraint: When the Court fails to show adequate deference to a State or to apply due restraint, it essentially deprives the national authorities of their proper decision-making competence and, conversely, oversteps its own role. This is most clearly the case when the Court acts like a fourth instance or, respectively, as a quasi-first instance. The Court assumes the role of a *fourth* instance when it reinterprets domestic law and second-guesses the domestic courts' proper proportionality assessments.[45] Especially if a judgment depends on normative considerations of political morality, as it is the case with the many judgments that must strike a 'fair balance' between competing rights and interests, it is far from obvious why the Court should substitute its moral view for the one of the domestic authorities, unless the domestic decision-makers disregarded well-established procedural or substantive standards, as we will see in Chapter 10.

A related issue arises when the Court decides as the *first* instance, that is, when the Court bases its judgments on more recent facts than were available for the final domestic decision.[46] This is problematic in view of the Court's procedural role. Articles 13 and 35(1) of the Convention embody the principle that the States must not be held to account before the Court before they have had the chance to correct matters through their domestic systems.[47] Thus, the Court breaches this principle of international law when, acting as a first instance, it establishes a State's international responsibility before the domestic authorities have had the opportunity to comply with their obligations under the most recent factual circumstances.

[45] Marc Bossuyt, 'Judges on Thin Ice: The European Court of Human Rights and the Treatment of Asylum Seekers' (2010) 3(1) Int-Am & Eur Hum Rts J 3, 213–215, 243.

[46] See eg *Udeh v Switzerland*, no 12020/09, 16 April 2013.

[47] *Selmouni v France* [GC], no 25803/94, para 74, ECHR 1999-V.

Undemocratic legislative activism: The Court further challenges the States' role within the Convention system when it engages in extensive judicial law-making. Doing so, it disrespects the legislative prerogative of the political branches within a State as well as the States' collective power to make and amend treaty law. More generally, when the Court engages in judicial law-making, it risks bypassing the democratic political process. Moreover, the Court's 'evolutive' interpretation of the Convention, which continuously expands the material scope of the Convention guarantees, means that the Court subjects ever more domestic policy areas to its control. It moves the boundaries between questions of politics and questions of law and imposes new legal obligations on the States, including positive obligations that require the States to take (political) action.[48]

Activist expansion of the judicial domain: While the just discussed problem results from the Court's judicial law-making in terms of substantive Convention law, sometimes the Court also unilaterally modifies the institutional and procedural structure of the Convention system. For example, the Court's generous application of admissibility criteria,[49] such as the requirement that an applicant has victim status[50] and the requirement that an applicant has already raised all complaints domestically before turning to the Court,[51] amounts to a certain self-empowerment. Not the treaty, but the judges decide what cases are heard. The Court has done so in a particularly blatant manner in the recent case of *KlimaSeniorinnen*: it quite openly acknowledged that it devises particular 'standing of associations in climate-change litigation', which has no basis whatsoever in the Convention, because it is urgent, in its view, that the States take legislative measures against climate change, viz the Court—in a grotesque reversal of the role and sequence of substantive and procedural law—reasoned that, because it wants to impose positive obligations to take legislative measures against the climate change on the States, it considers itself legitimized to create a new rule of standing for climate associations.[52] Few citizens of Switzerland seem to understand why the Court should be justified to claim authority to assess the country's climate protection measures in the name of an association financed by Greenepeace. Similarly brash is the Court's approach to specifying remedies beyond what is expressly provided for in Articles 41 and 46 of the Convention:[53] over time, the Court, on its own

[48] Lord Sumption, 'The Limits of Law' 27th Sultan Azlan Shah Lecture (Kuala Lumpur, 20 November 2013) 7–9.

[49] Sébastien Touzé, 'La complémentarité procédurale de la garantie conventionnelle' in F Sudre (ed), *Le principe de subsidiarité au sens du droit de la Convention européenne des droits de l'homme* (Anthemis 2014) 70–72, 77.

[50] See eg *Centre for Legal Resources on behalf of Valentin Câmpeanu v Romania* [GC], no 47848/08, ECHR 2014.

[51] See eg *GRA Stiftung gegen Rassismus und Antisemitismus v Switzerland*, no 18597/13, para 25, 9 January 2018.

[52] *Verein KlimaSeniorinnen Schweiz and Others v Switzerland* [GC], no 53600/20, paras 499–501, 9 April 2024.

[53] Jannika Jahn, 'Ruling (In)directly Through Individual Measures? Effect and Legitimacy of the ECtHR's New Remedial Power' (2014) 74(1) ZaöRV 1, 29–35.

initiative,[54] departed from issuing declaratory judgments (finding that there either was or was not a Convention violation)[55] and expanded its role in the implementation of its judgments, such that it became—to the detriment of actors under the States' control[56]— 'a major player' in the execution process.[57]

Many of the Court's landmark cases and many of its doctrines and practices have become the subject of criticism. The Court's transformative power thus appears as a main cause of the recent wave of criticism. Indeed, in view of the Court's activist development of the Convention law and system and its role therein, it has been observed that the States, their officials, and their citizens, increasingly feel like 'bystanders' and experience 'detachment'[58] or even 'estrangement'.[59] Given that these sentiments correspond to the themes of diversity and local self-government identified as common to different understandings of the principle of subsidiarity in Chapter 2, the normatively loaded calls for a 'more subsidiary' Court appear as directly related to the Court's own transformation of the Convention system.

b) Pushback

It is likely that none of the just discussed points of criticism against the Court would, on its own, have led to anything more than ordinary critical remarks. However, the various misgivings coalesced into a narrative according to which the Court has become too powerful, adjudicates in an occasionally arbitrary (ie overly discretionary and unpredictable) manner, intrudes too far into the States' orders, and overreaches its proper role *qua* international court, as a result of which it must be put in its place. Domestic judges, scholars, and national politicians have espoused this narrative and taken various forms of action to counter the Court's power.

For example, a number of the States' highest courts have developed more or less coherent and robust counter-limit doctrines aimed at protecting national constitutional sovereignty against undue intrusions of European human rights law, among them the German Federal Constitutional Court, the Italian Constitutional Court, and the Supreme Court of the United Kingdom.[60] In a

[54] See ibid 11.

[55] *Marckx v Belgium* (n 19) para 58.

[56] Elisabeth Lambert-Abdelgawad, 'The Court as a Part of the Council of Europe: the Parliamentary Assembly and the Committee of Ministers' in A Føllesdal, B Peters, and G Ulfstein (eds), *Constituting Europe* (CUP 2013) 281.

[57] ibid 278–279.

[58] Søren Pape Poulsen, 'Opening Speech (abstract)' in *Conference Report* (High-Level Expert Conference '2019 and Beyond: Taking Stock and Moving Forward from the Interlaken Process', Kokkedal, 22–24 November 2017) 4 <https://perma.cc/2WM6-356V> accessed 30 June 2024.

[59] See Armin von Bogdandy, 'In the Name of the European Club of Liberal Democracies: How to Evaluate the Strasbourg Jurisprudence' (*EJIL Talk!*, 20 December 2018).

[60] See Marten Breuer (ed), *Principled Resistance Against ECtHR Judgments* (Springer 2019).

spirit of 'sovereigntist constitutional supremacy', all of them laid down certain constitutional counterlimits, for the purpose of resisting the Court in exceptional circumstances.[61]

Attempts to substantially reduce the Court's authority have been proposed by domestic political actors, some of which have even threatened to leave the Convention system and taken steps to do so.[62] In the United Kingdom, the Conservative Party first issued a party manifesto containing the promise to replace the 1998 Human Rights Act, which incorporates the European human rights guarantees into the domestic law, and later effectively introduced a 'Bill of Rights' Bill.[63] In the Netherlands, the Dutch Party for Freedom proposed to withdraw from the Convention.[64] Switzerland de facto voted to leave the Convention system,[65] and has recently discussed its participation in the Convention system anew,[66] after the Court rendered its highly contentious *KlimaSeniorinnen* judgment.[67] In France, a '*Groupe de hauts fonctionnaires*' argued in one of the country's leading newspapers that withdrawing from the Court was a '*impératif démocratique*'.[68] Turkey opted for a reduction in its financial contributions to the Council of Europe, a move which—given that Russia, which had still been member at that time, had already stopped paying large parts of its contributions—plunged the Council of Europe in a veritable budgetary crisis.[69] Compared to all of this, the Danish government's attempt to reduce the Court's judicial independence seems quite harmless.[70]

There have also been more subtle political responses to what is considered an overly activist Court. For example, the States have recently tended to elect comparatively deferential, 'State-friendly', judges to the Court,[71] and anecdotal evidence suggests corresponding changes in the State governments' practices of nominating judges. It seems that the States have recently preferred to nominate and elect candidates who promise to be alert to the separation of the legal

[61] Helen Keller and Reto Walther, 'The Bell of Görgülü Can't Be Unrung—Can it?' (2020) 19 GCYILJ 83.

[62] Kanstantsin Dzehtsiarou, 'The United Kingdom and the European Convention on Human Rights: Together Until the End?' (2024) 5(1) ECHR L Rev 1.

[63] Bill 117, introduced at Session 2022–23.

[64] Kamerstukken II 2012/13, 33400 V, no 9.

[65] Federal popular initiative 'Swiss Law Instead of Foreign Judges (Self-Determination Initiative)', Federal Gazette 2019 5931.

[66] Parliamentary requests 24.3503 and 24.3515 of 29 and 30 June 2024, respectively.

[67] *KlimaSeniorinnen Schweiz v Switzerland* [GC] (n 52).

[68] Groupe Plessis, 'Cour européenne des droits de l'homme: pourquoi en sortir est un impératif démocratique' *Le Figaro* (Paris, 21 June 2016).

[69] Committee on Rules of Procedure, Immunities and Institutional Affairs (Petra de Sutter, rapporteur), 'Modification of the Assembly's Rules of Procedure: The Impact of the Budgetary Crisis on the List of Working Languages of the Assembly' (12 March 2018, Doc 145111) paras 3–6.

[70] 'Draft Copenhagen Declaration' (prepared by the Danish Chairmanship of the Committee of Ministers for the High Level Conference 'Continued Reform of the European Court of Human Rights Convention System—Better Balance, Improved Protection', 5 February 2018) paras 26, 41, 54. b), available at <https://perma.cc/3LUK-ZXJ2> accessed 30 June 2024.

[71] Øyvind Stiansen and Erik Voeten, 'Backlash and Judicial Restraint: Evidence from the European Court of Human Rights' (2020) 64(4) Intl Stud Q 770.

and the political powers—that is, to the judicial as opposed to the political role—such as national judges in lieu of human rights scholars, lawyers, or civil society activists. For example, scholars have speculated that Belgium recently chose to nominate candidates with judicial expertise in the hope of nominating someone less activist than the former judge Françoise Tulkens who, according to observers, 'appeared to be an activist judge'.[72] This suspected trend is reminiscent of the States' early preference for politically and diplomatically sensitive judges, noted previously, and corresponds, at least partially, to social scientists' findings.[73]

Examples of influential domestic actors who have considered the Court as overly powerful and taken counteraction exist also among scholarly writers. Especially, certain senior judges writing extra-judicially openly question the Court's authority. The late Sir John Laws, former Lord Justice of Appeal, questioned the Court's role as the authoritative interpreter of the Convention because '[t]here may perfectly properly be different answers to some human rights issues in different states on similar facts'.[74] The former Belgian Constitutional Court judge Marc Bossuyt suggested that the Court might not be the right institution to adjudicate asylum cases, raising the prospect of establishing a 'separate European Asylum Court' which would exercise jurisdiction only over those States that 'explicitly recognize it, possibly for a fixed period of time'.[75] This suggestion calls to mind the early Convention system, in which the Court's jurisdiction was optional. To give one last example, Hansjörg Seiler, a former judge at the Swiss Federal Supreme Court, insinuated that the Court has imposed an arbitrary rule of autocratic judges on the States.[76]

We can summarize the gist of the criticism addressed to the Court in three points. First, there is a fairly widespread perception of the Court as too intrusive: members of governments and parliaments as well as judges and scholars in several countries criticize the Court for pushing too far. Second, the Court's detailed review practice—sometimes called proportionality fine-tuning—is seen to contradict the originally intended structure and design of the Convention system. Third, many critics see the solution to this discontent in a stronger, more clearly 'primary' role for their domestic authorities, the necessary flipside of which is a reduced, more markedly 'subsidiary' role for the Court.

[72] See Koen Lemmens, '(S)electing Judges for Strasbourg: A (Dis)appointing Process?' in M Bobek (ed), *Selecting Europe's Judges* (OUP 2015) 112.

[73] Erik Voeten, 'The Politics of International Judicial Appointments: Evidence from the European Court of Human Rights' (2007) 61(4) IO 669.

[74] John Laws, *The Common Law Constitution* (CUP 2014) 83–84.

[75] Marc Bossuyt, 'The Court of Strasbourg Acting as an Asylum Court' (2012) 8(2) EuConst 203, 243–245.

[76] Hansjörg Seiler, 'Menschenrechte—Das trojanische Pferd des demokratischen Rechtsstaats' in J-B Zufferey, J Dubey, and A Previtali (eds), *L'Homme et son droit* (Schulthess 2011) 523.

c) Paradigm shift?

The criticism that has been addressed against the Court from within the States has not remained without consequences on the international and diplomatic level. When the British government held the Chairmanship of the Committee of Ministers between November 2011 and May 2012, it moved forward with resolute demands for a markedly subsidiary Court. To do so, it put the focus of its chairmanship on 'reforming the European Court of Human Rights and strengthening implementation of the European Convention on Human Rights'.[77] To that end, an informal conference on a '2020 Vision for the European Court of Human Rights' took place at Wilton Park in November 2011 before a ministerial conference was held in Brighton in April 2012.

The Wilton Park discussions suggested 'broad agreement that *radical* reform is needed for the Court'.[78] What the British chairmanship understood by 'radical reform' became clear with then-Prime Minster David Cameron's speech to the Parliamentary Assembly of the Council of Europe and the leaked draft of a ministerial declaration to be adopted at the Brighton Conference. Cameron suggested that the Court 'should not act as a small claims court', but should 'be free to deal with the most serious violations of human rights'. He thus hoped 'to get consensus on strengthening subsidiarity—the principle that where possible, final decisions should be made nationally', since, in his view, 'where an issue ... has been subjected to proper, reasoned democratic debate and has also met with detailed scrutiny by national courts in line with the Convention the decision made at a national level should be treated with respect'.[79] In this spirit, the British government's draft Brighton Declaration proposed to emphasize the 'fundamental principle of subsidiarity' and to underline that the Court should act 'in accordance with its subsidiary jurisdiction to interpret and apply the Convention'. In this view, the principle of subsidiarity requires stricter admissibility criteria and a 'considerable margin of appreciation' for the States.[80]

Indeed, although the Brighton Declaration upon which the States finally agreed reads more benevolently than the rather hostile British draft, they adopted an epochal decision at the Brighton Conference.[81] In order to give effect to the essence

[77] 'Priorities of the United Kingdom Chairmanship of the Committee of Ministers of the Council of Europe (7 November 2011–14 May 2012)' (27 October 2011, CM/Inf(2011)41).

[78] 'Conference Report: 2020 Vision for the European Court of Human Rights' (2020 Vision for the European Court of Human Rights, Wilton Park, 17–19 November 2011), on file, 6 (emphasis added).

[79] David Cameron, 'Speech on the European Court of Human Rights' (Parliamentary Assembly of the Council of Europe, Strasbourg, 25 January 2012) available at <https://perma.cc/2N2S-2X2J> accessed 30 June 2024.

[80] 'Draft Brighton Declaration' (prepared by the British Chairmanship of the Committee of Ministers for the High Level Conference on the Future of the European Court of Human Rights, 23 February 2012) paras 3, 17, 23, available at <https://perma.cc/MAN2-58ZE> accessed 30 June 2024.

[81] 'Brighton Declaration' (High Level Conference on the Future of the European Court of Human Rights (Brighton, 19–20 April 2012)).

of their criticisms against the Court, the States decided to amend the Convention Preamble with an explicit reference to the Court's merely subsidiary role. With this amending Protocol No 15, formally adopted in 2013, for the very first time in the then sixty-year history of the Council of Europe's human rights system, the States decided to amend the Convention to the effect of restricting rather than expanding the Court's authority.[82] Whether this decision marked a paradigm shift in the practice of the relations between the Court and the States is not entirely clear, however: as we will see in the following section, there are reasons to doubt.

D) State indecisiveness and Court activism

Brighton and Protocol No 15 mark the advent of the Convention system's 'age of subsidiarity'.[83] For many observers, this has been the turning point when the States opted for a 'rebalancing' of the relationship between the Court and themselves, in response to the perception that the Court had become too powerful and intrusive.[84] This appraisal of the events around the Brighton Conference is pivotal to the present book. However, on its own it could be misleading as about the decisiveness of the States' backlash against the Court.

While the Court has continued to suffer criticisms for having become too powerful and intrusive, another issue remained topical too: the Court's case overload that has persisted since many years. These two problems are not completely unrelated, since the Court's struggle with its docket may partially explain its activism, at noted above. As the huge number of cases that reach the Court every year has its cause in systemic human rights problems within the States, the Court cannot but find its own ways to deal with its docket crisis, for example, by changing its remedial approach,[85] unless the States become willing and capable to solve the root causes of the problem. That is, to some extent, the States themselves bear responsibility for some of the Court's activist strategic decisions, which have become targets of criticism. As long as the States lack a clear vision for the Convention system and the Court's role in it, they must not complain about the Court's activist approach to redesigning the Convention system.

A decision that the States did not adopt in the context of the Brighton Conference is illustrative of this predicament. The obvious compromise solution to reduce the Court's caseload problem in line with the principle of subsidiarity

[82] Article 1 of Protocol No 15 amending the Convention for the Protection of Human Rights and Fundamental Freedoms of 24 June 2013, in force since 1 August 2021, CETS No 213.

[83] Robert Spano, 'Universality or Diversity of Human Rights? Strasbourg in the Age of Subsidiarity' (2014) 14(3) HRLR 487.

[84] Mikael R Madsen, 'Rebalancing European Human Rights: Has the Brighton Declaration Engendered a New Deal on Human Rights in Europe?' (2018) 9(2) JIDS 199.

[85] See eg *Burmych and Others v Ukraine* (striking out) [GC], nos 46852/13 et al, ECHR 2017 (extracts).

would be to direct the Court to apply more restraint and deference, while rendering fewer (violation) judgments, where appropriate. Such a solution had been on the table shortly before and during the Brighton Conference. Initially, the Council of Europe's expert, intergovernmental Steering Committee for Human Rights (CDDH) discussed a Convention amendment that aimed in this direction. According to this proposal, the Court would have been obliged to declare cases inadmissible that were decided by a national tribunal that applied the Convention law, unless that tribunal had manifestly erred or the case raised a new question of Convention law.[86] Shortly after the CDDH released its report with this proposal, at the Brighton Conference, the British government tabled an almost identical—slightly more generous, viz 'state-friendly'—suggestion for a new admissibility criterion.[87]

These proposals closely reflected the political sentiments that shaped the Brighton Conference.[88] As the CDDH noted in the report that contained its proposal, the proposal would have highlighted the subsidiary nature of the Court's supervision, that is, the idea that the Court should not second-guess domestic decisions that applied the Convention law as interpreted by the Court and were based on a full and fair in-depth examination and a balancing exercise that, by definition, can fall either way.[89] In the analysis of the CDDH, it is implicit that, if the Court were to increasingly abstain from re-examining domestic balancing exercises, in cases where the domestic authorities have carefully weighed all competing rights and interests, it might simultaneously acquire a tool for handling its docket more effectively and avoiding the impression that it acts—as its critics would have it—like an obtrusive prig by second-guessing domestic decisions in cases that 'may fall either way',[90] as the Steering Committee put it.

However, although the States called for a more subsidiary Court and, correspondingly, a more prominent role and greater latitude for themselves, they shied away from taking a clear step in this direction by adopting a variant of the proposed new admissibility criterion: they reached agreement on the subsidiarity principle's enshrinement in the Convention preamble, but they could not agree on a legally more concrete decision to add a new admissibility criterion to the Convention.[91] This suggests that the States *qua* collective master of the treaty lack a coherent

86 Steering Committee for Human Rights, 'CDDH Final Report on Measures Requiring Amendment of the European Convention on Human Rights' (15 February 2012, 74th mtg, CDDH(2012)R74 Addendum I) para 28.
87 'Draft Brighton Declaration' (n 80) para 23. c).
88 David Milner, 'Protocols no. 15 and 16 to the European Convention on Human Rights in the Context of the Perennial Process of Reform: A Long and Winding Road' (2014) 17(1) ZEuS 19, 26–31.
89 Steering Committee for Human Rights, 'CDDH Final Report on Measures Requiring Amendment' (n 86) para 2 (p 38).
90 ibid.
91 See Milner (n 88) 30.

vision about what role the subsidiarity principle implies for the Court vis-à-vis the State authorities.

In view of the—somewhat paradoxical—coincidence of firm pushback and indecisiveness on the part of the States, it seems that the Court decided to take matters in its own hands. In times of widespread and serious discontents, the Court implemented what Robert Spano, a former Court president, in 2018, described as one of the most important jurisprudential developments of the past decade. In essence, the Court implemented what was proposed as new admissibility criterion but had not found the States' unanimous consent. That is, the Court's has increasingly shifted its 'focus from its independent assessment of the "Conventionality" of a domestic measure towards an examination of whether the issue has been properly analysed by the domestic decision-maker in conformity with [settled ECHR standards]'. According to Spano, this type of procedural review is 'the mechanism by which the Court implements the principle of subsidiarity in practice'.[92] What the Court in principle does, in applying this 'mechanism', is to waive its competence to reassess a domestic measure's Conventionality on the condition that the national authorities have already done so properly.[93] Thus, the Court started to work with a doctrine that comes close to the admissibility criterion that the States discussed without reaching agreement. The main difference to the proposal discussed by the States is that the Court chose to implement the idea of procedural review not (only) at the admissibility stage, but (also) at the merits stage of a case.

It remains to be seen whether, at some point in the future, the States can agree on a codification of the idea that a solid and effective domestic application of the Convention law justifies inadmissibility decisions on the part of the—in this sense subsidiary—Court. For the moment, it would appear that the Court is once again (or still) taking the lead in developing, if not reforming, the Convention system: as happened before with some of the Court's practices, the States approved the Court's procedural review practice later on. On the occasion of the 2018 Copenhagen Conference, the States generally noted that the principle of subsidiarity 'guides the way in which the Court conducts its review', followed by an explicit endorsement of the Court's process-based review.[94] Accordingly, the States endorse the Court's approach to approving national decisions in cases that do not raise new or difficult questions of interpretation and application of the Convention if the domestic authorities decided in conformity with Convention standards. In other words, in 2018, the States openly approved a judicial doctrine that essentially implemented

[92] Robert Spano, 'The Future of the European Court of Human Rights—Subsidiarity, Process-Based Review and the Rule of Law' (2018) 18(3) HRLR 473, 477–481.

[93] See eg *Von Hannover v Germany (no 2)* [GC], nos 40660/08 and 60641/08, ECHR 2012.

[94] 'Copenhagen Declaration' (High Level Conference 'Continued Reform of the European Court of Human Rights Convention System—Better Balance, Improved Protection' (Copenhagen, 12–13 April 2018)) para 28.

the admissibility criterion that those same States had yet not been willing to add to the Convention five years earlier. The upshot of all of this is that the Court capitalized on the idea of a new admissibility criterion in order to soothe the States' most forceful opposition while, in fact, preserving full judicial discretion.

E) Subsidiarity: what's in a name?

The last ten to fifteen years have led to a widely accepted, although often only tacitly acknowledged, recognition that a rebalancing of the relationship between the Court, which had steadily gained authority over several decades, and the States, which had faced a significant loss in influence during the same period, is needed. At the same time, it has become clear that the States are either unwilling or, due to a lack of agreement, unable to get into the driving seat. They have contented themselves with, at best, roughly specifying the direction of travel. The State-led reform process did not lead to any major changes in the concrete operation of the Court system:[95] the decision to make the Court's merely subsidiary role explicit in the Convention text is, albeit abstract in its wording, clear in principle and by far the most important and high-level decision that was taken.

In light of the developments that led to the decision to enshrine the principle of the Court's merely subsidiary role in the Convention Preamble, it is beyond question that the entrenchment of the principle of subsidiarity in the Convention Preamble is intended to elevate it to the rank of a structural principle with normative force.[96] The Court itself seems to share this view, as its recent jurisprudence—namely, the introduction of process-based review—suggests. However, the question of what guidance the much-cited principle of subsidiarity can provide to the overarching issue of clarifying the Court's mandate vis-à-vis the States has largely been left open. As Stefanos Xenofontos has remarked: 'while the role of the Court has been a recurring topic during the reform process, this age-old question remains substantially unanswered and thus ambiguous and open for ongoing contestation'.[97] To make sense of the principle of the Court's subsidiary role, the next chapter seeks to attain greater clarity about the principal concerns that have motivated the States' decision to formally enshrine the Court's subsidiarity in the Convention text.

95 See Steering Committee for Human Rights, 'Contribution of the CDDH to the Evaluation Provided for by the Interlaken Declaration' (11 December 2019, CM(2019)182-add).

96 See Committee of Ministers, 'Securing the Long-Term Effectiveness of the System of the European Convention on Human Rights' (4 November 2020, 130th Sess, CM/Del/Dec(2020)130/4) 4th recital.

97 Stefanos Xenofontos, 'The End of the Interlaken Process: A (Yet Another) Missed Opportunity to Guarantee the Long-Term Future of the ECtHR' (*Strasbourg Observers*, 29 April 2020).

4
The Concerns Behind the Court's Subsidiary Role

A) Introduction

The criticisms against the European Court of Human Rights (the Court, ECtHR) that led to the codification of the principle of subsidiarity in the Preamble to the European Convention on Human Rights (the Convention, ECHR),[1] can, for all intents and purposes, be summed up in the accusation that the Court is overly activist. In general, judicial activism denotes the behaviour of a court whose jurisprudence is characterized by strict scrutiny, little deference to other institutions, weak doctrines of non-justiciability or the like, heavy engagement in judicial law-making and standard setting, 'liberal' or 'progressive' interpretations of the law, tenuous reasoning and decisionism, and a permissive approach to precedents. The concept of judicial activism is thus spectral and multifaceted.[2] In the present context, it has a descriptive component when it refers to the Court's transformative power, which has shaped the Convention system considerably, as the previous chapter showed. However, when used by the Court's critics, it also has evaluative and normative components. The reproach is that the Court *qua* international supervisory body has shown a degree of judicial activism that is excessive and must be restricted, in order to ensure the national leeway necessary to maintain effective democratic self-government of the States. Chapters 2 and 3 suggest that the subsidiarity principle owes its recent rise in the Convention system to concerns about the member states (the States) democratic self-government and the room required for national diversity. However, these critical voices meet with resistance from those who emphasize that the Court's international control and common European human rights standards are of central importance when it comes to the Court's—at least partially self-chosen—*raison d'être*: supporting the States in the fight against human rights abuses, but also rendering justice in as many individual cases as possible.

[1] Convention for the Protection of Human Rights and Fundamental Freedoms, as amended, of 4 November 1950, in force since 3 September 1953, 213 UNTS 221, CETS No 005.

[2] See Fuad Zarbiyev, 'Judicial Activism in International Law—A Conceptual Framework for Analysis' (2012) 3(2) JIDS 247, 249–257.

Subsidiarity, Legitimacy, and the European Court of Human Rights. Reto Walther, Oxford University Press.
 DOI: 10.1093/9780198921455.003.0004

Recently, harsh critiques of judicial activism against the Court were thus counterbalanced to the point of stalemate. Most importantly, a proposal to introduce a new admissibility criterion, which promised to lessen the Court's human rights fine-tuning, failed to secure unanimous acceptance (see Chapter 3). An attempt to make sense of what the Court's subsidiary role really implies can, therefore, succeed only if it manages to achieve greater clarity about the principal concerns that are at stake on the side of the Court's critics and of those who counterbalance these critics. That is, developing a fuller understanding of subsidiarity *qua* principle underpinning the entire Convention system makes it necessary to abstract from the minute expressions of criticism discussed in Chapter 3. It demands conceptual clarity at a higher level: the question is what the principal concerns are of those who call for a more subsidiary Court and what the opposing concerns are. Recall that the principle of subsidiarity, despite its preference for local government and its valuing of the corresponding pluralism, does not simply oppose decision-making at the higher level. As we saw in Chapter 2, subsidiarity is also about the support that the higher level provides to the lower level. We can thus understand the subsidiarity principle as a reconciliatory device in a field of tensions, some of which pull downwards, while others pull upwards.

This chapter seeks to map the tensions that animate the subsidiarity principle in the Convention system. Despite the general approach of juxtaposing concerns with counter-concerns, we focus on the concerns pulling downwards. This is because, although the subsidiarity principle is bidirectional, both its emergence and its recent ascendancy within the Convention system are doubtlessly the result of worries about too much decision-making occurring at the higher level. Hence, at their core is a demand for increased decision-making at the lower level. Moreover, given that the pertinent scholarship is, on the whole, rather sceptical of the principle of the Court's subsidiary role, it is more interesting to ask what concerns may speak for the Court's subsidiarity than to preach to the choir (see Chapter 1). Finally, as noted in Chapter 1, we are not concerned with the philosophical question of how an ideal European human rights system would look like. Instead, we enquire how we, lawyers, must understand and explain the Court's role which, *de lege lata,* is subsidiary, viz how subsidiarity *qua* principle of Convention law must be interpreted, especially, in light of its object and purpose as it emerges from the drafting history.[3]

The previous chapters pointed towards three concerns guiding proponents of a subsidiary Court: state sovereignty, pluralism (or national leeway allowing for diversity), and democracy. Sceptics of the Court's subsidiary role oppose these concerns with the need for international control, common standards, and judicial review based on the Convention's catalogue of liberal rights. This chapter discusses

[3] See Article 31(1) Vienna Convention on the Law of Treaties (VCLT) of 23 May 1969, in force since 27 January 1980, 1155 UNTS 331.

each of these three concerns and counter-concerns, in turn. It shows that none of the concerns advanced by the proponents of Convention subsidiarity is unjustified per se, even though in the context of the international Convention system's rights-based judicial oversight mechanism, the counter-concerns are, of course, also justified.

B) State sovereignty and the Court's control

Critics who call the Court 'too intrusive' or 'too powerful' mean by this that the Court intrudes too far into the States' sovereign orders, that is, that the Court exercises too much control over the States' sovereign realms. There is a substantive and an institutional side to this claim. Substantively, the argument endorses national leeway in policy choices concerning, for example, the coordinate protection of competing religious freedoms in societies where various religions coexist. Institutionally, the argument relates specifically to the separation of the legal and political powers. Some constitutional traditions put great emphasis on a counter-majoritarian judiciary that tightly controls politics, whereas others are wary of such a counter-majoritarian institution that significantly constrains the democratic political process. An activist Court may appear more problematic if seen through the lens of a constitutional culture without a strong tradition of counter-majoritarian judicial review. From this perspective, the existence of an activist Court not only produces interference with substantive policy choices, but also has unknown implications for the separation of the legal and political powers in the domestic sphere. Some degree of state sovereignty is important on both counts. On the one hand, it enables national diversity, in terms of substantive policy choices. On the other hand, it makes possible to respect each State's unique institutional organization and secures room for decision-making via domestic democratic channels, which are themselves products of domestic democratic decision-making.

In a number of States, including France, Germany, Italy, Lithuania, Switzerland, and the United Kingdom, political, legal, and/or academic critics of the Court advance some variation of the argument that the State must regain sovereignty lost to the Court. In some of these States, institutional worries are dominant—consider the British and Swiss traditions of, respectively, parliamentary sovereignty and popular democracy—whereas substantive disagreement with Strasbourg judgments has been more prominent in other places. Elsewhere, Helen Keller and I describe this phenomenon as a 'spirit of sovereigntist constitutional supremacy'.[4] This development is problematic in light of the supremacy of international law and the

[4] Helen Keller and Reto Walther, 'The Bell of Görgülü Can't Be Unrung—Can it?' (2020) 19 GCYILJ 83.

international rule of law.[5] Some might even question whether state-sovereignty-based arguments against international law are justifiable at all. They could argue that it is the very purpose of international law—and especially of international human rights law, with its basis in normative individualism—to check the states. Human rights advocates have therefore frequently argued against state sovereignty and the consent principle in international law.

However, state sovereignty is not without value, even if judged in light of the premise of normative cosmopolitan individualism, which assumes that all individual human beings and only individual human beings (rather than groupings or subsets of individuals, such as states) are of ultimate moral concern and indeed of concern to everyone.[6] The argument is not that state sovereignty is valuable in and of itself. Instead, state sovereignty is instrumentally valuable, insofar as it facilitates the individual and the common good of the members of a political community.[7] Consider first that state sovereignty is, at present, a prerequisite for genuine political democracy and therefore instrumentally valuable insofar as democracy promotes the flourishing of the individual and their interests. This is because, for example, only in democratic orders do all individuals and their interests count the same. Second, state sovereignty benefits value pluralism and is therefore valuable to the extent to which value pluralism is conducive to individual flourishing. These two considerations are linked: individuals and their communities know their interests best and should therefore be allowed to choose autonomously, that is, regardless of the choice made elsewhere, how to order competing values. Thus, some measure of state sovereignty is indispensable if one sees value in a democratic polity's free choice of its value system, viz in its free ordering of its collective, inter-subjectively shared preferences for goods that it, *qua* collective, deems worth striving for by means of purposeful action.[8]

Human rights treaties generally acknowledge this. They recognize that the comprehensive politico-legal order of a sovereign democratic state provides the necessary unit within which individuals in constant disagreement about political, social, and moral questions can reconcile their divergent views. This is why, for example, Articles 8–11 of the Convention contain limitation clauses in their second paragraphs which allow rights restrictions that are necessary in a democratic society (see Chapter 10). As disagreements about political, social, and moral questions also touch on issues of individual rights, human rights, too, depend on a political order that allows its members *qua* political equals to govern themselves, including on issues of rights.[9] Human rights treaties, which take seriously the individual's

[5] Gerald Fitzmaurice, 'The General Principles of International Law Considered from the Standpoint of the Rule of Law' (1957) 92 RdC 1.

[6] Thomas W Pogge, 'Cosmopolitanism and Sovereignty' (1992) 103(1) Ethics 48.

[7] George Duke, 'Sovereignty and the Common Good' (2019) 17(1) I•CON 66, 70, 73.

[8] See Jürgen Habermas, *Between Facts and Norms* (MIT Press 1996) 255.

[9] Samantha Besson, 'Human Rights: Ethical, Political … or Legal? First Steps in a Legal Theory of Human Rights' in DE Childress III (ed), *The Role of Ethics in International Law* (CUP 2012) 243.

place within human society, therefore permit, to the extent 'necessary in a democratic society', restrictions of individual rights on grounds of public interest and allow the coordination of competing individual interests. International human rights law thus acknowledges that it is ultimately the state, not international human rights regimes, that allows individuals to coexist in self-determined political communities under collectively negotiated sets of rules which enable the overcoming of social conflicts.[10]

By securing the conditions for democratic self-government, state sovereignty allows us to heed value pluralism,[11] that is, the idea 'that there is a plurality of irreducibly distinct values' which can be ordered in several equally correct ways.[12] Recall the Steering Committee for Human Rights' suggestion that the Court should leave a decision to the domestic authorities in cases where the just balance between the competing rights and interests may fall on either side.[13] To the extent that reasonable disagreement about values and their comparative importance persists and to the extent that the institutional, political, and social context matters for the precise scope, content, and justification of a conception of rights and justice,[14] value pluralism deserves support if one holds the autonomy of individuals and their communities in high esteem.[15] State sovereignty allows different communities to arrange their societal lives according to their different value systems, traditions, and existing institutional arrangements and practices. From this perspective, state sovereignty is a precondition for a tolerant, liberal international order, one that recognizes that different values may be ordered in different, equally valid ways.[16]

None of this means that anything goes, however. In order to be justifiable, any sovereign state's arrangements and value choices must represent the views and interests of the individuals who live under its jurisdiction. States 'exist for the sake of human individuals'.[17] At a minimum, this excludes the justifiability of sovereign political regimes that commit systematic and widespread abuses of basic individual interests, but it may also justify the exceptional imposition of new human rights duties on otherwise sovereign states.[18] Since the argument is about the instrumental value of state sovereignty for the individual and common good of a political community and its members, it is limited in scope: it can defend state

[10] See Duke (n 7) 81.

[11] ibid 79–81.

[12] John Tasioulas, 'Human Rights, Legitimacy, and International Law' (2001) 58(1) Am J Juris 1, 19.

[13] See Chapter 2.

[14] See Andrea Sangiovanni, 'Justice and the Priority of Politics to Morality' (2008) 16(2) J Pol Phil 137.

[15] Tasioulas (n 12) 20.

[16] Joseph Raz, 'The Future of State Sovereignty' in W Sadurski, M Sevel, and K Walton (eds), *Legitimacy* (OUP 2019) 80–81.

[17] Samantha Besson, 'The Authority of International Law—Lifting the State Veil' (2009) 31(3) Syd L Rev 343, 361.

[18] See Shai Dothan, 'In Defence of Expansive Interpretation in the European Court of Human Rights' (2014) 3(2) CJICL 508.

sovereignty only to the extent to which this sovereignty does, in fact, promote the good of the individuals subject to its authority. In cases where a state's sovereignty impedes the promotion of the individual and common good, the present argument does not provide a defence of it.

The more a state protects and promotes individual well-being, the more it can justifiably claim sovereignty from international human rights courts; the more an international human rights regime improves the individual good, the more it is justified in interfering with an otherwise sovereign state's domestic order.[19] This is how state sovereignty and international control simultaneously call for and limit the Convention system's subsidiarity: in one case, they demand international interference; in the other, they preclude it. That is, state sovereignty, and hence the line between justified and unjustified international control, is contestable.[20] For the Court, this means that its task is 'that of finding the tenuous passage between undue interference with the sovereignty and autonomy of national authorities ... and the effective protection of the rights guaranteed under the Convention'.[21]

Because the course of this 'tenuous passage' is often reasonably controversial, it is not, in principle, misguided to invoke the States' sovereignty against specific rulings of the Court—the Court may have gotten things wrong. Neither the States' sovereignty nor the Court's international control provide any clear answers to the question of how much of each is needed for any given State to be a 'good state'.[22] Because being a good state is a function of a state's promotion of both the individual and the common good, individuals and their communities must have a say in what counts as a good state. This requires a political community's democratic self-determination and, hence, a measure of state sovereignty that enables different political communities to opt for different value orderings, if they so choose.

C) National leeway and European standards

'Sovereigntist' voices advocating an outright rejection of any form of European human rights law and supervision are rare and marginal. Although there are always zealots and villains whose commitment to human rights is a mere fig leaf for their malevolent plans, generally speaking, calls on the Court to pay more respect to its subsidiarity do not amount to calls to abandon the Court in favour of absolute state sovereignty in human rights matters. The debate about the Court's

[19] See Andreas Føllesdal, 'The Principle of Subsidiarity as a Constitutional Principle in International Law' (2013) 2(1) GlobCon 37, 61.

[20] Samantha Besson, 'Sovereignty' in Rüdiger Wolfrum (ed), *Max Planck Encyclopedia of Public International Law* (April 2011, OUP) mn 78–80.

[21] Stefan Trechsel, 'Preface' to Howard C Yourow, *The Margin of Appreciation Doctrine in the Dynamics of European Human Rights Jurisprudence* (Martinus Nijhoff 1996) xiii.

[22] cf Timothy Endicott, 'The Logic of Freedom and Power' in S Besson and J Tasioulas (eds), *The Philosophy of International Law* (OUP 2010) 252.

subsidiary role is thus not about whether there should be a Convention system or not, but about how exactly that system should operate vis-à-vis the States. This can be seen particularly clearly in the criticisms concerning the Court's standards of review and interpretative approach. Yet, the Court has additional levers which it may use to advance common European human rights standards at the cost of the States' leeway, and its usage of these levers has also been subject to criticism.

The primary practical means for adjusting the respective degree of international control and state sovereignty consists in varying the breadth (scope) and depth (strength) of the Court's control. The former refers to the extent of the subject matters that falls under the Court's supervision, the latter to the relative judicial power, especially the degree of substantive detail, with which the Court exercises its control and standard-setting functions. The broader the issue areas over which the Court exercises its control, the more specific the standards it sets, and the stricter the scrutiny it applies, the less discretion the States enjoy in implementing a judgment and the fewer areas the Court leaves for discretionary decision-making to the States.

The Court's activism hinges not only on the scope and depth of its substantive case law, since questions ostensibly unrelated to the scope and depth of the Court's substantive review also matter—for example, how the Court interprets the admissibility criteria or participates in the remedial process. The stricter its application of the admissibility criteria, the fewer issues come under its review or, conversely, the more precise its remedial orders are, the narrower the States' discretion in the implementation process. Indeed, critics have reproached the Court for its admissibility decisions and remedial practices. The Court's pre- and post-judgment practice may thus affect the scope and depth of its control quite independently from the Court's more general interpretative practice. When the Court orders highly specific general measures that a respondent State must take to implement a judgment, it is of no benefit to that State if the Court, in the abstract, has laid down only rough standards. Therefore, calls for a more subsidiary or less activist Court may plausibly also concern these aspects of the Court's practice.[23] By virtue of these 'levers' related to its international control, the Court enjoys broad latitude concerning the degree to which it reduces (or expands) the States' leeway.

Those who criticize the Court for its activism in a certain case assume that it could have been decided differently—that the case could have been decided 'either way' as the Steering Committee put it—and that the Court should therefore have left the matter to the respondent State's authorities. Critics of judicial activism are not alone when it comes to the first part of this assumption: those who lament that the Court is too lenient and abdicates its mandate to protect individuals' rights against the State also base their claim on the premise that the Court could have

[23] See Chapter 1.

decided differently. Although the two sets of critics will usually complain about different cases, both sides assume that rights issues can be decided in different ways, and therefore implicitly recognize that many issues before the Court are the subject of disagreement. Indeed, a large number of the Court's judgments that are not decided unanimously, roughly 70 to 90 per cent,[24] and the relatively few separate opinions where the judicial majority is outrightly accused of having decided wrongly[25] suggest that many issues before the Court are subject to reasonable disagreement—unless we call the judges themselves unreasonable.

The prevalence of reasonable disagreement about the proper reading of Convention law points to an argument for giving leeway to the States: where there is a range of different but equally reasonable solutions to a rights issue, these different solutions should be allowed to coexist out of respect for the self-government of different political communities. Here, judicially imposed conformity would risk undermining Europe's value pluralism and suffocating the States' democratic self-government.

Conversely, leaving the States to govern unchecked would render the Court's control meaningless, which would be at odds with the instrumental and limited justification of the States' sovereignty. The Convention law itself, in the Preamble, sets forth the vision of 'greater unity' and a 'common understanding' of human rights. This may be seen as contradicting the argument just made and suggesting, instead, that the Court system has been set up to harmonize diverse views on rights issues. Yet a closer look at Convention law and practice indicates that these preambular references are of greater aspirational than practical value. Consider, first, the recent addition of a reference to national leeway ('margin of appreciation') to the Preamble. This amendment of Protocol No 15 clearly speaks against reading the Convention as imposing a uniform human rights law on the States. Such a reading of the Preamble would, moreover, also contradict the purpose and function originally bestowed upon the Convention and its institutions.[26] In line with this, the Court has held that 'the main purpose of the Convention is to lay down certain international standards to be observed by States but ... this does not mean that absolute uniformity is required'.[27]

The Convention system is thoroughly based on the idea of diverse domestic human rights practices. This is most clearly visible from the limitation clauses to Articles 8–11 of the Convention and the Court's implied-limitations doctrine.[28] Both allow each State to choose to restrict the Convention rights in the pursuit

[24] Robin C A White and Iris Boussiakou, 'Separate Opinions in the European Court of Human Rights' (2009) 9(1) HRLR 37, 50.
[25] See Laurence R Helfer and Erik Voeten, 'Walking Back Human Rights in Europe?' (2020) 31(3) EJIL 797, 812.
[26] See Chapter 2.
[27] See eg *Independent News and Media and Independent Newspapers Ireland Limited v Ireland*, no 55120/00, para 120, ECHR 2005-V (extracts).
[28] See eg *Golder v the United Kingdom*, 21 February 1975, para 38, Series A no 18.

of sufficiently important public interests. As a result, the States' human rights policies may permissibly vary: some may take the political decision to restrict any given Convention right in the pursuit of a public interest, while others may make different choices. To give an example from the recent past, consider that Switzerland, in contrast to many other European States, never chose to impose strict confinements on its population in response to the Covid-19 pandemic, but this does not necessarily mean that the other States' confinements were in breach of Convention rights.[29] Moreover, even when two or more States pursue the same public interest by restricting the same right, this does not mean that they are implementing identical rights-restricting measures. Still, each policy may be compliant with the Convention. In other words, the Court does not generally enforce what it considers the single best policy choice. Within the Convention system, one may reasonably—within a 'margin of reasonableness', as it were—disagree about whether certain public interests are sufficiently weighty to justify a specific rights restriction. We will further discuss this point in Chapter 10.

This connects to the conclusion reached above: if the Court's task consists in finding the tenuous passage between undue interference with state sovereignty and effective protection of human rights, then there is also a need to draw 'the line between what is properly a matter for each community to decide at the local level and what is so fundamental that it entails the same requirement for all countries'.[30] This means that arguments to the effect that the Court drew this line incorrectly are, in principle, justifiable in light of current Convention law and practice: it is not self-evident what individual interests are 'so fundamental' that there remains no, or only very limited, leeway for the States.

Note that there are not only different views about permissible restrictions of Convention rights, but also about these rights themselves and their scope. From the criticism addressed to the Court, it appears that a significant part of the existing (reasonable) disagreement about the leeway that the Convention leaves to the States concerns the question not of how the States must protect and, conversely, may limit a Convention right, but of whether an individual's interest is protected *qua* Convention right—and whether the government correspondingly limited it—at all. The critics in question are concerned about the Court's generally rights-expanding evolutive interpretation. They worry about the shrinking domain of subject matters not under the Court's control and/or fear a rights inflation that trivializes human rights. Because the scope of Convention rights determines, together with other criteria, whether a complaint falls within the Court's jurisdiction at all, the interpretative determination of the scope of Convention rights is of great importance in fixing the leeway that the States retain in the face of their Convention

[29] See *Terheş v Romania* (dec), no 49933/20, 13 April 2021.

[30] Paul Mahoney, 'Marvellous Richness of Diversity or Invidious Cultural Relativism?' (1998) 19(1) HRLJ 1, 1.

obligations. Determining those individual interests that the Convention and its Protocols protect as 'rights' can therefore be a major bone of contention.

Interpretative questions concerning the scope of the Convention rights cannot be excluded from the debate about the Court's subsidiarity. They are crucial to the question of the Court's proper degree of activism and, respectively, the States' retention of leeway by keeping certain subject-matter areas under their sovereign control. This is not to suggest that the scope of Convention rights should vary from State to State. The point does not concern national discretion, but rather the States' participation in the interpretative determination of the scope of the Convention rights: because the right amount of international control is the inverse of the sovereignty that the States need to be good States—viz democratic polities that benefit both the individual and the common good—and because the States' democratic institutions may have advantages over the Court in determining the nature of the individual and the common good, an argument may be made for understanding the Convention's principle of subsidiarity in such a way as to give the States a say in the interpretative determination of the scope of Convention rights and, conversely, in the determination of the subject-matter areas in which their sovereignty is not limited by their Convention membership. The Court's current and long-standing practice of making its interpretative expansion of the Convention rights depend on corresponding national policies—known as the European consensus method—conforms to this point. We will discuss the European consensus method in Chapter 10.

If it is debatable where the line ought to be drawn between state sovereignty and international control, as well as between acceptable and unacceptable variances in different States' value orderings, the question concerning the subject-matter areas over which the Convention system extends can therefore not be taken for granted either. The determination of the scope of the Convention rights is a crucial lever for extending the reach of the Court's control. If arguments against the Court's (allegedly) excessive harmonization in a certain subject-matter area are valid, they must be valid a priori in relation to the Court's practice of bringing new subject-matter areas under its control. Of course, the same argument holds with regard to non-substantive Convention provisions, notably concerning the admissibility of an application and the implementation of the Court's judgments, which may also affect the Court's potentially harmonizing control, as has been explained.

D) Democratic politics and judicial review

So far, this chapter has suggested that states that are sovereign in a limited sense may benefit the individual and the common good because they allow—in accordance with Europe's value pluralism—for different democratic polities to make different, but equally permissible value choices. This section explains why the Court's critics have a point when they suggest that the Court's review poses a challenge to the States' democratic politics. This requires addressing the question of why a political community's democratic value choices would promote the individual and common good better than the judges with 'high moral character' sitting on the Court's bench.[31] In other words, the question is why the democratic process may fare no worse, at least, than the (international) judicial process in deciding rights issues in a manner conducive to the individual and the common good. If democratic politics had no advantages over the judicial process in this regard, the line of thought pursued here would lead to a dead end. Advocates of a markedly subsidiary Court indeed question that controversial issues affecting a respondent State's society at large should be decided by the international Court in the place of the concerned individuals themselves through their political community's democratic institutions. As the discussion will show, there are a range of reasons why one may doubt that the resolution of controversies about rights issues should simply be left to the Court. However, the discussion will not provide one right answer to the question of how political and judicial responsibility for decisions about rights should be shared.

a) The Court's review as a challenge to political democracy

Some of the Court's critics assert that it takes ever more issues out of the realm of political decision-making. They express discontent arising from the perception that societal conflicts are in the last instance increasingly being resolved through legal instead of political avenues and that institutions of international law play an important role in this. The main complaint is not that the Court decides in a way that is substantively wrong, but that it is not clear why the Court would render better decisions than the States' democratic institutions and, therefore, why it should decide controversial issues that affect society at large, instead of these societies themselves.[32]

It is by no means obvious which matters fall into the respective domains of political and (international) judicial decision-making. Different constitutional traditions have opted for quite different models of the separation of legal and political powers.[33] In some systems, the judiciary has the final word in all constitutional issues and itself determines the reach of the constitutional domain. Parliament, or the voting citizens, are 'sovereign' in other systems which, accordingly, refrain from establishing systems of constitutional review that would allow courts to override

[31] Article 21 ECHR (Criteria for office).

[32] See eg Adam Tomkins, 'The Role of the Courts in the Political Constitution' (2010) 60(1) UTLJ 1, 4.

[33] Christoph Möllers, *The Three Branches* (OUP 2013) ch 1.

decisions taken by parliament or popular vote. From the perspective of these latter systems, in particular, a court system such as that set up under the Convention, where the States retain little control over the general direction in which the court and its judicial practice evolves, looks like an anomaly.[34]

To be sure, States without established systems of constitutional review have, like all others, ratified the Convention and submitted to the Court's control. However, although this consideration should give pause to sceptics of the Court's democratic legitimacy, it does not suffice to set aside the debate about the proper role of the Court's review. This 'ratification defence' of the Court's international control may end discussions about the 'whether', but not about the 'how' of the Court's review.

Because the Convention and its protocols formulate their human rights guarantees in an extremely vague and open-ended manner, while many procedural, institutional, and organizational questions are left entirely to the Court's discretion, the Court's critics tend to understand the Convention system as a system where judicial supremacy reigns. This perspective highlights the fact that the Court exercises its review in such a way as to settle interpretative questions definitively and authoritatively for the entire legal-political system, namely by being quite specific about what policies the supreme law (ie the Convention law) requires although these questions are subject to reasonable disagreement such that answering them differently than the Court does would be equally reasonable.[35] That is, these critics assume that the generalizable parts of the Court's judgments have binding effect for all State parties, which is sometimes called *erga omnes inter partes* effect;[36] otherwise, viz if the Court's judgments were only of an isolated effect in the individual case, their complaint would make no sense. Although it remains a matter for debate whether the Court's judgments indeed enjoy such an effect,[37] this assumption is widely shared, also among the many Court scholars who are not critical, but favourable of this idea.

However that may be, to counter the idea of the Court's judicial supremacy, one might object that its judgments are de facto no more consequential than any given State's domestic law and practice allows them to be. Moreover, one could argue that, *qua* members of the Committee of Ministers, the States may 'dilute' what a judgment requires from the respondent State in terms of remedial measures, when taking the respondent State's discretion in the implementation of a judgment

[34] Andreas Føllesdal, Birgit Peters, and Geir Ulfstein, 'Introduction' in A Føllesdal, B Peters and G Ulfstein (eds), *Constituting Europe* (CUP 2013) 13.

[35] cf Stephen Gardbaum, 'What Is Judicial Supremacy?' in G Jacobsohn and M Schor (eds), *Comparative Constitutional Theory* (Edward Elgar 2018) 22–24; Jeremy Waldron, 'Judicial Review and Judicial Supremacy' (November 2014) NYU School of Law Public Law & Legal Theory Research Paper Series No 14-57, 27–32.

[36] Samantha Besson, 'The Erga Omnes Effect of Judgments of the European Court of Human Rights—What's in a Name?' in S Besson (ed), *The European Court of Human Rights After Protocol 14* (Schulthess 2011) 129–132.

[37] See Chapter 8.

into account.[38] Yet, these objections do not stand up to closer scrutiny if examined through the prism of general international law and 'traditional' Convention law—what a reading of Convention law based on its recent subsidiarity principle suggests is a question to be answered in the course of this book. From the perspective of international law, domestic law must not serve the States as an excuse for disregarding their legal obligations under Convention law.[39] Similarly, according to Convention law, Strasbourg judgments are binding on respondent States[40] and the Committee of Ministers is tasked with enforcing—that is, supervising the execution of—these judgments, not with reinterpreting them,[41] although there may remain room for different views on what a judgment requires in terms of implementation.[42] Finally, if one looks to the States' domestic laws, one must observe that the Convention is, as a matter of fact, incorporated and enjoys direct effect, in most States, today.[43] In short, the Court compares 'to that of even the most powerful national constitutional courts'[44] and counts among the world's most successful in terms of the frequency, significance, and impact of its policy decisions.[45]

The critics who deplore that the Court takes ever more matters away from the realm of political decision-making not only assume that the Court yields strong powers of review, but also that persistent, reasonable disagreement prevails about most rights issues that come before the Court.[46] In their view, the political rather than the judicial process should settle controversial issues that concern society at large and that may deeply divide it.[47] Their point is that the (interpretative) specification of individual rights often concerns society at large and may be as politically contested as any other policy question.

Despite the accuracy of this point, one must not forget the many cases decided by the Court that doubtlessly fall into the domain of the legal branch. Many of the Court's cases are resolved through legal technicalities and/or well-established legal rules. The Court thus renders a vast part of its judgments based on 'well-established case-law' by unanimous committees of three judges according to

[38] See Rule 6(2)(b) Rules of Committee of Ministers for the Supervision of the Execution of Judgments and of the Terms of Friendly Settlements of 10 May 2006, 964th mtg, as amended.

[39] Article 27 VCLT; Fitzmaurice (n 5) 85–88.

[40] Article 46(1) ECHR.

[41] Article 46(2)–(3) ECHR; Rule 10 Rules of Committee of Ministers for the Supervision of the Execution of Judgments and of the Terms of Friendly Settlements.

[42] See Başak Çali and Anne Koch, 'Foxes Guarding the Foxes? The Peer Review of Human Rights Judgments by the Committee of Ministers of the Council of Europe' (2014) 14(2) HRLR 301, 308, 312.

[43] See Chapter 8.

[44] Alec Stone Sweet, 'On the Constitutionalisation of the Convention: The European Court of Human Rights as a Constitutional Court' (2009) Yale Law School Faculty Scholarship Series no 71 14, published in French as Alec Stone Sweet, 'Sur la constitutionnalisation de la Convention européenne des droits de l'homme: Cinquante ans après son installation, la Cour européenne des droits de l'homme conçue comme une Cour constitutionnelle' (2009) 20(80) Rev trim dr h 923 (Michel Puéchavy, tr), 944.

[45] Martin Shapiro, 'The Success of Judicial Review' in SJ Kenney, WM Reisinger, and JC Reitz (eds), *Constitutional Dialogues in Comparative Perspective* (Palgrave MacMillan 1999) 201.

[46] Generally, Jeremy Waldron, *Law and Disagreement* (OUP 1999).

[47] Generally, see eg JAG Griffith, 'The Political Constitution' (1979) 42(1) MLR 1, 16.

Article 28 of the Convention.[48] Similar observations are apt with regard to those Convention violations that can appositely be called abuses or crimes because they clearly violate standards protecting an individual's physical integrity.[49]

However, the point remains that the Court is heavily engaged in judicial law-making, as we will see in some detail in Chapter 6. Due to the diversity between the States under its control, it is more often than are national courts confronted with cases whose core controversy can be accurately described neither as a legal technicality nor as a human rights crime or abuse, but which rather involves new issues that 'may be qualified as policy disputes that revolve around different interpretations of what a given right requires in specific circumstances'.[50] Such cases concern the respondent State as a whole, but the standards that the Court establishes in any one case will later usually also apply to other States.

When deciding new, controversial rights issues of this type, the Court—as any court that assumes constitutional functions—restrains the sphere of action of the political authorities, who are bound to respect the Convention's quasi-constitutional rights in accordance with their judicial interpretation. As Joseph Raz noted, in complex, pluralistic societies rife with disagreement, the most important effect of the entrenchment of rights is not substantive, but procedural and institutional: it concerns the allocation of power between political and judicial authorities.[51] This is no different in the Convention system, where the States *qua* political communities are expected to comply with the Court's judgments. The Convention's entrenchment of rights therefore comes down to giving the Court, rather than other bodies, including the States' parliaments, the power to settle controversies concerning entrenched matters, including controversies over how these matters should change over time. In short, the greater the extent to which the Court decides highly controversial issues in a broad range of areas of social life in a strictly binding manner and the more specific the standards it outlines, the more it impinges on the domain of the States' law- and policy-makers.

This consideration connects on to the discussions in the previous sections. The further-reaching and the more prolific and specific the Court's standard setting, the more acute the tension between Strasbourg's judicial and the States' political decision-making. But it is also the Court's location, watching over the States from a position external to any of the States' democratic polities, that further exacerbates the tension between judicial and political decision-making. Assuming that withdrawing from the Convention system is no realistic option for the States,[52] the Court, because it lacks a constant, ordinary political counterpart, as we will see in

[48] European Court of Human Rights, 'Analysis of Statistics 2023' (January 2024) 3–4.
[49] Andreas von Staden, *Strategies of Compliance with the European Court of Human Rights* (University of Pennsylvania Press 2018) 8.
[50] ibid.
[51] Joseph Raz, 'Rights and Politics' (1995) 71(1) Ind LJ 27, 42.
[52] See eg Armin von Bogdandy and Ingo Venzke, *In Whose Name?* (OUP 2014) 124–125.

Chapter 6, may be said—to adapt Mark Tushnet's allegory[53]—to take the constitution even further away from the people than powerful domestic courts do. Once the Court has resolved an issue, it is definitely removed not only from the realm of each State's ordinary politics, but also from the realm of each State's constitutional politics, as well as, by virtue of the unanimity requirement of amendments to the Convention, to a large extent from the States' *demoi*-cratic politics.[54]

This is rightly considered problematic insofar as political revisability—and, more generally, the contestability of public authority—are hallmarks of democratic legitimacy. Thus, as we will discuss in Chapter 6, in particular, the Court may seem not less, but rather more, susceptible than national constitutional courts are to the difficulties of the one-sidedness that it is hardly accountable to law-makers and little bound to (more or less) determinate legal provisions, whereas its jurisprudential principles restrict the realm of democratic politics. Strong demands for a markedly subsidiary judicial role might follow, since, as Conor O'Mahony observes, the more difficult it is to amend entrenched constitutional law on the political level and the more controversial the issues at stake, the stronger the arguments of political democracy for judicial restraint and deference.[55]

Before we come back to the institutional question of the Court's legitimacy to take constitutional law-making decisions, it is worth to consider to what extent the Court is institutionally and procedurally capable and suitable to render such decisions. This assessment reveals that the Court's superiority in this regard vis-à-vis political decision-making bodies, namely parliaments, is rightly controversial. This, in turn, emphasizes and leads back again to the important question of the Court's democratic legitimacy to take constitutional law-making decisions.

b) The over-representation of the few and under-representation of the many in the Court

A first characteristic of judicial decision-making to consider is that judicial proceedings, unlike political debates, focus on the resolution of an individual dispute. Their creation of legal normativity that extends beyond the concrete case at issue tends to be neglected, with the effect that judge-made law risks suffering from an excessive inclination towards the applicant's interests, as well as towards a legal regime's specific subject-matter area and predetermined value choices. This

[53] Mark Tushnet, *Taking the Constitution Away from the Courts* (Princeton University Press 1999).

[54] See Alec Stone Sweet and Thomas L Brunell, 'Trustee Courts and the Judicialization of International Regimes: The Politics of Majoritarian Activism in the European Convention on Human Rights, the European Union, and the World Trade Organization' (2013) 1(1) J L & Cts 61, 81.

[55] Conor O'Mahony, 'If a Constitution Is Easy to Amend, Can Judges Be Less Restrained? Rights, Social Change, and Proposition 8' (2014) 27 Harv Hum Rts J 191, 241.

narrow inclination runs afoul the general function of law-making.[56] That is, when courts set new legal standards in a leading judgment, they do not consider their decision 'as part of a general programme of government and with regard to its knock-on effects for other policy areas' as legislative law-makers would usually do.[57] Arguments that emphasize that law-making should primarily remain a matter for the democratic political process and that, therefore, sound a note of caution as regards the Court's review are, above all, concerned with this problem of the 'under-representation of the many' and the 'over-representation of the few' in the judicial, as compared to the political process. In terms of constitutional separation-of-powers theory, the 'over-representation of the few' and the 'under-representation of the many' is a crucial difficulty of constitutional review: when courts engage in judicial law-making and have the final say in matters that concern society at large, only those few who participate in the judicial proceedings have a say in the outcome, while the vast majority of those who will live under the newly established rule are excluded from the debate. To be sure, the over-representation of the applicant is a desired characteristic of judicial decision-making, understood as an individual corrective to general political decision-making. Yet, this does not make this feature of the judicial process less problematic in the face of judicial law-making.[58]

This representation problem is also an issue in the Convention system, where the respondent State's polity, represented by the government, appears before the Court. Although the problem is thus reduced before the Court, the point remains that courts are the most unrepresentative of all three branches given that they consist exclusively of legal experts, with their own particular way of thinking and reasoning.[59] The legislative branch—the forum through which and in which the citizens can participate most equally and where they are represented most directly—is not involved in the proceedings before the Court. When 'the State' appears before the Court, it is embodied by the executive; more precisely, by its *agent de gouvernement*, who usually belongs to a specialized legal office belonging to the ministry for foreign affairs, for justice, or some such government unit. The long-standing observation that international courts cause the legislative branch to lose power relative to the other branches of the *trias politica* corresponds to this.[60] Nonetheless, in functioning democracies, the government must be taken to represent a democratically elaborated conception of the public interest, such that

[56] Armin von Bogdandy and Ingo Venzke, 'Beyond Dispute: International Judicial Institutions as Lawmakers' in A von Bogdandy and I Venzke (eds), *International Judicial Lawmaking* (Springer 2012) 24–26.

[57] Richard Bellamy, *Political Constitutionalism* (CUP 2007) 246.

[58] Carol Harlow, 'Public Law and Popular Justice' (2002) 65(1) MLR 1, 2; Bradley W Miller, 'Majoritarianism and Pathologies of Judicial Review' in G Webber and others, *Legislated Rights* (CUP 2018) 196.

[59] Christ Hanretty, *A Court of Specialists* (OUP 2020); Cass R Sunstein, *Legal Reasoning and Political Conflict* (2nd edn, OUP 2018) ch 1.

[60] Jochen von Bernstorff, 'Authority Monism in International Organisations: A Historical Sketch' in J Mendes and I Venzke (eds), *Allocating Authority* (Hart 2018) 109.

its participation in the proceedings before the Court reduces the representation problem to some extent.

The concession that the problem is reduced in Strasbourg would not go far enough for some of the Court's most ardent defenders. They would submit that the over-representation of the few and the under-representation of the many in the law-making process of last instance courts would be outrightly desirable, because this would counter the power imbalances in the political process. This argument assumes that litigation is less affected by collective-organization problems and, therefore, more diffused than political lobbying, and that international adjudication provides a forum for those who lack legal and political clout domestically, since it may shed light on a State's treatment of vulnerable and minority groups.[61]

It is not clear, however, that the procedure before the Court does, in fact, equalize differences in political power in any satisfactory way. To be sure, in some cases the Court offers a corrective, but this risks bringing about a power imbalance of its own: if the Court recognizes an individual's interest claim as constituting a right protected under Convention law, the power balance is basically turned on its head, because the ruling cannot be challenged—or only with the utmost difficulty and minimal chances of success. The position of those who have succeeded in having their interest protected by the Court's interpretation of the Convention becomes largely exempted from effective contestation. The sole practical avenue available to those who disagree with a final Strasbourg ruling is to challenge it before the Court, which becomes possible only once an actionable situation based on suitable circumstances allows someone who is willing to litigate to raise the issue anew. Thus, the Court's entrenchment of an individual right amounts to an allocation of power in itself, since it limits the power to effectively raise anew a rights issue that may concern society at large to certain—ex ante unknown—individuals, that is, to those (un)lucky few who find themselves at some point of time in the position of claiming the 'victim status' necessary to bring an issue before the Court.[62] *Actiones populares*, by contrast, are inadmissible.[63]

More generally, it is unclear how much better than politics the Court system fares in terms of power imbalances stemming from resource problems and how grave the problems posed by the legal opportunity structures themselves are (eg standing and access, financial resources, expert support, and the receptivity and openness of the Convention law to new issues).[64] In order to litigate successfully (or at all) —just like in order to succeed at politics—the necessary resources and opportunities must be available.

[61] Dia Anagnostou, 'Law and Rights' Claiming on Behalf of Minorities in the Multi-Level European System' in D Anagnostou (ed), *Rights and Courts in Pursuit of Social Change* (Hart 2014) 3.

[62] Article 34 ECHR.

[63] See eg *Roman Zakharov v Russia* [GC], no 47143/06, para 164, ECHR 2015.

[64] See Ellen A Andersen, *Out of the Closets and Into the Courts* (University of Michigan Press 2005) 6–14.

That is, the same difficulties that prevent materially deprived, socially marginalized individuals from advocating for their interests in the political process may also stop them from bringing effective legal action. The means necessary to pay for litigation, including qualified legal counsel, are a notorious obstacle to justice, which may be especially difficult to overcome at Strasbourg: the Court's legal aid scheme is rightly described as minimal and restrictive.[65] Above all, legal aid is available only from an advanced stage of the admissibility proceedings onwards,[66] which means that no legal aid and, therefore, no qualified legal counsel, may be available during the admissibility stage of the proceedings that sifts out the vast majority of all applications. This casts doubts about whether the idea of the autonomous individual capable of bringing a case to the Court which, on an ideological level, firmly grounds the Convention system, as shaped by the Court and its predecessor institutions, corresponds to legal reality.

In other words, those who have the resources and support to defend their interests through effective litigation are unlikely to be those that have the least say in the political process.[67] Rather, they can seek to achieve their ends through the process that seems more favourable to their cause, while, if they are defeated, they can then try the other avenue.[68] A recent example of extremely costly and resource-intensive strategic litigation is the much debated case of *KlimaSeniorinnen*,[69] orchestrated and financed with more than 1 million euros by Greenpeace, which can hardly be said not to be a big-name actor. However, in general, it is difficult to estimate how many landmark cases are litigated, even if unsuccessfully, before the Court by parties that are genuinely structurally weak. Connections between individual applicants and non-governmental organizations, which are active in various roles before the Court, are not always discernible: civil society organizations often operate behind the scenes.[70] However that may be, as several scholars note, NGOs that are powerful enough to successfully mobilize the courts are unevenly distributed in society and pursue only select causes: the risk remains that the needs of those least privileged may remain uncared-for,[71] which may become aggravated through sorts of scale effects that cause well-established groups to continuously gain more support.[72]

[65] Andrew S Butler, 'Legal Aid Before Human Rights Treaty Monitoring Bodies' (2000) 49(2) ICLQ 360, 363.

[66] Rule 105(1) Rules of Court of 28 March 2024, in force since 28 March 2024.

[67] See eg *Big Brother Watch and Others v the United Kingdom* [GC], nos 58170/13 and 2 others, 25 May 2021.

[68] See Harlow (n 58) 17.

[69] *Verein KlimaSeniorinnen Schweiz and Others v Switzerland* [GC], no 53600/20, 9 April 2024.

[70] Loveday Hodson, 'Activists and Lawyers in the ECtHR: The Struggle for Gay Rights' in D Anagnostou (ed), *Rights and Courts in Pursuit of Social Change* (Hart 2014) 184.

[71] Bellamy (n 57) 245; Andreas Føllesdal, 'Why the European Court of Human Rights Might Be Democratically Legitimate—A Modest Defense' (2009) 27(2) Nord J Hum Rts 289, 302; Mark Tushnet, *Weak Courts, Strong Rights* (Princeton University Press 2008) 253–254.

[72] Claus Offe, '"Homogeneity" and Constitutional Democracy: Coping with Identity Conflicts Through Group Rights' (1998) 6(2) J Pol Phil 113, 137–138.

All of this may ground the fear that the Court offers a forum where everyone is given a voice only in theory, while, in reality, this forum remains as closed as the political arena to many individuals. In any case, the argument that the less-than-perfect representation and participation in the Court's proceedings is justified, since it simply provides redress for political inequalities, cannot fully convince. Conversely, the functioning of the Convention system offers a clear basis for the concern that the Convention system contributes to shifting political issues away from perhaps imperfect, but at least genuinely political forums—that is, the States' own democratic institutions—into a forum that suffers from similar problems in terms of opportunity structures, but also from a lack of conformity with democratic ideals, such as representativeness and everyone's chance of participation.

c) The Court as an epistemologically superior 'forum of principle'?

We have noted that it might be close to impossible to receive qualified legal counsel for financially poor applicants before the Court due to the Convention system's inadequate legal aid scheme. This poses a problem not only to individual justice but also to the public interest in a good jurisprudence: only if both sides of a case can submit proper arguments to the Court can it fully assess the impugned measure.[73] Only when everyone can bring a case under fair conditions will the Court be able to develop a set of jurisprudential rules that could aspire to develop into a just body of European human rights law. The point that good judgments require both litigant parties to be in a position to present their strongest possible case touches on considerations related to the epistemology of decision-making and to differences between judicial and political reasoning. Proponents and opponents of judicial review, such as those whose works we will discuss in Chapter 7, usually suggest that their 'favoured' decision-making body, that is, the constitutional court or parliament, has comparative advantages over its rival in terms of reaching just decisions about controversial rights issues.

A comparative argument suggesting that the Court would fare better or worse than the States' parliaments would not be possible here given the plurality of highly diverse parliamentary systems that we would need to consider. Given our focus on reasons for the Court's subsidiarity, all we can do is to draw attention to some of the Court's problems, which go often neglected. Thus, we do not argue that the Court fares worse than the (or any one of the) national parliaments do, but merely that assuming the opposite, as many Court scholars seem to do at least implicitly, is equally inadmissible.

[73] Butler (n 65) 363 (his note 10).

The perhaps most popular defence of rights-based judicial review is that judges are, on the whole, simply better at reasoning about rights than the participants in the political process. This argument holds that courts are 'forums of principle', concerned with justice, fairness, and morality, and therefore better suited to dealing with the normative issues raised in connection with individuals rights than politics is, since the latter is supposed to be single-mindedly focussed on optimizing the collective aggregate of individual interests.[74] Due to the judges' independence and impartiality, their relative isolation from ephemeral public trends and their high moral character, courts are said to render more just decisions than political bodies, most importantly parliaments.[75]

However, the respective normative value of judicial reasoning versus political reasoning remains controversial. As has been noted, 'legal reasoning and skill should not be confused with [the] moral reasoning and insight' asked for in deciding hard cases about rights and justice.[76] The dissimilar functioning of different courts and parliaments renders general arguments weak, but some of the Court's peculiarities cast doubt on the plausibility that this Court's reasoning about rights and justice, in particular, is superior to that of political debate. These peculiarities concern the Court's international setting, its judges, its resources and, finally, its adjudicative method.

At first sight, the Court's international setting means that it is well isolated from the political processes operating within the individual States. That is, it might be particularly reliable in making the correct decisions about rights because of its isolation from politics and the vagaries of short-term electoral accountability. Yet due to its peculiar enforcement mechanism, domestic political and diplomatic constraints are crucial for swift compliance with its judgments.[77] Anticipating these constraints is probably important for the Court's viability.[78] It is thus doubtful that the Court is really as isolated from domestic political trends as it seems to be at first sight.

Concerning the Court's judges, questions about the professional aptitude of some of them have not disappeared until today,[79] and the Court's reasoning and decision-making will not be significantly better than that of its individual members. A first problem is that a large number of the Court's judges come from countries whose commitment to liberal democracy appears unstable and that lack a

[74] Ronald Dworkin, 'The Forum of Principle' (1981) 56(2–3) NYU L Rev 469, 517–518.

[75] Ronald Dworkin, *Law's Empire* (Belknap Press 1986) 375.

[76] Alec Walen, 'Judicial Review in Review: A Four-Part Defense of Legal Constitutionalism: A Review Essay on Political Constitutionalism, by Richard Bellamy' (2009) 7(2) I•CON 329, 334.

[77] Courtney Hillebrecht, *Domestic Politics and International Human Rights Tribunals* (CUP 2014).

[78] See eg Tom Ginsburg, 'Political Constraints on International Courts' in CP Romano, KJ Alter, and Y Shany (eds), *The Oxford Handbook of International Adjudication* (OUP 2013).

[79] Christoph Grabenwarter and Matti Pellonpää, '"High Judicial Office" and "Jurisconsult of Recognised Competence": Reflections on the Qualifications for Becoming a Judge at the Strasbourg Court' (2020) 80(1) ZaöRV 13, 33–34.

long tradition of the rule of law, such that there may be doubts about some judges' familiarity with what these values entail for a judicial mandate.[80] A second problem is that there are relatively few proper expert judges on the Court's bench, since relatively few judges are recruited from among the States' highest judiciaries.[81] More generally, the Council of Europe's procedure for electing the Court's judges is probably sub-par.[82] However, even if the Court's judges would all be good judges at the domestic level, all but one of the judges on the bench are usually unfamiliar with the local circumstances of a case. Therefore, a third problem is that the Court's judges do not usually know much about the relevant domestic legal and factual situation of a case.[83] This is likely to unduly strengthen the weight of the national judge's opinion and the role of the case lawyers, who are also nationals of the States and who, because of the necessity of understanding the national law and language underlying a case, may be assumed to work often on cases concerning their home State.[84] Considering this, a fourth problem consists in risks of national bias and partiality:[85] the judges are elected on behalf of a particular State,[86] of which they are commonly nationals, for which they often served as legal, political, or diplomatic officials prior to their judicial mandate, whose actions they then judge (in most cases, even as a judge rapporteur[87]) and upon which their future careers may depend.[88] A final, again impartiality-related problem of the Court's judges consists in the fact that roughly one-fifth of them maintain affiliations with non-governmental organizations that work in the field of human rights and represent applicants before, or submit third-party interventions to, the Court. In dozens of cases, judges have sat on the bench in spite of affiliations with a human rights organization that appeared in the case, thus raising questions about the Convention law's impartiality and objectivity.[89] In this situation, the 'absence of prior emotional attachment to a case' required by judicial impartiality is doubtful.[90]

A further reason that casts doubts on the Court's nature as a 'forum of principle' is the Court's huge caseload, which is aggravated by its more general resource-related difficulties that result from severe financial constraints. The Court's budget

[80] George Letsas, 'The ECHR as a Living Instrument: Its Meaning and Legitimacy' in A Føllesdal, B Peters, and G Ulfstein (eds), *Constituting Europe* (CUP 2013) 131.
[81] Grabenwarter and Pellonpää (n 79) 32–33.
[82] Letsas (n 80) 130–131.
[83] See Article 26(4) ECHR; Rule 29(1) Rules of Court.
[84] cf Ledi Bianku and Peter Kempees, 'The European Court of Human Rights' in F Baetens (ed), *Legitimacy of Unseen Actors in International Adjudication* (CUP 2019) 111.
[85] See Luis López Guerra, 'The National Judge and Judicial Independence: The Case of the Strasbourg Court' (2017) 24(4) Maast J Eur & Comp L 552, 554–559.
[86] Article 22 ECHR.
[87] López Guerra (n 85) 559.
[88] ibid 557–558.
[89] Gaëtan Cliquennois, *European Human Rights Justice and Privatisation* (CUP 2020) 159–160.
[90] Frédéric Mégret, 'International Judges and Experts' Impartiality and the Problem of Past Declarations' (2011) 10(1) LPICT 31, 43.

per case is only a fraction of that of comparable courts.[91] This means, the Court's judges may mostly be more concerned with their daily struggle against their case overload than with the deep reflections on the legal and political morality of human-rights issues that the Court's preferred adjudicative method of deciding cases based on a fair-balance test would ideally involve. The casuistic weighing up of what are, in reality, incommensurable rights and interests is an inherently normative exercise that is not susceptible to clear legal answers. Instead, decisions are reached through a balancing exercise and, thus, based on moral reasoning. So, even if the Court's judges had plenty of time available for deep moral reflections of this type, it would be debatable whether they—or lawyers in general—have a comparative epistemic advantage in this exercise: it is not evident why international or constitutional lawyers would be especially well qualified for this task of moral reasoning.[92]

Many critics of constitutional review would indeed suggest otherwise. As a popular argument against judicial review goes, the political process is more open and comprehensive than court proceedings are because political debate is less constrained and much more often conducted in public forums than the judicial process. Since political deliberation is less formal than legal argumentation, it allows all types of arguments and reasons to be brought forward, and it is not cloaked in obfuscating jargon or constrained by certain semantic and argumentative structures.[93]

Importantly, this is not to suggest that political majority rule reveals a Rousseauian general interest. To be sure, many, if not all, of the forty-six States' democratic process are less than perfect. Thus, the problems of the Court's decision-making excellence raised above do not in any conclusive sense mean that it fares worse in making the moral choices that it must make when dealing with the cases before it than do political bodies. In particular, democratic majority voting will always leave a defeated minority that is compelled to accept the majority's choice, even if that choice is in fundamental opposition to their interests. Clearly, this is a danger against which judicial control may protect in some cases. Yet, apart from the fact that the Court suffers from certain significant decision-making problems, we must not assume that this is so in any case simply because the protection of vulnerable individuals is the role of the Court after all: justifying the claim that the Court knows best how to construe and protect the Convention's human-rights guarantees by pointing to the Court's legal mandate[94] would be reminiscent of

[91] See Elisabeth Lambert-Abdelgawad, 'The Court as a Part of the Council of Europe: the Parliamentary Assembly and the Committee of Ministers' in A Føllesdal, B Peters, and G Ulfstein (eds), *Constituting Europe* (CUP 2013) 293.

[92] Miller (n 58) 195.

[93] See eg Jeremy Waldron, 'The Core of the Case Against Judicial Review' (2006) 115(6) Yale LJ 1346, 1380–1386.

[94] See eg Geir Ulfstein, 'The European Court of Human Rights and National Courts: A Constitutional Relationship?' in OM Árnardóttir and A Buyse (eds), *Shifting Centres of Gravity in Human Rights Protection* (Routledge 2016) 50.

Justice Jackson's famous pun,[95] which reminds us that we must not think of the Court as infallible merely because it is a final instance.

d) The Court's judicial supremacy as a prerequisite of political democracy?

Justice Jackson's dictum—we are not final because we are infallible, but we are infallible only because we are final—recalls that conditions of reasonable disagreement and epistemic uncertainty prevail in real-life conditions. That is, it is generally unclear and controversial what the right, most just, or otherwise best solution is. There 'is no "canonical" meaning of any particular rights … they are merely shorthand ways of referring to a bundle of entitlements that correspond to certain values [and] people disagree about the proper balancing of those values'.[96] To justify the Court's ultimate interpretative authority over the Convention with the argument that the Court and its decision-making process is superior to democratic alternatives when it comes to finding the 'best' rights interpretations is all the more difficult if, as Wojciech Sadurski suggests, the (specific) meaning of rights is ultimately the result of a discursive social practice.[97]

This leads to what is, for present purposes at least, the central argument for settling controversial rights issues that concern society at large through the channels of democratic politics instead of in the courts: namely that everyone should be equally involved and equally responsible, as it were, for the ordering of society's collective life. This argument is one of procedural justice and it builds on the idea that democratically made choices are superior to other choices in the sense that only democratic decisions can claim to be morally binding for all members of the political community, because they all had an equal say in them.[98] At the most fundamental level, political democracy leads to an equal—and in this sense intrinsically fair—distribution of political power: democratic politics is the only way in which every member of a political community can fundamentally have an equal say with regard to the innumerable choices between conflicting interests and values that societal life entails. The point is not that political equality is a more important form of equality than substantive equality, but that simple majority rule at least makes it possible to firmly and visibly commit to the 'prior acceptance of a strongly egalitarian premise'.[99]

Interestingly, the perhaps most important and popular defence of rights-based judicial review also taps into this justificatory potential of political (ie democratic)

95 See Supreme Court of the United States, *Brown v Allan*, 344 US 443, 540 (1953).
96 Wojciech Sadurski, *Rights Before Courts* (2nd edn, Springer 2014) 46.
97 ibid 47–48.
98 See Wojciech Sadurski, *Equality and Legitimacy* (OUP 2008) ch 2.
99 ibid 90.

equality. This line of argument attempts to negate the democratic difficulties of rights-based judicial review by presenting rights as indispensable prerequisites of democracy itself: it holds that rights are a prerequisite of democratic politics, and therefore need to be protected by an institution that is external to the democratic process and that, to be effective, must be superordinated to this process. Those who call for a markedly subsidiary Court based on fears that the Court's international control undermines the States' democracies would turn out to be hypocrites, on this account, since their own demand would have to be taken as an attack on the indispensable prerequisites of democracy, and therefore on democracy itself.

However, there is a fundamental difficulty with this justification of (international) rights-based judicial review as an indispensable democratic prerequisite. For just as one may disagree about rights and justice in general, one may also reasonably disagree about what rights democracy presupposes.[100] Moreover, even if all Europeans agreed that democracy presupposes exactly those abstract rights listed in the Convention, it remained unclear what these rights precisely mean and require. The Court itself is very well aware of this: it leaves considerable discretion to the States in cases concerning their democratic processes.[101]

Thus, what Sadurski calls the 'standard defence' of rights-based review will not convince those who hold to the democratic principle according to which questions that concern all members of a polity should be decided through that mechanism which aggregates individual choices into a social choice in a way that is most responsive to the members' individual interests and that most visibly treats all individuals equally, namely: simple majority voting.[102] Simple majority voting is the only way of 'aggregating' the opinions of individuals who disagree into a collective preference that respects the equal value of each vote, while maximizing its weight.[103] Such equal decision-making is, in and of itself, a requirement of justice, if the equal advancement of everyone's fundamental interests is the most basic principle of justice and people are in disagreement about what this requires.[104]

This is not to suggest there could be a legitimate democratic process without individual liberty rights. The point is that the reverse argument is valid too: there are no legitimate rights without democracy determining these rights and while there must be limits on democracy, democracy requires that these limits be contestable.[105] The latter argument evokes the worries about judicial domination compellingly formulated by republican political theorists[106]—that is, fears of 'undemocratic liberalism'[107]—suggesting that judicial rights determinations must not

[100] Neil Walker, 'Constitutionalism and the Incompleteness of Democracy: An Iterative Relationship' (2010) 39(3) Rechtsfilosofie & Rechtstheorie 206, 221.
[101] See eg *Ždanoka v Latvia* [GC], no 58278/00, para 103, ECHR 2006-IV.
[102] Sadurski, *Rights Before Courts* (n 96) 46.
[103] Jeremy Waldron, *The Dignity of Legislation* (CUP 1999) 148.
[104] See Thomas Christiano, *The Constitution of Equality* (OUP 2008) chs 1 and 3.
[105] Chantal Mouffe, *The Democratic Paradox* (Verso 2000) 4.
[106] See eg Bellamy (n 57).
[107] Yascha Mounk, *The People vs. Democracy* (HUP 2018) ch 2.

rule a democratic society. The former argument, by contrast, raises concerns about political tyranny or 'illiberal democracy',[108] suggesting that democratic majorities must not be unchecked in a liberal, rights-based society.[109]

Contemporary liberal-democratic thought has downplayed the problem, which we discuss in the next chapter, that the aspiration to combine liberalism, viz individual freedom from government and state-approved or state-tolerated interference, and democracy, viz collective self-government through the aggregation of individual preferences, seeks to unite two political goals that have never smoothly coexisted. There are many alternative approaches to tackling the dilemma that equal liberal rights should spring from the free choice adopted by political equals, whereas such free choices can only be made among equals when they enjoy equal guarantees that secure their freedom in making up their own minds. Some of the most brilliant legal and political thinkers have reasonably disagreed about the best solution to this problem—no wonder, one may also disagree as regards the role of the Court as judicial constraint vis-à-vis the States' democratic institutions. In fact, the Court's location outside of any of the democratic polities under its control gives the debate an extra edge, as we will see in Chapter 6.

E) Democratic concerns as justification of the subsidiarity principle

Although most scholars of Convention law have been hostile to the idea of underlining the Court's merely subsidiary role, it is not, in principle, unreasonable to argue for a markedly subsidiary Court, viz to argue against judicial activism, based on democratic concerns. In deciding about rights issues, neither the superiority of the judicial process nor that of the political one can be taken as established. No doubt, both processes usefully complement each other, but one may reasonably disagree about the best way to arrange their complementarity, about how the Convention system combines political and judicial processes, and about whether a more activist or a more subsidiary Court would be preferable. While the previous chapters tentatively connected calls for more subsidiarity on the part of the Court to the States' democratic self-government, to the requisite conditionality of the Court's interventions, and to value pluralism, this chapter confirmed that such concerns can justifiably provide support to the Convention's principle of subsidiarity. However, legitimate objections must be borne in mind: State sovereignty must not be absolute, but find its limits where a State mistreats the individuals under its control; the Court system could not control these limits if the States'

[108] ibid ch 1.

[109] András Sajó and Renáta Uitz, *The Constitution of Freedom* (OUP 2017) ch 9.

leeway was unbounded, that is, if there were no common European standards; and the States' democracies depend on liberal rights that are practically guaranteed.

As there is no one right answer to the question of how political and judicial responsibility for decisions about individual rights and justice should be shared, the following chapter must examine in more detail the complicated relationship between liberal rights and democracy. Furthermore, we will enquire into the reconciliation of the respective concerns behind the liberal and the democratic principle through the institutionalization of distinct legal and political powers, so as to understand the special difficulty that rights-based judicial review poses to this endeavour. Only then will it be possible to discuss and assess possible solutions to the problem at hand, in the form of a developed understanding of the subsidiarity principle's normativity.

5

Liberal Rights and Democratic Politics

A) Introduction

With the European Court of Human Rights (the Court, ECtHR) having been accused of being too activist, the system set up under the European Convention on Human Rights (the Convention, ECHR),[1] is trapped in a tension between concerns about state sovereignty and international control, national leeway and common standards, and democratic politics and rights-based judicial review (see Chapter 4). It would appear that the latter component of each of these three interrelated 'pairs' expresses the very object and purpose behind the Court system: it was set up in order to exercise judicial control over the member states (the States) based on common human rights standards of international law. The founding of the Convention system was strongly motivated by the goal of preventing Europe from falling back into nationalistic political totalitarianism. When many of the States most heavily afflicted by this horrible past set up new constitutions and established powerful constitutional courts as their guardians, the Convention system was created as an additional bulwark.

As Chapter 3 shows, the Convention system has become judicialized, over the course of several decades. In the first decades of its existence, the dominant actors were political, rather than legal authorities, namely, the States' governments. This founding period foregrounded the States' political commitment to respecting the tenets of liberal democracy over reliance on the constraints of judicial reason. Hence, to maintain that the concerns motivating recent calls for more subsidiarity on the part of the Court are new or foreign to the system would be to show one's ignorance of the Convention system's longer-term development: these concerns may have been largely dormant for a long while, but they were always inherent in the system. The preambular amendments made by means of Protocol No 15 merely emphasize long-standing jurisprudential principles by codifying them.

Still, the decades prior to 2010 were shaped by a Court that gradually built up the Convention into a veritable 'cordon' within which the States' domestic laws and politics must remain, comparable to national constitutional cordons.[2] The States have, by and large, accepted this development. Thus, today, Convention law is

[1] Convention for the Protection of Human Rights and Fundamental Freedoms, as amended, of 4 November 1950, in force since 3 September 1953, 213 UNTS 221, CETS No 005.

[2] cf Martin Loughlin, *Sword and Scales* (Hart 2000) 232.

Subsidiarity, Legitimacy, and the European Court of Human Rights. Reto Walther, Oxford University Press.
 DOI: 10.1093/9780198921455.003.0005

constitutional law in this sense, and the Court, determining the course that the Conventional cordon takes and watching over trespassers, is a constitutional court insofar as it takes on the function that domestic constitutional courts fulfil at the national level.

In line with the perennial controversies about the democratic legitimacy of constitutional review, the previous chapter suggested that the Court's mission is a delicate one, if great value is placed not only on international judicial human rights review but also on the States' democratic character. It touched upon this delicate point when it noted the paradox that democratic institutions depend on individual freedom, viz on liberal rights, but that, in a democracy, liberal rights, to be legitimate, themselves depend on their legitimation through the democratic process.

This is the great dilemma of liberal-democratic constitutionalism: on the one hand, no collective political process can exercise legitimate democratic authority over the individual without the protection afforded by just individual freedoms ('liberal principle'); on the other hand, no individual can justifiably claim rights over and against the political community and other individual citizens unless these rights have been collectively legitimized ('democratic principle').[3] As Samantha Besson suggests, this is also a problem of justice (morality) and legitimacy (democracy),[4] reflecting a tension between a respect for each individual's equal moral value, that is, for justice in the individual case, and a respect for the political community's collective choices concerning the general ordering of the common life. This tension points to the challenges that a system of liberal-rights adjudication—of constitutional justice—such as that of the Court, may pose to democracy.

It is not possible for liberal-democratic constitutionalism to avoid this predicament, and it seems difficult to find ways of combining democratic and judicial rights-based decision-making without placing undue emphasis on either the democratic or the liberal principle: establishing a system of constitutional justice tends to result in the supremacy of liberal rights, and hence of the conception of justice held by whoever interprets those rights, while, in the opposite case, the majoritarian democratic will reigns supreme. Each of these configurations raises a different problem. It is not surprising, therefore, that regardless of the choice of system in each case, the detailed arrangement of judicial liberal-rights protection and democratic politics can never be settled once and for all. The development of the Convention system provides ample evidence for this claim: the subsidiarity principle gained prominence due to a renewed upsurge of concerns about

[3] In detail, Christoph Möllers, *The Three Branches* (OUP 2013) ch 2.

[4] Samantha Besson, 'International Judges as Dispute-Settlers and Law-Enforcers: From International Law Without Courts to International Courts Without Law' (2011) 34(1) Loy LA Int'l & Comp L Rev 33, 42.

the Court's (allegedly excessive) limitation of the States' democratic prerogatives after a period of widespread support for an ever-increasing judicialization of the Convention system.

A sound grasp of the predicament of liberal-democratic constitutionalism is important for obtaining a full understanding of the difficult questions that Conventional *qua* constitutional review raises, in terms of both the challenges it poses and the complementarity it promises to democratic institutions. The present chapter starts with a discussion of the vexed relationship between liberalism and democracy, before turning its attention to the institutional, that is, legal and political, instantiation of liberal rights and democratic politics, noting in particular the difficulties that result from the odd position that constitutional authorities—or 'constitutional guardians'—occupy in liberal-democratic separation-of-powers theory.

B) Liberalism and democracy

The liberal idea of individual freedom rights and democracy have come to be understood as nearly synonymous, and the staple response to the question of how human rights are best protected has become 'by democratic government'. The Convention Preamble and the Court's dictum that democracy is the only system of government compatible with the Convention[5] testify to this. However, the relationship between democracy and protected individual freedoms is, in reality, more complicated and not susceptible to an easy answer.

Before we go on with this discussion, we should recall some caveats. The tensions between democratic politics and protected liberal rights have been the subject of immense debates among, in particular, scholars of philosophy and political theory. Thus, as lawyers we must not venture into this debate in the naive belief that we can advance these fields or solve these tensions. The aim of this section is no more than to set out a sort of dialectical framework for the remainder of the book which illustrates in a clear and concise form the tensions between the liberal and the democratic principle and the two fundamentally opposite ways theorists can go to find a way out of these tensions. The accounts of liberal-democratic theory that we look at in the following were thus chosen not because these are the most convincing accounts of liberal-democratic theory, but because they serve the purpose just described: as accounts that are markedly liberal-*democratic* and *liberal*-democratic, respectively, they are well suited to illustrate the fundamentally opposed procedural and substantive logic of the democratic and liberal principles, clarity about which is crucial for the further discussion and, especially, a sound

[5] See eg *United Communist Party of Turkey and Others v Turkey* [GC], 30 January 1998, para 45, Reports of Judgments and Decisions 1998-I.

understanding of the different roles and functions of legal and political decision-making that follows these two contrary logics.

a) Pretentious judges and circular democrats

Critics of the current Convention system who call for more subsidiarity fear that the Court overly constrains the States' political democracies in the name of liberal rights. This suggests an understanding of the relationship between liberal rights and democracy as a sort of zero-sum game, in which more democratic choice comes at the expense of liberal rights and in which greater protection of rights entails less room for democratic self-determination. We will discuss this aporetic understanding of liberal-democratic constitutionalism by drawing on Andrew Levine's *Liberal Democracy: A Critique of Its Theory*, which offers a clear and concise account of the—for present purposes—central difficulty of the combination of liberal rights and democratic politics.

According to Levine, liberal-democratic constitutionalism—that is, constitutionalism built on the twin justificatory concepts of just individual freedom and legitimate collective self-determination—is internally incoherent because it is impossible to reconcile its two components. As he puts it, the liberal principle 'holds that there are aspects of an individual's life, including certain of his actions, which are private and with which others [especially the state] can never rightfully [justly] interfere',[6] whereas the democratic principle requires 'that political decisions [to be legitimate] should be determined collectively, and that collective decisions should be, at least indirectly, functions of individuals' choices among the options in contention'.[7]

Framing the liberal principle as a procedural decision-making rule, one may say that it gives each individual a prerogative: within the private sphere delimited for him or her, the individual is 'sovereign'. In this domain, the individual's choice is the social choice.[8] The public sphere, in which the democratic choice rules, is thus limited—but not made redundant—by each individual's 'sovereignty' over her or his private sphere.[9] In Jeremy Waldron's provocative words, this understanding of liberal rights, 'make[s] individuals dictators on the issues these rights cover'.[10] This way of putting it is helpful insofar as it also makes it possible—in contrast to formulations in terms of non-interference—to account for individual choices for state action, which require all others *qua* constituent members of the state community

[6] Andrew Levine, *Liberal Democracy* (Columbia University Press 1981) 93.
[7] ibid 1.
[8] See Amartya Sen, 'The Impossibility of a Paretian Liberal' (1970) 78(1) J Pol Eco 152.
[9] Levine (n 6) 95, 102.
[10] Jeremy Waldron, 'Rights of Majorities and Minorities: Rousseau Revisited' in JW Chapman and A Wertheimer (eds), *Majorities and Minorities* (NYU Press 1990) 66.

to act. Given the Court's abundant and controversial positive-rights jurisprudence (see Chapter 6), this aspect is important.

The democratic principle, for its part, is grounded in the insight that individuals benefit from public authority and a well-ordered state, if that state operates in such a way as to promote the best interests of those individuals who live under its authority. This is why a collective decision-making procedure must combine individual interests into social choices.[11] In order to maximize the aggregate interest of a group of individuals, majority voting is best: it is most neutral with regard to the competing options and most responsive to the voters' choices.[12] That is, it produces the most preferred and hence strongest outcome.[13]

The scope and content of the liberal principle answers the question about the just limits of the scope of application of the democratic principle: it determines those parts of an individual's life that are protected from interference by the state and others or—conversely and more broadly formulated—it determines those individual interests which the political community must secure for its individual members whether it likes it or not.[14] In order to be effective, the liberal principle requires determinate substantive content; if it is to be successful, liberal-democratic theory 'must non-arbitrarily delineate the domains of [its] two components'.[15] Neither individual assertions of private spheres of freedom nor the general postulation of a rebuttable presumption in favour of individual freedom can, however, provide a clear, legitimate answer to the question about the limits to democratic decision-making: if it were otherwise, the Court would have to approve of all rights claims submitted to it, and the German Federal Constitutional Court, the custodian of a general right to liberty,[16] would never be confronted with difficult cases.

Liberals have undertaken manifold attempts to delineate the private sphere of individual freedom from the public sphere of democratic decision-making. There is no way to adequately and justifiably protect individual freedom from democratic decisions unless the scope and content of the former is clearly and non-arbitrarily determined.[17] The search is for such a principled delineation that must not itself depend on what it is to do: the rule that delineates the liberal (private) and the democratic (public) domain must not itself derive from the public institutions and practices of, or the opinions and intuitions held by, the dominant members of the

[11] Levine (n 6) 20–21, 25–27.

[12] Kenneth O May, 'A Set of Independent Necessary and Sufficient Conditions for Simple Majority Decision' (1952) 20(4) Econometrica 680; see also Kenneth J Arrow, 'A Difficulty in the Concept of Social Welfare' (1950) 58(4) J Pol Eco 328.

[13] Wojciech Sadurski, *Equality and Legitimacy* (OUP 2008) 70–73.

[14] See Levine (n 6) 13.

[15] ibid 94.

[16] Federal Constitutional Court of Germany, *Elfes*, no 1 BvR 253/56 of 16 January 1957 (published in BVerfGE 6, 32).

[17] Levine (n 6) 102–103.

society (whether numerically or otherwise) to which it applies its constraining effect.[18]

The task at hand would be easy if it was not for the fact that there is essentially no individual conduct that does not affect others: every individual action affects others except for, perhaps, the most trivial actions of inner consciousness—there is hardly any purely self-regarding conduct. Because an individual whose freedom and interests are affected by another's actions has an interest in the regulation of the latter's conduct, conflicting individual spheres of freedom and interest must be delineated. The liberal-democratic assumption that everyone is the best judge of his or her own interests, viz that everyone is equally rational,[19] complicates matters: if select individuals are charged with this delineation, the outcome would depend on their subjective (arbitrary and undemocratic) choice, which would—due to its violation of the democratic principle that no one knows better than anyone else how to govern society[20]—appear 'condescending',[21] as Waldron puts it, or 'pretentious' in the sense given to the term in Friedrich Hayek's Nobel Memorial Lecture. The lecture, entitled 'The Pretence of Knowledge', warned against the 'scientistic' pretence to precise and comprehensive knowledge based on an expert's own pet theories about how to better the social order in cases where there cannot be such knowledge due to society's complexity.[22] Although Hayek seems to have been sympathetic to some forms of judicial review,[23] we will use the term 'pretentious' throughout the rest of this book to refer to this particular scientistic-elitist attitude of claiming to know better than the rest of society what is good for the individual and the collective. The alternative to this pretentious approach to solve the problem at hand would consist in appealing to the norms and intuitions that prevail in the democratic community, which would, however, defeat the purpose of delineating a domain in which individual choice governs regardless of social choice: since those whose freedom is to be limited (the democratic rulers) would determine the limits themselves, this strategy would be circular.[24]

Appealing to the concept of rights in order to make this delineation does not solve the problem. The exercise of individual rights is, just like any exercise of individual freedom, basically always other-regarding. Claiming one's own rights nearly always means restricting others' freedom to pursue what they consider their best interests: exercising a right requires others, often represented by the state, to

[18] ibid 107–109.

[19] See ibid ch 4.

[20] See Stephen Holmes, *Passions and Constraint* (Chicago University Press 1995) 26.

[21] Jeremy Waldron, 'The Constitutional Conception of Democracy' in his *Law and Disagreement* (OUP 1999) 303.

[22] Friedrich A Hayek, 'The Pretence of Knowledge: Nobel Memorial Lecture, December 11, 1974' (1989) 79(6) Am Econ Rev 3.

[23] See Friedrich A Hayek, *Law, Legislation and Liberty, vol 3* (Routledge & Kegan Paul 1982) ch 17; Anthony I Ogus, 'Law and Spontaneous Order: Hayek's Contribution to Legal Theory' (1989) 16(4) J L & Soc 393, 399–403.

[24] Levine (n 6) 118.

refrain from certain actions or, less commonly, to engage in certain actions that are beneficial to the right-holder's personal interests. At the latest, the exercise of legally protected individual rights becomes other-regarding, engaging the entire political community as represented by the state, when it requires the activation of the resource-limited government's machinery of law administration and enforcement.[25]

Thus, rights too must be determined either on the basis of a pretence, that is, by pretending to be mere objective readings of the law,[26] in fact based on a subjectively held normative theory—this is what human rights theorists do when they put forward various lists of human rights[27]—or in a circular manner, namely, based on the opinions of the social majority.[28] The Court's jurisprudence contains evidence of the judges' attempts to navigate between these equally imperfect options, such as when they occasionally note that a Convention guarantee must not be 'made conditional on its being accepted by the majority'[29] and, on other occasions, base their interpretative development of the Convention law on a 'European consensus' among the States.[30]

In the final analysis, liberal-democratic constitutionalism is incoherent, according to Levine, because there is neither a non-pretentious nor a non-circular way to distinguish the domains in which the free individual and the free democratic choice respectively rule. Although individual freedom and the equal distribution of the possibility of personal self-realization are widely recognized as important, conceptions of the proper domain of protected individual freedom may diverge significantly. What the 'right' liberal domain is and what is 'right' when divergent views concerning this question collide is a problem of justice that may lead to bitter societal conflicts. Taking decisions about the private sphere in a circular manner, by majority rule, is dangerous. But taking this decision based on a certain theory about what is right and just is dangerous, too: as Karl Popper gloomily reminds his readers, 'making heaven on earth ... only succeeds in making it a hell'.[31]

b) Rights as democratic self-constraints?

Those sceptical of a more restrained Court and, conversely, less critical of the democratic legitimacy of rights-based judicial review may oppose calls for a more decidedly subsidiary Court on the basis of an account of liberalism and democracy

[25] See Judith Resnik, 'Courts and Economic and Social Rights/Courts as Economic and Social Rights' in KG Young (ed), *The Future of Economic and Social Rights* (CUP 2019) 259–260, 267.
[26] See Oliver W Holmes, 'The Path of the Law' (1997) 110(5) Harv L Rev 991, 994.
[27] See eg James Griffin, *On Human Rights* (OUP 2008).
[28] cf Jean-Jacques Rousseau, *The Social Contract* (OUP 1994) 73.
[29] See eg *Bayev and Others v Russia*, nos 67667/09 and 2 others, para 70, 20 June 2017.
[30] See Chapter 8.
[31] Karl Popper, *The Open Society and Its Enemies* (Princeton University Press 2013) 157.

that is quite different than Levine's, one that presents liberal rights less as constraining than as promoting democracy. Simply put, they may argue that better protection of individual rights makes for better democracy, presenting liberalism and democracy as mutually beneficial components of a dual constitutionalism.

Stephen Holmes' account of liberal-democratic theory, *Passions and Constraint: On the Theory of Liberal Democracy*, defends this view. The liberal constraints that some take to tend towards unduly constraining democracy are, if looked at through his lens, simply indispensable enabling conditions of democratic politics. Holmes' account thus virtually turns the critical argument on its head, suggesting that it is wrong to mainly think of liberal rights as constraints on democracy and arguing that they instead play a crucial role in enabling the democratic process.[32]

Holmes' argument starts from the presumption that all individuals rationally pursue their individual self-interest. A commitment to the moral value that everyone is equal inheres in the assumption that everyone rationally pursues their own self-interest: if all human beings are taken to be equally rational optimizers of their self-interest, no one is better suited to rule than anyone else.[33] This claim underpins the idea of constitutionally constrained democratic government, because if all humans are self-interested and partial, the rulers, too, need to be ruled. Whoever rules must be subject to constraints that ensure that their rule serves not their own partial interests, but rather common, socially desirable goals.[34]

How is it possible, then, in large, modern societies for the people who know their interests best to act collectively at all and how is it possible for them to retain a say in, and control over, their government? The answer, of course, is that public discussion about political matters and political participation must be defended against attempts on the part of the ruling elite to capture the state for their own interests; rules and procedures must guarantee the competitive elections and free political debate that are necessary to ensure the democratic rule of the popular sovereign.[35]

Paradoxically, in order to guarantee these individual freedoms, the exercise of public authority by the very same government that is to be constrained proves indispensable.[36] In order to succeed in its cooperative enterprise, a political community must, through its governmental authority, provide tangible security guarantees, effectively enforce individual rights, and provide political and other minorities with reliable guarantees of equal treatment that safeguard their participation in public affairs on fair terms. Otherwise, those who are defeated and

[32] Holmes (n 20) xii–xiii, 9.
[33] ibid 26.
[34] ibid 4–5, 63–66.
[35] See ibid 8–9, 35, 167–172.
[36] ibid 19, 135–136.

oppressed are unlikely to accept common decisions, rules, and institutions. They may instead resist and cause turmoil.[37]

Holmes attempts to solve this (apparent) paradox by distinguishing between two different temporal perspectives, claiming that it is only a question of the time horizon applied as to whether liberal 'constraints' actually constrain or enable democracy: while liberal constraints limit democratic majorities in the short term, they enable democracy in the longer term.[38] According to Holmes, successful democracies have learned to collectively constrain themselves, to agree on 'a kind of collective *stare decisis*' that 'help[s] them to limit the range of options they have readily available' and that continues to legitimately constrain political majorities because it enjoys enduring popular consent.[39] In this view, the depoliticization of certain highly divisive matters, in the sense of their exclusion from the political battleground and from the realm of public interest more generally, is crucial, because unless a political community puts to rest its fiercest conflicts stemming from pervasive disagreements, it will not succeed in its cooperative, mutually beneficial enterprise.[40]

For Holmes, the conclusion of this line of argument is that the question of why a ruling collective would bind itself, that is, of how liberal constraints and democracy go together, can be answered by appealing to the insight that self-constraints ultimately have not an authority-limiting, but rather an authority-enhancing effect.[41]

c) Self-constraints and reasonable disagreement

The explanatory force of Holmes' account may legitimize the Convention system to some extent, as an institution that contributes to the States' long-term viability as democracies. However, the justificatory potential of his theory only goes so far, since he disregards a problem that he is clearly aware of, namely, the need to specify—and to solve conflicts between—the only prima facie uncontroversial rights that his theory implies.[42] In real life, controversies abound about precisely what forms of self-constraint democracy requires in areas such as religious toleration, judicial fairness, free speech, minimal economic guarantees, or appropriate state protection against threats of private violence. For example, the Court's practice shows that the religious domain, where tolerance has historically been decisive for social peace and cohesion, is a fiercely contested subject matter, as the illustrative example of *Lautsi*, which lists an impressive list of third-party interveners with an interest in the matter, shows.[43] Consider also that the forty-six political

[37] ibid 29–31.
[38] ibid 9–10.
[39] ibid 10 (original italics).
[40] ibid 102–106, 120–122, 211, 216.
[41] ibid 150–153.
[42] See ibid chs 7–8.
[43] *Lautsi and Others v Italy* [GC], no 30814/06, ECHR 2011 (extracts).

communities united within the Convention system may have quite different needs in terms of toleration and depoliticization: each State's successful internal political cooperation may depend on different constraints because their domestic societal conflicts may concern different issues and occur in different contexts. For instance, the Court's judgment in *Leyla Şahin* that did not find a headscarf ban in violation of the Convention must be read within the relevant context of Turkish society, where religious matters play a very different role than, for example, in the five Nordic countries.[44] From the latter, almost no cases concerning religious freedom reach the Court, whereas trade union rights under Article 11 would appear to be a comparatively important issue in Scandinavia. This means that democratic agreement about liberal rights usually, and especially in an international treaty system, holds only at a very high level of abstraction.

A political community that is forced to come to an agreement about what to do in the face of controversies concerning the scope and content of its liberal commitments essentially has two options available: either the citizens themselves (or their representatives) can resolve the controversies by majority rule or they can leave them to a 'counter-majoritarian' body, usually a constitutional court. Both solutions are imperfect. The former option weakens the prospective and constraining element of the notion of self-*constraints*. Here, the self-constraints risk degenerating into arbitrary ad hoc rule: if the meaning of constitutional constraints is determined afresh by majority rule whenever they are applied, what are they good for?

The latter option suffers from another problem. If liberal rights were *self*-constraints negotiated among political equals in an attempt to delineate the common ground upon which they can build their common political and social life, the relevant rights system would need to be part of the democratic polity itself. However, this is not, or only in a very limited sense, the case in the Convention system, which subjects State-level politics to 'external' European-level constraints. The *inter*-national character of the Convention system undermines the endogenous nature of the States' 'self-constraints': in particular, the more substantially the Court interprets the Convention rights, the less those rights appear to be democratically willed, as per Holmes' account, and the more they become exogenous in the sense that a trustee's decision cannot be said to be the decisions specifically willed by the trustor.

Consider, in this regard, the words Susan Marks chose to conclude her investigation into the conditions that made possible the Court's remarkable *Belilos* judgment, where the Court as the first international tribunal ever declared a member State reservation to a treaty invalid.[45] Suggesting that the States intentionally built the structural conditions that allowed Convention law to take on a life of its own

[44] *Leyla Şahin v Turkey* [GC], no 44774/98, ECHR 2005-XI.
[45] *Belilos v Switzerland*, 29 April 1988, Series A no 132.

and that decoupled it from its progenitors' democratic volition into the treaty system, she writes:

> If those provisions [i.e. the Convention rights] have come to take on a life of their own – not necessarily following the precise path mapped out for them by their creators, but finding instead their own more unswerving, more efficacious path for reaching the desired ends – then the Convention has surely served its purpose.[46]

Marks claims neither that the Convention system simply executes the will of its creators nor that the Convention system has taken on a life of its own against the will of the States. Does this make it possible to avoid both the problem of circularity and the problem of pretentiousness noted above?

Marks essentially offers a variant of the much-discussed defence of constitutional review that presents constitutional entrenchment and its entrustment to the judiciary as a form of self-commitment on the part of society: an actor which grasps the danger of taking wrong decisions in the future takes precautionary measures which precommits it to the right actions and precludes it from taking the wrong ones.[47] Following this logic, a political community, knowing that it could potentially destroy the foundations of its own democratic self-government, could preventively choose to transfer control over the abstract liberal constraints it deems indispensable for its democracy's viability to another party. On this reading, the very purpose of a State's submission to the Court's control could potentially be to give away its authority over decisions about the liberal rights it considers essential to its survival as a democratic polity, that is, to delegate the authority about these liberal constraints to judicial trustees 'given independent authority to make decisions according to their best judgment'.[48]

That said, however prudent this decision might be, the liberal constraints in question can no longer be plausibly understood as *self*-constraints as the quotation above makes clear. Without going into the details, it suffices to note the following two issues. First, it is doubtful whether a political community can actually *agree* on constitutional precommitments. Unlike in the case of the individual trustor, a collective is likely to disagree about the precise nature of the precommitment to be made: in order to overcome this problem, precommitments may be framed vaguely, so as to allow all participants to understand them in their preferred sense, which is one explanation for the open formulations usually adopted in negotiations

[46] Susan Marks, 'Reservations Unhinged: The Belilos Case Before the European Court of Human Rights' (1990) 39(2) ICLQ 300, 327.

[47] See eg Samuel Freeman, 'Constitutional Democracy and the Legitimacy of Constitutional Review' (1990) 9(4) Law & Phil 327, 353–354.

[48] Karen J Alter, 'Agents or Trustees? International Courts in Their Political Context' (2008) 14(1) Eur J Intl Rel 33, 35.

of treaties such as the Convention.[49] While this is not a problem per se, it means that some parts of the precommitment may not feel like self-imposed constraints for some members of the collective and that other parts of it will not feel like self-imposed constraints for other members of the collective. This is essentially what can be observed when a State government argues that it never committed to this or that reading of the Convention.

Second, problems arise from changes in the identity of the members who compose the entity that precommits itself: younger generations are bound by precommitments entered into by earlier generations, which is particularly troublesome if it is difficult or nearly impossible to make changes to the original precommitment. The original precommitment would then appear to be something of a power play on the part of a one-time majority, representing the entrenchment of the values and decision-making procedures that that majority holds dear.[50] This resonates with the argument that human rights treaties have been a means employed by incumbent governments to 'lock in' the status quo.[51] Again, this is not necessarily a problem—there is nothing bad about locking in liberal-democratic constitutionalism—but it does not fit well with Holmes' attempted reconciliation of liberal constraints with democracy, which depends on these constraints being *self*-imposed.

This conclusion brings Levine's arguments about the internal contradictions of liberal-democratic constitutionalism back into focus. If controversies about a democracy's liberal self-constraints are resolved by majority rule, this leads to the problem of circularity, since the liberal constraints will lack a credible constraining effect. If disputes about a democracy's liberal self-constraints are resolved by an external authority, however, this leads to what we called a problem of pretentiousness. Here the vexing questions are why a democratic polity should give up parts of its self-government at all and, more specifically, why it should entrust its own survival as liberal democracy to a specific body—why, that is, it should trust this body's pretence that it is more adept at figuring out what liberal constraints a democracy needs to function successfully in the long run.

d) A matter of approach?

Holmes and Levine arrive at quite different understandings of the (in)compatibility of liberal rights and democracy, even though they draw to a significant extent on the same ideas of political thought and their intellectual precursors. Enquiring

[49] Ed Bates, *The Evolution of the European Convention on Human Rights* (OUP 2010) 92–93.
[50] Jeremy Waldron, 'A Right-Based Critique of Constitutional Rights' (1993) 13(1) OJLS 18, 47–48.
[51] Andrew Moravcsik, 'The Origins of Human Rights Regimes: Democratic Delegation in Postwar Europe' (2000) 54(2) IO 217, 225–229, 232–233.

into the reasons for this divergence is insightful. It explains why Holmes' theory gets into trouble once there is substantive disagreement, and, more importantly, it draws attention to the different logic behind the liberal principle and the democratic one. This then makes it possible to link liberal rights and democracy to legal (judicial) and political (legislative) decision-making, respectively.

The works of Levine and Holmes approach liberal-democratic constitutionalism very differently. Levine addresses the procedural question of whether one can combine processes of collective and individual decision-making, without undermining the one or the other. Holmes, by contrast, discusses the substantive issue of whether the protection of certain individual freedoms is compatible with, or even required by, the common interest in effective collective self-government. These two different approaches produce contrasting views, a result which can be explained by appealing to the different natures of the liberal and the democratic principles: whereas the democratic principle, which is procedural and concerned with collective decision-making, presumes that the choices it produces are initially unknown and eternally contestable, the liberal principle, which is substantive and concerned with certain protected individual choices, presumes that certain questions concerning the distribution of spheres of freedom are predetermined, as though they were pre- or apolitical.

Democracy is basically a theory of legitimate authority, whereas liberalism is basically a substantive theory of rights and justice. That is, if one argues in line with the liberal principle, then one essentially invokes a substantive domain of individual freedom and focusses on the protective scope of rights, thus imposing substantive limits to what the government may or may not do. By contrast, if one argues in line with the democratic principle, then one operates with a procedural concept of collective self-determination and focusses on the source of legitimate government power. A commitment to both principles at the same time will inevitably lead to difficulties in certain cases, as Richard Wollheim's paradox of democracy suggests:[52] as a democrat one must accept democratic decisions due to the fact that they come from a legitimate source, even if they may not correspond to what one considers right and just in substantive terms; conversely, if one insists on the realization of one's preferred normative theory about rights and justice, it is necessary to accept that this may require disregarding democratic decisions despite their procedural legitimacy.

Thus, insofar as Holmes' democratic polity agrees on the content and meaning of the liberal rights upon which it decided in its attempt to constrain itself for the sake of sustaining its democracy, his theory works. But as soon as his citizens start to disagree about the constraints that they mutually imposed upon themselves, Levine's aporia surfaces: either the citizens themselves decide as a collective, in

[52] Richard Wollheim, 'A Paradox in the Theory of Democracy' in P Laslett and W Runciman (eds), *Philosophy, Politics and Society* (Blackwell 1964).

a democratic but circular manner, or they vest this power in another body which raises concerns about pretence. One must commit either to the democratic process or to one's subjectively preferred normative theory about the substantive constraints imposed on it.

This dilemma sheds light on the debate about the principle of subsidiarity in the Convention system. Those who are concerned about an activist Court often argue with essentially procedural arguments: they complain about an overly narrow margin of appreciation (ie too little national leeway), and about the Court's excessively strict scrutiny, they admonish the Court's practice of interpreting the Convention in an evolutionary manner, they bemoan legal uncertainty resulting from the Court's casuistry, they take issue with judicial orders of remedies, and they complain that the Court applies the admissibility criteria too leniently, so as to deprive the respondent State of its chance to settle the issue in its preferred manner. More generally, their main point primarily concerns decision-making authority, that is, the question of who is the legitimate decision-maker: relying on a theory about the legitimacy of democracy, their answer often points to the State authorities rather than the Court. The argumentative pattern of those who defend a more activist Court is usually quite different. This camp mostly suggests that the Court should have recognized this or that right, should have protected this or that act of individual freedom, or should have intervened to block this or that policy. For example, the authors of the case-law-focussed *Strasbourg Observers* blog identify a case where the Court should have enhanced the Convention's protective scope—in their terminology a 'missed opportunity'—about twice a month. Those who argue along these lines must rely, at least implicitly, on a theory of rights and justice.

Substantive concerns can, of course, be coupled with procedural criticism: for example, when the Court's admissibility practice is criticized on the grounds that the Court would thereby fail to do justice to the weakest members of society,[53] the argument remains primarily one about rights and justice. Conversely, procedural arguments about decision-making authority may depend on the nature of the substantive issue at stake: for example, when judicial restraint on matters of social justice, public morals,[54] or 'watershed questions of nation building and collective identity'[55] is demanded with the argument that everyone's view must matter equally, the main point is still a procedural one related to questions of decision-making authority.

[53] See eg Helen Keller and Aurore Garin, 'Câmpeanu: quo vadis? Le recours individuel en péril' (2017) 28(111) Rev trim dr h 485.

[54] See eg *James and Others v the United Kingdom*, 21 February 1986, para 46, Series A no 98; conversely, *Dudgeon v the United Kingdom*, 22 October 1981, para 52, Series A no 45.

[55] Ran Hirschl, 'The New Constitutionalism and the Judicialization of Pure Politics Worldwide' (2006) 75(2) Fordham L Rev 721, 723.

Liberal rights, by virtue of their claim to trump democratic decisions in cases of conflict, suggest that individual freedom should enjoy normative priority over collective self-determination. Only the individual is ultimately of normative value, after all. However, because individuals may enter into conflict as a result of the free pursuit of their individual interests, collective rules of coordination that supersede individual freedom, so as to coordinate conflicting individual choices, are indispensable for peaceful societal life. This is why liberal rights, if they are to be effective and legitimate, depend on procedures of collective decision-making. While this might suggest that collective self-determination has normative priority, such a conclusion would, in fact, raise great difficulties: a polity is collectively self-determined only if its collective choices are made through a non-arbitrary procedure guaranteeing that the outcome is an aggregative function of the member's free individual choices. That is, the democratic choice refers back to individual freedom. It may thus not come as a surprise that, as Levine complains, liberal-democratic theorists often seem to 'defang' democracy to such an extent that their theories become highly liberal, while remaining only marginally democratic.[56] Holmes is a case in point, insofar as his work is much more about making democracy liberal than about making liberalism democratic.

However, although some liberal theorists and advocates of constitutional review do indeed appear to be great sceptics of democracy, a fear of 'tyrannical' majorities or the like need not be the primary explanation for the phenomenon that Levine deplores. The actual reason why most liberal-democratic theories seem to make democracy liberal rather than liberalism democratic lies instead in the respective inner logic of the liberal and democratic principles, as well as in their interplay. The same explanation may, conversely, also exculpate those sceptics of (international) rights-based review who emphasize the value of democracy from the accusation of advocating unconstrained majority rule.

The liberal principle, in order to be meaningful, depends on substantive content. Thus, in light of this purpose of liberal rights, it seems difficult to theorize about their substantive content without evoking the impression that one is engaged in an attempt to 'defang' the reach of the democratic process. Conversely, it is not easy to 'democratise' the liberal principle, without coming across as an apologist for circularly self-constrained—meaning ultimately unconstrained—democracy.

Taking all of this into consideration, along with the point that the Convention's subsidiarity principle is about reconciling (State-level) democracy with (European-level) liberal-rights review, it follows that the normative guidance given by the subsidiarity principle must be such that democracy's procedural (democratic-authority-related) and liberalism's substantive (individual-justice-related) demands both receive their due in the Convention system.

[56] See Levine (n 6) 7, 151.

C) Law and politics

Clarity about the fundamentally opposed procedural and substantive logic of the democratic and liberal principles helps us understand and assess the institutional differences between legal and political decision-making that are crucial to answer questions about the division of decision-making authority between judicial and political bodies. Christoph Möllers' work on the separation of powers shows that, in principle, judicial decision-making adheres to liberal logic, and political decision-making to democratic logic.[57] The establishment of separate branches following these two different systems of logic may thus be the way for a polity to reconcile its dual commitment to liberalism and democracy.

a) Political and legal decision-making

Democratic politics, as a process of collective opinion-forming and decision-making, is prospective in its orientation and initially indeterminate as regards its substantive outcome. At stake is what a collective of equals wants at the moment or at some later point in time. Any anticipation of the result would risk undermining the principle that each participant has an equal say. The democratic process is therefore inherently *ergebnisoffen* (open-ended as regards its outcome).[58]

Liberal rights, by contrast, which postulate protected spheres of equal individual freedom, must be determinate in their substance. If individual freedoms were not prospectively delineated, there would be no basis for distinguishing protected individual acts from unprotected ones. For the individual actor, this would entail uncertainty, a state of arbitrariness in which it is impossible to rationally decide what is in one's best interest, because one cannot foresee the consequences of those actions. Because an individual's decisions do not manifest themselves outside the individual's mind before the corresponding action is taken, only the actualized, outward-directed exercise of individual freedom can be protected. That is, liberal rights can protect only the external manifestation of an individual's will-formation: legal protection can therefore only be afforded retrospectively.[59]

Beyond these differences in temporality and determinacy, political and legal decisions also diverge in their scope and reach. Here, the element of individual equality inherent in both the liberal and the democratic principles is crucial. The liberal principle holds that everyone's presumed rational pursuit of self-interest is morally equivalent. It follows that individuals deserve equal treatment whenever they pursue their individual interests equally in equal situations. The law thus

[57] See Möllers (n 3) 80–106.
[58] See ibid 71–76.
[59] See ibid 68–69.

protects individual freedom in individualized and specific circumstances: it can only meaningfully govern concrete incidents involving identifiable individuals.[60]

The democratic principle is also built on the equality of all individuals, since the democratic imperative of the political equality of each and every individual follows from the premise that everyone's interests count the same and that no one knows better than anyone else what is in the best interest of the collective. Therefore, in matters that concern everyone, the interests and preferences of each individual should be given the same weight: everyone should, as much as possible, have the same opportunities to co-determine the rules that govern the political community, including the distribution and delineation of competing spheres of individual freedom. This requires a decision-making process whose scope is potentially general and comprehensive.[61] If certain aspects of common life were a priori excluded from the democratic process, the principle of public equality would be violated,[62] coming with the danger that the preferences of some are prioritized over those of others.

b) Political and legal authority

Institutional arrangements, such as the Convention system, that vest courts engaged in rights-based review with the power to cordon off certain issues against politics, to take issues away from politics, as critics of the Court put it—even though the participants in the political process consider these topics to be important parts of their political argument—obviously contradict the logic of the democratic principle. Because this type of judicial decision-making does not apply democratically made and revisable law, but rather determines itself the scope of democracy, it virtually invites political threats to push back against the judiciary.

In other words, this institutional set-up challenges the logic of political decision-making based on retrospective, individual, and substantively determinate demands raised in the form of legal rights claims. This, in turn, brings into focus the particular nature of the authority of bodies engaged in the administration of constitutional constraints, which limit the ordinary democratic process. The Court, too, exercises this type of control: it may de facto even review a State's constitutional-level democratic politics.

The institutional characteristics of courts correspond to the logic of legal decisions that implement the liberal principle, while the institutional characteristics of legislatures correspond to the logic of political decision-making in line with the democratic principle. Courts are set up and well equipped to apply

60 ibid 69.
61 See ibid 71–76.
62 cf Cass R Sunstein, *The Partial Constitution* (HUP 1993).

(relatively) determinate legal rules retrospectively to individualized cases.[63] Legislatures, by contrast, are institutionally orientated towards the formation of a future-oriented collective will expressed in decisions that are, as regards their substance, initially non-predetermined and, as regards their scope of application, general.[64] Judicial authority is justified because it ensures the equal freedom of all individuals as specified and delineated in democratically made laws, whereas political authority is legitimate because it is democratic, that is, because its decisions are, at bottom, the result of a process in which everyone's interests count equally.[65] This is how the coexistence of separate legal and political power makes the coexistence of liberal and the democratic decision-making logic possible, at least on some level.

c) Constitutional authority as hybrid

At the constitutional level, the difficulty remains that the relevant authority ought to enjoy liberal and democratic authority at the same time. Liberal-democratic constitutionalism thus assumes constitutional authority to be democratic and liberal ab ovo, as it were. As constitutional law, granting liberal rights and prescribing legal procedures that guarantee individual self-determination, constitutional authority legitimizes the political process, making it equal and thus democratic; as constitutional politics, viz as a continuously reaffirmed political commitment—the polity's foundational pledge, so to speak—it contains the basic democratic (political) choice for liberal constitutional constraints. This coincidence remains a fiction that is impossible to realize.

The international order suffers from the same difficulty, as Martti Koskenniemi has drawn attention to.[66] The problem consists in the 'schizophrenic insistence that international law must be both grounded in the free-willed consent of sovereign States ... and binding on every individual State despite its immediate will'.[67] In relation to the Court system, the *Belilos* case, which concerned the validity of the respondent State's reservation, is perhaps the best illustration. The Court was faced with the hard choice of either masking its disregard for the respondent State's avowed democratic will or admitting that its control is, at the end of the day, dependent on the willingness of the controlled to be controlled (it chose the former, as everyone who read Chapter 3 might have guessed).[68]

[63] Möllers (n 3) 89.
[64] ibid 84.
[65] ibid 78–79.
[66] See Martti Koskenniemi, *From Apology to Utopia* (CUP 2006) 5, 17–23.
[67] Akbar Rasulov, 'Review: From Apology to Utopia: The Structure of International Legal Argument' (2006) 18(8) L & Pol Book Rev 583, 587.
[68] See *Belilos v Switzerland* (n 45).

If, following liberal-democratic theory, the constitution depends on liberal-legal and democratic-political legitimacy, it appears that it can be legitimate in neither sense, since there is neither a pre-constitutional liberal legal framework that could legitimize the democratic polity nor a pre-constitutional democratic polity that could legitimize the legal framework. It is logically impossible for the constitution to simultaneously provide the legal framework of liberal rights that ultimately grounds, controls, and legitimizes political democracy and to represent the outcome of that same democracy's political process that grounds, proclaims, and legitimizes all valid law. Although liberal-democratic theory takes its two constituent elements to be normatively coequal, in practice, there is no way to avoid conceiving of either constitutional politics or constitutional law as somehow prior to, or more foundational than, the other. It is similarly impossible for the Convention to be the product of the States' democratic volition and to control each State in a binding manner, regardless of its concrete will.

D) The Convention system between undemocratic liberalism and illiberal democracy

In domestic constitutional practice—and *pace* the many scholarly claims to the contrary—constitutional authority is primarily vested either in a judicial body, that is, one that primarily functions according to legal logic, or a political body, that is, one that primarily functions according to democratic logic. Usually, the proverbial guardian of the constitution is, in the last instance, either a court or parliament.[69] But because the constitution is expressive of legal and political authority, of individual liberal rights and collective democratic government, the constitutional guardian's role necessarily traverses the separation between the legal and political powers. Möllers thus describes constitutional courts as politico-legal hybrids which cannot help but make political decisions:[70] they cannot but render legislative decisions, since their leading judgments concern new issues which are not yet governed by a determinate set of legal rules, and they inevitably have prospective and general effects. In systems of political supremacy the opposite holds. Where parliaments guard the constitution in the last instance, they must sometimes render decisions that are actually of a legal nature because they are based on positive law and concern individualized circumstances that lie in the past.

Full coherence within liberal-democratic constitutionalism is impossible, difficulties always persist. Broadly speaking, too much protection of Convention rights hollows out democratic self-determination, whereas too little control over the

[69] Graham Gee and Grégoire C N Webber, 'What Is a Political Constitution?' (2010) 30(2) OJLS 273, 294–298.

[70] Möllers (n 3) 141–142.

States' political democracies endangers individual freedom; conversely, too little control on the part of the Convention comes with the risk that the States' political democracies are captured or become unfree or illiberal, while a Convention law that does not reflect the popular will lacks democratic legitimacy. 'Illiberal democracy' looms on one side of the abyss and 'undemocratic liberalism' on the other.[71] Whoever assumes the role of the 'guardian of the constitution' must walk a tightrope between respecting the legal constitution and respecting the political one.

Liberal-democratic constitutionalism implies that constitutional authority is legal authority legitimizing politics *and* political authority legitimizing law. Yet, in reality, constitutional authority normally appears in either a judicial or a political guise. Each comes with its own problems: systems of constitutional justice are bound by a democratic law-making process only to a limited extent and cannot help but engage in their own law-making; a sovereign political body, by contrast, is hardly bound by the liberal constraints that secure the individual's moral due against the majority's will. How this *problématique* manifests itself in the Convention system's practice is the subject of the next chapter. It will discuss how the Court, without being embedded in a fully-fledged politico-legal community, engages in judicial law-making.

[71] Yascha Mounk, *The People vs. Democracy* (HUP 2018) 9–14.

6
The Court Between Law and Politics

A) Introduction

A state's inclination towards legal or political constitutionalism grows and develops over time as a result of politico-legal culture and historical contingencies. Since the Second World War, the entire European Continent has decidedly moved towards the legal-constitutionalist model. In the course of this pan-European legal development, even countries such as the Netherlands, the United Kingdom, Switzerland, and the Nordic states have established modest forms of constitutional review.[1] This is mostly ascribed to Europe's shared history. World War II and the Soviet regime created a strong impetus towards the protection of individual rights and democracy by systems of constitutional justice, motivating the rise of legal constitutionalism.[2] It is still the case today that the idea of protecting the individual's fundamental interests—and democracy itself—against the state, even if it is currently democratic, lends strong support to the legal-constitutionalist paradigm.[3] At the international level, a similar trend can be seen, as Chapter 3, tracing the judicialization of the system set up under the European Convention on Human Rights (the Convention, ECHR),[4] illustrated.

The previous chapter showed that when questions of constitutionality are at issue, they must be resolved by either the political or the juridical process. This poses problems in light of liberal-democratic constitutional theory. Liberal-democratic constitutionalism holds that constitutional authority comprises both legal authority, legitimizing democratic politics, *and* democratic authority, legitimizing the law. Yet, the institution that administers and embodies constitutional authority cannot but assume either a juridical or a political guise. Both options are problematic: systems of constitutional justice are bound by democratic law-making processes only to a limited extent, while a sovereign political body is hardly bound by legal constraints. This chapter further explores this issue with regard to the Convention system.

[1] See Helen Keller and Alec Stone Sweet (eds), *A Europe of Rights* (OUP 2008).

[2] See Andrew Moravcsik, 'The Origins of Human Rights Regimes: Democratic Delegation in Postwar Europe' (2000) 54(2) IO 217, 232–233.

[3] See Mauro Cappelletti, 'Repudiating Montesquieu? The Expansion and Legitimacy of "Constitutional Justice"' (1985) 35(1) Cath U L Rev 1, 31–32.

[4] Convention for the Protection of Human Rights and Fundamental Freedoms, as amended, of 4 November 1950, in force since 3 September 1953, 213 UNTS 221, CETS No 005.

Subsidiarity, Legitimacy, and the European Court of Human Rights. Reto Walther, Oxford University Press.
 DOI: 10.1093/9780198921455.003.0006

B) The Court's judicial law-making

Liberalism and democracy are based on the recognition that everyone is free and equal. To the problem that free and equal individuals may clash in the pursuit of their interests, liberal-democratic constitutionalism responds with two basic rules, one pertaining to law and the other to politics. On the one hand, everyone has an equal right, first, to live in a self-determined manner unless a particular behaviour is legitimately prohibited and, second, to receive protection in the exercise of those individual freedoms that have legitimately been granted such protection. On the other hand, both legal protections and prohibitions of individual acts of freedom concern everyone and are legitimate only if they were instated by an act of democratic self-determination.[5] Spheres of individual freedom defined in this way can be considered as reciprocally guaranteed by all citizens and, therefore, as intersubjectively valid, as we will see in Chapter 8.

As regards the former rule, the main concern is with the distribution of legally protected spheres of individual freedom. It is in these determinate domains that an individual choice can be said to be a social choice, that is, in which the individual is said to become the 'dictator'.[6] Individual rights and their legal enforcement in concrete cases are the institutional means used to implement this liberal arrangement. Competent judicial institutions become active when an individual alleges a violation of his or her protected sphere of freedom. They are charged with determining whether this allegation is justified. Whether it is depends on the presence of a pertinent freedom-protecting rule that has been duly enacted. Vindicating specific claims of individual freedom that lie in the past is precisely what occurs in the judicial process of individual rights protection, such as before the European Court of Human Rights (the Court, ECtHR). The judicial protection of rights takes its legitimacy from this procedural vindication—as opposed to an absolute substantive guarantee—of an individual's claim to freedom. It takes its legitimacy from guaranteeing every individual's equal enjoyment of his or her legally guaranteed individual freedom in concrete cases.[7]

The other rule is institutionalized in the democratic political process. This is not the place to delve into democratic theory: the focus must remain on international judicial review. Suffice it to say, in order for politics to count as democratic, it must give (nearly) every adult individual who is a permanent and rightful member of the political community an equal opportunity to participate in competitive-voting and decision-making procedures, as well as in the preceding opinion-building processes, so that the government's responsiveness and accountability are ensured.[8]

[5] See Christoph Möllers, *The Three Branches* (OUP 2013) 70.
[6] See Chapter 5.
[7] Möllers (n 5) 71.
[8] See eg Andreas Føllesdal, 'Tracking Justice Democratically' (2017) 31(3) Soc Epistemology 324, 325.

The process of distributing protected spheres of individual freedom—that is, the process of regulating, by coordination, the community's societal life—takes its legitimacy from collective self-determination, from the guaranteeing of everyone's equal participation in the determination of coordinative and distributive rules that apply equally to all.

a) The politics of rights-based review

Little explanation is required in order to see that when courts decide on the distribution of protected spheres of individual freedom, as constitutional courts do when they interpret abstract rights clauses, this does not correspond to the theory outlined above. Judicial proceedings are individualized. Merely a handful of the members of the political community have a say in the deliberation and reaching of court judgments, even if a judgment concerns them all because it determines questions of constitutional law.[9]

When, in the context of resolving a legal dispute, constitutional courts interpret and develop the constitution *qua* foundation of all law and all politics, their decisions are inevitably politico-legal hybrids. They are legal insofar as they (in) validate the individual positions in contention based on the (judge-made) law, and political in their effect of (further) determining future (constitutional) legal positions of an unknown and indeterminate number of individuals.

Judicial specifications of rights determine far-reaching distributive questions on the basis of broad considerations in a general and forward-looking manner. This has often been highlighted in relation to socio-economic rights and positive duties, which are sometimes still considered political, non-justiciable issues. The view is that these issues are 'appropriate only for political resolution [and that it] would be anti-democratic for unelected, unaccountable judges to impose positive duties on elected legislators'.[10] However, as the Court's jurisprudence has made abundantly clear, the reality is that civil and political rights, too, give rise to a range of positive obligations with socio-economic implications. Thus, if the specification of socio-economic rights is inherently political, it would appear that the specification of civil and political rights is often quite political too. Any decision to depoliticize certain issues is inherently political. Accounts that describe the principle of proportionality as concerned with the 'optimisation of the common good, which includes both rights as protected interests and other interests'[11] and reject a 'firm formal distinction between "rights" and the other normative goals pursued by the state'[12]

[9] See Chapter 4.
[10] See Sandra Fredman, *Human Rights Transformed* (OUP 2008) 180–182.
[11] Julian Rivers, 'Proportionality and Variable Intensity of Review' (2006) 65(1) CLJ 174, 181.
[12] Eoin Daly, 'Republicanizing Rights? Proportionality, Justification, and Non-Domination' in E Herlin-Karnell, M Klatt, and HA Morales Zúñiga (eds), *Constitutionalism Justified* (OUP 2019) 214.

suggest as much. Similarly, the idea that individual rights are not merely subjective entitlements 'to be left alone', but objective legal principles expressive of value choices that underpin the entire constitutional order,[13] underlines the programmatic character of rights. Samantha Besson has accordingly argued that except for '[c]onstitutive procedural rules and democratic rights', civil and political liberties, just like socio-economic rights, should only be loosely entrenched, in order not to 'cut [them] off from democratic deliberation and change'.[14]

The observation that the judicial specification of all but perhaps the most minimal interpretations of negative rights in the liberal tradition tends to cross over the boundary into law-making is not novel. However, legal scholarship continues to negate, downplay, or conceal this phenomenon. The widely used German expression '*richterliche Rechtsfortbildung*' is telling: it utterly disguises judicial law-making by referring to it as 'judicial development of the law'.[15] If parliament legislates on issues of human rights or decides how to implement constitutional provisions that are as vague as rights clauses, no one would ever refer to this as 'developing' the law—it is law-making, plain and simple. The idea of 'evolving' or 'dynamic' interpretation has similarly misleading effects. Any interpretation entails an element of change and consists of an act of volition, a choice, that is, between different possible meanings which Hans Kelsen famously ascribed to the realm of policy-making.[16] In short, courts, whether they are said to 'develop', 'change', or 'make' the law, engage in 'the generation of legal normativity for third parties not involved in the dispute'.[17] The areas of the Court's practice discussed below provide ample evidence of how those who are vested with the task of specifying rights are de facto vested with a *mandat de légiférer*.[18]

To be more analytically precise, rights-adjudicating apex courts engage in law-making when their decisions:[19] (1) potentially concern anyone beyond the parties to the dispute, by creating 'general spheres of freedom and obligation';[20] (2) have prospective effects and may require the initiation of a legislative process; (3) are, due to the generally vague and open formulation of rights clauses, the result of judicial discretion rather than of clear and determinate legal norms or conclusive interpretative methods. When courts lay down standards with general and

[13] Federal Constitutional Court of Germany, *Lüth*, no 1 BvR 400/51 of 15 January 1958 (published in BVerfGE 7, 198) para 25.

[14] Samantha Besson, *The Morality of Conflict* (Hart 2005) 325–328.

[15] Armin von Bogdandy and Ingo Venzke, 'Beyond Dispute: International Judicial Institutions as Lawmakers' in A von Bogdandy and I Venzke (eds), *International Judicial Lawmaking* (Springer 2012) 14.

[16] Hans Kelsen, *Introduction to the Problems of Legal Theory* (Clarendon Press 1992) § 38.

[17] von Bogdandy and Venzke, 'Beyond Dispute' (n 15) 14.

[18] See Hans Kelsen, 'La garantie juridictionnelle de la Constitution (La Justice constitutionnelle)' (1928) 45 RDP 197, 241.

[19] von Bogdandy and Venzke, 'Beyond Dispute' (n 15) 9–20.

[20] Möllers (n 5) 79.

prospective effects on the basis of textually vague provisions and in the context of a legal process geared towards the individual applicant, the purpose of the separation of powers, according to which legal decisions are made by courts and political decisions are made by democratic bodies, is upset. Judicial authority of this kind, even if exercised in the name of individual rights, must not be overly unconstrained, uncontrolled, and detached from democratic politics to enjoy legitimacy, because its leading decisions potentially concern everyone.

b) The Court's practice

In the case of human rights courts, the just discussed problem is particularly grave. On the one hand, they seek to defend individual interests against certain majoritarian excesses, which requires their independence from politics. On the other hand, the legal basis upon which they decide is usually extremely open such that it may cover almost any issue of human life and their jurisprudence may entail thoroughgoing law and policy reform. Taken together, this necessarily makes courts engaged in rights-based review into judicial legislators. Thus, paradoxically, 'while the protection of basic rights is the most significant and most debated function of constitutional courts ... it may also be the most questionable one', if looked at from a separation-of-powers perspective.[21] The Court, too, is heavily engaged in judicial law-making, as the following discussion of the most pertinent areas of its judicial practice, in particular, show. In all of them, the Court's discretionary jurisprudence (ie its judicial choices) has significant general and prospective effects.

First, the reach of the Court's jurisprudence beyond the individual applicants' legal position is evident in so-called *multi-polar rights cases*: whenever one individual's right comes at the expense of another individual's right, even negative rights in the liberal tradition reach quite conspicuously beyond the right-claimant's sphere of freedom.[22] When settling such issues by balancing competing rights and interests, such as rights to privacy and media freedoms, courts cannot help but defend one private sphere of freedom, while at the same time delimiting and coordinating competing spheres of freedom and interests in a more general manner. The Strasbourg judges have developed an extensive body of pertinent case law[23] with value choices that unfold general and prospective (if only precedential)

[21] ibid 134–139.

[22] See eg *Von Hannover v Germany*, no 59320/00, ECHR 2004-VI; *Von Hannover v Germany (no 2)* [GC], nos 40660/08 and 60641/08, ECHR 2012; *Von Hannover v Germany (no 3)*, no 8772/10, 19 September 2013.

[23] See eg Stijn Smet and Eva Brems (eds), *When Human Rights Clash at the European Court of Human Rights* (OUP 2017).

effects which—in a democratically problematic manner—may challenge the Court's member states' (the States) established domestic value orders.[24]

Second, the Court's law-making directly competes with the States' legislation in the domain of *procedural rights*. As David Kosař's illustrative examples of France's abandonment of its *avocats généraux* at the *Conseil d'État*,[25] the abandonment of Turkey's Military Security Courts,[26] and the British Constitutional Reform Act 2005[27] show, the Court's case law has had a massive impact on the States' judiciaries.[28] These judicial design choices potentially remain effective for a long time into the future and concern everyone under a State's jurisdiction. As Kosař thus observes, the Court has become 'a key player in domestic judicial politics'.[29]

Third, a similar effect than the Court's judicial design choices has its recognition of positive rights and corresponding positive obligations. In the domain of *socio-economic rights*, in particular, the standards established through the Court's jurisprudence have obvious implications for an entire polity, since they concern its resource allocation, which—as 'power of the purse'—has therefore traditionally been a matter for parliament. In Ida Koch's words, the Court's pertinent practice has not only 'radical consequences ... with respect to the legislature's liberty to freely adopt and uphold legislation ... [but also] affect[s] the possibility of the legislature and of the executive to freely take decisions regarding financial resources'.[30]

In this area of the Court's judicial practice, its judicial law-making is particularly audacious and problematic, since the Convention does not explicitly guarantee socio-economic rights.[31] Quite to the contrary, within the Council of Europe, a deliberate decision was made to establish, on the one hand, the Convention system with the right to property and the right to education separated out and included in the optional Protocol No 1[32] and, on the other hand, a distinct system of socio-economic rights protection based on the European Social Charter.[33] Thus, when the Court reads socio-economic rights into Articles 2–14 of the Convention, it

24 See Angelika Nußberger, 'Subsidiarity in the Control of Decisions Based on Proportionality: An Analysis of the Basis of the Implementation of ECtHR Judgments into German Law' in A Seibert-Fohr and ME Villiger (eds), *Judgments of the European Court of Human Rights* (Nomos 2014) 174–178.

25 See *Martinie v France* [GC], no 58675/00, ECHR 2006-VI.

26 *Incal v Turkey* [GC], 9 June 1998, Reports of Judgments and Decisions 1998-IV; *Çıraklar v Turkey*, 28 October 1998, Reports of Judgments and Decisions 1998-VII; *Şahiner v Turkey*, no 29279/95, ECHR 2001-IX.

27 See also Diana Woodhouse, 'United Kingdom: The Constitutional Reform Act 2005—Defending Judicial Independence the English Way' (2007) 5(1) I•CON 153, 154.

28 David Kosař and Lucas Lixinski, 'Domestic Judicial Design by International Human Rights Courts' (2015) 109(4) AJIL 713, 715–716.

29 David Kosař, 'Nudging Domestic Judicial Reforms from Strasbourg: How the European Court of Human Rights Shapes Domestic Judicial Design' (2017) 13 Utrecht L Rev 112, 123.

30 Ida E Koch, *Human Rights as Indivisible Rights* (Martinus Nijhoff 2009) 255.

31 See ibid 4.

32 Marco Duranti, *The Conservative Human Rights Revolution* (OUP 2017).

33 European Social Charter of 18 October 1961, in force since 26 February 1965, CETS No 035; European Social Charter (revised) of 3 May 1996, in force since 1 July 1999, CETS No 163.

expands the Convention into areas that were, by an act of explicit political will, excluded from the Court's (mandatory) jurisdiction. In spite of all of this, the Court has for many years firmly held to the view that socio-economic entitlements must follow from the Convention's civil and political rights if the latter are to be practical and effective.[34] However, this long jurisprudential history cannot belie the tension between the effective realization of a certain (judicial) conception of social justice and due respect for the States' democratic choices in the domain of social policy.[35]

Fourth, the Court has used positive rights and obligations to promote a *horizontal rights protection* (ie their protection between private parties). To promote the horizontal protection of rights, the Court has admitted complaints whenever a State's active (or omissive) regulation or validation of private legal relations impinges on individual interests that enjoy Convention protection.[36] The State must then give reasons for doing so that are proportionate to the harm suffered by the individual applicant.[37] Broadly speaking, the effect of this is that any exercise of public authority regulating or validating private relations must be compatible with the Convention. In effect, the Court has thus used positive obligations to require that the States establish certain frameworks of private law.[38]

A fifth area of case law with potentially immense repercussions on an entire polity consists of the Court's jurisprudence concerning questions at the heart of the States' democratic system, notably their *elective processes*.[39] A political community has many competing and equally reasonable conceptions of democracy available:[40] for this choice, the domestic context is of the utmost importance and a State may pursue different, potentially competing, goals with the design of its democratic system.[41] Thus, when the Court, on the basis of individual rights claims, makes decisions in this field, it often decides on controversies that invariably concern the entire political community, viz on the respondent State's future form as a democratically self-governed polity.

This area of the Court's case law brings the difficult relationship between individual freedom and democracy discussed in the previous chapter to the forefront again: it seems as straightforward to call for strict judicial scrutiny in this domain as it is evident that questions concerning the organization of the political system

[34] *Airey v Ireland*, 9 October 1979, Series A no 32; *Artico v Italy*, 13 May 1980, Series A no 37.

[35] Ingrid Leijten, *Core Socio-Economic Rights and the European Court of Human Rights* (CUP 2018) 1.

[36] See Claire Loven, '"Verticalised" Cases Before the European Court of Human Rights Unravelled: An Analysis of Their Characteristics and the Court's Approach to Them' (2020) 38(4) Neth Q Hum Rts 246, 247, 249.

[37] Jan Zglinski, 'Doing Too Little or Too Much? Private Law Before the European Court of Human Rights' (2018) 37 YEL 98, 103.

[38] See eg *Howald Moor and Others v Switzerland*, nos 52067/10 and 41072/11, 11 March 2014.

[39] In detail, Rory O'Connell, *Law, Democracy and the European Court of Human Rights* (CUP 2020).

[40] See eg David Held, *Models of Democracy* (3rd edn, Polity 2006).

[41] O'Connell (n 39) 265.

affect everyone and should thus be decided in a process in which everyone has an equal say.

Finally, two more transversal practices of the Court deserve attention: its proportionality-balancing and its remedial approach. In the Court's practice, *proportionality* operates as a methodological and, derivatively, substantive standard that any exercise of public authority by the States must respect. Proportionality serves as the basis for a large part of the Court's interpretation[42] and application[43] of Convention law.[44] Based on the proportionality principle, the Court has developed standards of legal certainty and foreseeability,[45] requirements to establish guarantees and remedies against human rights abuse,[46] and positive obligations.[47] Most importantly, perhaps, the Court increasingly imposes on the States' legal and political authorities obligations to apply proportionality as their default method of assessing fundamental rights issues.[48] This ubiquitous resort of the Court to proportionality has several far-reaching implications.

First, together with an increasingly expansive interpretation of the right to private and family life (Article 8 of the Convention)[49] and the anti-discrimination clauses[50] (Article 14 of the Convention and Article 1 of the optional Protocol No 12),[51] the principle of proportionality brings a great number of legal and political decisions that somehow affect an individual's life choices or somehow classify an individual as opposed to others under the Court's control. That is, the Court increasingly controls any exercise of public authority by the States based on proportionality *qua* basic Convention principle, which is finally specified and applied by the Court, not unlike the way in which the German Federal Constitutional Court controls all State action, on the grounds that all State action must respect the constitutional principle of human dignity, which the Constitutional Court specifies and applies in the last instance.[52]

[42] See Jonas Christoffersen, *Fair Balance* (Martinus Nijhoff 2009) 44–68.

[43] See eg Alastair Mowbray, 'A Study of the Principle of Fair Balance in the Jurisprudence of the European Court of Human Rights' (2010) 10(2) HRLR 289.

[44] See also Yutaka Arai-Takahashi, 'The Margin of Appreciation Doctrine: A Theoretical Analysis of Strasbourg's Variable Geometry' in A Føllesdal, B Peters, and G Ulfstein (eds), *Constituting Europe* (CUP 2013) 69–78.

[45] Sébastien van Drooghenbroeck, *La proportionnalité dans le droit de la Convention européenne des droits de l'homme* (Bruylant 2001) mn 426–429.

[46] ibid mn 430–442.

[47] Christoffersen (n 42) 94–110.

[48] van Drooghenbroeck (n 45) mn 443–448.

[49] Maris Burbergs, 'How the Right to Respect for Private and Family Life, Home and Correspondence Became the Nursery in Which New Rights Are Born: Article 8' in E Brems and J Gerards (eds), *Shaping Rights in the ECHR* (CUP 2014) 315–316.

[50] See eg Charilaos Nikolaidis, *The Right to Equality in European Human Rights Law* (Routledge 2015) ch 2.

[51] Protocol No 12 to the Convention for the Protection of Human Rights and Fundamental Freedoms of 4 November 2000, in force since 1 April 2005, CETS No 177.

[52] FCC, *Lüth* (n 13).

A second result of the Court's ubiquitous resorting to proportionality is that it systematically decides new questions before it in a manner reminiscent of legislative decision-making: competing interests and preferences of individuals and their political community are recognized as relevant, weighed and balanced against each other, before a choice between them is made.

A third implication has been noted by Alec Stone Sweet and Jud Mathews. They observe that, '[e]levated ... in this way to a meta-principle of governance, proportionality emerges as a fundamental element of constitutional legitimacy'.[53] Importantly, this increasingly holds not only at the European but also at the domestic level of the Convention system: because the Court may reassess a vast array of domestic judicial and political decisions based on proportionality as methodological-cum-substantive standard, the Court has essentially implanted its conception of the proportionality principle into the States' domestic orders. Basically, the effect of this comes down to a constitutional law-making decision that the Court (incrementally and indirectly) imposed on the States. Under Convention *qua* constitutional law, no exercise of public authority is legitimate unless it is proportionate.[54]

However, it becomes perhaps most evident that the Court's practice blurs the boundaries between the logic of legal decision-making, evaluating individual acts of freedom *ex post facto* and on the basis of predetermined legal provisions, and the logic of political decision-making, establishing general rules that determine the nature of societal life with prospective effect, when we look at its *remedial practice*. When the Court renders pilot judgments, or judgments known as Article 46 or quasi-pilot judgments,[55] it deviates from the principle—anchored in Article 41 of the Convention—that its judgments are declaratory in nature[56] and decisively recommends, or even orders, remedial measures to implement the judgment.[57] Remedial measures that do not aim at the remediation of the rights violation that the applicant suffered but rather serve broader goals[58] correspond to the logic of political decision-making, since they do not have a retrospective-compensatory character, but rather a prospective-preventive one:[59] they specify how the respondent State must proceed, in the Court's view, in order to improve rights protection for the future.

[53] Alec Stone Sweet and Jud Mathews, *Proportionality Balancing and Constitutional Governance* (OUP 2019) 35.

[54] See also Chapters 8 and 10.

[55] Generally, Alastair Mowbray, 'An Examination of the European Court of Human Rights' Indication of Remedial Measures' (2017) 17(3) HRLR 451.

[56] *Marckx v Belgium*, 13 June 1979, para 58, Series A no 31.

[57] See eg *Assanidze v Georgia* [GC], no 71503/01, pt 14(a) (operative part), ECHR 2004-II.

[58] Valerio Colandrea, 'On the Power of the European Court of Human Rights to Order Specific Non-Monetary Measures: Some Remarks in Light of the Assanidze, Broniowski and Sejdovic Cases' (2007) 7(2) HRLR 396, 397–398.

[59] ibid 408–409.

This practice not only results in judicial law-making but also has the effect of undermining the 'cooperative political' logic of the process concerning the implementation of the Court's judgments, as set out in Article 46 of the Convention.[60] Thus, this is perhaps the area in which the Court acts most openly as a 'positive legislator' since, to put it succinctly, it makes the domestic legislature the executor charged with implementing what it considers to be the measures most suitable to solving wider societal problems. It is this jurisprudence that best illustrates the choice of words adopted in the previous chapter: it has something pretentious in it when select legal experts claim to know best how to improve society.

c) The Court as a politico-legal hybrid

When rights-reviewing constitutional courts, such as the Strasbourg Court, engage in law-making, this is problematic, because, according to liberal-democratic theory, rules with prospective and general effect must be determined through a democratic process of collective self-determination. Whereas ordinary law legitimately binds everyone, because it is made through a democratic process in which everyone has an equal opportunity to participate, (quasi-)constitutional rights are specified through an individualized, exclusive judicial process, which makes it hard to say that the spheres of individual freedom defined in this way are mutually guaranteed and intersubjectively justified. The problem becomes evident when one compares the ordinary politico-legal process with the functioning of rights-reviewing constitutional courts: in the former case, the courts apply law made by the democratic legislator, while in the latter case, the constitutional court administers a number of extremely vague rights clauses that were democratically laid down decades beforehand. Of course, an element of interpretation, of judicial creativity, is present in any judicial decision-making process, but, in the latter case, the legal principles that the courts 'apply' are virtually impracticable due to their concision and abstractness until the court 'translates' them into legal rules that lend themselves to application in concrete legal cases. Rights-based constitutional review is thus aptly described as a politico-legal hybrid. Ordinary courts are legitimate because they apply democratically made law in an impartial manner to individual cases, thus respecting the democratic principle and the liberal principle, public equality and individual equality, and collective self-determination and individual freedom. Rights-based constitutional review, by contrast, largely lacks what is known as the legality of the judicial process: the legitimacy that the judicial process derives from its being bound by democratically made law—rights-based

[60] Markus Fyrnys, 'Expanding Competences by Judicial Lawmaking: The Pilot Judgment Procedure of the European Court of Human Rights' in A von Bogdandy and I Venzke (eds), *International Judicial Lawmaking* (Springer 2012) 353.

constitutional review—only weakly respects the democratic principle, public equality, and collective self-determination. What is more, in the case of the Convention system, the Court, as we noted in Chapter 4, has, in contrast to many other domestic and international courts, great discretion also with regard to procedural, institutional, and organizational questions, that is, with regard to the important question about how it proceeds to reach its judgments.

C) The Court's democratic vacuum

The legality problem resulting from judicial law-making on the basis of vague rights clauses is considerable in the Court system. As is the case with any constitutional court, the Court is heavily engaged in judicial law-making and operates on the basis of weak legality, in the sense just discussed. An imbalance in the mutual legitimation of law and politics results from the strong position that constitutional courts occupy in their respective constitutional orders. Yet, in the Convention system, the imbalance is further accentuated by the Convention system's lack of developed democratic politics.

Although the Court often fundamentally challenges acts enjoying highest democratic legitimacy, namely, parliamentary laws, unlike domestic constitutional courts, it is not embedded in a fully fledged political community. The political side of the Convention system consists primarily of the Parliamentary Assembly and the Committee of Ministers. Both have only weak political powers. In the Council of Europe, all law-making other than the making of soft and judge-made law occurs between the States, as equal sovereign subjects of international law. The Parliamentary Assembly and the Committee of Minsters may only adopt resolutions and other documents with the character of soft law. Both are weak in the sense that they primarily operate through diplomatic channels and cannot create hard law by means of majority voting; the Committee of Ministers can merely 'consider the action required to further the aim of the Council of Europe, including the conclusion of conventions or agreements'.[61] Hence, neither body has law-making competences with regard to the Convention system—only the States *qua* collective master of the treaty have. Substantive Convention law is limited to the Convention and its protocols as interpreted by the Court, while additional procedural, organizational, and institutional rules are laid down in the judge-made Rules of Court. At most, the Committee of Ministers may take some influence on these questions through the adoption of resolutions that concern procedural issues, such as the pilot judgment procedure.

[61] Article 15(a) Statute of the Council of Europe of 5 May 1949, in force since 3 August 1949, 87 UNTS 103, CETS No 001.

The activities of the Convention system's international political actors are much more limited with respect to time, subject matter, and specificity than those of national political branches: the Convention is not a comprehensive system of political value choices and lacks the robust foundation of a uniform political culture that could instruct and underpin the Court's interpretative work.[62] That is, the Court cannot base its judicial law-making on a complete constitutional system—it cannot read the Convention in light of the comprehensive value system contained in a fully fledged politico-legal constitution. The Court's lack of embeddedness in a full-grown politico-legal order also means that its jurisprudence is not situated within the enclosed deliberative forum of a largely self-contained political community: due to the comparatively weak international deliberative space, it is presumably much less the subject of political debate than are domestic constitutional court judgments.[63] A related point is that there is much more heterogeneity present in the Convention system than within any of its States' politico-legal orders: the common ideology underpinning the Convention and tying the States together is much thinner than the common beliefs, values, and traditions reflected in state constitutions.[64] All of this suggests that the Court's judge-made law is not subject to the same legitimacy-enhancing mechanisms of public justifiability that are at work domestically.

The Convention system suffers from the democratic separation-of-powers problem inherent in any system of constitutional review. However, the problem is aggravated in the Convention system because it is not a fully fledged politico-legal order, but essentially reduced to the liberal-legal half of a liberal-democratic constitutional order.[65] The Court system is a strong judicial branch accompanied by a political branch that is only somewhat developed.[66] Whereas the Court has developed into a permanent, impressively effective and productive international judicial body, its political counterpart still consists of an intergovernmental process whose forty-six States do not always effectively act in concert during their sporadic meetings. The States, and with them their political and diplomatic representatives at the Council of Europe, are still primarily national actors operating against the background of their different domestic contexts and diverse legal and political traditions. The Convention system *qua* process of constitutional law is unified (in Strasbourg) and operates transnationally (across international and domestic law),

[62] See Janneke Gerards, 'Margin of Appreciation and Incrementalism in the Case Law of the European Court of Human Rights' (2018) 18(3) HRLR 495, 495.

[63] See Laurence R Helfer and Erik Voeten, 'Walking Back Human Rights in Europe?' (2020) 31(3) EJIL 797, 802.

[64] Generally, Michel Rosenfeld, 'Is Global Constitutionalism Meaningful or Desirable?' (2014) 25(1) EJIL 177, 190–191.

[65] See also Oliver Gerstenberg, '(The Failure of) Public Law and the Deliberative Turn' in C Mac Amhlaigh, C Michelon, and N Walker (eds), *After Public Law* (OUP 2013).

[66] Generally, Armin von Bogdandy and Ingo Venzke, 'In Whose Name? An Investigation of International Courts' Public Authority and Its Democratic Justification' (2012) 23(1) EJIL 7, 19–23.

yet its political counterpart is dispersed (among the States) and concentrated at the national level—the Committee of Ministers and the Parliamentary Assembly are only weak representative institutions.

All of this suggests that the mutual legitimation of law and politics is weak in the Convention system. In fact, there is hardly any reciprocity at work. In one direction, the Court system resembles a strong current that continuously carries legal constraints downstream, depositing them into the States' political democracies. The Convention system *qua* system of constitutional law functions like a constantly evolving, judge-made rulebook for each State's politico-legal order. The Court acts as the umpire that perennially watches over the States to see if they respect the rules of the game. Upstream, however, the flow is in reality little more than a trickle. There is neither an ongoing democratic process of Convention law-making nor anything close to a robust, continuous process of democratic constitutional politics. All that occurs in this regard is the States' infrequent affirmation of their ratification decisions when they adopt an optional or amending protocol.

D) Two opposite assessments

Chapter 4 argued that those who call for a more subsidiary Court take issue with the imposition of common European standards of judge-made human rights law on the States' political democracies. Judicial law-making, as it commonly occurs in the course of rights-based review, is indeed problematic from the point of view of democratic legitimacy: in the course of this practice, courts delimit and assign spheres of individual freedom with general and prospective effect, despite the individualized character of their procedures. They render decisions that concern potentially everyone based on individual rights claims and through a process that fails to respect everyone's equal right to participate. This is difficult to reconcile with the requirement of the democratic principle that decisions that concern all should be made through procedures in which everyone has an equal chance to participate.

The Court's exercise of international review aggravates this problem of democratic legitimacy. Convention law may appear to some as a 'law without a State'.[67] As Besson puts it:

> In the absence of other institutions and especially of a legislature with which to interact, and, more generally, of a political community to represent, the judiciary cannot play its interpretive and judicial law-making role. Such a judiciary is neither checked by nor accountable to any institution or community. Judicial

[67] Tim Koopmans, 'Federalism: The Wrong Debate' (1992) 29(6) CML Rev 1047, 1051.

> law-making as a reasoning and discursive exercise requires law *tout court* and judges cannot be asked to interpret and develop international law without that law being clearly identified for them.[68]

Importantly, however, the Court's situation at the international level, where it is beyond any State's politico-legal order, may not only aggravate problems of democratic legitimacy but also provide institutional safeguards that mitigate these problems. The relevant peculiarities of the Convention system compared to domestic systems of constitutional review will have to be considered more carefully than has been the case so far. In particular, in Chapters 9 and 10, we will have to discuss the Court's doctrines of restraint and deference, as well as other mechanisms that enable the States to have a say in the development (interpretation and application) of Convention law.

That said, those who call for more subsidiarity and those who oppose this call may arrive at quite different assessments of the Court's position in a 'democratic vacuum'.[69] The next chapters must inquire into these opposite assessments because different roles for the (subsidiary) Court and the other actors of the Convention system may follow. We will see that those who oppose a more restrained Court may not merely take the Court's democratic vacuum as unproblematic, but that they may consider it downright desirable. This view hinges on the argument that the Court's quasi-legislative specification and protection of rights is democratically legitimate because democracy would not be viable, or at least would be worse off, without it. Unsurprisingly, those on the other side of the debate argue for the opposite view.

Thus, those who defend an activist Court worry about democratic de-democratization and democratic illiberalism, whereas those who favour a more restrained Court worry about undemocratic liberalism and the elitist imposition of a less-than-just (neo-)liberal order along the lines of republican fears of judicial domination. In the former view, the Court is part of the solution *because* it operates from within a democratic vacuum that presumedly isolates it from the danger of democratic de-democratization. The latter perspective considers the Court as a possible problem *because* it operates in a democratic vacuum and thus potentially contributes to undemocratic liberalism.

[68] Samantha Besson, 'International Judges as Dispute-Settlers and Law-Enforcers: From International Law Without Courts to International Courts Without Law' (2011) 34(1) Loy LA Int'l & Comp L Rev 33, 49 (original italics, footnote omitted).

[69] Möllers (n 5) 213.

7
Rights
Moral Truths or Political Claims?

A) Introduction

The European Court of Human Rights (the Court, ECtHR) cannot exercise its rights-based judicial review without engaging heavily in the quasi-legislative specification of the European Convention on Human Rights' (the Convention, ECHR)[1] vaguely worded rights clauses. While the situation is no different in the case of domestic constitutional courts, the Court is distinctive in that it is located at the international level, where there is no fully-fledged politico-legal order. That is, the Court lacks political counterparts at a similar level of development, as well as embeddedness in a comprehensive political community whose value choices and public political discourse could confer democratic justifiability on its jurisprudential principles. Furthermore, Convention law—as specified by the Court's interpretation of the Convention—is, for all practical purposes, removed from politics: the member states' (the States) past practice has shown that amendments to the Convention's substantive provisions are virtually impossible, just like in constitutional states with constitutions that are so rigidly entrenched that the judicial interpreter is, in effect, the sole authority capable of revising constitutional law. As a result, Strasbourg's judicial process alone is capable of revising substantive Convention law.

The previous chapters discussed the underlying liberal-democratic predicament: if the constitution shall not be at the whim of the political process, resulting in a problem of circularity, the constitution must be entrusted to judicial guardians, who pretend—and/or are assumed—to know best how to solve the moral dilemmas that every society faces when significant private and public interests conflict. In other words, international judges determine what liberal rights the Convention imposes on the States in order to constrain the national democracies from within a 'democratic vacuum',[2] lest those who are constrained, that is, the States, decide for themselves what these constraints should be.

If human rights are taken to represent the liberal-democratic state's main source of legitimacy, it appears advantageous to give them judicial protection at

[1] Convention for the Protection of Human Rights and Fundamental Freedoms, as amended, of 4 November 1950, in force since 3 September 1953, 213 UNTS 221, CETS No 005.
[2] Christoph Möllers, *The Three Branches* (OUP 2013) 213.

Subsidiarity, Legitimacy, and the European Court of Human Rights. Reto Walther, Oxford University Press.
 DOI: 10.1093/9780198921455.003.0007

a *supra*-national level: this means that the liberal-democratic state cannot freely dispose of its legitimation basis, because it offers normative legitimacy that is substantively, as well as procedurally and institutionally, separate from the state. In this view, entrusting the prerequisites of the legitimate liberal-democratic state, namely, liberal individual rights, to an external authority is the best thing one can do to secure them against political temptation in a secular age. If, by contrast, one sees the solution to the liberal-democratic predicament in communal action on the part of every individual, in a joint effort to realize and sustain individual freedom and democratic self-determination, the main locus of securing liberal democracy must be the political community, which is today embodied by states. It is within states that civil society, civic engagement, political responsibility, etc. are most developed. It cannot be otherwise, so long as politics operates first and foremost within national boundaries. This would suggest that international human rights can do no more than provide support, within an *inter*-national framework, for a primarily domestic process, and therefore explain the subsidiarity of international human rights systems.

This chapter discusses a variant of each of these two views—call them *supra*-national legal constitutionalism and *inter*-national political constitutionalism—drawing on exemplary scholarly works. The second section discusses George Letsas' take on the Court system.[3] Letsas' account relies heavily on the work of Ronald Dworkin, an ardent and highly influential defence of rights-based judicial review. Their claim is that there are objective moral rights which one can apprehend rightly or wrongly, deriving from the basic principle that everyone has a right to equal concern and respect and that courts are better placed to get at this truth than politics is. Having clarified Letsas' view on the proper role of the Court, we discuss how this view potentially entails a near-infinite expansion of the Court's judicial reach, especially if it is situated within a teleological understanding of international human rights. Our critique marks the transition to the third section of this chapter and its discussion of the *inter*-national political constitutionalism's take on the problem at hand. On this account, which we will discuss on the example of Richard Bellamy's work, democratic politics plays a central role in securing liberal democracies. This could explain and justify the ascription of a merely subsidiary role to the Court.

B) *Supra*-national legal constitutionalism

To justify the view that human rights need judicial guardians at a *supra*-national level, Letsas develops an argument that basically consists of four steps. A first,

[3] See especially George Letsas, *A Theory of Interpretation of the European Convention on Human Rights* (paperback edn, OUP 2009).

essentially ontological claim is that there are discernible moral rights, in the sense of objective moral truths. The second claim has two parts, one essentially epistemological, the other essentially institutional: the idea is that one can get decisions about rights right or wrong (or at least that there are more and less correct solutions to rights issues) and that courts are best placed to discern this truth about rights (or at least that they are better at this task than political institutions). The third claim is that human rights derive, viz can be deduced, from the principle that everyone has a right to equal concern and respect. Finally, the belief, that human reason allows a continuously better understanding of what moral rights everyone has will always become available, demands that the rights-reviewing court incessantly develop the meaning of the human rights within its purview.

a) Moral rights

Letsas' view is underpinned by liberal political and moral rights theory that holds to the assumption that human rights are inherently moral rights. As such, they are not original entitlements conferred by positive, human-made law: the law-making process rather puts them at risk insofar as it may fail to recognize and respect them. That is, because, in this view, the purpose of international human rights is to unconditionally grant certain moral entitlements to everyone, these rights must be grounded not in positivist, politically alterable law, but in the unalterable empirical fact of everyone's humanity. The role of the Convention's protection of moral human rights that Letsas emphasizes conforms to this: the Convention system protects liberal rights *qua* constraints on democratic politics.[4] Hence, Letsas shares many liberals' traditional wariness about the dangers of democratic majority politics.

Letsas thus insists that the Convention is understood in a non-conventionalist way: its 'rights need not be the same as what the Contracting States (or the majorities in them) take them to be'.[5] According to him, Convention rights must mean what the Court's judges take them to mean, based on 'the best moral theory of human rights'.[6] In this view, concerns over the democratic legitimacy of human rights jurisprudence, the protection of expectations through legal certainty and predictability, and the frustration of public interests by human rights are irrelevant or at least unimportant[7]— 'the state' is conceived less as a political community of individuals than as an impersonal entity prone to violate human rights that have their basis in some substantive moral principle that justifies them.[8]

[4] ibid 18–36.
[5] ibid 40.
[6] ibid 55.
[7] See ibid 73.
[8] ibid 40.

b) Judicial reason

Grounding rights on some substantive moral principle, that is, on a non-positivist basis, leaves unclear and controversial what their real foundation is and what exactly follows from this abstract moral conception of rights on the level of specific, practically applicable human rights.[9] As Benjamin Barber notes, the predicament that results for the moral-rights theorist is that he needs 'norms external to the political process' that can solve the societal problem of conflicting interests that any society's political process must deal with.[10] Thus, Letsas needs a non-political theory about how one defines by way of interpretation the scope and meaning of the rights that the Convention protects, as well as about who has the best 'chances of reaching the right answer'.[11]

This question, concerning the 'who', is a 'no-brainer' for Letsas. Its answer can be short, since 'it is natural to assume that courts will normally reach better decisions than legislatures'.[12] Letsas' 'natural assumption' is tantamount to axiomatic trust in judicial expertise. Dworkin, upon whose work Letsas builds, defended this view with the questionable argument that, if rights were determined in the political process, the majority would be the judge of its own case. Dworkin essentially established a simple duality between, on the one hand, the individual rights-claimant, who is in need of protection, and, on the other hand, a unitary government, which he describes as homogenous and hostile.[13] Dworkin did not explain why he thinks the rights-reviewing judges are not part of what he considers the homogenous and hostile majoritarian state government, even though they are usually politically appointed or elected[14] and, for this and other reasons, part of the same (transnational) elite as politicians and other influential government officials.[15] Quite to the contrary, he simply claimed that a principled mode of juridical reasoning is available which allows courts to evade the making of political decisions.[16]

c) Liberal egalitarianism

It is along these lines, that Letsas calls on the Court 'to develop, through interpretation, a moral conception of what these fundamental rights [which individuals have against

[9] James Griffin, *On Human Rights* (OUP 2008) 13–15.
[10] Benjamin R Barber, *Strong Democracy* (20th anniversary edn, University of California Press 2003) 130.
[11] Letsas, *Theory of Interpretation* (n 3) 119.
[12] ibid.
[13] Ronald Dworkin, *Taking Rights Seriously* (HUP 1977) 143.
[14] See eg Article 22 ECHR.
[15] Mikael R Madsen, 'The International Judiciary as Transnational Power Elite' (2014) 8(3) Intl Pol Soc 332.
[16] See eg Ronald Dworkin, *Freedom's Law* (HUP 1996) 1–38.

their government] are'.[17] According to Dworkin and Letsas, the objective moral principle from which the judges must derive all human rights *qua* shields against democratic politics is everyone's 'fundamental right to equal concern and respect'.[18] At the most abstract level, according to this understanding, human rights require everyone to be treated equally without reference to personal traits and life choices.[19] In Letsas' words, the human rights that the Convention guarantees protect against 'policies enacted on the basis that some people should be deprived of their [rights] on the basis of who they are'.[20]

This understanding of Convention rights seems simple, insofar as it is based on a single fundamental principle, namely, that the States must treat everyone under their jurisdiction with equal concern (ie recognize everyone's equal moral worth) and respect (ie show equal deference to everyone's free choices concerning how to live their lives). In other words, according to this understanding, rights protect against majorities that despise someone's life, consider it offensive, immoral or, for other reasons, worth less than those of others; viz they guard against interference in someone's life on the basis of impermissible reasons of this kind.[21] This understanding of Convention rights appears to draw a clear line between those exercises of public authority that are based on permissible reasons and those based on impermissible reasons, according to the underlying deontological ethic. 'Courts are not asked to establish what interests human rights should serve, in what ways, and to what extent', Letsas writes, and he describes his rights theory as comparatively minimalist and easy to apply.[22]

However, it is largely unclear how saying that human rights are those rights that derive from an equal concern to everyone and, especially, respect for everyone's free choice concerning how to live their lives differs from recognizing general and indeterminate rights to equal treatment[23] and to liberty:[24] both allow applicants to complain essentially about any exercise of public authority with the result of bringing almost any exercise of public authority under the control of the rights-reviewing court.[25]

[17] George Letsas, 'Strasbourg's Interpretive Ethic: Lessons for the International Lawyer' (2010) 21(3) EJIL 509, 540.

[18] Dworkin, *Rights* (n 13) 273–274; Letsas, *Theory of Interpretation* (n 3) ch 5.

[19] Ronald Dworkin, 'Liberalism' in his *A Matter of Principle* (HUP 1985) 191–192.

[20] Letsas, *Theory of Interpretation* (n 3) 113.

[21] ibid 117.

[22] ibid 104.

[23] cf Article 1 of Protocol No 12 to the Convention for the Protection of Human Rights and Fundamental Freedoms of 4 November 2000, in force since 1 April 2005, CETS No 177.

[24] cf Federal Constitutional Court of Germany, *Elfes*, no 1 BvR 253/56 of 16 January 1957 (published in BVerfGE 6, 32).

[25] See Mattias Kumm, 'Who Is Afraid of the Total Constitution? Constitutional Rights as Principles and the Constitutionalization of Private Law' (2006) 7(4) Germ LJ 341, 349; Oliver Lepsius, 'The Standard-Setting Power' in M Jestaedt and others, *The German Federal Constitutional Court* (OUP 2020) 84.

Consider, for instance, that and with which reasons Letsas agrees with the Court's *Hirst (no 2)* judgment. In this judgment, the Court held that the United Kingdom must extend the franchise beyond the then-applicable British blanket ban on prisoners' voting rights, which was found to be in breach of the right to free and fair elections.[26] Letsas justifies this finding with the argument that 'it is reasonable to view the ban as based on moralistic ideas [ie ideas that question everyone's equal moral status] about how to treat prisoners'.[27] This reasoning leaves open the option of reading the Convention as requiring the abolition of further restrictions on the franchise. For example, it could be considered moralistic to disenfranchise those with certain cognitive disabilities due to their allegedly inferior rationality, those aged sixteen to eighteen, as well as long-term non-national residents.

Letsas' understanding of the Convention rights and their proper judicial interpretation has the potential to come close to allowing the Court to examine complaints about basically any exercise of public authority. This understanding allows individuals to complain about basically any act of public authority; first, against any act of public authority, that somehow interferes with individual liberty, which is assumed to be limitless in principle and limitable only exceptionally; second, against any act of public authority that does not enable one to make use of an opportunity, which potentially allows for far-reaching positive rights and, correspondingly, positive obligations; and, third, against every differentiated (non-indiscriminate) act of public authority, which by definition involves the unequal treatment of different individuals. If we take into account other scholars' works on equality and human rights, it confirms the hunch that Letsas' theory has the potential to expand the Court's reach almost infinitely. As Charilaos Nikolaidis argues, the principle that the States must equally respect everyone's free choices as to how to live their life can reasonably be understood to require protection against social oppression[28] and, together with the principle of equal concern, 'freedom from prejudice and stereotyping, as well as the need for reasonable accommodation of difference'.[29] The result is a substantive conception of equality[30] involving demands for redistribution, recognition, structural transformation aimed at creating a diversity-accommodating society, and social and political participation.[31]

[26] Article 3 of Protocol to the Convention for the Protection of Human Rights and Fundamental Freedoms of 20 March 1952, in force since 18 May 1954, CETS No 009.

[27] George Letsas, 'Proportionality as Fittingness: The Moral Dimension of Proportionality' (2018) 71(1) CLP 53, 85.

[28] Charilaos Nikolaidis, *The Right to Equality in European Human Rights Law* (Routledge 2015) 3.

[29] ibid 5.

[30] ibid 15.

[31] Sandra Fredman, *Discrimination Law* (2nd edn, OUP 2011) 22–33.

d) Liberal meliorism

The expansive judicial reach that results from Letsas' understanding of rights and the judicial role has especially robust consequences as it is embedded in a narrative of progress, a belief that reason allows for the continuous, perhaps indefinite,[32] betterment of the human condition.[33] In this spirit, Letsas suggests that the Court's evolutive interpretation of the Convention is *required* whenever a 'better understanding of the nature of human rights and the principles that justify them' becomes available.[34] As Michael Perry explains, a commitment to moral growth requires that courts deal with fundamental politico-moral issues by using non-interpretative methods and abstaining from grounding their conclusions in conventional moral views, on the grounds that the political branches fail to do so due to re-election pressures.[35] That is, courts must seize the opportunities that come their way to promote moral progress, in whatever sense the judges at the apex of the judiciary understand this progress, following their moral evaluation of the issue at hand.[36]

e) Judicial activism

For Letsas, the Convention protects moral rights against the failure of a State to recognize and/or to protect these rights. These rights are, according to him, objective moral truths that derive from the principle of equal concern and respect. Their identification and specification, through their derivation from this liberal-egalitarian principle, is a matter of moral reason. As courts are superior moral reasoners to political bodies, according to Letsas, the identification and protection of rights must be entrusted to them. This is an ongoing task: whenever a better understanding about what the principle of equal concern and respect requires in terms of Convention rights becomes available, these rights must be given new content: evolutive interpretation is called for. Whenever the State exercises public authority—including, for example, when it acts as a private-law legislator[37]—it must respect

[32] Marquis de Condorcet, 'The Sketch', in S Lukes and N Urbinati (eds), *Condorcet: Political Writings* (CUP 2012).

[33] See Thomas Skouteris, 'The Idea of Progress' in A Orford and F Hoffmann (eds), *The Oxford Handbook of the Theory of International Law* (OUP 2016) 940–941.

[34] George Letsas, 'The ECHR as a Living Instrument: Its Meaning and Legitimacy' in A Føllesdal, B Peters, and G Ulfstein (eds), *Constituting Europe* (CUP 2013) 139.

[35] Micheal J Perry, *The Constitution, the Courts, and Human Rights* (Yale University Press 1984) 100–102.

[36] ibid 110–113.

[37] *Redfearn v the United Kingdom*, no 47335/06, 6 November 2012; George Letsas, 'Rescuing Proportionality' in R Cruft, SM Liao, and M Renzo (eds), *Philosophical Foundations of Human Rights* (OUP 2015) 336 (his note 41).

what the principle of equal concern and respect requires, but what that means in practice largely depends on the circumstances of the individual case.

In sum, according to Letsas' theory, the domain of the Convention's 'constitutional justice' and thus the domain of the Court's control over the States is 'radically expanded'[38] to encompass basically any exercise of public authority, to allow an evolutive interpretation that finds its 'limits' only in the Court's best attempt to arrive at the objective moral truth and to largely deny relevance in the Convention system to the volition of the States *qua* sovereign, self-governed political democracies.[39] Some might call this 'undemocratic juristocracy', Letsas would probably prefer to call it 'a commitment to complete constitutional justice'.[40]

f) The problem of ideolatry

Letsas suggests dissolving the tensions behind the principle of subsidiarity one-sidedly, in favour of international control, common standards, and rights-based judicial review, while, according to the terminology of Chapter 5, his theory is pretentious insofar as it supports constraints on democracy that are limited only by Letsas' subjectively preferred moral theory of liberal rights—or whatever the Court judges' make of it. As Dean Spielmann, a former judge and president of the Court, laconically puts it in the preface to Letsas' *Theory of Interpretation*: 'The role of the judge, and his or her personal choice, is not to be underestimated'.[41]

A theory that considers the Court competent to interpret the Convention in light of an abstract objective moral principle of everyone's equal moral worth and freedom is apt to justify a far-reaching expansion of the Convention's protective scope, and therefore of its scope of control. To some extent, the Court has engaged in such expansive interpretivism. It has thus been observed that it may undermine its legal legitimacy, at least from the perspective of those with a more positivist bent than Letsas'.[42] Unsurprisingly, this seems to be the position of a majority of the States. As Nikolaidis suggests, their hesitance in the ratification of Protocol No 12 is explicable in terms of their reluctance to allow the Court to adjudicate essentially any exercise of public authority.[43] As of today, less than half of the States have recognized the general right to equality and the concomitant expansion of the Court's jurisdiction. However, for theorists such as Letsas, who consider it the point and purpose of the Convention system to defend the moral principles behind the

[38] cf Kumm (n 25) 346.
[39] See Letsas, *Theory of Interpretation* (n 3) 90–98.
[40] See Kumm (n 25) 368–369.
[41] Dean Spielmann, 'Foreword' to George Letsas, *A Theory of Interpretation of the European Convention on Human Rights* (paperback edn, OUP 2009) vii.
[42] See Nikolaidis (n 28) 63.
[43] ibid 85.

Convention rights, irrespective of the States' democratic volition, the interpretative expansion of the Court's reach is not merely unproblematic, but represents the singularly right adjudicative approach for the Court.

The equality of all individuals that the Court should realize, according to Letsas, is a utopian assumption, a moral ideal that can never fully materialize, an ideal that one cannot help but betray, even when fervently fighting for it.[44] Secularized and enlightened—that is, purged of God, as well as of divine, and natural, law—the ideal of equality depends on a moral argument, the nub of which is this: each human individual possesses by virtue of their equal moral worth and human dignity, certain equal liberal rights that do not fall within the purview of the authority exercised by political power-holders.[45] This claim of political morality intends to create 'legal compulsion ... solely from the compulsion of philosophical reason'[46] or, in other words, to produce legal normativity simply 'because of [its] self-evident rationality'.[47] It has no authoritative source, but rests entirely on the foundation of philosophical argument.[48] It is 'essentially an appeal to some fundamental set of rights that inhere in the individual and demand recognition whether or not they have been enacted in the law of particular states', quite like earlier appeals to natural rights.[49] To the extent that one considers courts to be forums for moral reason and democratic politics to be theatres of warring interest groups and selfish factions, democratic politics poses a danger to these rights, whilst courts protect them. Transferred beyond the state, this view conveys a distrust of states and a belief that international courts serve to rein in the states *qua* dangerous political actors.[50]

This account views the Convention favourably, as institutionalizing pre-existent moral human rights. Thus established and entrusted to the Court, the moral character of Convention rights permeates the entire legal and political order. Domestic constitutional and sub-constitutional law is no longer the result of democratic volition, but a matter of *supra*-national judicial moral reason. This view disregards the fact that the authoritative judicial interpretation of *supra*-constitutional law is no less an act of volition than a political body's decision. To paraphrase Bernhard Schlink, the anti-positivist bend of the theorists who adhere to this view impedes them from realizing that they are propagating a 'constitutional court positivism': their anti-positivism negates the judicial making of positive law, which we discussed in Chapter 6, because they fail to perceive the authoritative judicial

[44] Vividly, Michael Walzer, *Spheres of Justice* (Basic Books 1983) xi.
[45] Martin Loughlin, *Sword and Scales* (Hart 2000) 202.
[46] Jürgen Habermas, 'Natural Law and Revolution' in his *Theory and Practice* (Beacon Press 1973) 86.
[47] Martin Loughlin, 'What Is Constitutionalisation?' in P Dobner and M Loughlin (eds), *The Twilight of Constitutionalism?* (OUP 2010) 61.
[48] See even Ronald Dworkin, *Justice for Hedgehogs* (HUP 2011) 37–38.
[49] Martin Loughlin, *The Idea of Public Law* (OUP 2004) 126.
[50] See Jens T Theilen, *European Consensus Between Strategy and Principle* (Nomos 2021) 74.

interpretation of the law as such.[51] Their paradigm and their assumption that law is always just if it is only rightly interpreted, largely frees rights-reviewing courts from otherwise-applicable constraints of legal argumentation, substituting the judicial for the democratic legislator's responsibility to realize justice:[52] some liberal-egalitarian moral principle, some argument that the state's conduct did not fit its normative role, will always be available to turn an issue into a justiciable rights issue.[53]

As a result, it becomes possible to address, on the basis of moral reasons, innumerable rights claims to the political community, the only limit being that of one's moral imagination.[54] Severing the linkage between law and (democratic) volition also facilitates the idea of *supra*-national law.[55] Letsas' failure to see any difficulty with common human rights standards that all States must implement testifies to this.

The problem is that, in practice, most rights claims are potentially contentious and conflicting. The resulting controversies are inherently political, to the extent that they concern society at large. The view that these conflicts are best entrusted to international courts operating in a democratic vacuum is convincing only to the extent that one accepts several controversial and to some degree implausible assumptions. The first of these assumptions is that all these conflicts have a single correct solution that can be identified by moral reasoning. The second is that courts are the main *locus* of moral reasoning, and thus best placed to find these uniquely correct solutions. The third is that rights are 'simply' easy-to-apply guarantees against the state *qua* malign homogenous political majority, such that they are best controlled by a non-political authority external to the state. The fourth is that the understanding of 'law as right', that is, the understanding of law in a melioristic teleological sense, suggests that courts can indefinitely continue unpacking the true moral meaning of human rights, and thereby incessantly contribute to bettering the human condition. If accepted, these assumptions wholly vindicate the Court's existence in a democratic vacuum: they justify a *supra*-national legal constitutionalism and allow for a certain carefreeness as regards international judicial human rights control over democratic states and uniform standards of ever-growing scope and ever-increasing depth.

However, there are obvious issues with each of these assumptions. The problem with the first is that even if there is an objective moral truth that indicates that there is a single correct answer to every rights issue, conflicts would persist, due to

51 Bernhard Schlink, 'Die Entthronung der Staatsrechtswissenschaft durch die Verfassungsgerichtsbarkeit' (1989) 28(2) Staat 161, 168–169.

52 See Kumm (n 25) 349.

53 See Schlink (n 51) 168–169.

54 See Richard Bellamy, *Political Constitutionalism* (CUP 2007) 148.

55 Loughlin, *Public Law* (n 49) 127–128.

the lack of a generally accepted method for arriving at this truth.[56] The crux of the second assumption is related to this point. Aside from the questionable assumption that judges are somehow motivated differently in their choices than any other individual,[57] it is not clear that courts are the most capable of resolving issues of political morality for the methodological reason just given. This is even more the case, the more numerous and diverse the conflicting concerns are and the less an issue is simply a matter of defending one individual against a hostile homogenous political majority. In such circumstances it is at least questionable whether courts are best placed to decide. The two-party set-up of litigation makes it quite probable that the umpire fails to accurately grasp all of the competing interests at stake, as we noted in Chapter 4.

The problem with the third assumption is that human rights cannot be properly understood as easy-to-apply defences against homogenous and hostile political majorities. Governments must do and are used to do more than merely abstain from oppressing political minorities. Thus, an important part of the Court's jurisprudence is based on a positive understanding of the Convention rights. As a consequence, many issues of 'individual' rights concern broad circles of society. Making decisions about such issues is inherently political, as we saw in Chapters 5 and 6, in particular, since it means arbitrating with prospective effect between competing social, political, and cultural interests about which no consensus exists and to which no answer may be found that all sides would accept as right.

Finally, the problem with meliorism is that the belief in progress depends on a normative criterion which cannot be objective. The difficulties are essentially the same as those that beset the first assumption. A political community can share a belief in, and a narrative of, progress only insofar as it agrees on the pertinent evaluative criterion, the relevant data points, and their linkage: the stronger the disagreement about questions of political morality and empirical social developments—for example, about the superiority of liberal egalitarianism, its effects, and their normative assessment—the weaker the societal consensus about questions of progress. The appeal of populist 'illiberal democrats' to a non-negligible part of the citizens of many European countries testifies to this: these people reject elements of the morality held dear by liberal-egalitarian democrats, such as Letsas. However, there are also certain kinds of liberal-egalitarian democrats who, due to their doubts about the assumptions that underpin the *supra*-national legal constitutionalism sketched in this section, challenge this paradigm. They favour what may be called an '*inter*-national political constitutionalism', as will be discussed in the next section.

[56] See Jeremy Waldron, 'Moral Truth and Judicial Review' (1998) 43(1) Am J Juris 75.

[57] See Richard A Posner, 'What Do Judges and Justices Maximize? (The Same Thing Everybody Else Does)' (1993) 3(1) Sup Ct Econ Rev 1.

C) *Inter*-national political constitutionalism

The previous section discussed a view that proposed restricting democracy based on a general normative programme. On this account, the purpose of the Court system is to constrain the States' democracies based on a certain interpretation of the Convention rights, one that follows a specific moral rights theory. If one is favourable of this view, there is no reason to take issue with the Court's position in a democratic vacuum, since democratic volition has no role to play in rights protection in Europe anyways. On this account, it appears awkward, to say the least, to ascribe only a subsidiary role to the Court.

However, this approach to the liberal-democratic predicament may be understood to diminish secular achievements, because it appears to somehow replace earlier religious legitimation of political authority with a sort of quasi- or civil-religious legitimation, namely, a normative theory that claims objective validity. In response to this fear, proponents of neo-Roman republican theory, sometimes described as republican liberalism or democratic liberalism, consider another solution to the liberal-democratic predicament: they believe that the key to sustaining liberal democracy lies in the people themselves, that is, in their recognizing that their only chance to freedom is to assume the task of maintaining and cultivating the liberal-democratic order themselves. On this account, democratic politics plays a central role in securing the States' liberal democracies, which could explain and justify the ascription of a merely subsidiary role to the Court.

We will illustrate this take on the problem via a discussion of Richard Bellamy's work. This choice was a relatively easy one, given the shortage of contemporary scholars who have elaborated a decidedly sceptical stance on rights-based judicial review in favour of universal participation in democratic politics. Bellamy has not only consistently argued for political constitutionalism, but he has also applied his arguments to the context of European human rights protection.

Bellamy is critical of attempts to constrain democracy based on what are supposed to be objectively true liberal principles. His key arguments roughly reflect the controversial assumptions identified in the previous section's concluding critique. First, for Bellamy, liberal rights are not prior to, and constitutive of, democracy, but rather derive from democratic politics. Second, for Bellamy, democratic politics offers a better forum to settle rights issues than judicial proceedings do, because democratic politics makes it possible 'to build community by negotiating reciprocal compromises between conflicting views'.[58] Third, Bellamy's main concern is not to guarantee a minimal set of liberal rights, but to secure a society free from social domination by elites. Fourth, Bellamy argues that the liberal belief

[58] Richard Bellamy, 'Introduction' in his *Rethinking Liberalism* (Pinter 2000) xii.

in progress has been proven fallacious, because the potential for conflict has increased with the emergence of modern, pluralistic societies.

a) Political rights

Bellamy offers both a defence and a generalized normative model of the Westminster system as a democratic model sceptical of legal governance.[59] In this view, rights are 'utterly man-made and worldly'[60] and their juridification only obscures the intractable political controversies behind them.[61] Bellamy argues that one can hardly distinguish issues of rights and justice from matters of ordinary politics, the pursuit of group interests, and social welfare. Due to Rawlsian 'burdens of judgment' that result from factual and normative epistemic uncertainties, different personal experiences, and the inevitable choices a community must make,[62] rights issues are subject to reasonable disagreement and political contestation.[63]

In the context of the Strasbourg system, Marco Duranti's history of the Convention illustrates the reality of political controversy behind the determination of rights. Duranti shows how conservative political forces quite successfully sought to forestall 'leftist' policy change by including some, but not other rights in the Convention.[64] In a more expansive analysis, Danny Nicol studied how international regimes have sought to constitutionally protect neoliberal capitalism at the international level. He argues that neoliberal national elites, eagerly supported by the transnational judiciaries they set up, have been happy to allow international constraints on national politics, as long as these constraints 'loc[k] in neoliberal reforms against the vagaries of democracy'.[65] Recently, indeed, some pertinent criticism has been levelled against the Court. According to Kári Ragnarsson, the Court's jurisprudence in post-2008 austerity cases has been dismissive of social justice concerns and overly deferential to the austerity demands of the neoliberal political and economic elites. In this area, the Court's control is largely toothless, Ragnarsson argues, due to its acceptance of general goals, such as the protection of the public purse, as legitimate State aims and the application of a wide margin of appreciation.[66]

59 See JAG Griffith, 'The Political Constitution' (1979) 42(1) MLR 1.

60 Adam Tomkins, 'In Defence of the Political Constitution' (2002) 22(1) OJLS 157, 174; but cf Quentin Skinner, *Liberty Before Liberalism* (CUP 2012) 19–21.

61 See Eoin Daly, 'Republicanizing Rights? Proportionality, Justification, and Non-Domination' in E Herlin-Karnell, M Klatt, and HA Morales Zúñiga (eds), *Constitutionalism Justified* (OUP 2019) 198–206.

62 John Rawls, *Political Liberalism* (expanded edn, CUP 2005) 54–58.

63 Richard Bellamy, *Liberalism and Pluralism* (Routledge 1999) 59–63.

64 Marco Duranti, *The Conservative Human Rights Revolution* (OUP 2017).

65 Danny Nicol, *The Constitutional Protection of Capitalism* (Hart 2010) 154.

66 Kári H Ragnarsson, 'The Counter-Majoritarian Difficulty in a Neoliberal World: Socio-Economic Rights and Deference in post-2008 Austerity Cases' (2019) 8(3) GlobCon 605, 614–615.

Corresponding with Bellamy's view, these examples suggest that rights may be used to entrench certain interests against political reforms that would benefit other interests, because it is not a priori clear which concerns justifiably enjoy protection as rights.[67] Thus, Ran Hirschl explains the 'expansion of judicial power through constitutionalization and the corresponding acceleration of the judicialization of politics'[68] as being 'driven primarily by political interests to insulate certain policy preferences from popular pressures'.[69] In institutional terms, this means that the authority of those who decide about the scope and meaning of rights is problematic, insofar as this authority takes on a moral guise, with the effect of disguising the political reality that everyone pursues 'political ends which are far narrower, more limited, and more short term, than those abstractions' found in bills of rights.[70]

b) Relational rights

As Bellamy explains, it lies in the nature of rights, namely, in their relational and triangular structure, to fall within the 'circumstances of politics', the domain where, despite reasonable political disagreement, common decisions must be made.[71] The triangularity of rights means that there exist not only a right and its individual bearer, but also someone—usually the state collective—who is charged with respecting or securing the right. Rights are inherently relational, in that they constitute and define a relation of right and obligation between two or more individuals.[72] Thus, rights specifications always have effects beyond the rights-bearer, whether limiting someone else's freedom, requiring someone to undertake positive action, necessitating institutional and procedural measures, or otherwise incurring social costs. For Bellamy, this means that rights should be the outcome of collective agreements among all those concerned by their benefits and burdens.[73]

Positive law, such as Articles 8–11 of the Convention, and legal practice reflect the view that justified rights claims must not follow only from the subjective interests they protect, but must also depend on their implications for society as a whole: they make the legal protection of rights dependent on the absence of weightier countervailing public interests, including the rights of others. In the Court's practice, which we will discuss in more detail in Chapters 9 and 10, most Convention rights do not protect against any interference, but only against disproportionate restrictions—that is, most Convention rights do not convey an

[67] See Bellamy, *Political Constitutionalism* (n 54) ch 4.
[68] Ran Hirschl, *Towards Juristocracy* (HUP 2004) 211.
[69] ibid 213.
[70] See Griffith (n 59) 16–18.
[71] Bellamy, *Political Constitutionalism* (n 54) 20–26.
[72] John Finnis, *Natural Law and Natural Rights* (2nd edn, OUP 2011) 200–202, 218–219.
[73] Richard Bellamy, 'Rights, Republicanism and Democracy' in A Niederberger and P Schink (eds), *Republican Democracy* (Edinburgh University Press 2013) 255.

entitlement to absolute protection, but only to such protection that takes due account of countervailing interests.

Seen from this perspective, rights are aspects of a set of institutional arrangements that must be justifiable in its entirety to a political community as a whole, so that it makes no sense to understand rights as somehow natural or pre-political. However, the task of arriving at a rights specification that is acceptable to everyone is difficult. This becomes evident from examples such as the protection of personal security. Any increase in security measures normally comes at the cost of individual freedom, privacy, and/or free speech, etc., and consumes resources, leading to shortfalls elsewhere. How to strike this balance is far from uncontentious. Similarly, the line between those socio-economic claims that civil and political rights protect (if any) and those that fall into the domain of ordinary political debate about social and redistributive measures is highly contentious.

As Bellamy notes, rights are not compossible, in the sense of dovetailing perfectly without giving rise to conflicts.[74] The solution to conflicting views about the best set of protected rights cannot lie in the rights themselves; rather, the problem ultimately results from disagreement about these very rights. Bellamy thus suggests that societal considerations of a utilitarian and communitarian sort are indispensable for specifying rights. For example, the limits of the right to free speech are determined by the value of free speech to the community—by the right's 'place within a complex set of collective structures and practices, from clubs to political institutions, which are held to foster the development of a certain quality of human flourishing and interpersonal relations'—and by the right's utility 'for communication and the benefits deriving from the unrestricted exchange of information, feelings and ideas'.[75]

The Court's case law makes clear that there is some truth in this view. Its leading *Handyside* judgment turned on respect for *public* morals which might be understood differently in different societies.[76] Other judgments concerned political speech which enjoys particular protection because of its value for the democratic process and hence the entire political *community*;[77] again others addressed blasphemy laws which have been accepted essentially due to their contribution to *social* (religious) peace.[78] Similar considerations can also explain the Court's lustration case law: according to the Court, restrictions on the political rights of (former) communists can be upheld only so long as these communists pose a significant threat to the post-Soviet democratic order in a given State,[79] viz only as long as the

[74] Bellamy, 'Introduction to Rethinking Liberalism' (n 58) xii.
[75] Bellamy, *Pluralism* (n 63) 170.
[76] *Handyside v the United Kingdom*, 7 December 1976, para 48, Series A no 24.
[77] See eg *Brasilier v France*, no 71343/01, para 41, 11 April 2006.
[78] See eg *ES v Austria*, no 38450/12, para 43, 25 October 2018.
[79] *Ždanoka v Latvia* [GC], no 58278/00, para 135, ECHR 2006-IV.

social costs of granting political participatory rights even to (former) communists are seen as outweighing the utility of doing so.[80]

c) Democratic equality

Since no unambiguous legal expertise is available when it comes to questions of competing values and societal considerations, Bellamy argues that the democratic process is the better forum for deciding on the specification of rights than courts are.[81] James Allan summarizes the underlying thought succinctly: because courts' institutional arrangements cannot suppress judges' personal, subjective vantage points, one can scarcely consider a majority of judges better suited to render decisions on contestable rights issues than a majority of citizens or their representatives, for it is implausible that 'judges are somehow morally superior or of greater perspicacity' than everyone else.[82]

As Jeremy Waldron suggests, people do not, as a rule, vote in ways they consider unjust or morally wrong simply because doing so would favour their personal, selfish interests.[83] Instead, people and their representatives may often, though not always, vote according to what they think is in the best interests of the community. The reality of existing bills of rights suggests as much. If political majorities were always decided in amoral ways, as Dworkin and Letsas suppose, there would never be any political backing for morally justified minority rights protections, which is not the case in Europe's politico-legal reality, where there are, for example, international agreements for the specific protection of minorities, such as national minorities and linguistic minorities.[84]

To be sure, majorities are not always right, but it would be wrong to think people will always narrowly and egoistically strive to maximize their own interest. Thus, assuming that there is no one right answer to intricate moral questions available, decisions on the part of the political majority will often have to be taken as reasonably moral or, at least, as equally reasonably moral as judicial decisions.

This suggests that rights and democracy are reconcilable thanks to widespread liberal moral convictions.[85] That is, Waldron proposes an essentially circular

[80] cf *Refah Partisi (the Welfare Party) and Others v Turkey* [GC], nos 41340/98 and 3 others, para 132, ECHR 2003-II.

[81] Bellamy, *Pluralism* (n 63) 174.

[82] James Allan, 'Bills of Rights and Judicial Power—A Liberal's Quandary' (1996) 16(2) OJLS 337, 348.

[83] See Jeremy Waldron, 'Rights of Majorities and Minorities: Rousseau Revisited' in JW Chapman and A Wertheimer (eds), *Majorities and Minorities* (NYU Press 1990).

[84] Framework Convention for the Protection of National Minorities of 1 February 1995, in force since 1 February 1998, CETS No 157; European Charter for Regional or Minority Languages of 5 November 1992, in force since 1 March 1998, CETS No 148.

[85] See Jeremy Waldron, 'The Core of the Case Against Judicial Review' (2006) 115(6) Yale LJ 1346, 1364–1366.

approach to the liberal-democratic predicament, which makes the limits of democracy depend on democracy. However, he does so in a sanguine spirit reminiscent of Stephen Holmes' account (see Chapter 6): rights and democracy are not seen as antithetical to each other since the participants of the political process are assumed not to vote selfishly, but rather according to liberal moral convictions. Bellamy subscribes to a similar view, when he advocates 'a form of politics that makes liberalism an aspect of the democratic process itself, rather than a normative constraint on the scope of democracy'.[86]

A Convention system in which an activist Court decides largely on its own which rights claims receive protection and which do not would be incompatible with this view, according to which rights are not something external to politics, but the outcome of a shared political practice. For Bellamy, an institutionally grounded distinction between the judicial responsibility for the individual case and the political responsibility for 'deciding a collective policy on rights that looks at the myriad ways different rights interact' is important therefore;[87] lest the law become an opaque business of experts, estranged from ordinary people and their moral and political views.[88]

For republicans like Bellamy, the legitimacy of rights-reviewing courts 'rests on their being servants of the public and responsible for administering law that ultimately has the public as its source'.[89] Since rights represent everyone's equal entitlements within their political community, they are intrinsically linked to political equality and, therefore, intrinsically democratic.[90] Only democratic politics respects political equality and only 'obliging citizens to deal on equal terms with each other as rulers and ruled in turn'[91] provides security against the danger that a political community's arrangements for the protection of certain interests, but not of others, as rights are decided not equally by all, but by overbearing rulers.[92] Thus, for a decision about rights to be democratically legitimate, on this account, everyone should be able to agree, if not with, then at least *to* the outcome, on the grounds of its procedural rightfulness as the product of legitimate decision-making process.[93]

Bellamy's argument for political decision-making about rights depends on a demanding conception of political participation. The key quality of a democratic system is, in his view, 'that the political process obliges decision-makers to "hear

86 Bellamy, *Pluralism* (n 63) 93.
87 Richard Bellamy, 'Political Constitutionalism and the Human Rights Act' (2011) 9(1) I•CON 86, 111.
88 See Jeremy Waldron, 'Can There Be a Democratic Jurisprudence?' (2009) 58(3) Emory LJ 675, 693–697.
89 Richard Bellamy, 'Public Law as Democracy: The Case of Constitutional Rights' in C Mac Amhlaigh, C Michelon, and N Walker (eds), *After Public Law* (OUP 2013) 132.
90 ibid 139.
91 Bellamy, *Political Constitutionalism* (n 54) 83.
92 See ibid 53.
93 ibid 164, 191.

the other side"'.[94] This demands more than simply putting up with other views—it requires the reciprocal accommodation of diverse values and interests.[95] Bellamy does not claim that his favoured process of public reasoning leads to consensus or agreement about moral rights issues, but rather that it is likely to produce negotiated compromises, 'as products of the mutual recognition by citizens of the reasonableness of their often divergent points of view by seeking to accommodate these various perspectives within a coherent programme of government'. The resulting compromises are less crude aggregations of majority votes than attempts to balance, weigh, and make compatible their various rights claims.[96]

According to Bellamy, democratic politics promotes compromise because it depends on the successful building of majorities. In his view, the 'competitive struggle for the people's vote', as theorized by Joseph Schumpeter,[97] promotes the broad inclusion of diverse concerns in reciprocal ways in different parties' programmes.[98] Unlike social movements concerned with single issues, parties are concerned 'with the overall fairness of the system as a whole',[99] since from competitive party-based elections the need arises to formulate comprehensive, coherent government programmes that are able to win (ideally) broad, stable, and enduring majorities. In other words, competitive party politics facilitates log-rolling and the creation of artificial political unity, as it were, despite pluralism and disagreement within society.[100]

Through the negotiation of widely accepted rules, political parties play an indispensable role: the successful negotiation of compromise rules will usually be possible only if all those involved hold multiple positions, making it possible for them to engage in repeated rounds of horse-trading until a compromise is reached. This is why Bellamy opposes the juridification of rights claims. He fears that entrenching the pet causes of some groups in the law, but not those of others, would create unequal negotiating positions and thereby undermine processes of compromise-building. In particular, organizations that are narrowly focused on a single goal lose incentives for compromise-building and for engaging in negotiations, including the associated log-rolling and coalition-building, when they have good chances of achieving their aims through litigation.[101]

Along similar lines, the Court noted in *SAS*, when it rejected a right to wear face-covering veils and found the corresponding French ban compatible with the Convention, that certain conventions may 'by virtue of an established consensus,

[94] ibid 176.
[95] Bellamy, *Pluralism* (n 63) 93.
[96] Bellamy, *Political Constitutionalism* (n 54) 192–193.
[97] Joseph A Schumpeter, *Capitalism, Socialism and Democracy* (5th edn, Routledge 2003) 269.
[98] Bellamy, *Political Constitutionalism* (n 54) 230–231.
[99] ibid 232.
[100] See Richard Bellamy, 'Schumpeter and the Transformation of Capitalism, Liberalism and Democracy' in his *Rethinking Liberalism* (Pinter 2000) 99–100.
[101] See Bellamy, *Pluralism* (n 63) 104.

for[m] an indispensable element of community life within the society in question',[102] thus observing that it 'falls within the powers of the State to secure the conditions whereby individuals can live together in their diversity'.[103] As the Court explains, '[p]luralism and democracy must also be based on dialogue and a spirit of compromise necessarily entailing various concessions on the part of individuals or groups of individuals'[104] and thus restricting 'the reach of pluralism'.[105]

However, the case of *SAS* raised a serious problem: the existence of a stigmatized group with whom no other groups will build coalitions. It is here, indeed, that Bellamy thinks courts play a legitimate role as contestatory forums, namely, by ensuring that the settled law is impartially and even-handedly applied and that everyone receives a fair hearing for his or her claims. More specifically, according to Bellamy, 'judicial review can track whether reasoned debate occurs, but need not substitute for an absence of such deliberation'.[106] That is, when courts consider the law to be deficient, they must, according to Bellamy, do no more than call on the law-makers to reconsider it how and when they see fit: courts must sound the 'alarm bell', but go no further. It remains the task of politics to react to and remedy the situation, or so Bellamy argues.[107]

d) Contingent liberalism

For Bellamy, liberal rights and freedoms are politically contestable and rightly so. In his view, due to a persistent value pluralism, '[n]o overarching moral theory can resolve all the tensions within' a functionally differentiated modern society.[108] Bellamy thus rejects the idea that one could devise a theory of political morality from the impartial perspective of a neutral Archimedean point.[109] In this view, the constitutional constraints that self-avowedly neutral liberals advocate are just as moralistic as the constitutional constraints proposed by other theorists.[110]

For related reasons, Bellamy does not believe that liberalism will naturally prevail over competing moral and political theories. He dismisses the melioristic liberal belief in moral progress as a mere ploy. According to his historical account of liberalism, modern liberals developed the story of ongoing moral progress as a social theory that serves to cover up the problem that the philosophical commitment

102 *SAS v France* [GC], no 43835/11, para 122, ECHR 2014 (extracts).
103 ibid para 141.
104 ibid para 128.
105 ibid para 153.
106 Bellamy, *Pluralism* (n 63) 122.
107 Bellamy, 'Public Law' (n 89) 148–149.
108 Richard Bellamy, *Liberalism and Modern Society* (Polity 1992) 261.
109 ibid 253.
110 See also Steven Shiffrin, 'Liberalism, Radicalism, and Legal Scholarship' (6) 30(1983) UCLA L Rev 1104, 1156.

to the liberal principle of the greatest possible liberty of all is not susceptible to an objective, uncontroversial interpretation. Liberals, in order to nonetheless posit their liberal theory as objectively right, supplemented their liberal philosophy with a sociological thesis, according to which there is a natural development towards the envisioned liberal society that will bring individual life plans into harmony and put an end to controversies about the liberal principle. That is, in order to justify their claim of a universally shared liberalism, liberals added the thesis that society will naturally develop in this direction.[111]

Bellamy prefers to rely on Max Weber's sociology to suggest that, although we may thanks to science discern the best means to an end, we are incapable of establishing a single correct value order: everyone must choose their goals, purposes, and values for themselves.[112] Thus, Bellamy is convinced that modern political life cannot be governed by an overarching moral framework, but is marked by persistent struggles between different ethical ideals.[113]

In today's Europe, there are unmistakable tendencies that strongly resonate with Bellamy's scepticism of liberal meliorism and, conversely, confirm liberalism's contestability. Liberal meliorism has suffered, in particular, from the rise of populism and related phenomena, such as the emergence of Eastern European 'illiberal democrats' and scepticism about the European integration process. The strongly exclusionary, inegalitarian, and anti-pluralist implications of populism are antithetical to liberal constitutionalism. All of this challenges the thesis, most famously expressed by Francis Fukuyama, that liberal democracy is the end state of the teleological political-ideological evolution of a rational humankind whose yearning to fulfil material desires and for equal recognition inevitably leads to the creation of capitalist liberal democracies.[114] Instead, the populist upsurge indicates a loss of the belief in liberal-democratic constitutionalism as the superior form of government. As Fukuyama himself observes: '[t]he "democratic" part of liberal democracy is ... rising up and taking revenge on the "liberal" part'.[115]

The liberal order might currently be undermining itself in a way reminiscent of Weber's belief that, in modern, highly rationalistic societies, only those who occupy leading positions in the main public and private organizations actually enjoy a high degree of freedom.[116] At the expense of the common good, the liberal political, legal, and economic order encourages strong, perhaps excessive, individual assertiveness. Because this same liberal order increases social inequality, it produces a deep divide between those who can afford their individualistic self-realization

[111] Bellamy, *Modern Society* (n 108) 2–3.
[112] ibid 184–185.
[113] ibid 204.
[114] Francis Fukuyama, *The End of History and the Last Man* (Free Press 1992) 211.
[115] Francis Fukuyama, 'America: The Failed State' *Prospect* (London, 13 December 2016).
[116] Max Weber, 'Die wirtschaftlichen Unternehmungen der Gemeinden', in W Schluchter (ed), *Max Weber-Gesamtausgabe* (Mohr Siebeck 1998).

and those who cannot, or only to a lesser extent.[117] The resulting frustration provokes backlash in the form of withdrawal from, loss of trust in, and action opposing the (international) liberal order, its institutions, and its individual proponents.[118] Supporting the illiberal constitutionalism of populists with an authoritarian penchant who promise nationalistic programmes for the benefit of 'those left behind' is one way to act against the despised liberal order.[119]

All of this suggests that liberal democracy ultimately lives from the widespread popular belief in it, which also depends on people's circumstances of life. Bellamy may well be right to reject dirigiste attempts to impose an ostensibly neutral liberal political morality upon society. Liberalism is no sure-fire success: the pretence of political, legal, and bureaucratic elites to possess knowledge about the betterment of society does not suffice to sustain a liberal order—proponents of liberalism must continuously convince the general public of its value and defend it against its competitors in the public, political discourse.[120]

The emergence of anti-liberal politics signifies a partial failure on the part of liberalism and its advocates, which may indicate a need for change. Recalibrating the balance between (national) democratic politics and (international) judicial review—that is, between processes that operate more from the bottom up and others that operate more from the top down—in favour of the former, as suggested by the subsidiarity principle, might be one component of such a change, or so Bellamy's work suggests.

e) *Demoi*-cratic control

This leaves us with the question about the role for the Convention system and, in particular, the Court that Bellamy foresees. The Convention system is best understood, according to Bellamy, as a 'produc[t] of popular and state sovereignty that [is] necessarily and justifiably under the joint and equal control of sovereign democratic peoples as part of an international political constitution'.[121] Bellamy's argument hinges on his contention that political constitutionalism is compatible with rights-based review *if* the underlying bill of rights is legislative in nature and the reviewing court embedded in a political democracy.[122] The Convention law has to

[117] See Paul Howe, 'Eroding Norms and Democratic Deconsolidation' (2017) 28(4) J Dem 15, 20–27.

[118] See Eric A Posner, 'Liberal Internationalism and the Populist Backlash' (2017) 49 (Special Issue) Ariz St L J 795, 814–818.

[119] Ronald Inglehart and Pipa Norris, 'Trump and the Populist Authoritarian Parties: The Silent Revolution in Reverse' (2017) 15(2) Perspectives on Politics 443, 445–447.

[120] See Julian Scholtes, 'The Complacency of Legality: Constitutionalist Vulnerabilities to Populist Constituent Power' (2019) 20(3) Germ LJ 351, 359–361.

[121] Richard Bellamy, 'The Democratic Legitimacy of International Human Rights Conventions: Political Constitutionalism and the European Convention on Human Rights' (2014) 25(4) EJIL 1019, 1023.

[122] ibid 1024.

be the people's law, and the Court must operate in a democratic context: judgments must be open to public critique and discussion, democratic politics must be the source of the law, judicial discretion must be limited in order to prevent judicial arbitrariness, and judicial review must enhance rather than substitute for the democratic consideration of rights.[123]

That is, for Bellamy, the Court serves to draw political attention to human rights problems, especially in case of legislative inconsistencies, the unforeseen consequences of legislation, and 'discreet and isolated minorities' that fail to be given a fair hearing in the democratic political process. Policy decisions must ultimately remain political, however, since the judicial process is unable to take into account the multifarious concerns of all individuals who live under a certain human rights regime. The political process is better suited to do so.[124]

On most accounts, the Convention system does not fit well with these ideas, contrary to what Bellamy suggests. The question then is whether, how, and why the Convention system can be understood in a way that reflects Bellamy's considerations. The question *why* the Convention system would be compatible at all with a political-constitutionalist outlook is relatively easy and may find broad acceptance. As Bellamy explains, the Court may enhance everyone's equal say in the political process, support the States in 'locking-in' their democracies,[125] address transnational challenges facing the States' institutions, and facilitate the States' learning from each other about how to improve their institutions and to counteract parochial biases.[126]

To the question of *how* the Convention system can satisfy political-constitutionalist standards, Bellamy replies with three points.[127] First, membership must be based on democratic consent. Second, the Convention system must ultimately remain under democratic control—specifically, under the control of States that are, if not democratic, at least credibly democratizing. Third, the Court system must enhance, not undermine the States' democratic processes: Bellamy demands that the Convention remain an intergovernmental system that is thoroughly embedded in a democratic process. Thus, according to him, as long as there is no European *demos*, the democratic legitimacy of the Convention system depends on the *demoi*-cratic control of the States' *demoi*. In his view, the Convention system indeed is subject to the *demoi*-cratic control of the States' representatives who, in turn, are subject to the democratic control of their domestic constitutional arrangements. However, this is not uncontentious and much of the remainder of this book will deal with the theme of the democratic control, viz the legitimizing

123 ibid 1027–1028.
124 ibid 1029.
125 See Andrew Moravcsik, 'The Origins of Human Rights Regimes: Democratic Delegation in Postwar Europe' (2000) 54(2) IO 217, 225–229.
126 Bellamy, 'European Convention' (n 121) 1032–1033.
127 See ibid 1032–1035.

influence that the States through their democratic process have on the Convention system: we will argue that the Court's merely subsidiary role is grounded in the fact that the Convention must take its democratic legitimacy from the States' political processes.

This leads to the question of *whether* the Convention system as it functions in today's practice corresponds, roughly at least, to these considerations. Bellamy's own answer is exceedingly brief. Still, he rightly notes that the considerable powers that the intergovernmental Committee of Ministers enjoys within the Convention system may be said to secure a sort of *demoi*-cratic control. Bellamy is also right to point out that the Court leaves room for national discretion and that it increasingly does so in a manner that chimes with considerations concerning the separation of powers and democratic quality.[128] However, there is much more to be said about the functioning of the Convention system that would appear to be in line with Bellamy's views, as the remainder of this book shows in arguing, first, that the Court's subsidiarity is justifiable in light of the value of political equality, in particular, and, second, that this understanding of Convention subsidiarity can explain and justify important aspects of Convention law and practice that those who are closer to Letsas than to Bellamy tend to downplay or oppose, because they allow for a major role to be played by the States.

f) The problem of naive trust

Bellamy's trust in the democratic process may appear naive and vulnerable to the objection that it ignores the reality of failing democracies and the existence of occasional democratic failures in generally well-functioning liberal democracies. Most importantly, Bellamy can scarcely be said to carefully consider the reality of highly unequal political power: one person, one vote does not suffice for a fair political process.

It should also be clear that Bellamy, just like the liberals he criticizes, offers an argument that is ultimately political: he advocates bringing current systems in line with his preferred political theory. Most importantly, he himself essentially argues for a form of constitutional entrenchment when he suggests that no deviation from competitive electoral democracy and simple majority rule among the representative members of parliament should be allowed.[129] In more substantive terms, Bellamy's argument is more neutral; it is very much focussed on procedure—that of a competitive, pluralist party democracy—and prescribes few substantive ends.

The main problem with Bellamy's procedural view is its highly sanguine take on the equality and inclusiveness of democratic politics. A charitable reading of

[128] ibid 1036.
[129] Bellamy, *Political Constitutionalism* (n 54) 174.

Bellamy's work suggests that he accepts the importance of rights to the democratic process: while he assumes that there is reasonable disagreement about rights, he does not consider rights nonsensical or unimportant. He also emphasizes the value of a functioning system of ordinary courts. More generally, though he advocates a version of democratic politics that some find objectionable, his democratic model corresponds to the canonical features of the contemporary understanding of democracy. However, Bellamy shows little fear of left-wing or right-wing populist demagogues leading the public astray with dangerous ideologies or of certain political interest groups succeeding in gaining unequal benefits at the expense of others. His apparent conviction that most people most of the time display the civic virtues necessary for a well-functioning democratic process, showing equal concern and respect to their fellows,[130] seems dangerously optimistic in view of historical examples of democratic collapse. This is, no doubt, the polar opposite of Letsas' general distrust of democratic politics.

Still, Bellamy's work is important in bringing politics back into the, at times, quite complacent liberal-legalist discourse on the Convention system. First, it recalls that human rights claims, Convention membership, and efforts to implement the Court's judgments all depend on political will and result from political struggles. Second, its emphasis on the triangularity and relationality of rights recalls that any meaningful and legitimate rights configuration must take into account considerations beyond individual freedom and equality: practical feasibility, the availability of resources, social and opportunity costs, competing individual and public interests, and the prevailing public opinion cannot be ignored. The best philosophical argument will not suffice to protect rights, if it meets with widespread opposition for whatever reason. Because the Convention rights correspond to obligations borne by the States and, hence, their political communities, Bellamy rightly emphasizes that the process of determining rights should be inclusive and open. Otherwise, important considerations may remain neglected and the moral justifiability that rights acquire from their mutual recognition by all would suffer. Third, Bellamy's challenge of liberalism's claim to neutrality, that is, of the belief that human and social developments inevitably lead society to converge on a desirable set of liberal convictions, emphasizes that the direction in which society moves is neither predetermined nor uncontroversial.

All of this makes clear that rights issues are not susceptible to an unambiguous answer derived from any one holistic value theory based on the liberal equality of all individuals. Rights must be constructed through a political practice of which the judicial process is merely one part. This may explain the principle of subsidiarity in the Convention system: the Court system provides solely for the judicial process' contribution to the specification of Convention rights, while it is only

[130] See ibid 253–256.

within the States that a fully-fledged politico-legal practice occurs upon which the rights arguably depend.

D) Equal freedom: normative, contestable, and political

Liberty and equality are the central values of liberal-democratic constitutionalism. Both Bellamy and Letsas argue with the principle of equal concern and respect, with the idea that, morally speaking, everyone should count the same and that everyone's autonomous choices should command equal deference. Individual autonomy cannot be absolute, however, since a society founded on liberty as licence, condemning any restriction on the capacity to do as one pleases, would not be viable. This shifts the focus from freedom per se to apportioned spheres of protected individual freedom and to the process through which these spheres are distributed. Once freedom is understood as a humanly apportioned sphere of individual autonomy, equality becomes important: justice demands that everyone enjoys equal freedom. Yet, if freedom is a normative concept, equal freedom is normative too. Moreover, equality itself is open to many different interpretations. The question is thus: what equality in what freedom?

The answers proposed to this question will often be subject to reasonable disagreement. If the equal moral worth of all individuals is taken seriously, then everyone's view should count the same in the resolution of this disagreement. However, what that means is controversial too and, because any reasonable answer will involve more than the arithmetical formula of 'one person, one vote'—namely, equality in freedoms such as speech, assembly, and association which, to be effective, depend on opportunities and resources—formal political equality alone cannot solve the problem. But neither can procedural equality be left out: if a conception of substantive equality was imposed on society through an unequal decision rule, equality would be violated to the same extent as if society would content itself with the barest formula of political equality.

Neither of the two positions discussed in this chapter advocates liberty as licence, neither rejects the view that liberty should be distributed equally, and neither denies that equality consists of substantive and formal elements. Yet, the two positions give very different weight to formal democratic equality and a more substantive liberal understanding of equality. In doing so, both theories border on the absurd or the fanatical. One invokes the belief that judicial reason leads to an ever-better understanding of the moral verities underpinning a comprehensive liberal egalitarianism. The other, by contrast, suggests that equality is best served by a virtually unlimited political struggle conducted within a democratic polity where what counts as democratic is, by and large, fought out in this manner too. The first perspective suggests that the Court's lack of equally developed political counterparts is unproblematic, as long as its jurisprudence roughly conforms to the favoured conception of liberal egalitarianism. By contrast, the second perspective suggests that the democratic vacuum in which the Court operates is a problem, because it means that the political dimension of the equality of all individuals may not receive its due.

Given that neither side of the debate categorically negates the importance of the other side's most cherished principle—liberal and democratic equality, respectively—we can assume that there is broad agreement that the Convention system must satisfy both concerns in a reasonably balanced way. This suggests that the Convention's subsidiarity principle serves to ensure that the Convention system respects a reasonable balance between, respectively, liberal and democratic equality, as institutionalized in the Court's rights-based review, and the States' democratic politics. The Court system alone, unlike a fully-fledged politico-legal order that is at the same time liberal and democratic, cannot respect the comprehensive liberal *and* democratic equality of everyone. The Convention system, if it is to respect the democratic equality of all, depends on the States' democratic polities. The Court system must not usurp the States' democratic politics, but only support them in such a way as to ensure due respect for the principle of the democratic equality of all. The demand that the Convention law respect not only the liberal, but also the democratic principle, and the resulting indispensability of the States explains and justifies the subsidiarity of the European level.

8
The Court's Subsidiary Role

A) Introduction

The European Court of Human Rights (the Court, ECtHR) operates in a 'democratic vacuum'.[1] This situation is—as we have seen in the previous chapter—susceptible to either a positive or a negative assessment. While a positive assessment is vulnerable to the objection that it is grounded in a pretentious and elitist understanding of liberal rights and judicial review, a negative assessment can be criticized for its naive trust in the virtues of democratic politics. The former position flirts with the idea of establishing a powerful Strasbourg juristocracy, whereas the latter position risks relegating the Court to the rank of a mere advisory body.

Leaving behind these radical, but illustrative positions, the fact remains that, at the European level of the system set up under the European Convention on Human Rights (the Convention, ECHR),[2] there is an imbalance between a fully operative system of rights-based judicial review, on the one hand, and mere vestigial remains of a democratic political process, on the other. In the absence of countervailing arrangements, the Court would exercise its constitutional function of rights-based review without being embedded in a democratic polity. The (liberal) moral equality of every person as expressed in everyone's equal sphere of protected individual freedom would be given substance through a juridical process that lacks parallel political mechanisms capable of ensuring respect for the democratic principle according to which everyone should have an equal say in the general delimitation of competing private spheres. This one-sidedness would be problematic, since liberal and democratic equality—that is, equality on the level of individual autonomy and equality on the level of collective self-determination—must be given equal weight. Otherwise, conflicts resulting from incompatible exercises of individual freedoms could not be legitimately resolved, nor could exercises of collective freedom be legitimately constituted. In this chapter, we argue that the Convention's principle of subsidiarity is explicable and justifiable due to this incompleteness, as it were, of the Convention system.

In its second section, we explore the idea that liberal equality (equal rights) and democratic equality (equal political say) are inseparable, insofar as they represent

[1] Christoph Möllers, *The Three Branches* (OUP 2013) 213.
[2] Convention for the Protection of Human Rights and Fundamental Freedoms, as amended, of 4 November 1950, in force since 3 September 1953, 213 UNTS 221, CETS No 005.

Subsidiarity, Legitimacy, and the European Court of Human Rights. Reto Walther, Oxford University Press.
 DOI: 10.1093/9780198921455.003.0008

two interwoven dimensions of everyone's right to equal concern and respect. The equal freedom accorded to each individual is an expression of the fact that they are morally equal to everyone else, but what this means more concretely must be specified through a process that itself respects the moral equality of each individual, which must, in this context, principally assume the form of political equality. Democracy, as the primary locus of the political equality of all individuals, operates predominantly at the state level. This is, in short, why the Court system can only be subsidiary if it is to heed its liberal-democratic commitments: unlike its member states (the States), it accounts for only half of the principle of the moral equality of all people *qua* the foundation of human rights.

Against this background, we examine the Court's role and highlight the importance of justification (ie reason-giving) in the third and fourth sections of this chapter. We argue that a justificatory ethos underpins the Convention system in such a way that it subordinates questions of formal authority to questions of persuasive, substantive justification. Institutional counterbalances ensure an ongoing justificatory dialogue about the Convention rights, which is why it is difficult—and rightly so—to classify the Court's review either as strong form or as weak form: a strict hierarchy of authority would undermine the parity needed for the functioning of this process. In the final two chapters, we will see how this theory fits important aspects of Convention law and practice that have caused bewilderment among scholars, but that make sense in light of the Convention's subsidiarity principle as theorized here.

B) The primarity of the state polity

Unless one rejects the Convention outright, one accepts some idea of liberal human rights. The Convention system reflects an understanding of human rights as equal rights of all, accompanied by correlative duties:[3] the Convention contains no special rights for particular subgroups of humanity,[4] and its jurisdictional reach has deliberately not been limited to citizens, residents,[5] or even to individuals located within the States' territories.[6] In short, if a State's jurisdiction according to Article 1 of the Convention is established, the same Convention rights apply to anyone under that jurisdiction and give rise to State duties, insofar as a certain right lends protection in the individual circumstances of a case.

[3] Joseph Raz, 'On the Nature of Rights' (1984) 93(730) Mind 194, 199–200, 210–211.

[4] See eg *Strand Lobben and Others v Norway* [GC], no 37283/13, para 9, 10 September 2019 (joint dissenting opinion of Judges Kjølbro, Poláčková, Koskelo, and Nordén).

[5] See Samantha Besson, 'The Extraterritoriality of the European Convention on Human Rights: Why Human Rights Depend on Jurisdiction and What Jurisdiction Amounts to' (2012) 25(4) LJIL 857, 863.

[6] See eg *Al-Skeini and Others v the United Kingdom* [GC], no 55721/07, paras 130–142, ECHR 2011.

As we will see in the following, whoever accepts the conception of human rights as equal liberal rights with correlative duties that all humans possess in virtue of their humanity ought to accept two further propositions as well: first, that all humans are inherently equal in some morally relevant sense ('moral status equality')[7] and, second, that all humans are equally capable of reason, understood as the faculty of free will, the capability of 'making deliberate choices about their own situations and of carrying out these choices in action'.[8]

The first of the two propositions results from persistent disagreement and uncertainty about the distinctive marks of human nature and the implications that follow from individual autonomy: if one holds to the idea that there are equal human rights but cannot (dis)prove that every human individual is equal with respect to any relevant factual property, then the equality that grounds equal human rights must be a normative moral equality of all humans.[9] Since human equality, thus understood, is a moral claim, if it is to be practically effective, it must be asserted and must gain general acceptance. As Richard Bellamy therefore correctly notes, 'the moral force of even the most basic human rights does not follow from our humanity per se but the moral theory we hold'.[10]

Human rights, rather than somehow being inherent, are expressive and constitutive of the equal intrinsic worth and social standing of, and the social relations between, all individuals.[11] Moral status equality is a relational concept, just like human rights. Human rights, which serve to ensure the equal moral status of all, give everyone the same enforceable rights to determine—in certain morally justified circumstances—the conduct of everyone else,[12] whose respective duties are, for practical reasons, mediated by the state.[13]

The question is thus that of the domains and situations of societal life in which moral status equality justifies imposing on everyone the duty to behave in accordance with an individual's autonomous choice. This boils down to the question of establishing which general human interests are so important that their protection as human rights is a condition without which people could not mutually regard each other as moral equals.

Whatever the exact process followed in answering this question, it must depart from rights claims, or 'candidate human rights'.[14] This leads to the second

[7] See Allen Buchanan, 'The Egalitarianism of Human Rights' (2010) 120(4) Ethics 679, 685–690.
[8] Charles R Beitz, *Political Equality* (Princeton University Press 1989) 93.
[9] Richard Dagger, *Civic Virtues* (OUP 1997) 27–28.
[10] Richard Bellamy, 'Public Law as Democracy: The Case of Constitutional Rights' in C Mac Amhlaigh, C Michelon, and N Walker (eds), *After Public Law* (OUP 2013) 137.
[11] See Elizabeth S Anderson, 'What Is the Point of Equality?' (1999) 109(2) Ethics 287, 312–315.
[12] HLA Hart, 'Are There Any Natural Rights?' (1955) 64(2) Phil Rev 175, 178.
[13] Samantha Besson, 'Human Rights and Constitutional Law: Patterns of Mutual Validation and Legitimation' in R Cruft, SM Liao, and M Renzo (eds), *Philosophical Foundations of Human Rights* (OUP 2015) 283.
[14] See Charles R Beitz, *The Idea of Human Rights* (OUP 2009) 139.

proposition mentioned above, concerning everyone's capacity to reason. If everyone is taken as an equally rational 'best judge' of their interest, every individual must be equally considered a 'self-originating source' of rights claims.[15] As Rainer Forst notes, human rights presuppose the moral person who has 'the right to and the capacity for' the reciprocal and general justification of everyone's human rights against all others.[16]

That is, because everyone is equally subject to the human rights regime in the making, everyone must be equally involved in its making. Equal rights and political equality are thereby inextricably intertwined.[17] No human rights regime can be legitimately configured absent a process of political democracy. The Convention system's lack of developed forums for democratic politics therefore explains why it must be subsidiary: the States 'primarity' is justified—indeed, normatively compelling—because the States' democratic polities are far ahead of the Convention system in terms of heeding the political dimension of the moral status equality of all individuals. With Samantha Besson, one may hence say that, as there 'is no international polity of equals[,] ... the domestic democratic legitimacy of states' is needed to specify, and to solve disagreement about, the scope and content of human rights in a legitimate manner.[18]

Human rights protect those interests that the members of a political community consider—due to the general, human nature of these interests—sufficiently important to mutually assure each other their protection. This mutual protection has politico-legal priority, which justifies the public duties, as well as the financial and other burdens, that correlate with this reciprocal guarantee.[19] The discursive process of identifying those fundamentally important interests whose protection the members of a political community generally and reciprocally guarantee each other, resulting in rights that all individuals have in relation to themselves as a collective, can only be institutionalized within a political context.[20] That is, they can only be institutionalized within a context in which a group of people with rival views and interests unite under a common rule for the practical purpose of realizing their shared interest in an orderly, civilized government. The latter essentially consists of the practical process through which the people's diverging views and interests are conciliated roughly in proportion to their importance in a way acceptable to everyone, because everyone is given a say.[21] Indeed, the 'ways in which

[15] See Henry S Richardson, *Democratic Autonomy* (OUP 2003) 80–81.

[16] Rainer Forst, 'The Basic Right to Justification: Toward a Constructivist Conception of Human Rights' (1999) 6(1) Constellations 35 (Jonathan M Caver, tr), 43–44.

[17] Jeremy Waldron, 'Can There Be a Democratic Jurisprudence?' (2009) 58(3) Emory LJ 675, 708.

[18] Samantha Besson, 'State Consent and Disagreement in International Law-Making. Dissolving the Paradox' (2016) 29(2) LJIL 289, 301.

[19] Samantha Besson, 'The Egalitarian Dimension of Human Rights' (2013) 136 ARSP Beiheft 19, 33–34.

[20] Forst (n 16) 725–726.

[21] Bernard Crick, *In Defence of Politics* (University of Chicago Press 1962) 16–19.

constitutions protect fundamental rights reflect national constitutional values, national traditions and legal culture'; thus, the values, tradition, and culture of a state's political community provide the context within which a specific set of rights may receive protection.[22]

No adequate alternatives to democratic law made via political processes are apparent when it comes to configuring a rights regime under conditions of universal equality. This is why human rights, such as the Convention guarantees, are politically legislated legal rights, in spite of their groundedness in the moral status equality of all individuals.[23] The Court's practice of 'majoritarian activism' corresponds to this: as Alec Stone Sweet and Thomas Brunell note, the Court often develops the Convention rights by the delivery of judgments that the States would likely adopt if they would specify the Convention by amendments under majority rule.[24]

The moral status equality that grounds equal legal rights must validate its scope and content through a democratic process that plays out between political equals, if it is to avoid being self-defeating. Human rights are thus best understood as the set of rights that realizes the right to be treated as someone endowed with equal moral worth and therefore also to have, at bottom, an equal say in what this moral status equality implies. Everything about the idea of equal human rights beyond this moral status equality, this right to equal concern and respect, cannot a priori be ruled out as a subject of reasonable disagreement.

This conception of human rights includes the central points of Bellamy's and George Letsas' respective morality- and democracy-centred views: it depends on a discursive political process of mutual justification and excludes pretentious human rights theories, but it also rejects any form of non-reciprocity and non-generality, and thus discrimination. Human rights are just as incompatible with political majorities that privilege their own concerns and interests over those of others as they are with allocating the *Deutungshoheit* (ie the sole interpretative authority) about their proper scope and content in a way that definitively removes it from democratic politics. It is the latter point that merits emphasis in the present context, because it explains why European-level human rights protection must be subsidiary to the States' domestic human rights practices.

Only a democratic polity can fully realize the right to equal concern and respect and settle disagreements about the meaning of the equal moral status of all: human rights are inherently democratic, because of the disagreements that surround

[22] Janneke Gerards, 'Margin of Appreciation and Incrementalism in the Case Law of the European Court of Human Rights' (2018) 18(3) HRLR 495, 495–496.

[23] Samantha Besson, 'Human Rights: Ethical, Political ... or Legal? First Steps in a Legal Theory of Human Rights' in DE Childress III (ed), *The Role of Ethics in International Law* (CUP 2012) 238–239.

[24] Alec Stone Sweet and Thomas L Brunell, 'Trustee Courts and the Judicialization of International Regimes: The Politics of Majoritarian Activism in the European Convention on Human Rights, the European Union, and the World Trade Organization' (2013) 1(1) J L & Cts 61, 81.

them, their structure as the equal rights of all individuals and their correlation with equal duties of all institutionalized in state obligations. The Preamble of the Convention correspondingly notes: 'the maintenance and further realisation of human rights and fundamental freedoms are best ensured' by political democracy. If human rights are thus inseparably linked with political democracy, this points to the state's primary role in human rights practices, since, at present, only states constitute actual democratic polities. In the Convention system, too, there is no democratic polity at the European level.

C) The subsidiary role of the Court

Although rights disagreements must be settled through institutions in which everyone has an equal say at some point, a democratic one-level world state might not actually fare better than a multi-level system consisting of primary units (states) and a superordinate level (including international human rights judiciaries). Not only would a single world state dangerously threaten diversity and plurality *qua* conditions of politics, but it would also lack any powers to control and check it, as well as any safety net in the event that it were to deprive someone of their right to equal concern and respect.[25] As Besson explains, based on a reading of Hannah Arendt's famous right to have rights, the right to have human rights, including the right to have an equal say in the specification of these rights, 'cannot be guaranteed exclusively from within a given political community', since it serves, after all, as constraint on democratic sovereignty and self-determination.[26] This suggests that institutions and processes above the state must, first and foremost, guarantee that no state fails to secure the equal moral status of all, consisting of everyone's right to participate as an equal in the intersubjective discursive determination of those rights that the members of a political community grant each other reciprocally and generally, as well as everyone's right to enjoy the resultant rights on equal terms with all others.

According to what has just been said, the primordial purpose of an international system for the protection of human rights, such as that established under the Convention, is to ensure that no one becomes a 'no-count',[27] that is, someone who counts as less than an equal, or does not matter at all, as well as to provide the requisite safety net. It is in the sense of this safety-net function that the Convention system may be understood as a collectively established 'conscience of Europe'

[25] See Hannah Arendt, *The Origins of Totalitarianism* (2nd edn, Meridian Books 1958) 296–299; Hannah Arendt, 'Karl Jaspers: Citizen of the World?' in her *Men in Dark Times* (Harcourt, Brace & World 1968) 81.

[26] Besson, 'Human Rights and Constitutional Law' (n 13) 286.

[27] See Joshua Cohen, 'Minimalism about Human Rights: The Most We Can Hope For?' (2004) 12(2) Pol Phil 190, 197–198; Jean L Cohen, 'Rethinking Human Rights, Democracy, and Sovereignty in the Age of Globalization' (2008) 36(4) Pol Theo 578, 586.

meant to sustain the (domestic) awareness of, and allegiance to, rights, without which the idea of human rights cannot be effective.[28]

The Court might thus appear as the moral exhorter, the embodiment of the Convention's safety net, reminding each State not to deviate 'from the political task of securing basic rights organizationally and institutionally'[29] from within its democratic polity. Yet, however crucial this function of the Court, it must not overshadow the fact that this exhortatory task largely operates on the moral plane of conviction. In order to be effective, the moral conviction that everyone deserves equal respect and concern must be borne by political will.[30]

Qua treaty, the Convention is expressive of such a political will, while, unlike other human rights bodies, the Court is meant to be a genuine court of law rendering binding judgments on the basis of hard treaty law. Foregrounding the possibility of viewing the Court as 'conscience of Europe', a moral instance that appeals to a respondent State's conscience in an attempt to exhort it not to make anyone a no-count would therefore be misguided. The Court's legal authority might well suffer if it came to be seen as a predominantly moral instance. Nonetheless, the imperative of a safety net that protects against a State's failure to treat everyone with equal concern and respect suggests that the Court's authority cannot completely depend on a respondent State's political volition. Thus, the Court's role gives rise to a puzzle: how can it exercise the persuasive moral force that it must exercise *qua* embodiment of the Convention system's safety net, without undermining its legally binding authority? And, conversely, how can it respect the States' political will, based on which it exercises this binding authority, without abdicating its moral responsibility?

In the following, we explore an answer to these questions based on the Convention system's premise that the protection of human rights depends on the responsibility of each individual State and of all the States as a collective. The idea is essentially that the Court plays a correspondingly dual role, which allows it to support the continuing democratic development of morally persuasive human rights standards, on the one hand, and to secure established minimum standards of European human rights law, on the other. However, before we can explore the idea of the Court's dual role, we must understand how legitimate international rights depend on democratically built parochial rights, which underpins the former idea.

[28] See Claude Lefort, 'Politics and Human Rights' in his *The Political Forms of Modern Society* (MIT Press 1986) 260.

[29] Jean L Cohen, 'Rights and Citizenship, and the Modern Form of the Social: Dilemmas of Arendtian Republicanism' (1996) 3(2) Constellations 164, 170.

[30] ibid 182–183.

a) Democratic parochial rights' legitimization of international rights

To understand the complex relation between domestic and international rights and, concomitantly, as we will see, the roles of the Court and the States, a distinction introduced by Ronald Dworkin is helpful. Dworkin proposed to distinguish between what he calls a 'political right to equal concern and respect', which pertains to state-level political morality and a state's individual domestic responsibility, and a 'human right' 'to be treated as a human being whose dignity fundamentally matters', which pertains to international political morality and the states' collective responsibility. He then argued that a state may respect a proper conception of the international human right even if its domestic rights configuration fails to meet whatever substantive conception of the right to equal concern and respect for all one personally considers right and just, namely so long as it adopts an 'intelligible, even if unconvincing, conception' of what rights are implicated by the equal moral status of all.[31]

Besson expresses a similar view about the relationship between domestic and international rights. On her account, international human rights are a guarantee of more concrete domestic rights, which are conceived as fleshed out versions of the former.[32] In terms of state obligations, international human rights primarily oblige the states to translate international human rights into more specific rights that are effective under domestic law so as to ensure no one remains without equal rights.[33]

Thus, on Besson's and Dworkin's accounts, a state's parochial set of rights goes beyond what is minimally required to ensure that no one becomes a no-count, which is what must be protected from outside any given state, viz at the international level. As suggested above, the primary purpose of international human rights protection is to avoid that anyone is denied the (minimal) rights Dworkin and Besson construe as international human rights, which would be tantamount to making that person a 'no-count', a person without effective rights, including the right to have an equal say in the further specification of these rights. Dworkin himself speaks of showing 'contempt', in order to express the idea of treating someone as a no-count, which he juxtaposes to the mere 'mistake' that a state commits when it errs (is unconvincing) in its (still-intelligible) transformation of international human rights into a more parochial set of specific political rights.[34]

Political democracy is needed to give specific scope and content to the equal moral status of all, as argued above, that is, to turn Dworkin's abstract international human right into increasingly specific rights under domestic law. This explains the widely accepted understanding of international human rights as abstract minimal

[31] Ronald Dworkin, *Justice for Hedgehogs* (HUP 2011) 335–338.
[32] See Samantha Besson, 'Human Rights and Democracy in a Global Context: Decoupling and Recoupling' (2011) 4(1) Ethics & Glob Pol 19, 25–26.
[33] Besson, 'Human Rights and Constitutional Law' (n 13) 287.
[34] Dworkin (n 31) 335–336.

standards which the states' domestic rights guarantees should specify and exceed as well as why international human rights are formulated in vague and abstract terms, which, before their concretization, merely point to 'sensitive areas' of political morality.[35] Their open-ended language allows these rights clauses both to function as abstract international human rights and to be more concretely fleshed out rights under domestic law.

We can link this distinction between parochial and international rights—the former located at the state level, the latter at the international level—to the Convention States' twofold, individual and collective, responsibility. This makes it possible to also ascribe to the Court system two different, though not neatly separable, roles. The Convention system *qua* State community bears a collective responsibility to act from without to prevent any individual member State from treating an individual as a no-count, which requires common standards (ie international human rights) that the States *qua* community must collectively secure vis-à-vis each other. But if the scope and content of these standards is to remain subject to the incessant democratic discourse without which they would lack the necessary specificity, democratic legitimacy, and responsiveness to society's dynamic evolution, each State is individually responsible for the continuous development, through its democratic process, of a parochial rights configuration that can then feed into the States' shared understanding of international human rights via horizontal convergence. Thus, a State's domestic rights practice serves the purpose not only of paying immediate respect to the international rights of individuals under its jurisdiction, but also of contributing to the development and legitimation of these standards.

Given the duality of domestic and international rights with the former feeding into the latter and the latter constituting the minimal content of the former, there is a sliding scale between thorough international human rights, that is, rights that have become firmly established as legally binding Convention standards that each State must respect as a minimum, and more far-reaching parochial rights, that is, rights that, as of yet, exist only under domestic law, although they may have been influenced by the Convention system's persuasive moral authority.[36] Consider, for example, that the Federal Constitutional Court of Germany recently developed an individual right under domestic law to protection against the one-sided deferment of constitutionally required reductions in greenhouse gas emissions to the disadvantage of younger and future generations, whereby it relied on Convention law.[37]

At one end of this sliding scale between firmly established international human rights and more demanding parochial rights, the Court, primarily acts as an

[35] ibid 337–338.

[36] See Anton Strezhnev, Beth A Simmons, and Matthew D Kim, 'Rulers or Rules? International Law, Elite Cues and Public Opinion' (2019) 30(4) EJIL 1281.

[37] Federal Constitutional Court of Germany, *Climate protection*, no 1 BvR 2656/18 of 24 March 2021 (translation available from the court).

adjudicator: it exercises its binding legal authority in a rigorous manner from the top down, based on a democratically legitimate basis of domestic political wills that converged from the bottom up. In an ideal world, this role of the Court would not be necessary at all: since these firmly established human rights standards, which the Court rigorously adjudicates, have developed bottom up, from within the States, the States would be expected to willingly respect these standards on their own; it should actually not be necessary that the Court needs to remedy domestic violations of these standards and even less so that it needs to substitute for the States' structurally deficient domestic human rights protection.

At the other end of the scale, the Court acts more as a norm-entrepreneur: it exercises a less robust, but more independent moral authority, insofar as its judgments in issue areas where a well-established *acquis conventionnel* has not yet emerged still have such persuasive force that it allows them to influence a State's further development of its parochial rights configuration. In this role, the Court acts in an 'enabling', instead of in a 'remedial' or 'substituting' manner, to use a terminology which we encountered when we approximated the theory behind the subsidiarity principle in Chapter 2: it facilitates the process through which the States democratically develop their parochial conceptions of human rights and, then, converge on common standards.

This spectral duality of the Court's role comes most clearly to the fore in what is usually described as the narrowing of the margin of appreciation as a function of a growing European consensus, that is, the Court's practice of making its development of the Convention rights dependent on corresponding developments within the States with the effect that the States become increasingly bound by specific Convention standards as a function of convergent State practice. But it is also apparent from the Court's interpretative incrementalism, viz its gradual development of the Convention law on a case-by-case basis. Furthermore, it explains, and it can be understood by looking at, the Court's oscillation between claiming more and less rigorous interpretative authority and precedential effect for its case law. For this reason, it is apt to understand the Court's jurisprudential authority as varied. The flipside of this, so to speak, is that the States bear interpretative obligations under the Convention which require them to secure in their domestic legal orders the conditions that are necessary for them to contribute to the interpretative development of Convention law. We will discuss these practices at some length in Chapters 9 and 10.

The result of all of this is a bidirectional process: the Court exercises top-down control over the States and operates as a coordinative forum in which the States' domestic rights interpretations converge from the bottom up. Of course, this is far from a neatly delineated two-way street with clear destinations at either end: the Convention system can bridge the gap between the moral force of human rights and their democratic grounding only by oscillating between enforcing legally binding common standards and allowing each State to develop its own democratic rights configuration under the influence of the moral reasons expressed by the Court and other participants in Europe's human rights praxis. The following two subsections outline how the Court system assists each State in its individual responsibility of developing a parochial rights configuration through democratic processes that can then feed into common Convention standards, and how this then functions to allow the States to assume their collective responsibility to check each other mutually on the basis of the common minimal standards upon which they have converged.

b) Enabler of the democratic development of rights

The first role of the Convention system concerns each State's individual responsibility for human rights. This role is concerned with providing support to each State in its specification of the scope and content of the equal moral status of everyone through the constitutional process of its democratic polity. That is, in this role, the Convention system supports each State individually in its parochial rights configuration: 'European human rights are ... necessarily incomplete norms that gain their democratic legitimacy from their reception in a national legal order through various reception mechanisms'.[38] The Convention system is subsidiary to each individual State, since it must take care to be supportive in a way that respects each State's democratic self-government.

Each State needs time and leeway to develop its domestic rights specification through a democratic process. This explains the procedural dimension of the principle of subsidiarity in the Convention system, viz why the Court must only deal with an issue after the domestic authorities have done so, according to Article 35(1) of the Convention, which requires the exhaustion of all domestic remedies before turning to the Court. It also justifies the substantive dimension of subsidiarity: the States enjoy a primary role as interpreters of the Convention due to the need to develop the Convention law from the bottom up from within the States' democratic polities. Finally, it explicates the remedial dimension of subsidiarity, which permits a State to decide itself how to modify its domestic practice in the course of implementing an adverse Court judgment, so as to enable that State to carry the dialogue about the proper understanding of the Convention rights further. The next chapters discuss relevant Convention practices in more detail.

The Court system *qua* 'facilitator',[39] or enabler, essentially supports each State in vesting rights with a scope and content, by providing it with further discursive

[38] Samantha Besson, 'European Human Rights, Supranational Judicial Review and Democracy: Thinking Outside the Judicial Box' in P Popelier, C van de Heyning, and P van Nuffel (eds), *Human Rights Protection in the European Legal Order* (Intersentia 2011) 135.

[39] See Samantha Besson, 'Subsidiarity in International Human Rights Law—What Is Subsidiary About Human Rights?' (2016) 61(1) Am J Juris 69, 100.

forums, extra argumentative space, and additional considerations that the domestic actors may want to take into account. For example, the Court may operate as an 'agent of the public', by giving a voice to groups who object to certain policies on rights grounds, but who have not been given a fair hearing in the domestic discourse.[40] Thus, individual applicants to the Court must have exhausted only those domestic remedies that are effective in giving them a voice.[41] The Court may also add 'reflectiveness' to a State's democratic rights discourse by acting as an 'interlocutor', with which domestic authorities 'can converse about an advantageous' rights specification,[42] or by helping a State to conform to its reflected moral commitments instead of acting on mere snap judgments or spontaneous moral opinions.[43] The interaction between the Court and domestic authorities may, in turn, lead to a broader public debate among citizens about rights issues.[44] This may also involve civil society organizations who, based on Article 36(2) of the Convention appear as *amicus curiae* before the Court, where they too have a chance to communicate their views effectively to the respondent State. In short, the Court's review may spur democratic deliberation about rights.

Because the primary sites of political will-formation are located at the State level and situated within the domestic context, the Court must engage with the States on an individual basis. This means, first, that the Court's jurisprudence is sometimes clearly tied to a certain domestic context,[45] and, second, that it makes sense to look at the bigger picture of convergent domestic views only when the States have individually made up their minds about what they consider a legitimate solution to a specific rights issue. That is, it makes little sense to draw comparative conclusions before most States have actually dealt with a rights issue, albeit the deliberate abstention from taking action may, of course, also count as a domestic policy.[46] When the States are still in the process of making up their minds on new rights issues, the moral authority of the Court's judgments may contribute to this process. The Court may also simply alert the States to a growing human rights problem.

A related and, with good reason, oft-repeated point is that an external perspective may help a democratic polity to identify biases, prejudices, and deep-seated stereotypes which give rise to unconvincing, or worse even unintelligible, conclusions about the equal moral status of all, viz about the respects in which equals

[40] See Alison L Young, *Democratic Dialogue and the Constitution* (OUP 2017) 153.
[41] See eg *Keegan v Ireland*, 26 May 1994, para 39, Series A no 290.
[42] See Fiona de Londras, 'International Human Rights Law and Constitutional Rights: In Favour of Synergy' (2009) 9(2) Intl Rev Con 307, 311.
[43] See WJ Waluchow, 'Constitutional Morality and Bills of Rights' in G Huscroft (ed), *Expounding the Constitution* (CUP 2008) 92.
[44] See Young (n 40) 154.
[45] See eg *Leyla Şahin v Turkey* [GC], no 44774/98, para 115, ECHR 2005-XI.
[46] See Shai Dothan, 'Judicial Deference Allows European Consensus to Emerge' (2018) 18(2) Chi J Intl L 393, 414.

must be treated equally and unequals unequally.[47] For instance, where there are clear indications of a case of a 'tyrannical majority', the Court's intervention can compel a State to have a second look at its impugned policy, this time through a lens that is less distorted by preconceived opinions. The Court's famous observation in *Hirst (no 2)*—namely that 'it cannot be said that there was any substantive debate by members of the legislature on the continued justification in light of modern-day penal policy and of current human rights standards for maintaining such a general restriction on the right of prisoners to vote'[48]—could be read in this light, for example.

Although not exhaustive, the foregoing illustrates how the Court system can beneficially contribute to a State's development of its parochial understanding of rights. In this role, the Convention system supports each of the States in its domestic implementation of the international human right to have rights—that is, in its specification of a parochial set of rights giving expression to the equal moral status of everyone. It helps each State to avoid what Dworkin calls mere 'mistakes', by assisting it with developing a constitutional rights configuration that, in the ideal case, is convincing and not merely intelligible.

Indeed, the Court's case law enjoys much persuasive force: the States take its views on rights issues seriously, sometimes making them effective beyond an individual case's decisional authority. Perhaps most importantly, the Court has repeatedly 'nudged' the States towards policy changes in favour of minorities or vulnerable groups. As Laurence Helfer and Erik Voeten's work on the rights of LGBT (lesbian, gay, bisexual, and transgender) people suggests, even if the Court is sensitive to social developments within the States and 'follows a strategy of "majoritarian activism," using the laws and policies of most member countries as a benchmark for developing international standards',[49] it retains judicial discretion—independent moral authority—which allows it to promote policy change. What Helfer and Voeten describe is influence through persuasion, not hierarchical command. The same goes for the Court's advisory opinions, which higher domestic courts may discretionarily request, as these opinions' non-binding character shows.[50] Both practices institutionalize what has been identified as a proactive form of judicial restraint and labelled 'active judicial participation':[51] the Court participates in, but does not authoritatively set forth, each State's domestic rights configuration.

[47] See Oliver Gerstenberg, '(The Failure of) Public Law and the Deliberative Turn' in C Mac Amhlaigh, C Michelon, and N Walker (eds), *After Public Law* (OUP 2013) 230.

[48] *Hirst v the United Kingdom (no 2)* [GC], no 74025/01, para 79, ECHR 2005-IX.

[49] Laurence R Helfer and Erik Voeten, 'International Courts as Agents of Legal Change: Evidence from LGBT Rights in Europe' (2014) 68(1) IO 77, 80.

[50] Article 5 Protocol No 16 to the Convention for the Protection of Human Rights and Fundamental Freedoms of 2 October 2013, in force since 1 August 2018, CETS No 214.

[51] Michael Heise, 'Preliminary Thoughts on the Virtues of Passive Dialogue' (2001) 34(1) Akron L Rev 73.

With regard to this role of the Court, Geir Ulfstein deserves support when he argues that the Court system is rightly conceived of as a *trans*-national, not as a *supra*-national or international-constitutional entity, because it functions as a transnational extension of a State's constitutional arrangements for the protection of rights.[52] As such it adds to the domestic rights protection and may bring about change through its persuasive moral authority, viz by convincing a State of what it considers a morally superior understanding of the demands of the equal moral status of all in a certain sensitive issue area. It does so through a process akin to domestic inter-institutional interaction: 'argumentations included in the ECtHR judgments may lead the state to correct its dysfunction in the protection of the rights and freedoms guaranteed by the Convention when shaping its own legal system'.[53] This process operates in parallel to each of the forty-six States. For example, a Strasbourg judgment may convince some, but not other non-respondent States of the need to change their laws and policies. Likewise, some States but not others may consider an advisory opinion rendered at the request of another State. Thus, there may come various reactions and responses from the States to a Court judgment.

Of course, this situation stands in a certain contrast to the Convention's preambular ambition of achieving a 'common understanding' of human rights. In order to achieve common standards, an element of 'verticalisation' is needed, which, however, must not do away with the Convention system's transnational character. If it did, it would suffocate the States' bottom-up input and eliminate an important source of the Convention law's democratic legitimacy.

Ulfstein, in describing the Court as an international court with constitutional functions and transnational practice, refers repeatedly to a vertical dimension of the Convention system, either explicitly or through references to the Court's 'supreme authority', its 'ultimate say' or the like.[54] Yet, he fails to convincingly explain how this fits together with certain principles of Convention law and practice of which he is well aware, especially the Convention law's abstention from claims of direct effect and supremacy, the States' varying degrees of compliance and, therefore, the Convention system's varying degrees of integration into the States' constitutional orders. It seems as though Ulfstein struggled to reconcile the perspectives of international and domestic law, while, at the same time, mediating between the

[52] Geir Ulfstein, 'Transnational Constitutional Aspects of the European Court of Human Rights' (2021) 10(1) GlobCon 151, 152.

[53] Adam Bodnar, 'Res Interpretata: Legal Effect of the European Court of Human Rights' Judgments for Other States Than Those Which Were Party to the Proceedings' in Y Haeck and E Brems (eds), *Human Rights and Civil Liberties in the 21st Century* (Springer 2014) 234, citing to Evangelia Psychogiopoulou, 'Strasbourg Court Jurisprudence and Human Rights in Greece: An Overview of Litigation, Implementation and Domestic Reform' (JURISTRAS State of the Art Report, Athens undated) 27.

[54] Ulfstein (n 52) 158–173.

attempt not to undermine the Court's international legal authority and the demand not to negate the Convention system's non-supranationality.

On the present account, this struggle cannot, as a matter of legal fact, and must not, as a matter of normative theory, be won by either side. The perennial character of this struggle is crucial to maintaining both the democratic legitimacy and the moral authority of the Convention system. The Court's role as an enabler of each individual State's domestic rights protection chimes with the values of diversity and domestic self-government, as it is marked by a process of influence by moral persuasion instead of legal command. The Convention system's ambitions for common standards and international control, by contrast, are primarily a matter for the States' collective responsibility and the Court's corresponding role. It is here that the claim for vertical hierarchy gets its just due.

c) Guardian of the *acquis conventionnel*

The Convention system serves to secure the international right to have rights under a State's jurisdiction—or, in other words, to guarantee that no one under the Convention's jurisdiction is subject to Dworkinian contempt. Here, the international dimension of the principle of moral status equality is at stake, that is, the requirement that no one is degraded to a no-count. This requires less in terms of rights protection than one might expect—or at least hope for—from the States in the domestic sphere. Article 53 of the Convention formalizes the point that the Convention's standards are only minimum standards which must not impede domestic rights configurations that offer more protection.

As Dworkin notes, it may be controversial whether a State's parochial rights specification can be considered as an (at least) intelligible (if unconvincing) domestic implementation of international human rights.[55] How the line should be drawn between Dworkin's notions of 'contempt' and 'mistake' is the crucial question here. Because international rights proper (and not their parochial interpretations) are at issue, references to the subsidiary role of the Convention system appear puzzling in this context. Statements such as 'the ECtHR—in accordance with the principle of subsidiarity—has the final say about the interpretation of the ECHR'[56] are correspondingly confusing.

In order to understand how the elements of subsidiarity and of 'primarity' (or supremacy)—referred to by expressions such as 'final say'—fit together, one needs to appreciate why and how the Convention system relies on the States *qua* collective of forty-six democratic polities when stipulating those firmly established Convention standards that all States must respect as a minimum.

[55] Dworkin (n 31) 336.
[56] Ulfstein (n 52) 170.

On a normative note, unless one accepts to draw the line between contempt and mistake based on a pretentious theory—that is, a subjective theory preferred by the Court's judges at any given time—which would fail to do justice to human rights' grounding in the equal moral status of all, that line must be democratically rooted. On a practical note, a pretentious theory would most likely not be effective in the long run, since, if it is to be effective on the ground in the States' domestic orders, it requires the normative force that it takes from its procedural democratic origins and its basis in international law *qua* politically willed body of rules.

In light of what has just been said, the answer to the initial question of where to draw the line between contempt and a mistake must lie in a process similar to the discursive process involved in the domestic specification of rights. When a State's parochial rights configuration necessarily develops through a democratic discourse that permits the equal participation of all individuals *qua* moral equals, the question of what counts as contemptuous treatment of an individual also requires a response that results from a discursive process involving the equal participation of all—hence, for example, each State has, in practice, a right based on Article 36(2) of the Convention to appear as a third-state intervener before the Court in order to participate in the development of the common Convention standards in cases to which it is not a party.[57] If the Convention's minimal standards were not developed democratically through a bottom-up process, the States' further development of these basic standards into more demanding parochial rights would not start from a basis that itself respects the equal moral status of everyone. In other words, the line between contempt and mistake must crystallise out of the States' convergent democratic views. It is the domestic rights interpretations—developed in each State with the support of the Convention system *qua* facilitating transnational extension of the States' domestic institutional arrangements—which grow in the forum offered by the Court system into a thicket of minimum standards, thus gradually converging into an *acquis conventionnel*, that checks each State in a top-down process.[58]

The Court thus plays, or should play, a 'harmonising role':[59] it provides a forum for (indirect) dialogue and coordination[60] with and among the States' domestic political and legal authorities.[61] It thereby enables what Seyla Benhabib calls 'democratic iterations', 'complex processes of public argument, deliberation, and

[57] Nicole Bürli, *Third-Party Interventions Before the European Court of Human Rights* (Intersentia 2017) 152.

[58] See Samantha Besson, 'Human Rights' Adjudication as Transnational Adjudication: A Peripheral Case of Domestic Courts as International Law Adjudicators' in A Reinisch, ME Footer, and C Binder (eds), *International Law and...* (Hart 2016) 57.

[59] *A, B and C v Ireland* [GC], no 25579/05, para 5, ECHR 2010 (joint partly dissenting opinion of Judges Rozakis, Tulkens, Fura, Hirvelä, Malinverni, and Paolelungi).

[60] See Alec Stone Sweet, 'A Cosmopolitan Legal Order: Constitutional Pluralism and Rights Adjudication in Europe' (2012) 1(1) GlobCon 53, 53.

[61] cf Antonios Tzanakopoulos, 'Judicial Dialogue as a Means of Interpretation' in HP Aust and G Nolte (eds), *The Interpretation of International Law by Domestic Courts* (OUP 2016) 93.

exchange—through which universalist rights claims are contested and contextualized, invoked and revoked, posited and positioned—throughout legal and political institutions'.[62]

The Court's practice of linking the margin of appreciation with the European consensus doctrine corresponds to this account: when the State-level discussion about what human rights minimally require in a certain area subsides, the standard upon which the States' democratic views converged becomes part of the *acquis conventionnel*, which functions as an elevated, but still 'minimal' check upon the States, and each State's individual room for manoeuvre diminishes. As regards this *acquis conventionnel*, the Court plays the role of a proper court of law: it acts as the judicial guardian of those standards of European human rights law on which the States converged and that, through this process, became democratically legitimate standards whose respect the Court must safeguard.

d) The Court's democratic vacuum: vice and virtue

It becomes clear now why what we have called with Christoph Möllers the Convention system's 'democratic vacuum' is a vice and a virtue at the same time. As concerns the Court system's role in preventing instances of Dworkinian contempt by imposing 'minimal' checks on the States, it must not be part of any State's democratic polity, because its very purpose is to act as an external check upon each State's political community. Recall that the concern is to prevent a State from making someone a no-count, which cannot be assured from within the State, but must be guaranteed by the States collectively *qua* Convention community. Similar to the exclusion of constitutional bills of rights from ordinary democratic politics, the Convention thus understood is positioned in a democratic vacuum for good reasons.

Yet, as concerns the Convention system's transnational role of assisting each State in its own discursive process bearing on the configuration of its parochial set of rights and, thus, in its prevention of Dworkinian mistakes, it cannot but be conceived as an extension to a State's democratic polity: 'states remain the "fundamental" subject of international law and the primary producers of norms'.[63] If the Convention system always and only operated in a democratic vacuum, it could not help usurp the States' political democracies and, by extension, their citizens' individual autonomy.

Contemporary international human rights systems are—happily for their legitimacy—not at loss about the minimal standards of liberal democracy. Instead of bootstrapping themselves, they can—and for reasons of democratic legitimacy

[62] Seyla Benhabib, 'The Legitimacy of Human Rights' (2008) 137(3) Daedalus 94, 98.
[63] Mireille Delmas-Marty, *Ordering Pluralism* (Hart 2009) 13.

and social acceptance must—draw on convergent historical experiences and traditions mirrored in standards that are widely shared between modern liberal-democratic states. For example, Geranne Lautenbach, in her study about the Convention law's conception of the rule of law, observes that the Court draws from pre-existent domestic standards to reinforce the State's rule of law.[64]

As regards the underlying assumption of the States' character as reasonably reliable liberal democracies, this appears justified, formally speaking, in the Convention system and is reflected in the Court's jurisprudence:[65] each State is required, according to the terms of membership, to be minimally democratic, based on the rule of law and respectful of liberal rights.[66] However, if a State failed to meet these standards, due to liberal-democratic backsliding or because it was erroneously admitted despite its illiberal and/or undemocratic government, the question must be posed as to what this means for its participation in the system and, conversely, as to the system's role as regards this State.

Allan Buchanan argues that only minimally liberal-democratic states may legitimately play a role in the further development of liberal-democratic standards, noting that these minimal requirements themselves develop from the bottom up.[67] This view roughly corresponds to the existent domestic practice, approved by the Court, of excluding 'enemies' of the liberal-democratic State from certain democratic institutions through restricting their participatory rights.[68] One might suggest proceeding in the same way, mutatis mutandis, with members of the community of Convention States. It would certainly seem reasonable to attach some consequences to a State's systematic disrespect of the *acquis conventionnel*, in order to prevent it from undermining the established level of common standards that the States mutually reimpose upon each other as a 'minimal' check.

It would be important, however, for such a response to unambiguously come from the peers of the State concerned and not merely from the Court. Only then will it be clear that the State has unequivocally fallen behind what have truly become robust and widely shared common standards. Just as the States (individually) are primarily responsible for their parochial rights, the States (collectively) are primarily responsible for international rights *qua* minimal mutual checks. Apart from the just-discussed normative considerations lying behind this primarity of the States, there is, of course, also the more trivial and pragmatic point that, to the extent that enforcement mechanisms are available at all, they are under the States' control, as will be discussed below.

[64] Geranne Lautenbach, *The Concept of the Rule of Law and the European Court of Human Rights* (OUP 2013) 12–13.

[65] See eg *Tchankotadze v Georgia*, no 15256/05, para 113, 21 June 2016.

[66] See the Preamble and Article 3 Statute of the Council of Europe of 5 May 1949, in force since 3 August 1949, 87 UNTS 103, CETS No 001.

[67] See Allen Buchanan, *Justice, Legitimacy, and Self-Determination* (OUP 2004) 188–190.

[68] See eg *Refah Partisi (the Welfare Party) and Others v Turkey* [GC], nos 41340/98 and 3 others, ECHR 2003-II.

e) The dialectical logic of the subsidiarity principle

To Andreas Føllesdal's claim that, when international human rights review helps in ensuring respect for the limits of relevant democratic decisions, it marks out the domain within which each State's domestic policy decisions must remain,[69] it should be added that this top-down check can be legitimate and operative only after some degree of rapprochement, some measure of bottom-up convergence, has occurred. Just as, if it is to legitimately bind all, the scope and content of the States' parochial sets of rights depends on the democratic legitimation and legal validation flowing from the all-inclusive domestic law-making process, the scope and content of Convention law, if it is to legitimately bind each State *qua* democratic polity, depends on the democratic legitimation and legal validation that stems from the bottom-up convergence of domestic standards through a process that conforms with (procedural) Convention law. Where else, if not from the States' democratic practice, in which the continuously changing social life of the individual rights-bearers is primarily lived, should the scope and content of the *acquis conventionnel* that checks the States legitimately come from?

This is not to say that every State's consent to a standard of Convention law is necessary for that standard to become a legitimately authoritative 'minimal' check. Domestic democracy does not require everyone's consent in order to establish legitimate legal standards either. Just as individuals come together in political communities in order to reciprocally guarantee each other's mutual rights, knowing that they will not always obtain their preferred rights configuration, so too can the political communities to which they belong unite to reinforce their domestic bills of rights, knowing that this may be prudent even if the resulting subsidiary bill of rights will not always correspond to their preferred rights configuration. The corresponding judicial practice may be best described as a combination of judicial 'deliberative engagement'[70] and 'majoritarian activism', in which the judges 'produce rulings that reflect outcomes that states might adopt under majoritarian, but not unanimity, decision rules'.[71] What counts and lends legitimacy to the result is that each State-participant is accepted as an equal and given equal opportunities to participate, although what that means precisely is itself subject to this same process.

It is important to be clear about the limits of judicial majoritarian activism. The Court should not mechanically develop the Convention law in accordance with the view held by a majority of the States. Instead, the Court itself also has a say in the discursive interpretation of the Convention that allows it to 'have some impact on emerging consensus'.[72] The presence of a legal trend within the States

[69] Andreas Føllesdal, 'Tracking Justice Democratically' (2017) 31(3) Soc Epistemology 324, 325.
[70] Stone Sweet and Brunell (n 24) 86.
[71] ibid 63–64.
[72] See Kanstantsin Dzehtsiarou, *European Consensus and the Legitimacy of the European Court of Human Rights* (CUP 2015) 156.

does not mean that the Court should simply accept that trend, while the absence of such a trend does not mean that each State can do as it pleases.[73] Recall that the Court system's roles as enabler and guardian are far from being neatly distinguished: there is a sliding scale along which the Court's jurisprudential authority varies, as we argue in more detail in the following chapter.

What matters is that each State's polity be given a feeling of ownership for the Convention, because it has, and feels that it has, a fair chance to partake in the Convention's dialogic interpretation, even if the Convention law ultimately develops in another direction than the one favoured by a majority of the population within a certain State.[74] This approach 'helps ... mitigate the legitimacy problems associated with judicial lawmaking under supremacy'[75] and contributes to the stability of the Convention system, since it ensures inclusive participation in the development of the Convention law such that the Convention is not at risk of becoming an 'alien' document.[76]

Some may think of the account of the Court's subsidiary role defended here as a foolhardy kind of human rights brinkmanship. In the sense of Ernst-Wolfgang Böckenförde's famous observation that liberal democracies are sustained by conditions they cannot themselves guarantee, this may well be true, but it is the unavoidable 'great gamble ... made for the sake of liberty'.[77] An amount of brinkmanship is unavoidable, if the commitment to the equal moral status of all, and hence to their legal and political equality, is to be maintained.

The Convention system's horizontal and vertical uniting of several dozen (presumably) liberal-democratic peoples comes close to the best of all practically possible safeguards against the latent danger of liberal-democratic self-dissolution, in that it creates and maintains horizontal and vertical pressures that work together in a democratically legitimate manner to sustain its members' liberal-democratic commitments. Despite its subsidiarity, the Court is a crucial, indispensable actor in this endeavour: in its role as enabler, it works towards ensuring that each State bears its individual responsibility, and, when reimposing convergent domestic standards as 'minimal' checks on the States, it arranges and maintains the ideological convergence needed in order to allow the States to bear their collective responsibility. The better the Court succeeds in its task of facilitating each individual State's liberal-democratic conviction, the more reliably each individual State will bear its responsibility, and therefore the more robustly the States will bear their collective responsibility.

73 ibid 29.
74 See ibid 4.
75 Stone Sweet and Brunell (n 24) 64.
76 See Neal Devins and Louis Fisher, *The Democratic Constitution* (2nd edn, OUP 2015) 325.
77 Ernst-Wolfgang Böckenförde, 'The Rise of the State as a Process of Secularization' in M Künkler and T Stein (eds), *Religion, Law, and Democracy* (OUP 2020) 167.

In sum, the general logic behind the Convention's subsidiarity principle is that, due to the political dimension of the equal moral status of all, which grounds the idea of equal individual rights, the State level must always—that is, even when standards upon which the States have converged are at stake—be primary for normative and practical reasons. Conversely, the Convention system is always subsidiary, either in the sense that it 'merely' complements each State's domestic discursive institutions or that it 'merely' supports the States in their joint enterprise to build a collective safety net to protect against any party's defaulting on its commitment and moral obligation to respect everyone's equal moral status. The normative reason for the Convention's subsidiarity principle lies in the equal moral status of all and democratic theory, while its practical and pragmatic reason lies in Europe's political division into forty-six States and in the insight that Convention standards, however persuasive, are dependent on their social acceptance and the political support of the States that flows from it. But despite its subsidiarity, the Convention system plays a crucial role: without it, no European rapprochement would be possible in relation to human rights, for convergence towards shared standards must be mediated and, once a degree of convergence is established, reinforced. The logic of subsidiarity is therefore a dialectical one: it describes a bidirectional—bottom-up and top-down—discursive process in which a State's views reach the Court (bottom-up), may be challenged by it (top-down), develop, and converge in response to this challenge (bottom-up) and become part of the Court's future argumentation (top-down). In the Convention system, the principle of subsidiarity must allocate responsibility in such a way as to keep this dialogue alive, 'to facilitate the adjustments and readjustments that characterise the harmonisation process'.[78]

D) The dialogic justification of rights in the Convention system

The previous sections of this chapter suggest that the roles of the Court and the States as guided by the principle of subsidiarity point towards a dialogic process which includes the States collectively *qua* Convention community and individually, with their domestic legal and political actors, and the Court. This dialogue makes the Court's subsidiarity possible in practice: it allows the Court to have an important say in the Convention system, even to adjudicate the *acquis conventionnel* in a rigorous top-down manner, without usurping the States' democratic polities. This dialogue is ongoing and remains in constant flux, although (temporary) convergence on standards that are widely and firmly accepted occurs. However, given this incessant discourse about how the Convention guarantees are

[78] Delmas-Marty (n 63) 44.

best understood and protected, there can be no such thing as an eternally right understanding of the Convention guarantees: if what is right is what is justifiable, what is right is subject to change as long as the argumentative discourse about what is justifiable goes on. Thus, a sort of discursive ethos relating to the scope and content of the Convention rights must be a constant that is more important and foundational to the Convention system than any specific understanding of the Convention rights.

The remainder of this chapter suggests that such an ethos is discernible in the Convention system and that the Court's merely subsidiary role entails that its interaction with the States' authorities approximates the inter-institutional interaction between constitutional authorities known from dialogue theories of constitutionalism. First, we discuss the proportionality principle and its crucial, ubiquitous role in the Convention system. Because the proportionality principle essentially offers a justificatory framework that structures the dialogue about the justification of right claims, this suggests that a culture of dialogic justification of rights reigns in the Convention system. Second, more generally, we argue that the Court system is downrightly designed for the ongoing dialogic justification of rights: since the supremacy neither of democratic politics nor of constitutional justice strictly holds in the Convention system, the Court and the States' political authorities are virtually compelled to maintain an incessant conversation about the proper understanding of the Convention guarantees. That is, checks and balances between them essentially take the form of their respective ability to continuously contest the others' reasoned decisions about the Convention rights.

a) Proportionality as discursive framework

Proportionality is—contrary to oft-repeated formulations equating what is proportionate with what is Convention-compliant, and vice versa—a 'central procedural component of rights adjudication' whose 'basic function is to organize a systematic assessment of the justifications that state officials must provide if they wish to limit the scope of a right in a constitutionally permissible way'.[79] In other words, proportionality is a doctrinal method (or process) first and a substantive standard only second and derivatively.[80] Proportionality, understood in the latter sense, would be entirely empty were it not for the content derived from proportionality in the former sense. However, in the Convention system and the domain of individual rights more generally, the principle of proportionality is basically all-decisive.

[79] Alec Stone Sweet and Jud Mathews, *Proportionality Balancing and Constitutional Governance* (OUP 2019) 3.

[80] See ibid 30, 48.

Broadly speaking, the proportionality principle means that when an infringement of a right's protective scope has been established, it is justified (legally permissible) if there is a valid legal basis for the infringement, if the infringement pursues a legitimate aim in the public interest, if the infringement is necessary to achieve this aim, and if a fair balance has been struck between the infringement and its purpose. This final test of whether a fair balance has been struck is sometimes also referred to as proportionality *stricto sensu*, and it is decisive of most of the Court's proportionality analyses. However, what a fair balance between the policy goal pursued and the right infringement is cannot be said in the abstract, since this is about the question which of two goods—the infringed right and the interest in whose service the right was infringed—outweighs the other. That is, the (judicial) authority in charge of this assessment must make a 'political or value-laden' choice.[81] Therefore, ultimately, judicial proportionality analyses are mainly about morality, as the influential former president of the Supreme Court of Israel Aharon Barak frankly put it.[82] If the Court rules, this means what is proportionate is what is moral from the Court's perspective.

Alec Stone Sweet and Jud Mathews thus essentially equate the authority of the proportionality principle with the authority of the reviewing court.[83] This stands in a contrast with traditional separation-of-powers theory, according to which the authority of legal rulings is backed by democratically willed law. Stone Sweet and Mathews accordingly note that judicial proportionality analyses cannot 'camouflage judicial lawmaking' and point out the importance of the justifications that courts submit for the policy choices they make when they decide based on the proportionality principle.[84]

What Stone Sweet and Mathews problematize is less of an issue for proponents of a 'culture of justification',[85] such as Moshe Cohen-Eliya and Iddo Porat. For them, what should be decisive is convincing justification of all government action, not formal (legal or political) authority. In a culture of justification, convincing substantive justifications for any exercise of public authority are more important than the answer to the institutional question of 'who decides?', and institutional hierarchies are for good reason comparatively diffuse.[86] We will come back to this latter point in the next section, where we discuss the Court system's oscillation between strong- and weak-form review.

[81] Aileen McHarg, 'Reconciling Human Rights and the Public Interest: Conceptual Problems and Doctrinal Uncertainty in the Jurisprudence of the European Court of Human Rights' (1999) 62(5) MLR 671, 695.

[82] Aharon Barak, *Proportionality* (CUP 2012) 342 (his note 9).

[83] Stone Sweet and Mathews (n 79) 4.

[84] ibid 30.

[85] Etienne Mureinik, 'A Bridge to Where? Introducing the Interim Bill of Rights' (1994) 10(1) SAJHR 31, 32.

[86] Moshe Cohen-Eliya and Iddo Porat, *Proportionality and Constitutional Culture* (CUP 2013) 476–477.

What matters for the moment is the explanation and defence of the proportionality principle's ubiquity that Cohen-Elyia and Porat offer.[87] Due to the importance that a culture of justification assigns to convincing justification of government action, in a culture of justification, basically every exercise of public authority should be subject to judicial review, the barriers to such a review should be low, and respect for rights should be a central, substantive 'benchmark' for assessing essentially all government action. This, in turn, requires that the protective scope of rights is expanded without much regard to the textual wording of the rights clauses. The Court's ubiquitous resort to proportionality reasoning makes much of this possible, as we saw in Chapter 6. Conversely, these key characteristics of a culture of justification have considerable explanatory force for the Convention system.

Note how they relate to several characteristics of the Convention system that we discussed earlier: first, to the many overlapping competences in the Convention system, second, to the insight that the Court's quasi-constitutional adjudication stands between the separation of the legal and the political powers and, third, to the Court's relatively generous, though arguably defensible, application of the Convention's admissibility criteria, the expansion of the Convention's protective scope, including to private law matters, in ways that render the treaty text largely irrelevant and, concomitantly, the increasing subjection of any exercise (and omission) of public authority to the control of the Court. Taken together, all of this means—as propagated by Cohen-Elyia and Porat—that the Court may review basically all government action. That is, it may incessantly and more or less directly interfere with the States' political choices in ways that requires it to convincingly justify its interferences by reasoning about and arguing with the scope and content of the Convention rights. The States' authorities, too, are, therefore, constantly required to interpret and apply—argue about and justify—the Convention rights and their concrete meaning in government practice.

As this justificatory discourse about the Convention rights essentially occurs within, and is structured by, the discursive framework that the principle of proportionality prescribes, the ubiquity of proportionality reasoning in the Convention system[88] testifies to the ubiquity of this dialogue about the Convention rights between the Court and the States' authorities, which occurs not only at the law-application stage, but reaches far into the interpretation of the Convention guarantees, since, in the Court's practice, proportionality review and law interpretation are all but distinct: as we will see in some detail in Chapters 9 and 10, the *acquis conventionnel*—the firmly established understanding of the meaning of the Convention rights—essentially emerges from the iterative application and review of the Convention rights in numerous cases, which happens through consecutive

[87] ibid 477–479.

[88] Sébastien van Drooghenbroeck, *La proportionnalité dans le droit de la Convention européenne des droits de l'homme* (Bruylant 2001).

proportionality analyses, rather than from standalone landmark rulings that give ready-made interpretative precedents.

When we will look more closely at this process in the next two chapters, we will see that argumentative persuasiveness is more important than strict, formal hierarchy. This is a good thing, since, as argued above, interpretations of the Convention guarantees that have lasting legitimacy become possible only through dialogic interaction between legal and political authorities at the European and the State level. Proportionality analyses manifest the continuous argumentative, discursive search for (the lack of) justification for governmental action that makes this dialogic interaction possible.

Thus, proportionality reasoning is an attractive and, generally speaking, rightly ubiquitous instrument for the Convention system, where subsidiarity commands a continuous interpretative dialogue about the scope and content of the protected rights: it helpfully structures this dialogue about rights and justified rights-interferences between the Court and the States' authorities without substantively determining it. The inter-institutional dialogue that proportionality reasoning inspires is of great value to the Convention system: it helps to reconcile the tensions between morality and liberal rights, on the one hand, and collective self-rule and democracy on the other,[89] that is, the tensions, common to all liberal-democratic systems, identified to be the main animating force behind the principle of subsidiarity in the Convention system.

b) The Court's review between weak-form and strong-form review

In order to reconcile the Court's international judicial rights protection with the States' democratic politics, proportionality *qua* justificatory framework must, on the one hand, make the States' political authorities take the Convention rights and the Court's interpretations of these into account and, on the other hand, constrain the Court to show respect to domestic authorities that do so. The result should be close interdependence, with bidirectional persuasive effects, between the Court's judge-made Convention law and domestic law- and policy-making.[90] Only through such an interaction can there emerge a 'collective judgment of reason about what the commitment to rights' implies.[91] Within a Convention system governed by the principle of subsidiarity, one should thus construe proportionality, following Stephen Gardbaum, 'as enhancing, not constraining, democracy', as being 'centrally about the democratic legitimacy of a

[89] Stone Sweet and Mathews (n 79) 55.

[90] See ibid 129, 131.

[91] Mattias Kumm, 'The Idea of Socratic Contestation and the Right to Justification: The Point of Rights-Based Proportionality Review' (2010) 4(2) L & Ethics Hum Rts 140, 168.

constitutionalized rights regime and an appropriate balance between judicial and legislative powers'.[92]

As we will see in the following, the Convention system, with its robust, but flexible authority in the States' legal orders, its virtually unamendable rights clauses, and its abundance of materially diverse case law, benefits from structural conditions that are conducive to a process of mutually influential Convention adjudication and domestic law- and policy-making. The latter operates its own proportionality assessments that may warrant judicial deference and restraint, while the former contributes additional considerations to the domestic law- and policy-making process. In fact, the Convention system may be particularly well suited for inter-institutional interaction, constitutional dialogue, since the supremacy neither of democratic politics nor of constitutional justice strictly holds in the Convention system, due to the varied jurisprudential authority of the Court and the partly political, partly legal process of the reception and implementation of Convention law and jurisprudence. For this reason, the criticism levelled against the notion of constitutional dialogue that is familiar from systems with some form of parliamentary supremacy—namely, that no actual dialogue takes place because parliament has the last word anyways—does not readily apply to the Convention system, whereas it is equally implausible to oppose the notion of dialogue in the Convention system with the argument, familiar from systems of judicial supremacy, that the judges have the final word anyways.[93]

To understand how the subsidiary Court interacts with the States' authorities and how this interaction relates to the democratic legitimacy of the Convention system, it is more apt to look at it through the lens of Gardbaum's New Commonwealth Model of Constitutionalism,[94] which encompasses those constitutional orders in which the notion of dialogue has gained the most traction. Dialogic constitutionalism's focus on how legal and political powers interact[95] fits well with subsidiarity *qua* normative principle structuring the responsibility sharing between the Convention system's national and international legal and political actors.

The New Commonwealth Model of Constitutionalism is distinct from legal and political constitutionalism in that it combines weak-form judicial review with some model of pre-enactment political rights review.[96] The Convention system conforms to both elements, though in its own way. Pre-enactment political rights review appears in the Convention system insofar as the authority whose act is subject to the Convention-based review, viz ultimately the State, is required to undertake

[92] Stephen Gardbaum, 'Proportionality and Democratic Constitutionalism' in G Huscroft, BW Miller, and GCN Webber (eds), *Proportionality and the Rule of Law* (CUP 2014) 260.
[93] See Young (n 40) 1–30 and chs 2–3.
[94] Stephen Gardbaum, *The New Commonwealth Model of Constitutionalism* (CUP 2013).
[95] Young (n 40) 84.
[96] Gardbaum, *New Commonwealth Model* (n 94) 25–27.

its own rights review before the Court exercises its control.[97] Apart from the pertinent admissibility rule, this can clearly be seen from judgments in which the Court's reasoning suggests that it found a Convention violation partly due to the respondent State's procedural negligence, that is, due to an insufficient assessment of the proportionality of the rights infringement at issue.[98] As regards the States' political authorities in particular, they are increasingly encouraged in virtue of the Court's jurisprudence to engage in a sort of pre-enactment political rights review.[99] Similar encouragement has come from the Parliamentary Assembly[100] and the Committee of Ministers.[101] To be sure, in most Convention States, there remains considerable room for improvement in terms of the systematicity and formality of pre-enactment political rights review,[102] although some procedure for ensuring rights conformity is usually in place.[103] In light of what has been said about the democratic basis of rights, the Convention's subsidiarity principle would indeed appear to demand that the States establish domestic practices of pre-enactment political rights review. This becomes especially clear from Strasbourg case law that deals with 'general measures', the Court's term for rights infringements resulting directly from domestic legislation or policy rather than from an individual decision adopted with case-based discretion by a judicial or administrative body. These cases demonstrate that the States' law- and policy-makers, if they are to take their role as first-line interpreters of the Convention seriously, need to already engage in a form of rights review during the law- and policy-making process.

This is crucial for operationalizing the bottom-up approach to the concretization of rights that the principle of subsidiarity demands. Procedures of pre-enactment political rights review ensure that the executive (when drafting bills), the legislature (when deliberating on bills), and the citizenry and civil society (in political debates about bills and party manifestos) develop and sustain a robust rights consciousness. This, in turn, promotes a bottom-up rights culture, in which the moral issues that underpin controversial questions of rights are the subject of a free, unrestricted, and inclusive debate of which records are kept that may then assist the judges in ascertaining the political motives behind a rights-restricting policy. What is more, serious political engagement with the rights issues raised by a legislative draft ensures that at least some assessment of the bill's implications

97 Articles 13 and 35(1) ECHR.

98 See eg *El Ghatet v Switzerland*, no 56971/10, para 52, 8 November 2016.

99 See eg *Animal Defenders International v the United Kingdom* [GC], no 48876/08, paras 113–125, ECHR 2013 (extracts).

100 Parliamentary Assembly, 'Resolution "National Parliaments: Guarantors of Human Rights in Europe"' (23 June 2011, 25th Sitting, Res 1823 (2011)) para 6.4.

101 Committee of Ministers, 'Recommendation to Member States on the Verification of the Compatibility of Draft Laws, Existing Laws and Administrative Practice with the Standards Laid Down in the European Convention on Human Rights' (12 May 2004, 114th Sess, Rec(2004)5) para 4.

102 Alice Donald and Philip Leach, *Parliaments and the European Court of Human Rights* (OUP 2016) 304.

103 Stone Sweet and Mathews (n 79) 135.

on rights has been made in case the enacted policy itself will never come to the courts, for example, because those most negatively affected by it lack the necessary means to litigate. Thus, although pre-enactment rights review is no explicit requirement under Convention law and is still in an embryonic stage in most States, the Convention's subsidiarity principle would appear to demand the widespread institutionalization of respective procedures.

Turning to the second characteristic element of Gardbaum's New Commonwealth Model of Constitutionalism, weak-form judicial review, the Court's control may be described as such a weak-form review, since it lacks the power to invalidate or disapply domestic legislation or other acts under domestic law.[104] More generally speaking, the Court does not have 'the final word', as constitutional courts do in systems of judicial supremacy. To be sure, the Court's judgments are binding by virtue of Convention law.[105] That is, although they must be transformed into the domestic orders, a process which involves a degree of (interpretative) discretion, they are not subject to a political override mechanism of the sort considered integral to Gardbaum's model. The Convention system does not and should not correspond to the model preferred by Bellamy, who advocates establishing a formal override mechanism under the control of the Committee of Ministers.[106] Then again, there are no 'hard' (and few 'soft') enforcement measures available to the Convention system.[107] Moreover, the binding character of the Court's judgments is, so to say, politically mediated. It is up to the Committee of Ministers to declare a judgment executed: despite the considerable legalization of the supervision process,[108] this remains a political decision in the final instance. Apart from awards of just satisfaction, the Court system essentially operates with 'weak remedies'.[109] Weak remedies, unlike highly concrete and strictly binding 'strong remedies' that may include time limits for their implementation, leave it to the political authorities to develop what are known as 'action plans' within the Convention system, that is, strategies for how to solve a rights issue within a reasonable period of time. So, the Convention's execution process indeed entails at least a considerable degree of 'decoupling of [Conventionality] review from judicial supremacy' as is characteristic of the New Commonwealth Model of Constitutionalism.[110]

[104] See Gardbaum, *New Commonwealth Model* (n 94) 26–27.
[105] See Articles 41 and 46 ECHR.
[106] Richard Bellamy, 'The Democratic Legitimacy of International Human Rights Conventions: Political Constitutionalism and the European Convention on Human Rights' (2014) 25(4) EJIL 1019, 1034, 1037.
[107] Andreas von Staden, *Strategies of Compliance with the European Court of Human Rights* (University of Pennsylvania Press 2018) 6.
[108] Başak Çali and Anne Koch, 'Foxes Guarding the Foxes? The Peer Review of Human Rights Judgments by the Committee of Ministers of the Council of Europe' (2014) 14(2) HRLR 301, 314.
[109] Generally, Mark Tushnet, *Weak Courts, Strong Rights* (Princeton University Press 2008) 248–249.
[110] Gardbaum, *New Commonwealth Model* (n 94) 88.

The Convention's system for the implementation of the Court's judgments operates as a 'constitutional counter-balancing mechanism'. Such mechanisms ensure, according to Alison Young, that no institution ever definitively has the final word. They thereby secure an important condition for inter-institutional dialogue. As Young explains: '[i]f it is the case that one institution always wins ... then it is difficult to see how any form of effective dialogue can take place'.[111] Inter-institutional interaction requires a form of institutional equality,[112] recognizing that judicial and political bodies play complementary roles in the specification of rights. Counter-balancing mechanisms, which enable one body to signal its view that the other has misused its powers, help secure such equality.[113]

The decoupling of the Court's review from judicial supremacy has become most evident in sensitive, politically high-profile cases, considered 'fit for lobbying',[114] in which the Committee of Ministers considered a judgment to have been executed irrespective of the fact that the respondent State's implementation was ludicrously minimal.[115] When this happens, the Committee of Ministers, on the initiative of the respondent State and possibly taking the views of civil society into account, essentially overrules the Court's view on what the applicable Convention right required in a certain case in a manner that is not quite so different from what marks judicial review as weak form in Gardbaum's New Commonwealth Model of Constitutionalism, where the political view about rights prevails over the judicial one by virtue of an override mechanism at the discretionary disposal of the political authorities. Similarly, the Convention practice described above corresponds to the view of dialogue theorists, according to which one may speak of dialogic constitutionalism also with regard to systems where a judicial decision may be subject 'merely' to political modification and avoidance.[116]

Considerations about this question in the Convention system are surprisingly intricate. For there is a certain mismatch between the Court's de jure powers, which do not include invalidating or disapplying domestic law, and the factual effects of its jurisprudence, which in practice regularly includes changes to the States' laws and policies. This divergence between the Court's legal powers and the factual authority of its jurisprudence is crucial. It makes the Convention system vacillate between judicial and political supremacy, such that an assessment of how 'strong' the Court's review really is becomes difficult: in the final instance, the answer may very well vary, depending on whether one takes the perspective of international law or of a certain State's domestic law, and depending on how one factors in the

[111] Young (n 40) 101.
[112] See Luc B Tremblay, 'The Legitimacy of Judicial Review: The Limits of Dialogue Between Courts and Legislatures' (2005) 3(4) I•CON 617, 630.
[113] Young (n 40) 114–115, 160.
[114] See Çali and Koch (n 108) 312–313.
[115] See eg *Hirst v UK (no 2)* [GC] (n 48).
[116] See Peter Hogg and Allison Bushell, 'The Charter Dialogue Between Courts and Legislatures (or Perhaps the Charter of Rights Isn't Such a Bad Thing After All)' (1997) 35(1) Osgoode Hall LJ 75, 79.

effect that Strasbourg jurisprudence has by virtue of its moral and political authority as opposed to the Court's formal legal powers.

The difference with Gardbaum's New Commonwealth Model of Constitutionalism is ultimately not that large. This is because unsolicited inter-branch respect is an essential aspect of that model's successful functioning in practice. Gardbaum's model does not postulate that the legislature should always or even merely regularly make use of its override power, and hence that the political view on rights should always or usually prevail over the judicial one. Instead, Gardbaum emphasizes the difference between 'the formal allocation of [this] power' and 'normative constraints on' its exercise. As he explains, 'in practice sometimes courts and sometimes legislatures will have the final word ... [i]n this way, there is a de facto division of authority that maintains the distinctness and stability of the [New Commonwealth Model of Constitutionalism]'.[117]

Hence, just as the Court's control would be senseless if the States regularly refused to comply, judicial review would be a hollow feature of the New Commonwealth Model of Constitutionalism if its outcomes were always legislatively overridden. Both systems thus crucially depend on what ultimately is nothing other than the sincere political will to engage with and take seriously the judicial views on rights issues, despite the lack of (hard) mechanisms to enforce the judicial opinion. As regards the Convention system, Pieter van Dijk and Fried van Hoof made this point plain long ago, when they noted that the success of the Convention system ultimately depends on the political will of the States, such that legal arguments, no matter how compelling, can never guarantee against State disobedience, in particular when allegedly vital national interests are at stake.[118]

The declaratory effect of the Court's judgments might then serve as a reminder of the 'declaration of incompatibility' that British courts can issue:[119] the declaratory judgment depends on political will to have its intended effects. Again, this is not to deny or downplay the binding effect of the Court's judgments, but to insist on what it means in practice and to explain why this reality may—normatively speaking—not be completely undesirable.

Overall, the Convention system comes quite close to Gardbaum's criterion of weak-form judicial review. The Court's review is 'weak' in the sense that the States, due to the absence of strong enforcement mechanisms, remain relatively free to disregard Court judgments partially or entirely, for example, because they consider the Court's jurisprudence incompatible with domestic constitutional law. However, just as legislative overrides have remained exceptional in systems that adhere to the New Commonwealth Model of Constitutionalism,[120] the Court's

[117] Gardbaum, *New Commonwealth Model* (n 94) 93–95.

[118] Pieter van Dijk and Fried van Hoof, *Theory and Practice of the European Convention on Human Rights* (2nd edn, Kluwer 1990) 618.

[119] Section 4 of the Human Rights Act of 1998.

[120] Gardbaum, *New Commonwealth Model* (n 94) 228–230.

judgments are well obeyed in practice, at least if measured by the standards of international courts.[121] As Ulfstein recently argued, the Court's claim of superiority is 'generally respected' despite its judgments' lack of direct effect.[122] Therefore, the Convention system conforms to Gardbaum's model insofar as one may describe it as having established a legally weak-form, but practically strong-form, mechanism of judicial review.

Having seen that Gardbaums New Commonwealth Model of Constitutionalism is apt to understand how the subsidiary Court and the States' political authorities interact, we must turn to the normative justification that Gardbaum provides for the institutional setup of his model. This is highly pertinent to the Convention system, since it is, according to Gardbaum, the combination of legally weak-form, but practically strong-form, rights-based judicial review which combines the judicial and political protection of rights that makes judicial rights protection not only effective, but also democratically legitimate.[123] This is in line with the present account of the Convention's principle of subsidiarity. The institutional structures just sketched ensure that the Convention system avoids the mechanical transformation of the States' domestic law into law compliant with the Convention as read by the Court, while still imposing powerful constraints on the States' sovereignty in the combined form of an influential legal discourse and international law obligations.

Call this human rights brinkmanship, but, again, it may be the only institutional choice available to reconcile concerns about liberal rights and political democracy in a balanced and sustainable manner. To borrow the terminology used in Chapter 5, wavering between the circular and the pretentious solution to the liberal-democratic predicament may be the best practical way to reconcile democratic politics and individual liberal rights, such that liberal-democratic constitutionalism becomes the paradox that Stephen Holmes claims it is. Holmes' argument is that constrained rule is more powerful than unconstrained rule, because the former has an edge over the latter in terms of social compliance and obedience. Successful democracies constrain themselves, in the sense that they limit their political options, so as to remain legitimate thanks to sustained popular consent. However, given the social and temporal contingency of the proper liberal limits to democracy, it is hard to imagine how this would be possible if democratic politics had no ongoing say in the determination of these limits. Hence, the best way to conceive of the relationship between the Court and the States' democratic politics is one of a continuous back and forth, a process in which the Court acts, on the one hand, as a forceful reminder of the liberal limits that have emerged as reasonable and mutually acceptable in the past, and thus, on the other hand, also as a

[121] Courtney Hillebrecht, *Domestic Politics and International Human Rights Tribunals* (CUP 2014) 11.

[122] Ulfstein (n 52) 156, 158.

[123] See Gardbaum, *New Commonwealth Model* (n 94) 36, 235–236.

participant in the ongoing discursive elaboration and modification of these limits for the future.

E) Legitimacy through dialogue

A perpetual dialogue, a dialectical conversation in which judgments about the political morality of rights are approached and refined through a process of shared elaboration, deliberative engagement, or democratic back and forth between the national and international legal and political actors involved in the Convention system is necessary for the Convention system to do justice to the grounding of human rights in the equal moral status of all. If the Convention system is to heed the principle of political equality, the development of Convention rights must occur from the bottom up, such that the States *qua* democratic polities play the leading, primary role. As this chapter suggests, the Convention rights are specified through a justificatory dialogue in which the authority question is subordinated to the requirement of convincing substantive justifications. The Convention system is best conceived as standing somewhere between strong-form and weak-form review, which is normatively justified because it combines judicial and political reasoning about rights in such a way as to make the Court system not only effective, but also democratically legitimate. The incessant justificatory dialogue that ensures that no one ever really has the final word about the proper construction of the Convention rights offers a way to make up for the Convention system's problem that the central judicial authority is not embedded in a democratic polity, with the concomitant formal and informal checks and balances. As such, it offers an indispensable alternative, ensuring that no one ever definitively has the last word. The inter-institutional interaction that Convention system's principle of subsidiarity commands, and that was sketched in this chapter, would appear to suit the notion of 'shared responsibility' which, as Chapter 2 suggests, has become a catchphrase to refer to the political-aspirational 'ought' of the States' and the Court's collaboration for the benefit of a democratic, effectively rights-protecting Convention system.

9
Interpretation and the Court's Subsidiary Role

A) Introduction

The political dimension of everyone's equal moral status that grounds human rights demands the democratic specification of these rights. A demand for their domestic interpretation then follows from the states, as the main *loci* of democratic politics. The international European Court of Human Rights (the Court, ECtHR), by contrast, plays a subsidiary role. On the one hand, it supports each member state in its development of a parochial conception of human rights. On the other hand, it supports its member states (the States) collectively in the task of achieving convergence with respect to a shared understanding of the European Convention on Human Rights' (the Convention, ECHR)[1] guarantees that it then reimposes on the States. This bidirectional process depends on a particular form of embeddedness of the Convention system's national and international levels. This chapter discusses relevant questions concerning the jurisprudential authority of Convention law (in particular, the Court's jurisprudence), the Court's interpretative approach, and the demands that the Convention law makes upon the States in terms of its domestic reception, as well as the related issue of how the States' domestic laws approach this question. In doing so, it suggests that various practices of Convention law that appear unprincipled are explicable and justifiable in terms of the Court's subsidiary role: its 'casuistry' (ie its highly case-based jurisprudence), its flexible approach to precedence, its abstention from claiming *erga omnes inter partes* effect, supremacy or direct effect for the Convention law and its jurisprudence, and its flexible European consensus doctrine are all expressive of the Court's oscillation between its two roles, as sketched in the previous chapter. Only the Court's oscillation between exercising a more strictly binding legal authority and a more persuasive moral authority makes it possible for Convention law, while developing from the bottom up, to serve as a top-down check on the States.

[1] Convention for the Protection of Human Rights and Fundamental Freedoms, as amended, of 4 November 1950, in force since 3 September 1953, 213 UNTS 221, CETS No 005.

Subsidiarity, Legitimacy, and the European Court of Human Rights. Reto Walther, Oxford University Press.
 DOI: 10.1093/9780198921455.003.0009

B) The Court's interpretation of Convention rights

A central issue we must discuss is the authority of the generalizable interpretations that the Court gives to the Convention rights: the stronger this authority is, the stronger is the harmonizing effect of the Court's judgments and the lesser room remains for the States' contribution to the interpretative development of the Convention rights. While it is clear that the operative provisions of the Court's case law are binding only *inter partes*—that is, they solely oblige the respondent State(s)[2]—the effects of the Court's general interpretations of the Convention rights are less clear and often treated no more than cursorily, if at all, in Convention scholarship. Speaking of an *erga omnes inter partes* effect, some scholars suggest that the Court's interpretation of the Convention in a particular case is authoritative for all States.[3] Perhaps more common is the notion of a *res interpretata* principle, which is used to express the same idea,[4] but illustrated by opposing it to the established principle of a judgment's *res judicata* effect.[5] However, matters are more complicated than some proponents of a strong Court would presumably like them to be.

a) Flexible interpretative authority and precedential effect

Other than the decisional authority of the Court's case law (*res judicata*), the interpretative or jurisprudential authority of the Court's reading of the Convention guarantees is not addressed in the treaty text. It does not clearly follow from Article 32 of the Convention—according to which '[t]he jurisdiction of the Court shall extend to all matters concerning the interpretation and application of the Convention'—that a reading of the Convention in a certain case henceforth binds all States. Nor are arguments that this follows, or can be inferred, from Articles 1 ('Obligation to respect Human Rights')[6] and 19 ('Establishment of the Court') (together with Article 32) of the Convention beyond doubt.[7] It would also be a

[2] Article 46(1) ECHR.

[3] See Samantha Besson, 'The Erga Omnes Effect of Judgments of the European Court of Human Rights—What's in a Name?' in S Besson (ed), *The European Court of Human Rights After Protocol 14* (Schulthess 2011) 130–131.

[4] See eg Janneke Gerards, 'The European Court of Human Rights and the National Courts: Giving Shape to the Notion of "Shared Responsibility"' in J Gerards and J Fleuren (eds), *Implementation of the European Convention on Human Rights and of the Judgments of the ECtHR in National Case-Law* (Intersentia 2014) 23.

[5] See eg Adam Bodnar, 'Res Interpretata: Legal Effect of the European Court of Human Rights' Judgments for Other States Than Those Which Were Party to the Proceedings' in Y Haeck and E Brems (eds), *Human Rights and Civil Liberties in the 21st Century* (Springer 2014) 224.

[6] 'The High Contracting Parties shall secure to everyone within their jurisdiction the rights and freedoms defined in Section I of this Convention.'

[7] See eg Bodnar (n 5) 227.

mistake to deduct the Court's unqualified interpretative authority from the notion of 'autonomous concepts', which holds that concepts of Convention law such as 'tribunal' do not necessarily correspond to the concept of the same name in a State's domestic law.[8] The claim that one must not equate a concept in Convention law with a concept of the same name in domestic law, in order to prevent States from simply evading their Convention obligations, does not yet indicate how these 'autonomous concepts' receive interpretative content—'autonomous concepts' are compatible with the process of dialogical interpretation discussed earlier: no doubt, when first called upon to interpret a notion such as 'tribunal', the Court's judges approached their task on the basis of their existing, domestic-law-inspired understanding of that concept.

The Court's jurisprudential authority is important for its subsidiarity. If the Court's jurisprudential authority was taken to mean that its interpretation of a Convention right, or concept, would settle the interpretative question to which it pertains definitely and with binding effect for the entire politico-legal order of all States, this would ascribe a judicial supremacy to the Court that would be incompatible with its substantive subsidiarity, since it would largely deprive the States of their say in the Convention interpretation. It is therefore normatively misguided to speak in unqualified terms of the Court's interpretative authority, as is implicit in the notions of *res interpretata* or *erga omnes inter partes*.

Unqualified claims concerning the Court's interpretative authority would appear to stand on shaky ground, even when taken descriptively. Apart from Article 46 of the Convention, which might be read by an argument from the contrary to exclude extending the Court's interpretative authority beyond an individual case, the Court has never claimed unqualified jurisprudential authority for itself. Quite to the contrary, it has consistently rejected the view that its mandate is to secure the uniform application of the Convention law. It seems only logical, therefore, that it has never used the notions *erga omnes inter partes* or *res interpretata*, contrary to certain judges' separate opinions.[9]

Definitively ascribing an *erga omnes inter partes* or *res interpretata* effect to the Court's jurisprudence thus implies an excessively general rigidity, with an overly high degree of certainty: on the one hand, this ignores the Court's moral, or persuasive, authority, viz the idea that the domestic authorities may follow the Court's reading of the Convention not because they are legally obliged to do so, but due to the persuasiveness of the Court's interpretative reasoning; on the other hand, the notion of *res interpretata*, due to its derivation from *res judicata*, has an overly rigid connotation which may belie the fact that human rights interpretations are never settled once and for all, but always in flux due to social change

[8] See eg Gerards, 'Shared Responsibility' (n 4) 23.

[9] See eg *GIEM SRL and Others v Italy* [GC], nos 1828/06 and 2 others, para 76, 28 June 2018 (partly concurring, partly dissenting opinion of Judge Pinto de Albuquerque).

and the particularities of each case's context. It therefore seems better to use the less misleading—and less likely to be misunderstood—terms 'jurisprudential' or 'interpretative authority', which allow for a more nuanced understanding of the authority of the Court's jurisprudence.[10]

The Court's dealings with the notion of precedent confirm our argument about its interpetative authority. The precedential effect of its interpretations is the flipside of its jurisprudential authority: the former refers to the binding authority of an interpretation for the Court itself, the latter to the binding authority of an interpretation for the States.[11] Just like the Court's interpretative authority, its precedential approach has been ambiguous, as transpires from its formulation that 'judgments issued in individual cases establish precedents albeit to a greater or lesser extent'.[12] The Court has not endorsed a doctrine of strict precedent, and we must assume that it has correspondingly abstained from claiming unqualified interpretative authority. Consistency demands that, if it claimed the latter, it would have to endorse the former too.

This view corresponds to the vague formulation chosen by the States' representatives in the Action Plan attached to the Interlaken Declaration, which holds that the States commit to 'taking into account the Court's developing case-law, also with a view to considering the conclusions to be drawn from a judgment finding a violation of the Convention by another State'.[13] It is hard to see how some scholars come to understand the soft expressions 'taking into account' and 'considering' as to set out 'with a high level of clarity'[14] an obligation 'to comply with the Convention as explained by the Court in its case-law, even if [a] state was not party to the case'.[15] 'To consider' means to contemplate, to think carefully, to note, to reflect, while 'to take into account' means to notice something, to take it as a contributory factor into consideration, according to the Oxford English Dictionary. One cannot help but surmise that some commentators' reading of these passages is influenced by their thinking about legal desiderata.

The bidirectional dialogic interpretation of Convention rights implied by the principle of subsidiarity can account for expressions such as 'considering' and 'taking into account'—and, more importantly, for the Court's corresponding equivocation about the precedential value and interpretative authority of its jurisprudence. Indeed, the understanding of the subsidiarity principle sketched in Chapter 8 vindicates the Court's approach, as justified in light of the principle of subsidiarity. Only a flexible doctrine of precedent and soft claims of jurisprudential

[10] See Besson, 'Erga Omnes' (n 3) 126–134.
[11] ibid 134–135.
[12] *Pretty v the United Kingdom*, no 2346/02, para 75, ECHR 2002-III.
[13] 'Interlaken Declaration' (High Level Conference on the Future of the European Court of Human Rights (Interlaken, 19 February 2010)) para 4. c) of the Action Plan.
[14] Bodnar (n 5) 232.
[15] Gerards, 'Shared Responsibility' (n 4) 23.

authority enable the Court to steer a middle course between the risks of legal uncertainty and unpredictability, the need for the bottom-up convergence of standards, and the danger of claiming unqualified interpretative authority in such a way as to make impossible the demand rooted in political equality that the States' democratic processes contribute to the specification of the Convention rights. In short, consistent case law requires a certain rigidity, but subsidiarity—not to mention the States' loyalty and devotion to the Convention system—requires flexibility. Thus, what the Court has called the 'orderly development of the Convention case-law' requiring that 'it usually follows and applies its own precedents',[16] is best understood as an attempt to bring together the demands for legal certainty and for the appropriate, democratically legitimate, bottom-up development of standards upon which the States converge.

Note, finally, that our argument is corroborated by the Court's principal adjudicative method, that is, the proportionality assessment. The Court's proportionality-based balancing of circumstances is hardly compatible with the idea of the unqualified interpretative authority of its jurisprudence. The highly casuistic balancing of all circumstances relevant to a case, upon which proportionality assessments hinge, can result in general Convention interpretations that are easily applicable to new cases only (if at all) after an unspecified, but usually considerable, number of balancing decisions have accumulated in a convergent way.[17]

b) Interpretative incrementalism

The balancing rods that the Court uses to walk the 'tightrope' between flexibility and rigidity are its margin-of-appreciation doctrine and its incremental approach to interpreting the Convention. We will discuss the Court's margin-of-appreciation-imbued review in the next chapter. Here, our focus is on the Court's interpretative approach.

In a book about the Convention's principle of subsidiarity, the Court's 'incrementalism' deserves the centre stage in this discussion.[18] Incrementalism refers to the gradual interpretation of the Convention through a step-by-step development of general principles. It denotes the idea and practice that the Court derives its general interpretations of the Convention gradually from a large number of cases which it decides through ad hoc balancing, making space for judicial sensitivity to the full context of a case. This means, of course, that it is difficult to distinguish

[16] *Cossey v the United Kingdom*, 27 September 1990, para 35, Series A no 184.

[17] See Alec Stone Sweet and Jud Mathews, *Proportionality Balancing and Constitutional Governance* (OUP 2019) 40–41.

[18] On the following, see Janneke Gerards, *General Principles of the European Convention on Human Rights* (CUP 2019) 506–512.

clearly in the Court's practice between interpretation and application of the law: the Court construes Convention law largely by deciding one case at a time, over and over again.

This inductive approach enables the Court to tread carefully, taking the States' reactions into account and responding to them,[19] and to increasingly reimpose the resulting shared standards on the States with the (gradually more robust) expectation that the domestic authorities will progressively abide by them—the Court may 'nudge' the domestic authorities towards compliance with its standards by enticing them with the prospect of deference—thereby legitimizing and validating these standards once again. The Court, in turn, may refine and readjust these standards several more times—in principle, infinitely many times, if need be—on a case-by-case basis. This permits the Court to calibrate its approach casuistically, at least until it has set out, often in Grand Chamber judgments, well-established principles and standards (dubbed 'general principles' by the Court), but probably even subsequently, since it may continue to adapt such well-established standards if legal demands or social change require. Janneke Gerards thus aptly describes the Court's incrementalism as 'disclosing a certain search for reflective equilibrium in that it shows a continuous movement from definition of general principles to refinement in individual cases, to redefinition of general principles, and further refinement in individual cases'.[20]

Since a case has usually been decided by the respondent State's authorities before it comes to the Court[21] and, in case of a violation judgment, it is sent back to the State authorities for implementation, this continuous movement is also an oscillation between bottom-up and top-down 'adjustment decisions',[22] as discussed in Chapter 8.

The Court's incrementalism has received rather little attention. However, in our account of the Convention system and its subsidiarity, it deserves to be considered as a central element in the Court's role and its corresponding practice. To do so, Alison Young's collection of constitutional doctrines that serve the purpose of 'procrastinating' on taking a robust judicial stance, in order to allow for inter-branch interaction, is helpful. These doctrines include the US Supreme Court's *Ashwander* principles (concerning an issue's 'ripeness' for judicial determination), different variants of judicial minimalism, and the idea of judicial warning shots directed at the law-maker ('flares').[23] As we will see, the Court, too, uses variants of all these doctrines as a means of interacting with the States' authorities. This can be explained with, and appears justified in light of, subsidiarity's demand that

[19] See eg *Lautsi and Others v Italy* [GC], no 30814/06, ECHR 2011 (extracts).
[20] Janneke Gerards, 'Margin of Appreciation and Incrementalism in the Case Law of the European Court of Human Rights' (2018) 18(3) HRLR 495, 511–512.
[21] Article 35(1) ECHR.
[22] D W Haslett, 'What Is Wrong with Reflective Equilibria?' (1987) 37(148) Phil Q 305, 306.
[23] Alison L Young, *Democratic Dialogue and the Constitution* (OUP 2017) 127–133.

Convention law be developed through a justificatory dialogue which gives the States a say.

To begin with Justice Brandeis' *Ashwander* principles, these principles serve to determine when the judge should avoid passing judgment in spite of the jurisdictional power to do so. Broadly speaking, Justice Brandeis laid down the following principles:[24] first, in 'friendly' proceedings, no new jurisprudential principles are laid down; second, issues are not decided unnecessarily or anticipatorily; third, rulings are narrowly tied to the facts of a case; fourth, cases are, where possible, decided without developing new jurisprudential principles; fifth, an applicant must have suffered some harm, otherwise the case is not admitted; sixth, cases of applicants who benefited from the alleged rights violation are not heard; and seventh, harmonious interpretation is applied wherever possible. We can observe all of these rules in the Convention system in some form.

First, the Court's friendly settlement decisions (Article 39 of the Convention) simply strike out a case without developing the case law, offering no more than a short account of the facts and the settlement reached.[25] Second, the Court regularly holds that it 'considers that no separate issue arises under Article ... ' (or similar), thus leaving questions open if it considers it unnecessary to rule on them.[26] Third, the Court's jurisprudence is (in)famously casuistic.[27] Fourth, sometimes the Court can, and does, avoid the most important legal questions raised in a case by solving it through less controversial (formal) rules. For example, in *Gross*, the Grand Chamber avoided the substantive issue concerning assisted suicide by declaring the case inadmissible, because it had not been duly informed that the applicant had meanwhile died.[28] Fifth, according to Article 34 of the Convention, cases are admissible only where an applicant can claim 'victim status'.[29] Sixth, the Court, when considering a case's admissibility, has sometimes taken into consideration that an applicant benefited from the rights issue raised in the complaint.[30] Finally, the Court does not, of course, exclude that domestic law can be brought into line with the Convention by interpretative means. It leaves this question open and entrusts it to national authorities.[31]

A second technique to promote dialogue that the Court has used is to strategically avoid sensitive social issues, until matters have been debated in the States and

[24] US Supreme Court, *Ashwander v Tennessee Valley Authority*, 297 US 288 (1936) paras 63–72 (concurring opinion of Justice Brandeis).

[25] Recently, eg *Paixão Moreira de Sá Fernandes v Portugal* (dec), no 44285/16, 8 April 2021.

[26] Recently, eg *Perovy v Russia*, no 47429/09, para 69, 20 October 2020.

[27] See eg Sarah Lambrecht, 'Assessing the Existence of Criticism of the European Court of Human Rights' in P Popelier, S Lambrecht, and K Lemmens (eds), *Criticism of the European Court of Human Rights* (Intersentia 2016) 544.

[28] *Gross v Switzerland* [GC], no 67810/10, paras 28–37, ECHR 2014.

[29] See eg *Centre for Legal Resources on behalf of Valentin Câmpeanu v Romania* [GC], no 47848/08, para 101, ECHR 2014.

[30] *Galović v Croatia* (dec), no 54388/09, para 71, 5 March 2013.

[31] See eg *Anchugov and Gladkov v Russia*, nos 11157/04 and 15162/05, para 111, 4 July 2013.

become less controversial, so that it can express its view on the safer ground of established domestic views.[32] A good example of this is the case law on issues concerning the beginning and end of life. The Court has so far refused to decide the questions when life begins and whether an embryo/foetus enjoys the status of a person, leaving this to the States and limiting itself to reviewing procedural aspects of such cases.[33] With regard to cases that concern the ending of someone's life, the Court has taken a similar approach:[34] it focuses on procedural issues and highlights the less controversial principle of personal autonomy.[35] However, it may well be that the Court *at some point* enters the debate on these questions with its own substantive take.

Third, we can assume that the Court engages in a certain amount of judicial 'agenda setting' at the admissibility stage: the Court's statistics suggest that the Court mainly 'picks' those cases for judgment that it considers an apt means for rebuking the respondent State. While it declares more than 90 per cent of all applications inadmissible, roughly 90 per cent of its judgments are violation judgments. Moreover, even if one looks at only chamber and Grand Chamber judgments—that is, excluding committee judgments that are usually concerned with systematic and repetitive human rights problems—the number remains high, at about 70 per cent. Convention law leaves ample room for this practice, due to the highly indeterminate, merit-based, 'manifestly ill-founded' inadmissibility criterion:[36] the Court's registry itself states that the 'reasons given for the inadmissibility decision in such a case will be identical or similar to those which the Court would adopt in a judgment on the merits concluding that there had been no violation'.[37] Judicial agenda-setting through inadmissibility decisions has a downside, however: although deciding not to decide is also a decision—to approve and legitimize the contentious measure—the parties and even the judges themselves have fewer chances to participate and influence the outcome of proceedings in cases in which the Court does not render a judgment. Thus, the Court's agenda-setting may not only be conducive to a dialogue about rights.

Fourth, as times change and society develops, issues may become ripe for judicial determination, and, like other courts,[38] the Court has used the technique of offering 'warning shots' in judgments where it has not yet found a Convention violation, but anticipates that its jurisprudence would probably change in the

[32] See Young (n 23) 129.
[33] See *Vo v France* [GC], no 53924/00, ECHR 2004-VIII.
[34] See *Lambert and Others v France* [GC], no 46043/14, ECHR 2015 (extracts).
[35] Daria Sartori, 'End-of-Life Issues Under the European Convention on Human Rights: The Value of Personal Autonomy Within a "Proceduralized" Review' (2018) 52 QIL 23, 38–41.
[36] Article 35(3)(a) ECHR.
[37] European Court of Human Rights, 'Practical Guide on Admissibility Criteria' (31 August 2025) para 386.
[38] See Ronald J Krotoszynski, Jr, 'Constitutional Flares: On Judges, Legislatures, and Dialogue' (1998) 83(1) Minn L Rev 1.

foreseeable future. In some judgments, it has expressed doubts about compliance of a measure with the Convention, while in others it anticipated social changes that could lead to a different assessment in the future. An example of the latter is *SH*, in which the Court admonished the Austrian parliament to 'undertak[e] a thorough assessment of the rules governing artificial procreation, taking into account the dynamic developments in science and society noted'.[39] *Sheffield* provides an example of an adumbration of legal change. In this judgment, the Court held that '[a]s to legal developments in this area ... [it] is not fully satisfied that the legislative trends' are sufficient for a change of jurisprudence, since 'there is [not] as yet a common approach'.[40] In the later *Goodwin* judgment, this had changed in the Court's view and it held 'that the respondent Government can no longer claim that the matter falls within their margin of appreciation'.[41] By issuing warnings, the Court invites the domestic policy-makers to (re)consider[42] certain factual and/or legal points and to undertake certain revisions in light of them,[43] thus respecting their primary responsibility for policy choices and human rights protection, without abdicating its own examination of a rights issue. As with some of the other strategies just discussed, the Court gains time and, meanwhile, gives the States the chance to develop their own views on a rights issue to which it may later respond.

Fifth, the Court also engages in the sort of judicial minimalism most famously written about by Cass Sunstein.[44] The idea is that, when a court issues narrow and shallow rulings—rulings that are limited to specific circumstances and leave foundational issues unanswered—it leaves the political authorities more room for their own deliberations and decision-making, as compared to judgments that lay down broad principles. The recent *Mugemangango* case illustrates this: although the Court was clear in its finding that the Belgian system of parliamentary responsibility for settling post-election disputes violates the Convention, under reference to the principle of subsidiarity and the States' wide discretion in matters relating to electoral systems and the separation of powers, it stopped short of 'tak[ing] a clear stand and [inferring] ... a proper obligation to provide for a judicial or quasi-judicial remedy in respect of decisions taken by a parliament in electoral matters', as two concurring judges lament.[45] For the Court, leaving deep, foundational questions open may help to secure the States' stable coherence, despite disagreement, as well as to avoid unnecessarily offending the fundamental convictions of

[39] *SH and Others v Austria* [GC], no 57813/00, para 117, ECHR 2011.

[40] *Sheffield and Horsham v the United Kingdom*, 30 July 1998, para 57, Reports of Judgments and Decisions 1998-V.

[41] *Christine Goodwin v the United Kingdom* [GC], no 28957/95, para 93, ECHR 2002-VI.

[42] See Guido Calabresi, 'Foreword: Antidiscrimination and Constitutional Accountability (What the Bork-Brennan Debate Ignores)' (1991) 105 Harv L Rev 80.

[43] See Young (n 23) 132.

[44] Cass R Sunstein, *One Case at a Time* (HUP 1999).

[45] *Mugemangango v Belgium* [GC], no 310/15, paras 2–3, 10 July 2020 (joint concurring opinion of Judges Turković and Lemmens).

a political community. At the same time, it allows for progressive jurisprudence that evolves in lockstep with social developments. What is more, if one plausibly assumes that the Court is, due to its temporal, spatial, and social remoteness from a case, a fallible decision-maker in certain respects, minimalist decision-making may be a means to keep the effects of potential flaws in its case-based and country-specific assessment as small as possible.[46]

In light of what has been said above, it appears that Sébastien van Drooghenbroeck may well have been right when he argued back in 2001 that the Court's casuistry and the resulting legal uncertainty and jurisprudential incoherence are, in no sense, pathologies. Rather they are, he surmised, the result of a deliberate judicial strategy of minimizing precedents with far-reaching and long-lasting consequences,[47] a deliberate decision against '*toute ambition pédagogique de systématisation et d'éclaircissement du droit conventionnel*'.[48] Our understanding of the Court's subsidiarity can explain and justify this practice.

c) Gradual convergence of an *acquis conventionnel*

Strict adherence to precedent would be sensible for the Court at most in some domains, namely, in those domains where Convention law has been developed through an incremental, interpretative dialogue between the Court and the States to the extent of being fairly comprehensively settled. We can call the Convention law upon which the States and the Court converged the *acquis conventionnel*, as suggested in Chapter 8. The idea of robust interpretative convergence finds support in Convention law and practice: most evidently, in the treaty-based notion of 'well-established case-law' which certainly forms the very heart of the *acquis conventionnel*, but also in the observation that some of the Court's violation judgments involve such clear legal rules that there remains, even in the eyes of the intergovernmental Committee of Ministers, no room for negotiation concerning their implementation.[49]

To be sure, it is inherent in the Convention law's incremental development that the boundaries between more and less well-established principles, and therefore the boundaries of such an *acquis conventionnel* can only be fuzzy. This is perhaps why scholars tend to be unclear about whether they are talking about the formal notion of 'well-established case-law' (Article 28 of the Convention) or merely about jurisprudence that has already converged into quite clear guiding principles.

[46] See Cass R Sunstein, 'Beyond Judicial Minimalism' (2008) 43 Tulsa L Rev 825, 832–834.

[47] See Sébastien van Drooghenbroeck, *La proportionnalité dans le droit de la Convention européenne des droits de l'homme* (Bruylant 2001) ch 6.

[48] ibid mn 850.

[49] See Başak Çali and Anne Koch, 'Foxes Guarding the Foxes? The Peer Review of Human Rights Judgments by the Committee of Ministers of the Council of Europe' (2014) 14(2) HRLR 301, 312.

For example, it seems difficult to reconcile Gerard's convincing account of the Court's incrementalism with her much less persuasive and insufficiently nuanced claim concerning the Court's jurisprudence's *res interpretata* effect. At times, she even fails to distinguish between the 'general principles' set out in the Court's leading judgments from the notion of 'well-established case-law', denoting those issues that are fit for unanimous committee judgment.[50]

What appears clear is that Convention interpretations forming part of the formal corpus of 'well-established case-law' have achieved a degree of robustness that can be seen as marking a sort of (temporary) end point in the dialogue about the proper construal of a Convention right. The notion of 'well-established case-law' is anchored in Article 28 of the Convention. This provision holds that unanimous committees of three judges may declare a case 'admissible and render at the same time a judgment on the merits, if the underlying question ... concerning the interpretation [of the Convention] is already the subject of well-established case-law'.[51]

Emphasizing the Court's incremental development of an *acquis conventionnel*—which certainly includes, but perhaps reaches beyond, the 'well-established case-law'—has advantages that accord with our account of the Convention system's subsidiarity. For one, it avoids the difficulty of needing to identify 'judgments of principle'.[52] This, in turn, makes it possible to circumvent the idea that singular judgments in and of themselves posit definite legal data points about what the law 'is', a claim which appears particularly misleading as regards the Court, with its highly casuistic interpretative approach. Rather than standing on their own, most landmark judgments mark a climax or turning point towards which a series of cases has incrementally led over time. This point bears emphasis: well-established principles normally emerge from an interplay between domestic reception and repeated application at Strasbourg, including by the Grand Chamber, and thus depend, not least, on the existence of several similar cases to which they could reasonably be applied in a by-and-large consistent manner. Moreover, the gradual development of an *acquis conventionnel* through a dialectical process of 'to and fro' between Strasbourg judgment and domestic reception conforms to the principle of subsidiarity, since it marks a collaborative process, whereas the classification of a singular judgment as one of principle falls, by and large, to the Court alone—for example, by selecting cases for publication in its case reports, by relinquishing, or accepting a request to refer, a case to the Grand Chamber, by using particularly principled language or by selecting a case for citation in other judgments and/or in its non-binding information documents.

50 See Gerards, 'Shared Responsibility' (n 4) 23.

51 Article 28(1)(b) ECHR.

52 'Report of the Group of Wise Persons to the Committee of Ministers' (979bis mtg (15 November 2006), CM(2006)203) para 68.

This is not to say that the judicial, scholarly, or any other kind of classification of an important judgment as a landmark should be avoided or considered without value. This highlighting is a fair means to argue for the high relevance of a case, to draw attention to it, and to stir up a particular debate. But this is exactly the debate-provoking potential of leading cases that underlines that these judgments give life to justificatory dialogue rather than bringing it to an end. Consider that so-called WECL-cases, governed by well-established case-law and decided by committees of three judges, by contrast, receive hardly any attention, because the underlying Convention law is considered settled beyond debate. In short, the argument is not against the notion of leading cases, but against taking singular landmark judgments as concluding the development of the Convention law. That is, in line with the defence of the Court's flexible interpretative authority, it is an argument in favour of patiently awaiting the actual end of the debate about the proper understanding of a certain rights issue, which can reasonably be assumed to have occurred only when the actors involved converge on a solution.

Note also that our argument does not question the Court's judgments' bindingness *inter partes*: a respondent State's domestic implementation of the Court's judgments is an essential step in the process of rights clarification. In this sense, the principle of subsidiarity's remedial dimension is related to its substantive (interpretative) dimension.[53] Neither do we mean to deny the general 'value of orientation'[54] that important Strasbourg judgments have: no doubt, the development of the Convention law occurs principally through Grand Chamber judgments and important chamber case law together with the domestic reception of this jurisprudence. The point is that the Court's jurisprudence may still be undergoing incremental change, and rightly so, even after a leading judgment has been rendered. It seems not only imprecise but also normatively problematic to ascribe leading judgments unqualified interpretative authority, since this would imply denying the States their contribution to the development of the Convention law that subsidiarity demands, as long as there are unsettled controversies both between the States and within the Court, that is, among the individual judges and/or between the organizational sections from which the chambers are formed. The situation is different where Convention law has become 'well-established', with the effect that the Court routinely applies it to new cases, unanimously, and without 'much new thinking',[55] such that it hardly provokes discussions at the State level, and that it should therefore never come to Strasbourg but 'tacitly' be dealt with domestically in line with the *acquis conventionnel* that emerged through a prior

[53] See 'Copenhagen Declaration' (High Level Conference 'Continued Reform of the European Court of Human Rights Convention System—Better Balance, Improved Protection' (Copenhagen, 12–13 April 2018)) para 28. c).

[54] cf Federal Constitutional Court of Germany, *Görgülü*, no 2 BvR 1481/04 of 14 October 2004 (published in BVerfGE 111, 307; English translation available from the court) para 39.

[55] Bodnar (n 5) 237.

interpretative dialogue. Indeed, most States are—in this sense—faithful compliance partners to the Court and hardly ever subject to committee judgments.

In short, since subsidiarity requires the Convention to be developed jointly by a collaborative process between the States and the Court, one cannot assume a strict precedential/interpretative authority of the Court's case law before that dialogical process of interpretation came to a halt by having produced well-established Convention interpretations. As Adam Bodnar observed, 'there is no significant theoretical difficulty from the point of view of [the] *res interpretata* value' as regards case law that is 'well-established' and fit for committee judgment.[56]

It is inherent in the process of dialogical Convention interpretation that the stages leading up to 'well-established' Convention law evade any sharp distinction. Illustrative of this ambiguity is former Court president Robert Spano's extra-judicial suggestion that more than 90 per cent of the cases the Strasbourg judges adjudicate in their everyday work are solved based on case law that is 'close to well established, at least as regards the general principles applicable to the issue at hand'.[57] This estimate is considerably more than the roughly 67 per cent of cases that are actually adjudicated (on the merits) by committees, but roughly corresponds to the fact that—due to joined applications—even more than 90 per cent of all applications decided on the meris by judicial formations are dealt with in the committee formation.[58] The interpretative and precedential value of the Court's jurisprudence is not susceptible to a simple dichotomy of, on the one hand, 'well-established case-law' and, on the other hand, all other jurisprudence. That is, there may be well-established Convention law apart from what formally qualifies (ie according to Article 28) and is treated as 'well-established case-law'. Our notion of an *acquis conventionnel*, which includes the corpus of 'well-established case-law', but may be broader so as to include, for example, also convergence that is robust in principle, but too abstract for the resolution of concrete cases, captures this Convention reality: there cannot but be a spectrum of more and less well-established Convention law, reaching from the well-established case-law fit for quasi-mechanical committee judgment to still entirely unresolved interpretative issues.

C) The States' interpretative obligations

In line with our argument of this and the previous chapter, Alex Stone Sweet has observed that in the Convention system '[n]o single organ possesses the "final

[56] ibid.

[57] Robert Spano, 'The Future of the European Court of Human Rights—Subsidiarity, Process-Based Review and the Rule of Law' (2018) 18(3) HRLR 473, 476.

[58] European Court of Human Rights, 'Analysis of Statistics 2023' (January 2024) 3–4.

word" when it comes to a conflict between conflicting interpretations of rights'; instead, there is an ongoing dialogue at work.[59] This is why the debate about an arguable *erga omnes inter partes* effect of the Court's jurisprudence misses the point. Much more relevant and to the point are inquiries into the conditions necessary for, and the practical functioning of, a meaningful dialogical interaction between the States' authorities and the Court about how best to understand and protect Convention rights. In this spirit, the previous section shed light on a number of strategies that the Court uses to respect the States' position as first-line defenders and interpreters of the Convention rights by postponing its own determination of a rights issue. Corresponding to the subsidiarity principle, the Court's cautious approach to developing the Convention law allows the States to partake in the endeavour of interpreting the Convention promoting domestic feelings of ownership for the Convention law. Understanding the Court's jurisprudential authority as varied accords with this, since the Court's variable interpretative authority is a precondition for the incremental interpretative specification of the Convention rights.

As there are always two involved in a dialogue, we must now discuss what it takes on the part of the States for a successful dialogue about the Convention rights. Then, the focus must shift to the Court again, in order to look more closely at the Court's reception of the States' views on the meaning of Convention rights.

Most fundamentally, as follows from the argument we developed in Chapter 8, in particular, the States are obliged to assume their interpretative obligations within the framework of a political democracy. Indeed, as the present account of the Court's subsidiary role hinges on political democracy *qua* normative imperative that is practically operative only at the State level, the justification of the Convention system's subsidiarity would vanish in lockstep with the demise of domestic democracy.

In more practical terms, the States' interpretative dialogue with the Court about the meaning of the Convention rights requires from the States essentially three steps. Domestic authorities concerned with a rights issue must determine whether the Convention applies at all and, if so, identify the relevant Strasbourg case law, if there is any. They then have to study (consider, take account of) this case law which is itself an act with an interpretative dimension, before they must apply the Convention law and jurisprudence to the problem at their hands. In light of the previous discussion of the Court's jurisprudential authority, the second step of the process just outlined appears central.

Importantly, taking the Court's jurisprudence into account does not mean strict, mechanical compliance, given the variability of the Court's interpretative authority. This would be impracticable anyways, since any application of a norm to a case itself involves an interpretative element—*'il n'y pas d'application*

[59] Alec Stone Sweet, 'A Cosmopolitan Legal Order: Constitutional Pluralism and Rights Adjudication in Europe' (2012) 1(1) GlobCon 53, 55.

sans interprétation'.[60] Still, there is well-established Convention law, which enjoys strong interpretative authority and leaves little room for discretion: if a State fails to abide by certain standards, a committee of Strasbourg judges will unanimously render a violation judgment. This means that the domestic authorities are required to ascertain the factors that determine the authority of a Convention interpretation given by the Court, as well as its relevance to the circumstances of the case at hand in good faith, in order to determine how closely they are expected to follow it. They must read, analyse, and (if need be) distinguish the relevant Strasbourg jurisprudence correspondingly, so as to produce a considered decision, and they must do so over and over again as new cases emerge, in order to maintain the dialogue about rights outlined in Chapter 8.

The domestic authorities' contribution to the development of the Convention standards thus consists in their well-reasoned decisions. Domestic decisions must at least comprise a proposition concerning the arguably right interpretation of the Convention susceptible to the subsequent consideration of the Court and (indirectly) the other States' authorities. The better, and more persuasively, the domestic authorities justify their reading of the Convention, the higher the demands on the Court in terms of its response, especially if it disagrees with the proposed reading of the Convention. It is not a priori problematic, therefore, if the Court reverses a previous finding because, in a later case concerning the same or another State, it has been persuaded by the domestic authorities' careful reasoning. There is a large middle ground between the undesirable extremes of mechanical compliance with and blatant disregard for Strasbourg jurisprudence. This middle ground allows domestic authorities to question, challenge, and criticize the Court's interpretations, and still apply, or at least have regard to, and distinguish the case at hand from earlier cases. Antonios Tzanakopoulos puts this well when he describes the relationship between an international decision and its interpretation by domestic actors as 'dialectical, creating a feedback loop' and notes that domestic law-interpreters 'seek to comply, and at the same time forge the understanding of the rule in the international legal order'.[61] This confirms that the interpretative authority of the Court's case law is rather elusive and rightly so: anything else would not fit well with the subsidiarity principle's demand that defining the scope and content of the Convention rights is a matter for the reciprocal exchange of views between the Court and the States.

It is important to be explicit about the obligatory character of the States' primary role in the interpretation of the Convention. As the States are duty-bound to protect the Convention rights as first-line defenders,[62] they also bear

[60] George Scelle, *Précis de droit des gens* (Sirey 1934) 488.

[61] Antonios Tzanakopoulos, 'Judicial Dialogue as a Means of Interpretation' in HP Aust and G Nolte (eds), *The Interpretation of International Law by Domestic Courts* (OUP 2016) 90.

[62] Article 1 ECHR.

interpretative obligations with regard to determining what their duties are under the Convention and what measures they must take to abide by them. While there is no reason to reproduce in detail Amrei Müller's analysis of what the States' obligation to interpret and develop the Convention rights includes,[63] as this would go beyond setting out the mainstays of the Convention's subsidiarity principle, the question about the Convention law's status in the States' domestic legal orders merits attention. This is, so to say, the cornerstone diametrically opposed to the one concerning the effect and authority of the Court's jurisprudence: just as the effect and authority of the Court's jurisprudence cannot be haphazard for a functioning interpretative dialogue as required by the subsidiarity principle, the States' domestic treatment of Convention law and jurisprudence, too, cannot be haphazard.

Needless to say, subsidiarity implies that it is, as a rule, up to each State how it governs the status of the Convention in its domestic order, as long as it performs the obligations, including those interpretative obligations, it assumed when it decided to accede to the Convention system by its free, democratic will. However, if, as argued above, convergence is possible concerning what the substantive Convention rights imply, convergence is also possible concerning the procedural question of what it takes on the part of a State to perform its institutional obligations *qua* member of the Convention system: there has been considerable convergence, for example, in relation to proportionality as the 'go to' test to assess rights issues. Quite some convergence has occurred also on the question concerning the domestic status of the Convention law.

First of all, as concerns the legal validity of the Convention in the States' domestic orders, all States have incorporated the Convention in some way, with the effect that it has become an integral part of their domestic laws, as happened with British Human Rights Act of 1998. Similarly, in all States, individuals can invoke the substantive Convention rights (or their domesticated counterparts) before the State's public authorities—that is, the Convention rights enjoy direct effect by virtue of domestic law in all States.[64]

This is not only unproblematic but even desirable in light of the Convention's subsidiarity. The States would have difficulties in engaging in a dialogue with the Court about the scope and content of the Convention rights if their domestic authorities could not, or could only with difficulty, apply—and in the process of doing so interpret—the Convention. Especially because the 'evolutive' or dynamic interpretation of the Convention is very much about the constant adaptation of its rights to the change that societies undergo—to 'present-day conditions and of the ideas prevailing in democratic States today', as the Court has been used to put

[63] Amrei Müller, 'Domestic Authorities' Obligations to Co-Develop the Rights of the European Convention on Human Rights' (2016) 20(8) IJHR 1058.
[64] Stone Sweet (n 59) 63, 66–67.

it[65]—it is indispensable for an authority to apply the Convention rights routinely in order to partake in this interpretative process.[66]

The question whether applicants before domestic courts can invoke the Court's jurisprudence just as they can invoke the Convention rights per se appears rather idle in light of all we have said above. Since domestic authorities must consider the Court's jurisprudence, it should be clear that the Court's case law can be pleaded by applicants and applied by the domestic authorities to resolve a case. At the very least, the Court's jurisprudence has the effect of improving the informational basis upon which a State's exercise of public authority rests. At the other end of the spectrum are cases raising issues governed by 'well-established case-law' which should be solved 'tacitly' at the domestic level, in order to avoid burdening the Court with cases that do not raise any controversial legal questions. Thus, for suitable cases, possibilities under domestic law to reopen a case after a negative Strasbourg judgment deserve support.[67] Overall, then, the variability of the Court's jurisprudential authority means that an applicant's reliance on the Court's jurisprudence before domestic authorities is, in any case, an important legal argument, but not tantamount to a legal 'trump card' that always wins whatever the countervailing arguments are.[68]

Compared to the questions of incorporation and direct effect, the comparative picture is more nuanced as regards the Convention's rank within the States' domestic legal orders.[69] Still, two principles have emerged. First, the Convention can be opposed to domestic legislation everywhere but in the UK.[70] Second, the Convention enjoys firm *supra*-constitutional status virtually nowhere.[71] The precise rank that the Convention law occupies in the different States within these two guardrails need not be elaborated here,[72] since, from the perspective of the Convention's principle of subsidiarity, the *supra*-legislative, but *non-supra*-constitutional, rank that it has in practice merits commendation for two reasons.

The democratic rationale of the Convention's subsidiarity principle requires that even the political branches, including parliament, ordinarily be bound by the Convention. Only then are they encouraged, or indeed obliged, to take it

[65] *Tyrer v the United Kingdom*, 25 April 1978, para 31, Series A no 26.

[66] See Samantha Besson, 'Human Rights' Adjudication as Transnational Adjudication: A Peripheral Case of Domestic Courts as International Law Adjudicators' in A Reinisch, ME Footer, and C Binder (eds), *International Law and ...* (Hart 2016) 62–63.

[67] See Committee of Ministers, 'Recommendation to Member States on Re-examination or Reopening of Certain Cases at Domestic Level Following Judgements of the European Court of Human Rights' (19 January 2000, 694th mtg, Rec(2000)2).

[68] See Christos Giannopoulos, 'The Reception by Domestic Courts of the Res Interpretata Effect of Jurisprudence of the European Court of Human Rights' (2019) 19(3) HRLR 537.

[69] See Stone Sweet (n 59) Appendix 1, column 2.

[70] Samantha Besson, 'The Reception Process in Ireland and the United Kingdom' in H Keller and A Stone Sweet (eds), *A Europe of Rights* (OUP 2008) 50, 53.

[71] Stone Sweet (n 59) Appendix 1, column 2.

[72] See eg Cedric Marti, *Framing a Convention Community* (CUP 2021) 181–195.

into account, to interpret, and apply it in the course of their law-making. This speaks for giving the Convention a *supra*-legislative rank. Because the domestic authorities are, of course, also bound by their constitution—and possible constitutional jurisprudence—the institutionalization of some sort of roughly coequal 'Conventionality review' would appear apt for the same reason: only if the constitution does not mechanically prevail over the Convention is a regular practice of domestic Convention interpretation secured also at the level of domestic constitutional authority. If the constitution were to strictly prevail in practice, domestic authorities engaged in constitutional interpretation could ignore the Convention. For example, in Switzerland, right-wing political forces unsuccessfully sought to introduce strict constitutional supremacy, precisely with the aim of eliminating the need to consider the Convention when constitutional matters—especially popular votes on constitutional amendments—are at stake.[73] If the Convention has a quasi-constitutional status, by contrast, the constitution and the Convention must be taken into account, such that reaching conformity, by harmonious interpretation or the like, is encouraged.[74] This would suggest that countries adhering to a principle of parliamentary sovereignty and lacking a formal distinction between ordinary and constitutional politics, notably the United Kingdom, should ensure that the Convention enjoys a status, however it is called, that compels parliament to legislate so as to achieve 'harmony' with the Convention.[75] Similarly, in Switzerland's system of popular, direct democratic constitutional law-making, it would be desirable to emphasize that the '*pouvoir constituant*' (the People and the Cantons) must take the Convention into account when exercising its constitutional powers. Were the Convention to strictly prevail over constitutional law, this would risk eliminating the States' bottom-up input, for they might become mechanical domesticators of—that is, deprived of a means of constructive opposition to—the Court's views on the proper scope and content of human rights, which would represent an excessive challenge to the democratic principle.[76]

In sum, then, the Convention is ideally given a rank coequal with that of the constitution, so as to bind all domestic authorities, including legislative and constitutional powers, but still allowing them to actually interpret the Convention through a reception process, especially in the course of interpreting the domestic constitutional bill of rights. This best allows for a collaborative *trans*-national, top-down, and bottom-up interpretation of human rights in which substantive justification, rather than formal authority, takes centre stage, as the Convention's subsidiarity principle demands, according to the previous chapter.

[73] See Helen Keller and Reto Walther, 'The Bell of Görgülü Can't Be Unrung—Can it?' (2020) 19 GCYILJ 83, 94–95.

[74] See ibid 86–90.

[75] cf Sections 6(1) and 10 of the Human Rights Act 1998.

[76] See Armin von Bogdandy, 'Pluralism, Direct Effect, and the Ultimate Say: On the Relationship Between International and Domestic Constitutional Law' (2008) 6(3–4) I•CON 397, 412.

As regards the authority of the Court's interpretations of the Convention within the domestic legal order, it would appear that the answer has been given already when suggesting that the Court's jurisprudential authority varies: it would make little sense to give incongruent answers here. However, in principle, each State should remain free to make the decision to give 'interpretative priority' to the Court's reading of the Convention. This might be a reasonable 'default position' for a democratic polity that generally adheres to a principle of political primacy and has, therefore, decided against constitutional review, but still seeks the benefits of a (moderately strong) system of rights-based judicial review. The only caveat that the democratic principle, and by extension the Convention's subsidiarity principle, would appear to call for is that this decision ought to remain reversible either as the general rule or merely in exceptional cases.[77]

Still, a rule granting interpretative priority to the Court's reading of the Convention should be applied cautiously. First, strict application of such a rule appears ill-advised, for it seems unlikely that a strong feeling of ownership for the Convention could be retained by a political community that has completely, albeit reversibly, entrusted the making of the Convention law to the Court. Second, because the domestic interpretations of the Convention have been important in the past for the continuous development of Convention rights, a State's valuable contribution could be lost.[78] This is also why the British 'mirroring principle'—the idea that the domestic courts must 'keep pace with the Strasbourg jurisprudence as it evolves over time: no more, but certainly no less'[79]—appears ill-suited from the perspective of the Convention's subsidiarity principle. Thus, a practice of generally following the Court's reading of the Convention that still leaves some room for disagreeing with the Court and for going beyond Strasbourg's minimum requirements would appear preferable.

D) European consensus

The dialogue about rights requires that the Court listen and respond to the States when they apply and interpret the Convention. If the Court were to fail to be receptive to the States' views on the proper reading of the Convention, it could hardly expect them to be open to its own views. Dialogical interaction is a two-way process, a process that is reciprocal and bidirectional. The Court's interpretative incrementalism serves the Strasbourg judges as a means of awaiting the States' views

[77] See also Supreme Court of the United Kingdom, *Manchester City Council v Pinnock* [2010] UKSC 45 para 48.

[78] See Shai Dothan, 'Judicial Deference Allows European Consensus to Emerge' (2018) 18(2) Chi J Intl L 393, 409; Stone Sweet (n 59) 76, 79.

[79] United Kingdom House of Lords, *R v Special Adjudicator, ex parte Ullah* [2004] UKHL 26 para 20.

and reactions, in order to consider and respond to them. However, apart from the 'incrementalist' judicial strategies discussed above, the Court uses two more distinct doctrines to take account of, and respond to, the States' interpretations and applications of the Convention. First, it does so through the combined 'living instrument' and 'European consensus' doctrine.[80] Under this method, a 'comparative analysis of the prevailing legal trends and common understandings of a right, with a principal focus on the national legal orders of the signatory parties',[81] serves to identify the contemporary understanding of a Convention right that deserves priority in the teleologically motivated dynamic interpretation of the Convention, because it corresponds to a majority of the States' evolved domestic human rights practices.[82] Second, as we will see in the following chapter, it does so by exercising restraint and deference. Showing judicial restraint and deference allows the Court to adjust the strictness of its scrutiny reflecting its status as an international body that is less democratically legitimate and, on occasion, less well placed to decide than the domestic authorities.

The need to treat the Convention as a 'living instrument' that must be interpreted dynamically and read in light of contemporary circumstances is per se hardly contestable and has little to do with the Court's merely subsidiary role, a point which becomes clear from the corresponding domestic judicial practice.[83] The interesting and controversial questions are how and to what extent the Court is justified in developing the States' obligations under the Convention.

The European consensus doctrine, an interpretative method, is the 'central piece in the living-instrument architecture' of the Convention system.[84] According to this doctrine, the Court makes its development of the Convention rights dependent on corresponding developments within the States. Its relevance to the present work quickly becomes clear from a reading of Kanstantsin Dzehtsiarou's leading study on the European consensus doctrine. Most importantly, perhaps, Dzehtsiarou defends the Court's approach to make its evolutive interpretation of the Convention dependent on convergent State practice, observing that its alternative would be 'adjudication based on the moral standpoint of the judges', which meant adjudication based on a subjective and in this sense arbitrary standard. According to Dzehtsiarou, the development of the domestic view on the scope and

[80] See *Dudgeon v the United Kingdom*, 22 October 1981, Series A no 45; *Marckx v Belgium*, 13 June 1979, Series A no 31; *Tyrer v UK* (n 65).

[81] Panos Kapotas and Vassilis P Tzevelekos, 'How (Difficult Is It) to Build Consensus on (European) Consensus?' in P Kapotas and VP Tzevelekos (eds), *Building Consensus on European Consensus* (CUP 2019) 7.

[82] See Kanstantsin Dzehtsiarou, *European Consensus and the Legitimacy of the European Court of Human Rights* (CUP 2015) 1–2, 138–142; Luzius Wildhaber, Arnaldur Hjartarson, and Stephen Donnelly, 'No Consensus on Consensus? The Practice of the European Court of Human Rights' (2013) 33(7–12) HRLJ 248, 248.

[83] See eg Vicki C Jackson, 'Constitutions as "Living Trees"? Comparative Constitutional Law and Interpretive Metaphors' (2006) 75(2) Fordham L Rev 921.

[84] Angelika Nußberger, *The European Court of Human Rights* (OUP 2020) 87.

meaning of the Convention rights is 'one of the most objective criteria available' to the Court when it needs to determine whether the time is ripe for an evolution of the Convention law.[85]

Dzehtsiarou's work confirms our understanding of the European consensus doctrine, according to which this method allows the Court to engage in a dialogue with the States.[86] Moreover, in line with our argument to the effect that the Court system's subsidiarity requires an interpretative dialogue because the Convention law would lack a sufficient democratic basis otherwise, Dzehtsiarou suggests that the European consensus doctrine is a way to enhance the Court's democratic legitimacy by offering a means for the Court to engage in an inter-institutional dialogue with the States' more democratically legitimate authorities.[87]

The European consensus doctrine does not determine the Court's interpretative specification of the Convention to a high degree and rightly so: one must not forget the element of comprehension involved in any act of listening. The Court, like anyone on the receiving end of an act of communication, may merely comprehend what it is willing to hear and is capable of understanding given its own social position. That is, its comprehension of the States' views on a rights issue involves an active element of construction, just as there is an element of subjective construction involved when legal scholars discern the 'prevailing opinion'.[88] In any case, in both situations, a subjective element is already present in the choice to apply this methodological approach. Conversely, it is also true that the approach, once chosen, does have a constraining effect, since the audience in question will plainly not accept any outcome.[89] This partial subjectivity and partial objectivity of the European consensus doctrine is not a problem, however. Quite to the contrary, it ensures that the Court has a way of bringing its own understanding of a rights issue into dialogue with the States' views, a process that Chapter 8 argued is necessary for the Court to navigate between its moral and legal authority.

The European consensus doctrine's fit with the gradual dialogic development of the Convention law proposed here and the present account of the potential of the Convention's subsidiarity principle to justify this approach are evident in light of what has been said. This fit and justification, and its potential to suggest modifications to the Court's European consensus method merit further elaboration. We will discuss four points: the ubiquity, flexibility, methodology, and oft-criticized majoritarian character of the European consensus doctrine.

[85] Dzehtsiarou (n 82) 142.
[86] ibid 157.
[87] ibid 155–158.
[88] See Paul Johnson, 'Sociology and the European Court of Human Rights' (2014) 62(3) Soc Rev 547, 552–553.
[89] See ibid.

a) Ubiquity and flexibility

A first point to mention is the ubiquity of the European consensus doctrine. The Court has applied the European consensus doctrine to virtually all Convention provisions.[90] This is in line with what was said in Chapter 8, namely, that even what counts as Dworkinian 'contempt' requires interpretative specification; even the most basic human rights standards cannot develop from scratch, but depend on bottom-up input.[91] Similarly, Dzehtsiarou argues that, if the Court is to establish 'a set of shared rules and principles among European nations which are so fundamental that they form the foundation of European society', it can convincingly do so only if it bases its findings on the strong justification following from the fact that they are indeed 'shared and supported' by the States.[92] What has just been said leaves room for the application of the European consensus doctrine more often in one context, and less often in another one—specifically, it has been observed that the doctrine is most often applied in cases concerning Article 8 of the Convention.[93] This is unsurprising, given that Article 8 not only contains by far the broadest and most dynamic Convention right, but also addresses subject matters that are more easily subjected to comparative legal analysis than, for example, procedural issues under Article 6.[94]

A second point that deserves attention is the European consensus doctrine's flexibility. On the one hand, it must be emphasized that the Court, when applying this doctrine, does not actually require unanimity among the States, but is usually satisfied with a majority or a trend of convergence.[95] Clearly, the Strasbourg judges' subjective perception that it is time to push the Convention law forward will often stand at the beginning of an enquiry into corresponding majorities or tendencies, which, if found, then serve as persuasive arguments and justifications that the Court can use to gain support for, or at least acceptance of, its attempt to develop Convention law.[96] It would, of course, be an illusion to believe that there are hard-and-fast rules as to when the judges must engage in comparative legal analyses.

On the other hand, it is noteworthy that there is also a certain flexibility concerning the subject of what the Court takes as a European consensus. That is, the States' convergence can occur on a more or a less abstract level.[97] Abstract

[90] See Dzehtsiarou (n 82) 17–20; Wildhaber, Hjartarson, and Donnelly (n 82) 257.
[91] See also Wildhaber, Hjartarson, and Donnelly (n 82) 257.
[92] Dzehtsiarou (n 82) 75–76.
[93] Wildhaber, Hjartarson, and Donnelly (n 82) 257.
[94] Paul Mahoney and Rachael Kondak, 'Common Ground: A Starting Point or Destination for Comparative-Law Analysis by the European Court of Human Rights?' in M Andenas and D Fairgrieve (eds), *Courts and Comparative Law* (OUP 2015) 140.
[95] Anatoly Kovler and others, 'The Role of Consensus in the System of the European Convention on Human Rights' in European Court of Human Rights (ed), *Dialogue Between Judges* (2008) 15.
[96] See Conor Gearty, 'Building Consensus on European Consensus' in P Kapotas and VP Tzevelekos (eds), *Building Consensus on European Consensus* (CUP 2019) 459–460.
[97] Dzehtsiarou (n 82) 13.

convergence may be found at the level of principle—for example, while there is a consensus on the importance of the best interests of the child, 'perceptions as to the appropriateness of intervention by public authorities in the care of children vary from one Contracting State to another'.[98] More concrete convergence occurs on the level of legal standards (or rules)—for example, homosexual couples must 'have available a specific legal framework providing for the recognition and protection of their same-sex unions'.[99] However, once again, it would be naive to believe there could be clear criteria for determining when the States have converged on a level of specificity sufficient to support the development of a common European standard.

Taken together these two observations support the claim that the entire Convention law develops and crystallises through a flexible process of the States' increasing convergence. To be clear, the claim here is not that the European consensus doctrine serves to receive the States' consent, but rather that it serves to develop the Convention law through an incremental process consisting of a series of exchanges between the Court and the States that ensures their co-developing of the Convention law, so as to make the resulting interpretations mutually acceptable. When there is a robust European consensus of the more concrete type, in particular, the relevant standard of Convention law may well be understood as part of what has been called the *acquis conventionnel*, such that deviation, if permissible at all in certain exceptional cases, can be considered Convention-compliant only if the State in question submits highly persuasive reasons.[100] By contrast, when there is no more than a tendency and/or rough agreement on abstract principles, the process of the States' convergence is still ongoing and the Court should refrain from pushing ahead with top-down consolidation.[101] It is therefore not surprising if the Court, at some point, finds no more than an abstract consensus insufficient to resolve a rights issue on the European level,[102] but, at a later point, finds consensus on a level of specificity sufficient to do so.[103]

b) Methodology

The benefits of the European consensus doctrine, justifying the Court's interpretative development of the Convention law and entering into a dialogue about the

[98] *Strand Lobben and Others v Norway* [GC], no 37283/13, para 210, 10 September 2019.

[99] *Oliari and Others v Italy*, nos 18766/11 and 36030/11, para 185, 21 July 2015.

[100] See also Dzehtsiarou (n 82) 15–16; Thomas Kleinlein, 'Consensus and Contestability: The ECtHR and the Combined Potential of European Consensus and Procedural Rationality Control' (2017) 28(3) EJIL 871, 878.

[101] Wildhaber, Hjartarson, and Donnelly (n 82) 257.

[102] See eg *Chapman v the United Kingdom* [GC], no 27238/95, paras 93–94, ECHR 2001-I; *Coster v the United Kingdom* [GC], no 24876/94, paras 107–108, 18 January 2001.

[103] Compare, eg the case of *Oliari v Italy* (n 99) with the earlier judgment in *Schalk and Kopf v Austria*, no 30141/04, ECHR 2010.

proper understanding of the Convention rights with the States, materialize only when convergent State practice is established on a methodologically sound basis. The principle of subsidiarity as conceptualized here suggests certain methodological guidelines that the Court's practice should respect. First of all, because the Court's jurisprudence affects all States, all States should have an influence on it. Ideally, the Court would therefore regularly include in its comparative analyses all forty-six States. However, clearly this will often be unworkable in practice.[104] Thus, because the Court's comparative analyses are necessarily limited to a selection of the States, as will remain the case in practice, it is important that it publicly and transparently justify its selection,[105] not least because of the risk of a biased choice.[106]

While inclusiveness or, as second best, reasoned selectivity are important, the Court must also avoid over-inclusiveness. The Court often supplements its analysis of the States' domestic laws and practices with an examination of pertinent international treaties and non-binding instruments. Sometimes, it also takes a look at practices in non-European states. This is unfortunate, since both approaches raise concerns. On the present account, it is quite obscure how the Court could justifiably develop the Convention based on non-European practice: neither can the domestic practice of non-European states enhance the democratic legitimacy of the Convention law nor does the Court enter into a dialogue with these states about their domestic rights configurations.[107] What is more, the practice of including the view of non-European states raises quite insurmountable selection difficulties that bring with them the risk of bias, arbitrariness, and unpredictability.[108] Similar difficulties result from a reliance on comparative legal analyses submitted by third-party interveners from civil society,[109] who, of course, are pursuing their own political agendas which are reflected, more often than not, in the comparative analyses they submit.[110] There is no reason for the Court to rely on these documents' legal comparisons within the framework of its European consensus doctrine: to do so without the risk of falling prey to the third-party intervener's subjective agenda, the registry would have to verify the submitted analysis carefully, but if it did so, it could just as well put together its own comparative overview of domestic laws.

[104] Dzehtsiarou (n 82) 102–103; Wildhaber, Hjartarson, and Donnelly (n 82) 258.

[105] Dzehtsiarou (n 82) 104.

[106] Christian Djeffal, 'Consensus, Stasis, Evolution: Reconstructing Argumentative Patterns in Evolutive ECHR Jurisprudence' in P Kapotas and VP Tzevelekos (eds), *Building Consensus on European Consensus* (CUP 2019) 86; Dzehtsiarou (n 82) 102.

[107] See also Dzehtsiarou (n 82) 67, 70.

[108] In detail, see ibid 65–71; Laura van den Eynde, 'The Consensus Argument in NGOs' Amicus Curiae Briefs: Defending Minorities Through a Creatively Used Majoritarian Argument' in P Kapotas and VP Tzevelekos (eds), *Building Consensus on European Consensus* (CUP 2019) 101–105.

[109] Dzehtsiarou (n 82) 66.

[110] Nicole Bürli, *Third-Party Interventions Before the European Court of Human Rights* (Intersentia 2017) 81; Dzehtsiarou (n 82) 98–99.

As regards the Court's consideration of international law as a means to develop Convention law, different, but related problems arise. It is certainly true that international obligations and, to a lesser extent, non-binding documents adopted by the States can be indicative of their views on rights issues, as long as this practice can plausibly be taken to be representative of the States' views (which is not necessarily the case for reasons that we will discuss below). But there is considerable risk that this practice leaves the Court with excessive discretion. Indeed, the Court quite openly claims virtually unlimited discretion, when it states that it is for itself 'to decide which international instruments and reports it considers relevant and how much weight to attribute to them'.[111]

However, there are further problems, which result from the making of international law and its legal force and judicial control, or the lack thereof. It follows from the making of international law, that it is a rather bad indicator of a State's actual view on a rights-matter. Since international treaties are usually intergovernmentally negotiated commitments bearing on questions of principles, international law will be less reflective of a State's actual view than its domestic policy decisions. Thus, when the results of an analysis of domestic practice and of international obligations diverge, the Court should let the former prevail. When recent international law that has been concluded by many of the States corresponds to these States' domestic policy decisions, however, this may be taken as additional confirmation of the States' view about the issue at stake.

Quite often, documents of international law are of an aspirational nature: their legal force is limited and they certainly lack any sort of judicial control, which is why they may, in turn, be relatively far-reaching in substantive terms. Yet, the idea that some international law's aspirational nature can serve to propel the Convention law's progressive development is mistaken.[112] First, this idea is ignorant of the complementarity of constitutional and international rights protection that underpins the European consensus method. As we saw in Chapter 8, the States' domestic rights-conceptions should surpass, not merely match, international human rights standards—not vice versa.[113] Second, the Convention, unlike other international human rights documents, is not, and must not be aspirational, but rather a legally binding treaty, which, moreover, has a thoroughly judicial supervisory mechanism producing binding judgments. To disregard this difference between the Convention and other international human rights documents potentially undermines the Court system's peculiar international legal force. Thus, when the States adopt aspirational international law documents, since this is evidence of their hesitation to act on these aspirations in more robust ways, these aspirations must not be taken to circumvent their hesitation to enter new binding obligations by

[111] See *Tănase v Moldova* [GC], no 7/08, para 176, ECHR 2010.
[112] See Jens T Theilen, *European Consensus Between Strategy and Principle* (Nomos 2021) 250–251.
[113] See Mahoney and Kondak (n 94) 120; Wildhaber, Hjartarson, and Donnelly (n 82) 252.

instilling corresponding hard-law obligations through the 'backdoor' of dynamically interpreting binding, and even judicially controlled, treaty law. It appears problematic, therefore, when the Court, to give one recent example, adjudicates on the Paris Climate Agreement[114] by incorporating it into Article 8 of the Convention as it did in the *KlimaSeniorinnen* case.[115] If international courts start indirectly to adjudicate agreements that contain provisions of varied legal force,[116] that intend to operate bottom up,[117] and that certainly have not been vested with a judicial oversight mechanism, they not only disregard their mandate and subsidiary role, but also risk deterring states from concluding such agreements at all.

c) Majoritarianism

According to our argument, the European consensus doctrine deserves support, since it is an instrument for the democratic bottom-up development of the Convention law in a dialogue between the Court and the States. Quite contrary to this sympathetic view of the European consensus doctrine are views that fear this method undermines human rights *qua* counter-majoritarian and minority-protecting guarantees.[118] Clearly, developing Convention law in line with convergent State practice is a form of judicial majoritarian activism, as we have already noted. However, as we have argued in Chapter 8, human rights *qua* equal rights must be rooted in democratic politics, because they are only one side of the moral status equality that grounds them, the other side being the political equality of all. Thus, arguments such as the one made by George Letsas to the effect that the States, when establishing the Convention system, agreed to completely entrust to the Court the interpretation of the moral principles enshrined therein are normatively difficult.[119]

The Court is first and foremost a court of law and, as such, not mandated to pursue a certain subjective moral theory about human rights. We must not confuse human rights law with the political use of moral arguments of human rights.[120] The Convention system pertains to the former: the Convention is a binding document of positive law, and the Court is mandated with applying this law retrospectively to individual cases. Human rights politics is of crucial importance, but it is not a matter for the Court, as we will forcefully argue in the Epilogue. Legitimate

114 Paris Agreement of 12 December 2015, in force since 4 November 2016, 3156 UNTS 3.
115 *Verein KlimaSeniorinnen Schweiz and Others v Switzerland* [GC], no 53600/20, 9 April 2024.
116 See Lavany Rajamani, 'The 2015 Paris Agreement: Interplay Between Hard, Soft and Non-Obligations' (2016) 28(2) J Env L 337.
117 Johannes Reich and Nina Boss, 'Switzerland' (2022) 33(1) Yb Intl Env L 149, 149.
118 See eg Eyal Benvenisti, 'Margin of Appreciation, Consensus, and Universal Standards' (1999) 31 NYU J Intl L & Pol 843, 851.
119 See Chapter 7.
120 See eg Theilen (n 112) 426–428.

law depends on democratic politics. Thus, the view of the critics of the European consensus doctrine appear all the more out of place if one considers that 'common rules and principles were anticipated by the drafters of the Convention [ie the Convention-law-makers] to be guiding principles for the development of human rights in Europe'.[121] Even ardent defenders of a vigorous Court such as Eva Brems admit that 'the ECHR is considered to be derived from the national systems of the European states'.[122]

The Convention system has been set up to 'intensify cooperation and collective protection of human rights'[123] based on the insight, expressed by Pierre-Henri Teitgen, one of the Convention's founding fathers, that the real danger to Europe's liberal democracies are not pan-European majority opinions, but cunning domestic minorities that suppress one freedom after another and asphyxiate the public conscience in order to disable levers of control.[124] Admittedly, if this idea is to convince, two premises must be plausible. Only together do they render convincing the claim that the European consensus doctrine usually works as a collective mechanism that enhances the individual State's protection of minorities and constrains individual States' deviant majorities.

The first premise is that the States must maintain liberal-democratic systems on the domestic level, with counter-majoritarian checks and balances—a collective of totalitarian States will surely fail to reap the benefits of democracy's epistemological acumen. More generally, unless the States' domestic procedures can be presumed to work sufficiently well to produce reasonable outcomes, it cannot be presumed that looking at their domestic practices collectively reveals reasonable outcomes.[125] Second, the States must be committed to the foundational values of the Convention system,[126] such that one may presume that a State's domestic take on a rights issue was adopted with regard to the Convention law. We may apply these assumptions in a way akin to legal presumptions[127]—given the corresponding requirements of membership in the Council of Europe—but, as we have noted in the previous chapter, the question of what to do with States that do not quite qualify as reasonably liberal, democratic, and rule-of-law-based clearly is important.

According to our argument, making the development of the Convention rights dependent on the States' domestic practices is only justified in cases where these practices are plausibly democratic, viz where these practices can credibly claim to represent the views of individual political equals.[128] Moreover, the logic that better

[121] Dzehtsiarou (n 82) 119 (his note 23).
[122] Eva Brems, *Human Rights* (Martinus Nijhoff 2001) 420.
[123] Dzehtsiarou (n 82) 120.
[124] See Arthur H Robertson, 'The European Court of Human Rights' (1960) 9(1) Am J Comp L 1, 10.
[125] See Dothan, 'Judicial Deference' (n 78) 413–414.
[126] Dzehtsiarou (n 82) 118–119 (referring to an interview with Lech Garlicki).
[127] See also ibid 129.
[128] See Shai Dothan, 'In Defence of Expansive Interpretation in the European Court of Human Rights' (2014) 3(2) CJICL 508, 516–517, 520–521.

outcomes result from a greater number of decision-makers only works if, among other things, all these decision-makers are roughly similar and aim for roughly similar goals.[129] This condition would not hold when, for example, some States are authoritarian instead of democratic, with the result that their governments pursue the interests of the ruling clique, rather than of the individual citizens. Thus, it merits discussion whether the Court, when applying the European consensus doctrine, ought to disregard the domestic practices of States whose conduct cannot reasonably be understood other than as outrightly flouting the foundational values of the Council of Europe.

That said, the explicit exclusion of some States' views would put enormous strain on the Court's acceptance in these States, unless this decision were not taken by the Court: as suggested in Chapter 8, the community of Convention States would have to take a decision, which the Court could then rely upon. The Court could, for example, argue that the position on rights issues of States whose participatory rights in the Parliamentary Assembly had been suspended must not figure in European consensus analyses since it is the very purpose of these analyses to root the development of Convention law in liberal-democratic polities.[130] The Court might then admit a carefully chosen, balanced selection of high-quality third-party briefs from civil society actors of these States as substitute in order to keep its forum open to these States' democratic voices.

Finally, when we consider arguments against the European consensus doctrine that operate with the protection of minorities and their rights, it is important to bear in mind that the proper specification of minority rights may also be controversial. Indeed, it may go to the heart of the vision that a community of political equals has of their culture and society, raising extremely difficult questions about what it means for equals to have to determine the content of their equality for themselves.[131] Thus, the alternative to taking account of the States' evolving domestic practices is also in this domain not unproblematic. For one, the legal entrenchment of new minority rights, if it is politically and socially premature, can be counterproductive and lead to a hardening of conflicting positions, a fact activists are well aware of.[132] For another, taking the judges' own moral standpoint as decisive entails various risks of unpredictability, as well as of arbitrariness and illegitimacy, as we discussed in previous chapters. This also means that the argument against the European consensus method that follows from the laudable goal of minority protection can be no stronger than the plausibility of the claim that

[129] See Dothan, 'Judicial Deference' (n 78) 404–405.

[130] See also Samantha Besson, 'State Consent and Disagreement in International Law-Making. Dissolving the Paradox' (2016) 29(2) LJIL 289, 306–307.

[131] See Vijay M Padmanabhan, 'The Human Rights Justification for Consent' (2013) 35(1) U Pa J Intl L 1, 57.

[132] See Roni Mann, 'Non-Ideal Theory of Constitutional Adjudication' (2018) 7(1) GlobCon 14, 17.

the judges themselves, who are recruited from and elected by the States' domestic politico-legal elites, are not affected by the same discriminatory attitudes that are supposedly reflected in the domestic practices[133] upon which the European consensus doctrine draws.[134]

d) In defence of European consensus

Overall, the European consensus doctrine merits support. Unless one takes the extreme position that the Court is mandated to develop the Convention law without rooting these developments in the States' democratic polities at all, one has to endorse the European consensus doctrine in principle—if only due to a lack of alternatives that fare better at, first, giving the Court epistemic support in finding good solutions to Europe's changing human rights challenges and, second, tying the Convention law's development back to the States' democratic volition. It is a tool that allows the Court to enter into such a dialogue with the States about the development of the Convention rights that is mostly indeterminate as regards its outcomes,[135] which is important to lend the process of Convention law-making democratic (procedural) legitimacy. More specifically, it is a means for the Court to listen to the States' views, and thereby to gauge whether the time is ripe for the development of the Convention law.[136] Unless the Court exaggerates its discretion in what it considers relevant to establishing convergence,[137] this may enhance the States' feeling of ownership for Convention law and lend democratic legitimacy to the continuous development of Convention rights. The doctrine is flexible, a situation which could not be otherwise given that the convergence of domestic practices is a gradual and uneven process. This once again explains and justifies the variable authority of the Court's jurisprudential standards[138] and the importance of the States' domestication of the Convention in a way that allows them to routinely engage with the Convention rights to contribute to their development. In other words, the Court's usage of comparative analyses once again illustrates the dialectic nature of the development of the Convention law—a process of oscillation between the Convention's ambition of reaching increasingly shared understandings of what the Convention rights demand and the reality of rights

[133] cf *Bayev and Others v Russia*, nos 67667/09 and 2 others, 20 June 2017 (dissenting opinion of Judge Dedov).

[134] Theilen (n 112) 91.

[135] See Djeffal (n 106) 92.

[136] See Nußberger (n 84) 88.

[137] See Geir Ulfstein, 'Evolutive Interpretation in the Light of Other International Instruments: Law and Legitimacy' in A van Aaken and I Motoc (eds), *The European Convention on Human Rights and General International Law* (OUP 2018) 91–93.

[138] See also Djeffal (n 106) 92–93.

interpretations as political choices between conflicting views on how to reconcile competing interests.[139]

E) Convention rights: ever in flux, ever contestable

In Spring 2025, notably in the context of (irregular) migration and fears of criminal foreigners, some States' governments have openly addressed the Court due to concerns about how Convention law matches these and other current challenges.[140] Recent discussions have indeed spurred two questions: first, about whether—and if so, how—the States may oppose the Court's development of Convention law; and second, about whether 'regressive' interpretations of Convention law may be permissible. These are important questions, but as concerns the broad lines of their answers, less vexed than one might think at first sight. Practices of (constitutional) principles of resistance[141] or counter-limits against the Convention law,[142] must not, in our view, be assessed overly negatively per se. Where they are the result of a credibly liberal-democratic State's rule-of-law-based domestic decision-making, opposition to a ruling of the Court can and should be understood as a (fierce) contribution to the dialogue about the proper reading of the Convention. There is little reason to fear, or normatively discredit, this type of constitutional opposition to Convention law if it occurs in singular cases, as 'episodic instances',[143] and is based on well-reasoned considerations that can plausibly be understood as arguments about human rights and democracy, viz as arguments faithful to the legal and political dimensions of everyone's equal moral status that underpins the liberal-democratic State. The situation is different if either the source of opposition and/or the opposition itself does not correspond to the qualitative criteria just mentioned. Unfortunately, there really are some States that have increasingly given grounds for general suspicions about their liberal-democratic credentials. The next chapter takes this point up when discussing the Court's growing case law under Article 18 of the Convention. There have also been exceptional—and luckily unsuccessful—attempts to push back against the Convention system in a way that would not

[139] See Paolo G Carozza, 'Uses and Misuses of Comparative Law in International Human Rights: Some Reflections on the Jurisprudence of the European Court of Human Rights' (1997) 73(5) Notre Dame L Rev 1217, 1236.

[140] Open letter on the initiative of Denmark and Italy of 22 May 2025; see also Joint Statement by 27 States of 10 December 2025 delivered to the Conference of Ministers of Justice of the Council of Europe.

[141] See eg Marten Breuer (ed), *Principled Resistance Against ECtHR Judgments* (Springer 2019).

[142] See eg Keller and Walther, 'Görgülü' (n 73).

[143] Alice Donald, 'Book Review: Principled Resistance to ECtHR Judgments—A New Paradigm?' (2020) 1(2) ECHR L Rev 297, 302.

appear compatible with the demands outlined here, since they operated with blanket threats to exit the Convention system.[144]

This chapter together with considerations that we have made in earlier chapters also allows for a short response to the question of whether a principle of 'non-regression' is part of the Convention law, such that 'regressive' interpretations of Convention guarantees would be impermissible. This point is often raised as a concern about the Court's European consensus method along the lines expressed in the question: what if the States cut back on human rights? Our response to this allegedly pressing problem would appear rather straightforward: where there is reasonable disagreement about the proper specification of a right, that is, about what the best interpretation of a rights clause is, there will also be reasonable disagreement about what counts as a 'progressive' and 'regressive' interpretation, respectively. In other words, an evolving reading of the pertinent Convention right may well be 'progressive' and 'regressive', viz approximating or moving away from the 'right' understanding of the respective Convention guarantee, depending on the observer's preferred moral theory. For example, enhanced preventive measures against terrorism may be negative or positive overall because, depending on the perspective taken, the loss of freedom on the part of suspected or convicted terrorists may be outweighed (or not) by the gains when it comes to the interests of others in security, order, and the resulting freedom. Of course, there are better and worse, more and less convincing moral theories of human rights, but it is not clear a priori which one these are and it would be naive to assume that any one theory that was, at one point of time, embraced by the Court is irreversibly the best one. Generally speaking, the dialogue between the Court and the States and, within the States, between the competing democratic political forces must always go on. As we argued, in particular, in Chapter 8 on a theoretical level and in this chapter on a more practical one, it is through this dialogue that convincing and democratically legitimate understandings of human rights develop. As we will see in the next chapter, the Court's review practice, which largely operates on the basis of a proportionality test that allows each State some leeway—a margin of appreciation—lends further strength to this argument. Chapter 10 shows that the permissible *qua* proportionate limitation of the Convention rights links these judicially controlled rights to the democratic process. That is, the Court's review method, just like its interpretative practice, contributes to the democratically legitimate development and application of the Convention rights. It, too, fits and justifies our argument about the proper—subsidiary—role of the Court.

[144] See eg Helen Keller and Reto Walther, 'Resistance in Switzerland: Populist Rather than Principled' in M Breuer (ed), *Principled Resistance Against ECtHR Judgments* (Springer 2019) 185–188.

10
Review and the Court's Subsidiary Role

A) Introduction

Proportionality analysis has become *the* method for constitutional and international adjudication almost everywhere. In Chapter 8, we have explained and justified this development with the argument that proportionality analysis offers a framework for structuring the justificatory dialogue about rights implied by a constitutional culture in which any exercise of public authority requires justification. The important question now is: how can the proportionality framework facilitate such inter-institutional interaction in, or dialogue about, the case-based concretization of the European Convention on Human Rights' (the Convention, ECHR)[1] guarantees effectively in line with the Convention's principle of subsidiarity? This chapter, developing an answer to this question, enquires into the role that national discretion and international judicial deference and restraint in the European Court of Human Rights' (the Court, ECtHR) proportionality assessment play in the Convention system's inter-institutional dialogue about rights.

B) Proportionality and separation of powers: some preliminaries

As a preliminary matter, we must remind ourselves that proportionality is the prima facie method for applying the Convention rights and not an interpretative doctrine. However, this distinction is rather elusive. This becomes obvious, for example, when the Court has resort to proportionality analysis in order to determine positive obligations, which is, in principle, a matter of interpreting the Convention guarantees.[2] More generally, the difficulty of the distinction between the (general) interpretation of the Convention guarantees and the case-based application of Convention law appears from statements such as the following of former Court president Robert Spano: '[t]he scope of a Convention provision ... must ... be determined on the basis of the underlying principles of the provision in question in light of a concrete case'.[3]

[1] Convention for the Protection of Human Rights and Fundamental Freedoms, as amended, of 4 November 1950, in force since 3 September 1953, 213 UNTS 221, CETS No 005.

[2] See eg *Osman v the United Kingdom*, 28 October 1998, para 116, Reports of Judgments and Decisions 1998-VIII.

[3] Robert Spano, 'The European Court of Human Rights and National Courts: A Constructive Conversation or a Dialogue of Disrespect?' (2015) 33(1) Nord J Hum Rts 1, 8.

Subsidiarity, Legitimacy, and the European Court of Human Rights. Reto Walther, Oxford University Press.
 DOI: 10.1093/9780198921455.003.0010

It is important that we bear in mind the impossibility of sharply differentiating between the interpretation and application of the law, because this insight bears on claims that the Court does not allow for national discretion in the interpretation of the Convention guarantees, but only in the application of the Convention rights to individual cases.[4] This recognition also corroborates the argument we made in Chapter 9 that the Court's interpretative authority must be understood as varied: the Court's casuistic case law results from the application of the Convention guarantees through (by definition) haphazard proportionality reasoning, which is possible only insofar as the prior interpretative specification of the Convention law left that law unclear or underdeterminate—that is, left room for the case-based weighing of competing interests—and which in turn further reduces the interpretative clarity of the Convention guarantees, namely, to the extent to which the casuistic application of the Convention rights feeds back into the interpretative specification of Convention law. In other words, due to the Court's incremental (individual-case-based, casuistic) interpretation of the Convention, the discretion that the Court grants to its member states (the States) at the stage of applying the law—when a domestic measure's compatibility with the Convention in the individual case is assessed and the Court shows restraint and/or deference—also bears on the (discursive, bottom-up) interpretative development of Convention rights.

This suggests an answer to the question why it is appropriate for the Court to allow for national leeway in the application of Convention law. Our answer to this question will primarily revolve around the insight that permissible restrictions of rights serve to bring about the implementation of separation-of-powers thinking in the domain of rights, too—viz to bring both the judicial realization of the liberal principle (ie individual claims to freedom) and the political realization of the democratic principle (ie a collective claim to self-determination) to bear on rights issues. Just as the States are generally expected to respect the Court's judgments, the Court is expected to show respect for the States' political choices. This is what the margin of appreciation—the States' discretionary margin—is about, and, as Stephen Gardbaum argues, this explains why rights can be justifiably overridden or limited in the first place.[5]

The question then is how and when the Court must take account of, as well as show restraint to, the views of a respondent State when applying Convention rights to an individual case. This question is about the judicial delineation of what Alec Stone Sweet and Jud Mathews call 'zones of proportionality, within which policy-makers enjoy meaningful policy discretion',[6] and about what Andreas Føllesdal describes as 'the acceptable domain of just outcomes'.[7] Yet, while these formulations

[4] See eg *Austin and Others v the United Kingdom* [GC], nos 39692/09 and 2 others, paras 65–68, ECHR 2012, and the joint dissenting opinion of Judges Tulkens, Spielmann, and Garlicki.

[5] Stephen Gardbaum, 'Limiting Constitutional Rights' (2007) 54(4) UCLA L Rev 789, 830.

[6] Alec Stone Sweet and Jud Mathews, *Proportionality Balancing and Constitutional Governance* (OUP 2019) 128.

[7] Andreas Føllesdal, 'Tracking Justice Democratically' (2017) 31(3) Soc Epistemology 324, 330.

convey an illustrative image of liberal rights as limits to the room for *manoeuvre* of democratic politics, they add little to answer our questions. That is, they say little about the Court's proper standard of review, and hence provide scant guidance when it comes to the pertinent questions of national discretion and of international judicial restraint.

The problem behind rights-based proportionality analysis as a method of judicial review is that it gives an (international) apex court, such as the Strasbourg Court, all the necessary tools to take over, to a considerable extent, the functions of the other branches of government—unless the judges apply doctrines of deference and restraint that allow other institutional actors to have their proper say by, among other things, granting them some discretion.[8] Julian Rivers thus suggests that we must specifically think about the separation of powers in the context of proportionality *qua* method of rights-based judicial review. That is, our enquiry into the role that national discretion and international judicial deference and restraint in the Court's proportionality assessment play in the Convention system's inter-institutional dialogue about rights, which we discussed in Chapters 8 and 9, must proceed against the backdrop of the complementarity of the institutional ability and legitimacy of the Court and of State authorities.[9]

Thus, we must briefly reconsider the value and justification of inter-institutional collaboration. In Chapter 4, we discussed relative strengths and weaknesses of judicial and political decision-making. We saw, first, that rights determinations made by elected political, and especially parliamentary, bodies enjoy higher democratic legitimacy than do those of the (especially international) judiciary. This superior legitimacy is grounded in political equality and electoral accountability characteristic of democratic politics. In principle, the political view of rights is more representative and results from a more participatory process than the judicial one. By contrast, the judicial process may play a valuable role in preventing or mitigating majoritarian pathologies, for example the unjustified disregard of the interests of individuals belonging to minority or otherwise vulnerable groups. More generally, the political and the judicial processes vary in terms of their opportunity structures. Some individuals and groups may have advantages in the political process, others in the legal process; some may have better chances to obtain what they seek to obtain in political forums, while others are better off in the judicial system. In this regard, issues of access play a role, but there are also epistemological (dis)advantages, different styles and modes of reasoning, and other sorts of institutional and procedural strengths and weaknesses that matter, including the counter-majoritarian function of judicial review. All of this suggests that legal and political decision-making about rights ought to be combined when a political community decides about rights and their limitations.

8 See Julian Rivers, 'Proportionality and Variable Intensity of Review' (2006) 65(1) CLJ 174, 182.

9 See ibid 175–176.

When we looked at some particularities of the Strasbourg Court *qua* international court, we discovered additional epistemic and normative arguments that speak in favour of (conditional) judicial deference and restraint. For one, the Court is temporally and spatially distant from the facts on the ground, including the domestic law and procedure applicable in a given case. Moreover, as we saw in Chapter 7, the specification of human rights has a relational, political, and social component, insofar as rights are based on (political) equality, which links them inextricably to democracy—to a political community's collective self-determination—and thus to a democratic polity, which the Court is not a part of, as we saw in Chapters 6 and 8. As the Court has repeatedly held, its subsidiary role is explicable by the general recognition that the national authorities are, 'by reason of their direct and continuous contact with the vital forces of their countries', better placed than itself 'to evaluate local needs and conditions'.[10]

The Court has regularly applied deference and restraint on the basis of the grounds just mentioned, and hence rightly so. This contrasts with, and essentially disproves, George Letsas' account of the Convention system:[11] it is neither descriptively nor normatively right to claim that it is the exclusive preserve of the Court to identify, specify, and defend absolute (ie unqualified), rights against the States *qua* majoritarian-tyrannical policy-makers. The Court confirms this non-absoluteness of all Convention rights when it holds that '[t]he search for [a fair] balance is inherent in the whole of the Convention'.[12] In reality and contrary to the widespread idea that there are at least some Convention rights that are absolute and impervious to any proportionality reasoning, the Court's practice subjects even so-called absolute or strictly inviolable rights to evaluative processes that involve the weighing of all relevant considerations. The Court does so, for example, to determine whether certain circumstances meet the 'minimum level of severity' that is required under Article 3, which prohibits torture and other inhuman or degrading treatment, or what amounts to an 'unfairness' in the sense of the procedural guarantees contained in Article 6 of the Convention.[13] Indeed, contrary to widespread beliefs, the Court applies deference and, sometimes, explicitly grants a respondent State a margin of appreciation even in cases under Article 3 of the Convention.[14]

Human rights, whose protective effect depends, in practice, on proportionality considerations, such as those guaranteed in the Convention, are thus *always* political in some sense: as we saw in Chapter 7, they must depend, to some degree,

[10] See eg *Dubská and Krejzová v the Czech Republic* [GC], nos 28859/11 and 28473/12, para 117, 15 November 2016.

[11] See Chapter 7.

[12] *Sporrong and Lönnroth v Sweden*, 23 September 1982, para 69, Series A no 52.

[13] See Steven Greer, 'Should Police Threats to Torture Suspects Always Be Severely Punished? Reflections on the Gäfgen Case' (2011) 11(1) HRLR 67, 79–80.

[14] See eg *HA and HA v Norway* (dec), no 56167/16, para 35, 3 January 2017.

not only on considerations concerning the moral worth of their individual bearer, but also on considerations of a utilitarian and communitarian sort. Perhaps this becomes clearest when we consider why the deliberate use of lethal firearms for purposes of self-defence and/or in order to rescue third persons, such as hostages, may be permissible, in very exceptional circumstances,[15] while it is never permissible to engage in even only minor conduct contrary to Article 3 of the Convention; as the example of the case of *Gäfgen* shows, it already amounts to a violation of the Convention to merely threaten a child abductor with treatment contrary to Article 3 of the Convention, in order to try to save the lives of innocent others.[16] In the former situation, viz when a hostage-taker is targetedly killed, this occurs in circumstances of relatively great clarity and certainty: the hostage-taker is clearly identified, the danger he poses is imminent and certain, the measure to be taken is as clear as it is consequential and the action (if properly executed[17]) is quite certain to be suitable and effective. By contrast, it is highly improbable that these conditions will ever pertain to the same degree in scenarios involving ticking bombs or abduction as in *Gäfgen*. In such cases, great doubts are likely to surface about issues such as the responsibility and knowledge of the suspected individual who is in police custody, the usefulness of inflicting harm upon him, and the imminence of the danger posed by the presumed bomb or the condition of the abducted person.[18] The risk of a slippery slope is therefore considerable here: allowing methods of interrogative torture may very well open floodgates that are best kept closed. Thus, the latter, but not the former, practice is subject to uncertainties that would inevitably undermine the rule of law in a way that is simply unacceptable to a society committed to certain civilizational values and interested in social peace and relations of trust between citizens and public authorities. This means we may explain and justify the stricter prohibition of torture than of exceptional targeted killings better with societal considerations than with arguments relating to isolated individual interests. It is therefore important to bear in mind that rights, especially if their protection depends on proportionality considerations as is basically always the case in the Convention system, are always matters that concern society as a whole and, hence, matters also for politics.

Finally, to approach the question how the Court should interact with and take into account the views of the States' political authorities in its assessment of a case by means of a proportionality analysis so as to respect their democratic functions, it is important to understand the multiple tiers in the Court's proportionality analysis, viz the analysis' sequential stages and their different characters. Rivers, for example, suggests that these different characters of the sequential test stages call for

[15] See eg *Ramsahai and Others v the Netherlands* [GC], no 52391/99, ECHR 2007-II.

[16] See *Gäfgen v Germany* [GC], no 22978/05, ECHR 2010.

[17] cf *McCann and Others v the United Kingdom*, 27 September 1995, Series A no 324.

[18] See also Sherry F Colb, 'Why Is Torture "Different" and How "Different" Is It?' (2009) 30(4) Cardozo L Rev 1411, 1464–1467.

different standards of review, because they may allow for, demand, and proscribe deference and restraint on different grounds.[19] We therefore treat the question of how the Court should apply variable standards of review in a way that facilitates its inter-institutional interaction with the national political authorities that the Convention's subsidiarity principle demands according to and in the order of the steps involved in the Court's multi-tiered proportionality assessment.

Our discussion begins with the legality requirement of a rights restriction (ie its legal basis), continues with the question of whether the contested measure pursues a legitimate aim, and proceeds to the question whether this measure is 'necessary' for the pursuit of the legitimate aim. Although the first two stages of the Court's test cascade are important, in most cases, the Court's review heavily centres around the third stage. This last stage of the Court's assessment itself also takes the form of a (rather obscure) multi-tiered test. Contrary to its abbreviated denomination as a 'necessity test', it usually turns less on empirical causality than on the normative counter-balancing of competing interests. Hence, in the Court's language, the test concerns whether a measure is necessary 'in a democratic society'. The final qualifier, referring to the normative concept 'democracy', brings the test's normativity to the fore. Finally, we will raise the question of whether the Convention law imposes such absolute or categorical limits on the limitation of rights, which the Court must strictly enforce no matter what.

C) Legality: link between rights and democracy

The Court, after its interpretative reading of an allegedly infringed Convention right has established that the alleged rights restriction did indeed infringe on the right invoked by the applicant, first examines whether the impugned measure is grounded in a legal basis of sufficient quality.[20] As previous chapters suggest, this test ensures that any measure affecting an individual's status as a morally equal member of the political community has a basis in democratically made law. The legality requirement of rights infringements epitomizes the important link between rights and democracy. Rights must be specified—granted and taken away—through a reciprocal process that plays out between individuals who are respected as equal moral reasoners, individuals who are equally knowledgeable about their individual and societal interests. Rights are constitutive of this equality: they enable it by giving everyone a fundamentally equal chance to participate in this reciprocal process of rights reasoning, which is why the members of a democratic polity must grant each other their rights on a reciprocal basis, as we noted in Chapter 8. Thus, rights limitations *qua* rights specifications must be rooted in a democratic

[19] Rivers (n 8) 195–206.
[20] See eg *Del Río Prada v Spain* [GC], no 42750/09, para 125, ECHR 2013.

process and be based on generally and equally applicable rules that are formulated in such a way as to allow all individuals to direct their conduct in accordance with these rules.

Indeed, past practice has shown that the Court's finding of a Convention violation on the ground of its lacking a proper legal basis may spur democratic debate and law-making. For example, in Switzerland, the Court's finding of the lack of a legal basis for the surveillance of social-insurance recipients by private investigators in *Vukota-Bojić* led to legislative amendments that were subject to considerable public debate, and eventually even a popular referendum on the new law.[21]

Beware, however, from overstretching the legality requirement. First, what matters is not that every rights infringement is based on parliamentary law, but that every rights infringement has its roots in the responsible State's democratic process, in generally and equally applicable rules originating from its democratic institutions.[22] This is also the case, for example, when a measure's direct legal basis is a duly-made executive decree, case law, or even a private regulation based on proper parliamentary delegation or incorporation of that rule.[23]

Second, the Court *qua* a subsidiary international judicial body with a limited mandate is not a further court of appeal. Thus, it ignores—and rightly so—possible errors of law (and fact) that have occurred domestically unless they raise issues of rights. This so-called 'fourth-instance doctrine', whose name refers to what the Court is not, corresponds to the Convention's subsidiarity principle: as we argued in Chapter 8, the Convention system operates in such a way as to assist and support the States only in cases where rights, viz issues that affect everyone's equal moral status, are at stake.[24] Where an applicant is simply not content with the outcome of the domestic proceedings, this does not mean that he or she was not respected as a moral equal. Everyone has a right to have his or her rights claims—his or her claimed spheres of individual freedom—taken seriously, but there is no general right to have these claims recognized and protected: the legality requirement serves to implement this two-tiered principle.

However, because equal moral status demands that everyone's autonomous choices meet with equal respect in this sense, the Court is justified in intervening when a domestic error of law (or fact) amounts to nothing less than arbitrariness.[25] Arbitrary exercises of public power make it impossible to direct one's free will rationally according to foreseeable consequences.[26] It deprives individuals

[21] *Vukota-Bojić v Switzerland*, no 61838/10, 18 October 2016; Amendments of 16 March 2018 on the Federal Act on General Aspects of Social Security Law, Official Compilation 2019 2829.

[22] See also Geranne Lautenbach, *The Concept of the Rule of Law and the European Court of Human Rights* (OUP 2013) 43, 85, 112–113.

[23] See eg *De Wilde, Ooms and Versyp v Belgium*, 18 June 1971, para 93, Series A no 12; *Kafkaris v Cyprus* [GC], no 21906/04, para 139, ECHR 2008.

[24] See eg *Perlala v Greece*, no 17721/04, para 25, 22 February 2007.

[25] See eg *Khlaifia and Others v Italy* [GC], no 16483/12, para 91, 15 December 2016.

[26] See eg *M v Germany*, no 19359/04, para 90, ECHR 2009.

of 'the chance to exercise their free will to choose rightly or wrongly', to choose to act within or against the legitimate law.[27] Arbitrariness therefore undermines the—normative-equality-generating—principled presumption that everyone is a rational, self-determined individual.[28] The same problem affects laws that have retroactive effect, as Article 7 (No punishment without law) of the Convention makes clear,[29] and policies of preventively detaining '*Gefährder*' (individuals suspected of being dangerous) on the basis of heteronomously ascribed future choices, that is, relatively low-threshold suspicions about what they might do in the future, which are incompatible with Article 5 (Right to liberty and security) of the Convention.[30]

As just noted, the Court's legality control is limited in scope. Another question concerns the strictness of this control. Since the principle of legality's requirements concern, first and foremost, the generality and equality of the law that provides a basis for a rights infringement, it raises a predominantly formal legal question. The Court is thus well suited to complement the States' law-appliers in maintaining these prerequisites of their domestic liberal democracies. While it must take account of the States' different legal systems, which may equally satisfy these requirements, there is no reason why it should apply restraint in its assessment of the question whether a contested measure satisfies the legality requirement. This is neither a policy question nor a question about the substantive content of the domestic law.[31] Geranne Lautenbach is right, therefore, when she admonishes the Court's aberrations in cases where it assesses the legality requirement only in a toned-down manner as part of an overall proportionality assessment. As she observes, 'legality provides a formal guideline for the manner in which human rights may be restricted', which has nothing to do with the question whether a rights restriction stands in a reasonable relation to the legitimate aim pursued.[32]

Because no pertinent considerations of legitimate authority, related to democracy and procedure, appear relevant here, there is, as explained, no reason for judicial *restraint* on the part of the Court at the legality stage of its assessment. Note, however, that this will generally be different when it is not the assessment of the fulfilment of the legality standard in the individual case that is at issue, but rather the interpretative question concerning what exactly this rule-of-law requirement implies: as we discussed in previous chapters, standards of Convention law have been, and continue to be, developed from the bottom up, which ensures their necessary democratic legitimacy. Further, the absence of grounds calling for judicial

[27] See Alec Walen, 'A Unified Theory of Detention, with Application to Preventive Detention for Suspected Terrorists' (2011) 70(4) Mar L Rev 871, 881.
[28] See Chapter 5.
[29] See eg *Kononov v Latvia* [GC], no 36376/04, para 185, ECHR 2010.
[30] See eg *Ostendorf v Germany*, no 15598/08, para 66, 7 March 2013.
[31] Lautenbach (n 22) 116, 122.
[32] ibid 117–118.

restraint does not mean that there are no reasons for judicial *deference* on the part of the Court. Deference, which is owed as the result of differences in institutional competence, knowledge, and expertise,[33] may be owed here to the extent to which the Court must rely on the domestic authorities' superior understanding of domestic law and of the domestic legal system. It cannot be expert in forty-six (forty-seven, if we count the European Union, or even more, if we consider some States' federal structure[34]) legal systems.[35] This finally leads to the substantive latitude, the *normative flexibility*, inherent in the legality requirement (and other Convention standards) which is due to, and necessary because of, these several dozen different legal systems that may ensure equally, but in different ways, the Convention's standards of legality, among other things.

D) Legitimate aims: purposes of a democratic community

Any restriction of rights—even if it is grounded in duly-made law—must have a legitimate purpose, lest it be 'patently unreasonable'.[36] In the Convention system, rights that are subject to permissible infringements at all may be justifiably limited only in the pursuit of a 'legitimate aim'. This is evident in those cases where the Convention's rights clauses are accompanied by express limitation clauses listing what counts as legitimate aims (especially Articles 2 and 8–11), but a similar logic applies to most other rights,[37] for example those protected in Articles 1–3 of Protocol No 1, relating to property, education, and elections.[38] Similarly, in the context of Article 12 of the Convention, the Court has observed: '[t]he Convention institutions have accepted that limitations on the right to marry laid down in the national laws may comprise formal rules, but also substantive provisions based on generally recognised considerations of public interest, in particular concerning capacity'.[39]

According to the Court itself, its 'practice is to be quite succinct when it verifies the existence of a legitimate aim',[40] and it only rarely finds that a State did not pursue a legitimate interest with a contested rights limitation. The Court's principle that it 'will respect the legislature's judgment as to what is "in the public interest", unless that judgment is manifestly without reasonable foundation',[41] deserves support.

[33] See Rivers (n 8) 177.
[34] See eg *Bosphorus Hava Yolları Turizm ve Ticaret Anonim Şirketi v Ireland* [GC], no 45036/98, para 143, ECHR 2005-VI.
[35] See eg *Winterwerp v the Netherlands*, 24 October 1979, paras 45–46, Series A no 33.
[36] Rivers (n 8) 195.
[37] See also Janneke Gerards, 'How to Improve the Necessity Test of the European Court of Human Rights' (2013) 11(2) I•CON 466, 466–467.
[38] Protocol to the Convention for the Protection of Human Rights and Fundamental Freedoms of 20 March 1952, in force since 18 May 1954, CETS No 009.
[39] *Delecolle v France*, no 37646/13, para 52, 25 October 2018.
[40] *SAS v France* [GC], no 43835/11, para 114, ECHR 2014 (extracts).
[41] *Jahn and Others v Germany* [GC], nos 46720/99 and 2 others, para 91, ECHR 2005-VI.

As the Court rightly notes, 'the notion of "public interest" is necessarily extensive [and] will commonly involve consideration of political, economic and social issues'.[42] This jurisprudence is in line with the present account of the Court's subsidiary role: the choice of a democratic polity's public interests ultimately concerns the purposes of that community and is, therefore, an inherently political question falling within the scope of the polity's political institutions, unless an alleged 'legitimate aim' falls manifestly outside of those broad interests that the States *qua demoi*-cratic makers of the international Convention law laid down as legitimate grounds for rights restrictions.

It is important to be clear about the reach of public interest considerations. Although there are 'absolute' rights which may not be directly limited in the pursuit of public interests, there are, frankly, no rights that are specified—and hence (de)limited—without having some regard for societal, public interest, considerations. As our earlier discussion of the *Gäfgen* case illustrated, *all* rights may be 'subject to limitations in the broad sense'.[43]

The notion that (unqualified) rights raise absolute barriers to 'the State'—whether the government, the democratic majority, the public, or another more or less diffuse entity with collective interests, needs, and sentiments—is hardly tenable given the public dimension of the justification of rights, which we discussed in Chapters 7 and 8. Indeed, public interest considerations are quite ubiquitous in the Court's practice, even in cases concerning rights clauses that do not follow the approach, known from Articles 8–11 of the Convention, of explicitly juxtaposing an individual's protected interest (ie right) against other rights and interests. However, since the determination of public interests is primarily a matter for a democratic polity's political institutions, 'the State' and its political authorities must play an important role alongside the Court in the case-based specification-by-limitation of virtually all Convention rights. As the following discussion shows, the Court's review of the aims pursued by a State through a rights restriction generally corresponds to this; we argue, however, that the Court should adopt a consistent practice of examining the pursued aim in the context of the contested measure, rather than examining it in the abstract.

a) Broad notions, succinct review

The Court's practice of 'succinctness' in assessing the presence of a legitimate aim appears to be generally justified in light of what we have just said. The determination of a polity's common interests should be left to the democratic process unless an alleged 'legitimate aim' falls manifestly outside the interests explicitly

[42] ibid.
[43] Stefan Sottiaux, *Terrorism and the Limitation of Rights* (Hart 2008) 40–41.

allowed for under a certain Convention right or, where there are no explicit limitation clauses, outside those interests that are reasonably compatible with the Convention's liberal-democratic programme. In addition to this ground for judicial restraint, there are also reasons for deference on the part of the Court: the determination of a society's common interests depends on a wide range of essentially non-legal considerations and circumstances which the domestic (political) authorities are better placed to identify and assess.

The uncountable public interests that a State may wish to pursue may explain and justify the very vague formulations of the legitimate aims included in Articles 8–11 of the Convention, as well as the absence of jurisprudence that significantly concretizes these formulations. As the Court once noted, '[p]luralism and democracy are based on a compromise that requires various concessions by individuals or groups of individuals, who must sometimes agree to limit some of the freedoms they enjoy in order to guarantee greater stability of the country as a whole'.[44] As we saw in Chapter 7, the States' political forums are more suited than the Court is to negotiating these compromises and deciding the concessions everyone must make in the first place.

This argument in favour of lenient review does not, however, entail that everything goes. It is clear that there are rights restrictions that are outrightly unreasonable, because they are incapable of being connected to legitimate aims in any way.[45] Perhaps no other of the Court's recent judgments shows this better than *Bayev*, which concerned Russian 'anti-homosexuality' laws that outlawed the 'promotion of homosexuality', for example protests for their rights by gay rights activists, among minors.[46] There, the government's argumentation was not only rationally implausible and self-contradictory—as well as devoid of any objective, scientific evidentiary basis—it was also in contradiction with European standards upon which the States have long converged.[47] Most importantly, however, by rejecting the Russian government's argumentation, the Court defended the principle that everyone should be allowed to publicly demand the protection of their interests *qua* rights that express the equal moral status of all. The measures at stake in *Bayev* sought to curtail precisely this basic right, by publicly denigrating certain individuals and denying them the opportunity to stand up for their moral equality.

The Court's lenient review of the public interests that a State pursues when restricting a Convention guarantee, albeit generally worthy of support, is often too indulgent in one respect. Unfortunately, the Court has not established a routine

[44] *Refah Partisi (the Welfare Party) and Others v Turkey* [GC], nos 41340/98 and 3 others, para 99, ECHR 2003-II.

[45] cf Rivers (n 8) 198.

[46] *Bayev and Others v Russia*, nos 67667/09 and 2 others, 20 June 2017.

[47] See Parliamentary Assembly, 'Resolution "Tackling Discrimination on the Grounds of Sexual Orientation and Gender Identity"' (27 June 2013, 26th Sitting, Res 1948 (2013)); Committee of Ministers, 'Recommendation to Member States on Measures to Combat Discrimination on Grounds of Sexual Orientation or Gender Identity' (31 March 2010, 1081st Mtg, CM/Rec(2010)5).

practice of including in its assessment a distinct analysis of a measure's suitability for achieving the end it is intended to realize.[48] This is a problem, since the Court's examination of a public interest pursued with a contested measure in light of this specific measure may contribute to a better understanding of a State's policy as a whole. As we can see on the example of the *Bayev* case, this analysis may be important to expose an aim as illegitimate: the aims advanced by the Russian government—the protection of public morals, health, and the rights of others—are legitimate, of course, but when looking at them in the context of the contested measures it quickly becomes clear that the proposed understanding of 'public morals' was fused with homophobic bias, that the protection of 'health' was understood as requiring combating homosexuality, and that the protection of the rights of others was considered as necessitating the protection of minors from 'positive presentations' of homosexuality.[49] Thus, the actual object pursued by a contested measure can only be understood when considering the way in which the measure is suitable or capable of contributing to effectuating change.

That is, for the Court, the question really must be whether a public interest as specified by a given policy choice is legitimate.[50] This may also be important in cases when the domestic policy-makers merely have failed without bad intentions to consider their actual aim and the measures adopted to realize this with sufficient care. Even a restrained and deferential assessment of the interconnected legitimate aim and suitability tests may suffice not only to weed out manifestly illegitimate aims, but also to identify policies that, although adopted in good faith, are manifestly unsuitable to achieve what that State actually hopes to achieve.[51]

b) Prohibition of bad-faith restrictions of rights

Given their social, relational, and political character, rights may justifiably be limited in the pursuit of a wide range of policies. It is important, however, that this occurs via a democratic process, as explained earlier. Having established, and acceded to, the Council of Europe and the Convention, the States 'decidedly rejected undemocratic forms of government',[52] such that 'democracy is the only political model contemplated by the Convention and, accordingly, the only one compatible with it'.[53] This excludes, most importantly, the dishonest, insincere, and pretextual limitation of rights which is obviously at odds with the requirement that rights

[48] Gerards, 'Necessity Test' (n 37) 471.
[49] See *Bayev v Russia* (n 46) paras 65–82.
[50] Rivers (n 8) 197.
[51] See eg *Bartik v Russia*, no 55565/00, para 49, ECHR 2006-XV.
[52] Helen Keller and Corina Heri, 'Selective Criminal Proceedings and Article 18 ECHR: The European Court of Human Rights' Untapped Potential to Protect Democracy' (2016) 36 HRLJ 1, 1.
[53] *United Communist Party of Turkey and Others v Turkey* [GC], 30 January 1998, para 45, Reports of Judgments and Decisions 1998-I.

are specified and delimited in a mutual process: 'ulterior purposes' and 'hidden agendas'[54] behind the limitation of rights fundamentally contradict democratic decision-making standards of equal participation, publicness, accessibility, etc.[55]

Such bad-faith restrictions of rights are prohibited by Article 18 of the Convention. This provision is meant to secure 'against undemocratic tendencies posing as legitimate rights restrictions which would, if uncontested, undermine and erode both human rights protections and the foundational principles of democracy'.[56] That is, Article 18 seeks to prevent the abuse of rights restrictions for political purposes, namely, in order to secure one's hold on power, such as when a ban on someone's right to political contestation is sought.[57]

Article 18 highlights the particular danger posed to liberal democracy by the deceitful limitation of rights on the basis of a feigned 'legitimate aim'. It goes without saying that, in this situation, there is no reason for judicial restraint on the part of the Court.[58] Quite to the contrary, a government's deceitful limitation of the rights of the individuals under its jurisdiction is blatantly undemocratic and illegitimate. To use the terminology of Ronald Dworkin again,[59] it inevitably happens that governments limit rights by mistake without having legitimate grounds, but when they intentionally limit rights on illegitimate grounds and seek to cover this up with pretextual, only superficially legitimate grounds, this is no mere mistake but displays utter contempt for the principle of political equality. It is urgent, then, for the Convention system to intervene and contribute to sustaining (or restoring) the domestic democratic process upon which rights depend.[60]

Still, there may be reasons for judicial deference, insofar as it may be difficult to ascertain with the Court's institutional competences whether a rights limitation has occurred in bad faith contrary to Article 18. Given that Article 18 violation judgments amount to serious accusations against the responsible State authorities[61]—quite apart from alleged risks of double-standards[62]—there are good reasons for the Court to tread carefully in the deployment of this provision.[63] The Court should carefully scrutinize cases where the circumstances make a violation of Article 18 plausible, but also make a violation judgment dependent on a

[54] See *Rasul Jafarov v Azerbaijan*, no 69981/14, para 153, 17 March 2016.

[55] Generally eg Lon L Fuller, *The Morality of Law* (rev edn, Yale University Press 1969) 46–96.

[56] Corina Heri, 'Loyalty, Subsidiarity, and Article 18 ECHR: How the ECtHR Deals with Mala Fide Limitations of Rights' (2020) 1(1) ECHR L Rev 25, 26.

[57] See eg *Selahattin Demirtaş v Turkey (no 2)* [GC], no 14305/17, 22 December 2020.

[58] Andrei Mamolea, 'Good Faith Review' in L Gruszczynski and W Werner (eds), *Deference in International Courts and Tribunals* (OUP 2014) 75.

[59] See Chapter 8.

[60] See Floris Tan, 'The Dawn of Article 18 ECHR: A Safeguard Against European Rule of Law Backsliding?' (2018) 9(1) GJIL 109, 120–121.

[61] See also *Khodorkovskiy v Russia*, no 5829/04, para 260, 31 May 2011.

[62] See Başak Çali, 'From Flexible to Variable Standards of Judicial Review: The Responsible Domestic Courts Doctrine at the European Court of Human Rights' in OM Árnardóttir and A Buyse (eds), *Shifting Centres of Gravity in Human Rights Protection* (Routledge 2016) 270–271.

[63] Heri (n 56) 55.

high standard of proof. This standard, however, must not exclude the possibility of (partly) shifting the burden of proof for procedural reasons onto the government, once sufficient doubts exist about a measure's good-faith motivations.[64] In sum, while the choice of a political community's interests must remain its own, the Court's role is to control for rights restrictions that in fact serve a government's ulterior purposes, or that are erroneous or misguided because they are clearly unsuited to achieving their ends.

E) Necessary in a democratic society

It is the point and purpose of rights that the interests they protect generally 'trump' legitimate interests of others or society as a whole that are not protected *qua* rights. As an exception to this rule, a rights infringement, even if it is duly grounded in the law and pursues a legitimate aim, is only justified and permissible if it stands in a relationship of a certain quality with the legitimate aim it pursues: the end of a right's restriction must outweigh the right upon which it infringes. Thus, while the first stage of the Court's proportionality assessment focusses on the contested measure (ie the infringement of a right) and the second stage's focus is on the public interest pursued (ie the legitimate aim), during the third and final stage, the Court's focus is on the quality of the relationship between the means and the end.

a) Rhetorical device rather than framework for dialogue

According to Convention law, for a rights restriction to be permissible, the relationship between the means and the end must be such that we can say the contested policy is 'necessary in a democratic society'. A democratic society is, according to the Court, a society marked by 'pluralism, tolerance and broadmindedness', viz a society ready to accept a plurality of diverse individual exercises of liberal rights. This mirrors the liberal—freedom-promoting—commitment of a liberal-democratic polity: restrictions on individual exercises of freedom must be limited to what is necessary for the collective to remain viable as a democratic polity that optimizes its individual members' freedom. This is not simply an empirical question as 'necessity' might suggest, but instead requires that a rights infringement correspond to a need that is 'pressing' within the societal context ('pressing social need') of a pluralistic, tolerant, and broadminded democracy, as the Court has usually put it. To prove this 'imperativeness', a respondent State must furnish reasons that are 'relevant' and 'sufficient'.[65]

[64] See Keller and Heri (n 52) 8–9.

[65] See eg *Handyside v the United Kingdom*, 7 December 1976, paras 48–50, Series A no 24; *Young, James and Webster v the United Kingdom*, 13 August 1981, para 63, Series A no 44.

Unfortunately, the Court's terminology is quite vacuous. In particular, it has remained unclear whether 'pressing social need' refers to the importance of the legitimate aim (end) pursued with the contested measure (means) or to that means' effectiveness.[66] If the latter, this would mean that the contested policy must be pressing due to the significant contribution it makes to achieving the end, which, albeit certainly legitimate, would not necessarily have to be highly important. For example, in the *Vavřička* judgment, the relevant paragraphs leave the reader confused about whether the Court deals with the policy aim's (protection of individual and public health) particular importance or the policy measure's (duty of vaccination against contagious diseases) effectiveness: the Court, concluding that there is a pressing social need to protect individual and public health (end) and to preserve a high vaccination rate (means), which obviously must not be an end in itself, vacillates between relating the imperativeness requirement to the end and to the means, respectively.[67] If the imperativeness related to the contested measure and its effectiveness, this would be reminiscent of the well-known requirement of constitutional law that only a least rights-restrictive—viz so to say, pressing *qua* most effective—means is permissible to achieve a certain end. However, this would not correspond to the Court's—justified, as we will soon see—common practice[68] of abstaining from requiring that a State adopt the least restrictive means to achieve a certain end.[69]

Moreover, the clarity of the necessity requirement also suffers from its conflation with the outrightly normative juxtaposition of the means and ends, which is aimed at balancing an impugned measure's costs and benefits in order to assess whether it is proportionate *stricto sensu*. Just like the requirement for a 'pressing' social need, the proportionality *stricto sensu*, or fair balance, test brings an evaluative element into the Court's assessment, which, in raising questions less of law than of political morality, is more valuative than legal in nature.[70] As Luzius Wildhaber, the first president of the permanent Court, and his co-authors, Arnaldur Hjartarson and Stephen Donnelly, observed, the Court's judgments are for a good part 'expressions of underlying value judgments and philosophies', including about institutional issues relating to the separation of powers,[71] rendered by judges who 'act like political theorists'.[72] The widespread reference to systems of rights-based review

[66] See Gerards, 'Necessity Test' (n 37) 467, 482.

[67] *Vavřička and Others v the Czech Republic* [GC], nos 47621/13 and 5 others, paras 281–284, 8 April 2021.

[68] See eg *National Union of Rail, Maritime and Transport Workers v the United Kingdom*, no 31045/10, para 103, ECHR 2014.

[69] See Eva Brems and Laurens Lavrysen, '"Don't Use a Sledgehammer to Crack a Nut": Less Restrictive Means in the Case Law of the European Court of Human Rights' (2015) 15(1) HRLR 139, 166.

[70] See John G Merrills, *The Development of International Law by the European Court of Human Rights* (Manchester University Press 1988) 149.

[71] Luzius Wildhaber, Arnaldur Hjartarson, and Stephen Donnelly, 'No Consensus on Consensus? The Practice of the European Court of Human Rights' (2013) 33(7–12) HRLJ 248, 252.

[72] David Robertson, *The Judge as Political Theorist* (Princeton University Press 2010) 348.

as systems of constitutional justice testifies to this idea that rights lie at the heart of just modern polities.[73]

The Court's approach to the necessity test is rather confused, as just explained: it applies, in an inconsistent and hard-to-comprehend manner, three different yardsticks— 'pressing social need', 'relevant and sufficient reasons', and 'proportionality' and 'fair balance'—under the formula 'necessary in a democratic society'. In particular, the Court does not strictly distinguish between a means–ends analysis concerned with empirical questions of the necessity of the contested measure with regard to the pursuit of the legitimate aim, on the one hand, and a proportionality analysis *stricto sensu* concerned with the normative balancing of the interests harmed against the interests served, on the other. Regrettably, as Eva Brems and Laurens Lavrysen accurately note, the Court, instead of applying a clear, multiple-tiered 'German tradition-like proportionality test', has traditionally undertaken a haphazard balancing exercise.[74]

What is more, looking for an explanation for the Court's fickle necessary-in-a-democracy test, one naturally comes to think about its practice of varying its scrutiny by means of granting a more or less wide 'margin of appreciation'. This, however, is just another infamous source of confusion. Over the decades, the Court's margin-of-appreciation practice has produced a difficult-to-comprehend doctrine, hardly worth this label,[75] that purports to complement—and specifically to calibrate the strictness of—the Court's review, yet that is barely distinguishable from the balancing exercise itself,[76] with the result that its effects are scarcely determinable.[77] It is therefore not clear whether the inconsistencies in the Court's necessary-in-a-democracy test are actually a function of the Court's varied standards of review, resulting from its margin-of-appreciation 'doctrine'.

In short, the Court's margin-imbued proportionality exercise frequently appears rather as a hotchpotch of various considerations that bear on the case and may legitimize the desired outcome than as a well-structured, coherent analysis. Angelika Nußberger, a former vice-president of the Court, describes this quite frankly, when she admits that proportionality decisions 'depend on personal preferences ... the Court has elaborated lists of factors to be taken into account ... Nevertheless, as potential human rights conflicts are too varied to bring them all under similar schemes, in most areas balancing will remain a free-hand exercise'.[78]

We may thus conclude with Janneke Gerards' observation that 'the test of necessity in a democratic society seems to be more important as a rhetorical device

[73] See Stone Sweet and Mathews (n 6) 10–12, 31.
[74] Brems and Lavrysen (n 69) 140.
[75] See Angelika Nußberger, *The European Court of Human Rights* (OUP 2020) 88.
[76] See eg Yutaka Arai-Takahashi, *The Margin of Appreciation Doctrine and the Principle of Proportionality in the Jurisprudence of the ECHR* (Intersentia 2002) 14.
[77] See eg Janneke Gerards, 'Margin of Appreciation and Incrementalism in the Case Law of the European Court of Human Rights' (2018) 18(3) HRLR 495, 504–505.
[78] Nußberger (n 75) 97.

than as an instrument that can help the Court to structure its argumentation'.[79] This lack of conceptual clarity and orderly structure is problematic, given that the proportionality analysis is supposed to provide the common justificatory framework that structures the inter-institutional discursive construction of Convention rights and their permissible limitation.[80] As Gerards, too, notes,[81] without a clear justificatory framework, there is significant risk that the domestic authorities and the Court talk past each other. This would frustrate any meaningful dialogue about rights.

b) Means–end relationship: reasonableness control

The discussion so far has raised the questions of, first, how the Court's assessment should be structured and, second, what review standards it should involve, so as to facilitate the specification of the Convention rights in a discursive process between the States and the Court, as demanded by the subsidiarity principle.

For the following discussion, it is important, once again, to be clear about the Court's 'necessary in a democratic society' test's confusion of causal means–end considerations and normative balancing exercises. The former puts a means in relation to the ends pursued with it, the latter weighs interests harmed (the infringed right) against interests served (the legitimate aim pursued). Means–end tests thus centre on empirical and factual questions concerning the adopted measure's effectiveness, in terms of its contribution to achieving the ends pursued by it. Proportionality balancing, by contrast, is a matter of value judgment.

It is crucial that the normative balancing assessment is not used to forgo the enquiry into the means–end relation. It would of course be possible to weigh the competing values—for example, individual self-determination about medical interventions and public health—*in abstracto* and come to the conclusion that one value is weightier than the other without having regard to the specific measure employed to promote the one value at the cost of the other. However, this approach risks overlooking a problem in the means–end relationship. The aim pursued may, in certain cases, only be properly understood in light of the measure adopted, as we saw above on the example of *Bayev*. Further, it may be the case that an enquiry into the means–end relation would reveal ways to circumvent the trade-off between the two independently valuable interests at stake.[82] The proportionality framework used to specify the Convention rights and their permissible restrictions must not, therefore, be taken to allow an exclusive focus on the balancing of the competing

[79] Gerards, 'Necessity Test' (n 37) 468.
[80] cf Rivers (n 8) 195.
[81] Gerards, 'Necessity Test' (n 37) 468.
[82] See ibid 471.

rights and interests. An enquiry into the means–end relationship must also be obligatory on the part of the Court.

This leads us to the question of what scrutiny the Court should apply to assess means–end relationships. Essentially, the decision must fall somewhere between whether the Court should only check that a contested measure can be taken reasonably to contribute to the pursued aim, or whether it should undertake a more stringent test, so as to examine whether the contested measure is necessary *qua* indispensable, because there are no other measures that would suffice to achieve the legitimate aim pursued. Note that even the former, more lenient type of assessment must include a 'non-restrictive means test' since, of course, no right must be limited in order to achieve a goal that could be achieved without such a limitation.[83]

To answer the question about the scrutiny properly applied by the Court, it is important to understand the normative judgment that 'tacitly' inheres in the otherwise empirical means–end test: what the end, that is, the policy aim, is and to what degree of satisfaction it shall be pursued requires the making of political choices, viz political value judgments. Thus, if the Court applied a stringent test, it would need a precise understanding of the end, including the desired degree of satisfaction, to which the means should lead. Otherwise, it could not determine whether there are equally effective, but less costly, alternative means available.[84] As the determination of the public interest is a predominantly political task that involves the making of a choice in light of a factual analysis of the prevailing circumstances, as we noted above, this consideration cautions against strict scrutiny on the part of the Court. The outcome of a least-restrictive-means test, in particular, inevitably depends on the assessor's understanding of the aim and proceeds, on this basis, to determine quite specifically the means that must be adopted in order to pursue that end, namely, *the* least restrictive but still sufficiently effective[85] means.[86] The latter determination is, at bottom, an empirical issue usually afflicted by considerable uncertainty, which policy-making bodies are better placed than courts to answer.[87]

In short, a least-restrictive-means test involves a number of complexities, including normative political choices, although, theoretically speaking, it has an objective empirical and factual nature. If the Court were to apply a least-restrictive-means test, it would therefore risk not only deciding issues on which it has less expertise than the domestic authorities have but also substituting its own policy assessment for the States' policy choices in a fairly intrusive manner. This would run contrary to the Convention's character as a document laying out legal minimum standards, which Chapter 8 expressed in Dworkin's terms as not proscribing parochial human rights specifications that are merely unconvincing on a certain

[83] See Gardbaum, 'Limiting' (n 5) 849.
[84] See Gerards, 'Necessity Test' (n 37) 474–475.
[85] See eg *Ashingdane v the United Kingdom*, 28 May 1985, Series A no 93.
[86] See Rivers (n 8) 199.
[87] ibid 200.

substantive theory of rights and justice, as long as they remain intelligible. Thus, the Court's refraining, under normal circumstances, from conducting a least-restrictive-means test would appear as its proper application of deference and restraint to the epistemically superior and democratically more legitimate domestic authorities.

Bearing in mind what we initially said about proportionality analysis and the separation of powers, these considerations suggest that the Court should indeed apply a reasonableness test when it examines the means–end relationship.[88] This assessment 'merely' serves the purpose of gaining a better understanding of a policy, so as to weed out measures that are erroneous in the sense that they do not serve a public aim to any reasonable extent,[89] that they, upon closer inspection, serve no legitimate public aim, or that they restrict rights avoidably because non-restrictive alternative measures would lead to the same goal. Despite this assessment's leniency, the improved policy understanding it brings about is important for the Court's further review and enhances a State's understanding of its policies in a valuable way. The more clarity that domestic authorities have about their policy decisions, the more 'illuminated' their views become about the proper construction of the Convention rights and their permissible restrictions. Thus, when the Court's review compels the domestic authorities to be clear about the means and ends of their policies, it potentially puts them in a better position to contribute to the discursive construction of the Convention rights' proper specification.

Note, finally that our argument does not suggest that there are no good reasons to encourage the domestic authorities to search for the least restrictive means sufficient to achieve their desired policy aims. Such encouragement could indeed mobilize institutional abilities that the domestic authorities possess to a higher degree than the Court, which would be welcome. As we will see in the following section, the Court should thus reward convincing domestic least-restrictive-means tests with deference and restraint during the normative balancing stage of its assessment.

c) Proportionality balancing: restraint on procedural grounds

This leads us to the question of how the Court should approach its proportionality balancing, which bears on the value judgment of how the interests harmed and the interests served by an impugned measure weigh against each other. If a democratically determined legitimate aim is pursued with what can—due to a reliable

[88] See Stephen Gardbaum, 'Proportionality and Democratic Constitutionalism' in G Huscroft, BW Miller, and GCN Webber (eds), *Proportionality and the Rule of Law* (CUP 2014) 274.

[89] See eg *Bartik v Russia* (n 51) para 49.

domestic least-restrictive-means test—be assumed to be the least restrictive means, there remain few grounds to justify the Court's second-guessing of a careful domestic balancing exercise, given the imponderability of this exercise.[90] The Court, finding a Convention violation, would not only substitute its own value judgment for that of the domestic authorities, but it would also risk proscribing the pursuit of a democratically chosen policy goal even though that aim was judged permissible ('legitimate') under the Convention. That is, if the Court found even the (what is presumed to be) least restrictive means to achieve what qualifies as a legitimate aim disproportionate—and hence in violation of the Convention—it would risk definitively preventing the State from achieving that aim on the basis of the mere substitution of its own value judgment for the equally reasonable judgment of the domestic authorities.

It is unclear how this could be justified. One would need a convincing argument for why the outcome of the Court's proportionality balancing *qua* 'free-hand exercise' can be presumed to be superior to the value judgment produced through the domestic balancing exercise. Unless one believes in the moral superiority of judges—a claim that runs afoul of the democratic premise that no one is morally superior to anyone else—such an argument may be persuasive only on a case-by-case basis: first, on procedural grounds, if it can be convincingly shown that the domestic authorities failed to engage in a careful balancing exercise; second, on substantive grounds, if it is clear that the domestic authorities' value judgment, despite a lack of procedural faults, deviates from value judgments that have become so widely shared among the States that they must be considered as having crystallised into a (partial) hierarchy of values that are compelling for the entire Convention system. The Court itself appears to share this view, namely, requiring 'strong reasons to substitute its assessment for that of the national courts' where the latter have duly assessed the case and carefully weighed the competing interests.[91] We may assume that this position prevails—and should be binding on the Court—today, since also the States endorsed this position in the Copenhagen Declaration's statement concerning what the principle of subsidiarity implies for the Court's review.[92]

The Court's practice shows that procedural and substantive types of domestic default occur every now and then. The most famous case of a domestic procedural default probably is the United Kingdom's failure to hold any actual debate on the proportionality of the then-valid British prisoner disenfranchisement regime which the Court found in *Hirst (no 2)*.[93] Examples of substantive value judgments

[90] See also Rivers (n 8) 201.

[91] Recently, *Guðmundur Andri Ástráðsson v Iceland* [GC], no 26374/18, para 251, 1 December 2020.

[92] 'Copenhagen Declaration' (High Level Conference 'Continued Reform of the European Court of Human Rights Convention System—Better Balance, Improved Protection' (Copenhagen, 12–13 April 2018)) para 28. c).

[93] *Hirst v the United Kingdom (no 2)* [GC], no 74025/01, para 79, ECHR 2005-IX.

upon which the States have converged, such that any (seemingly) procedurally flawless decision at odds with them would have to be considered in breach of the Convention, are numerous: recall that, as we noted in Chapter 9, a vast number of the Court's judgments are rendered on the basis of 'well-established case-law', viz unanimously and using a simplified procedure.

To sum up, our argument has been that the Court's standard of review must, in its default mode, be a lenient one, that is, roughly one of reasonableness, because the domestic (political) authorities are better placed to make and perform the choices and tests discussed above. However, regardless of this, the Court could always issue a rebuke in response to a domestic assessment based on its finding that the contested measure is not proportionate *stricto sensu*. Yet, as we just indicated, such findings may, in turn, raise difficulties in terms of the legitimacy of the Court's overruling domestic value judgments given the difficult-to-answer question of why one should take the Strasbourg judges' moral appraisals as more reliable than those of the States' authorities. The Court should, therefore, be cautious when it comes to overruling a domestic decision that was procedurally taken in a diligent, human-rights-respecting manner, which involves, most importantly, the serious consideration of alternative policies in a search for less restrictive, but sufficiently effective measure, on the one hand, and balancing all interests at stake against each other, on the other: the Court's task is to ensure that a contested measure is justifiable, not that it is correct in the judges' view. It is clear, however, that, where there are well-established substantive standards of sufficient precision to decide individual cases unequivocally, the Court must insist on these standards vis-à-vis aberrant State authorities.

d) Subsidiarity, restraint and deference, and procedural review

Our argument accords, on the one hand, with the Court's common practice of abstaining from conducting a least-restrictive-means test and, on the other, with its increasingly frequent practice of refraining from substituting its proportionality balancing for that of the domestic authorities if the latter's decision-making was procedurally diligent with respect to human rights, a condition which has become known under different names, including the procedural margin of appreciation[94] and the responsible or diligent domestic authorities doctrine.[95] The Copenhagen Declaration so to say 'codified' this practice, as Mikael Madsen noted.[96]

[94] Armin von Bogdandy, 'In the Name of the European Club of Liberal Democracies: How to Evaluate the Strasbourg Jurisprudence' (*EJIL Talk!*, 20 December 2018).

[95] See eg Çali (n 62).

[96] Mikael R Madsen, '"Unity in Diversity" Reloaded: The European Court of Human Rights' Turn to Subsidiarity and Its Consequences' (2021) 15(1) L & Ethics Hum Rts 93, 96.

As this section shows, the fact that procedural review plays an important role in the Court's review approach corresponds to, and is justified by, the theory of the Court's subsidiary role, as we developed it in Chapter 8. The general theory, related to the connection between democracy and rationalism, that stands behind procedural review, as Patricia Popelier has shown, fits our argument. Indeed, Popelier's account is broadly in line with the arguments we made in Chapter 8, suggesting that the discursive justification of all exercises of public authority crucially underpins the idea of human rights. As Popelier puts it, the 'participation of every person affected in rational deliberation and public debate' is a central procedural aspect of the idea taken from democratic theory that 'rationality is an important aspect of the legitimacy of government', rationality (or rationalism) referring to 'an ongoing process of rationalization, leading to decisions which are justifiable on the basis of present information and context and adaptable to changes in insight and environment'.[97]

According to Popelier, the Court, when it varies its scrutiny based on the quality of domestic decision-making, employs adjustable limits 'to the claimed primacy of politics while respecting the political balance of interests'.[98] This does not entail international-judicial prescriptions of specific procedural standards to be followed domestically, for example in parliament. All that the Court's procedural monitoring aims at is ensuring that all relevant evidence and competing interests are taken into account in a balanced, reasoned manner.[99] Put differently, the Court's procedural review is about ensuring that decisions concerning rights are based on reason-giving and deliberation—that is, that they occur through a process of argumentation and justification, in which opinions about values are actually formed—and that they do not just follow a crude logic of group interest, party politics, and majoritarian vote-counting where a priori fixed interests compete to gain the upper hand.[100]

The argument that the Court would unduly intrude on the preserve of parliament in requiring parliamentary debate of measures that impinge on Convention rights[101] is therefore unconvincing: given the Court's legal power to conduct its own fully-fledged substantive review of a contested measure,[102] an approach that merely controls for vaguely defined procedural requirements, such as that some reasonable proportionality balancing did occur, is clearly less intrusive. One

[97] See Patricia Popelier, 'The Court as Regulatory Watchdog: The Procedural Approach in the Case Law of the European Court of Human Rights' in P Popelier, A Mazmanyan, and W Vandenbruwaene (eds), *The Role of Constitutional Courts in Multilevel Governance* (Intersentia 2013) 249–251.

[98] ibid 252.

[99] See ibid.

[100] See Sandra Fredman, 'From Dialogue to Deliberation: Human Rights Adjudication and Prisoners' Rights to Vote' in M Hunt, HJ Hooper, and P Yowell (eds), *Parliaments and Human Rights* (Hart 2015) 450.

[101] See eg *Hirst v UK (no 2)* [GC] (n 93) para 7 (joint dissenting opinion of Judges Wildhaber, Costa, Lorenzen, Kovler, and Jebens).

[102] Articles 19 and 32 ECHR.

might even say that this approach does no more than check the plausibility of the political-constitutionalist assumption that political decision-making features quality reasoning about rights.

Since policy-making always involves an element of interest-based decision-making, all the Court's procedural review can aim for is to guarantee that, on the continuum between reason-based deliberation and interest-based powerplay,[103] decisions concerning rights fall not so far on the latter end of the spectrum that some relevant interests are not taken sufficiently seriously. In line with this, the Court has never, as far as I can see, scrutinized a parliament's internal decision-making process to any degree of detail. For example, in *Guðmundur Andri Ástráðsson*, the Court did not have to establish parliament's breach of the voting rules laid down in the domestic law, since the domestic courts had already done so.[104] Much less has the Court specified parliamentary decision-making rules,[105] which would hardly have been possible for international judges who watch over several dozens of different parliaments anyways.[106] Nor has it established a practice of finding a Convention violation only because of the procedural quality of parliamentary decision-making.[107] Instead, it sometimes suggests that a domestic decision could have been compliant with the Convention law, if it had been duly reasoned.[108]

In short, all that the Court has done is to apply restraint (or not) where it has (not) been shown that the domestic authorities—hence the legislature in case of general legislative measures—engaged in proportionality balancing or, in other words, took the Convention rights and their restriction seriously, when making and justifying policy choices. These are, so to say, the circumstances in which the Court does not need to substitute its courtroom for the domestic deliberative forum. In these conditions, there are no good reasons to assume that the Court's decision about the rights issue at stake will be better than that of the domestic authorities. We may understand this review standard of the Court as a form of intermediate scrutiny, stricter than checking only for manifest errors, but more lenient than checking compliance with the correct procedure.[109]

The importance of human rights diligence on the part of the States' political authorities to the Convention system is widely recognized, as noted in Chapter 8 when discussing pre-enactment political rights review. Matthew Saul thus expects the Court increasingly 'to make parliamentary process part of its move towards a deeper concept of subsidiarity'.[110] This development would deserve our support,

[103] See Cass R Sunstein, 'Interest Groups in American Public Law' (1985) 38(1) Stan L Rev 29, 48–49.
[104] *Ástráðsson v Iceland* [GC] (n 91).
[105] See eg *Parrillo v Italy* [GC], no 46470/11, ECHR 2015.
[106] Matthew Saul, 'The European Court of Human Rights' Margin of Appreciation and the Processes of National Parliaments' (2015) 15(4) HRLR 745, 752.
[107] Popelier (n 97) 257.
[108] See eg *El Ghatet v Switzerland*, no 56971/10, para 52, 8 November 2016.
[109] See Leonie M Huijbers, *Process-based Fundamental Rights Review* (Intersentia 2019) 128–130.
[110] Saul (n 106) 746.

since it corresponds to the account of the Court's subsidiary and the national authorities' primary role developed here. The more representative, participative, and inclusive, on a personal level, and the more comprehensive and transparent, on a substantive level, the debate about the proper scope and content of human rights is,[111] because it is conducted in a comparatively open political, instead of a more exclusive judicial forum, the more democratic legitimacy the resulting decisions will enjoy and the more restraint must be shown by the Court. Similarly, the Court should and does show more deference to national authorities if they base their decisions on a thorough assessment of expert knowledge and country comparisons, a careful weighing-up of a wide range of considerations and detailed debate.[112] Moreover, the Court has repeatedly emphasized that a measure must be assessed in light of contemporary circumstances, which suggests, especially in areas where matters are evolving quickly, that the domestic law-maker's reliability is heightened if it keeps an eye on relevant developments, so as to reconsider an issue if necessary, as a result of pertinent changes.[113]

Once again, this is roughly in line with our account of the Convention's subsidiarity principle. On the one hand, the sensitivity to ongoing developments fits to the point that the scope and content of rights is contingent on social developments that occur over time. On the other hand, comprehensive expertise-based policy-making represents (if combined with the justified presumption of the decision-maker's democratic legitimacy) the very circumstance in which it is generally hard to imagine why the Court should be better placed to decide than the domestic authorities are. Since domestic policy-makers have, in most respects, more epistemic capacities at their disposal than the Court has, if they make use of these resources and ground the value judgments inherent in rights issues in their corresponding knowledge base, it is hard to see what the Court can add besides a mere additional level of review.

Of course, because its subsidiary role allows the Court's procedural review to proceed only at a relatively high level of abstraction, there is a risk that the Court at times condones procedural flaws that negatively affect the proper discursive construction and justification of the scope and content of rights and their limitations.[114] However, if the Court were to seek to avoid each and every individual wrong, it would need to base its adjudication on a comprehensive and substantive theory of justice. This would also mean that the Court would overrule many domestic choices in spite of their reasonableness—or, to use Dworkin's expression, despite their intelligibility—simply because they fail to convince the Court's judges.[115] James Thayer made a similar point long ago when he suggested limiting

[111] See ibid 763–764.
[112] ibid 764–767.
[113] See eg *SH and Others v Austria* [GC], no 57813/00, para 117, ECHR 2011.
[114] Saul (n 106) 771.
[115] See Chapter 8.

judicial interference to instances where 'those who have the right to make laws have not merely made a mistake, but have made a very clear one, —so clear that it is not open to rational question'. His rationale was, just like ours, one of inter-institutional interaction, that is, of constitutional counter-balancing,[116] as becomes clear from his reasoning according to which constitutional review should ask 'what judgment is permissible to another department which the constitution has charged with the duty of making it'.[117]

Put more clearly, if the Court intervened whenever it finds a measure unconvincing despite its intelligibility, this would come at the cost of the democratic legitimacy of the entire Convention system. It would also, presumably, impinge on its social acceptance, with the effect that its political support would potentially erode. It is thus neither surprising nor unjustified that the Court's procedural approach to its review has been commended in the Copenhagen Declaration.[118] Because the notion of justice is often controversial—'the' just interpretation of the Convention's individual rights is often reasonably contestable—the idea that the Court can systematically render individual justice is misguided, in the sense that, if construing the Convention rights as legitimately as possible requires an ongoing discursive process concerning the scope and content of these rights, this process will inevitably include stages in which such uncertainties about the right interpretation of a Convention guarantee persist so that no more can be said about the rightness of a decision other than that it appears reasonably, or plausibly, just (ie justifiable), although not necessarily correct on any given substantive theory.

F) Limits on the limits?

In this book, we are concerned with subsidiarity in the Convention system, a procedural principle: we deal with questions of authority, not of justice. This means we neither assess the Court's jurisprudence substantively, nor argue for a certain 'correct' understanding of the scope and content of the Convention rights. Nor do we, therefore, develop an account of substantive 'red lines', in the sense of an account of that 'core substance'—if it exists at all—of the Convention that the Court should always and regardless of any grounds for deference and restraint, subject to its own fully-fledged merits review in order to prevent any infringement of it. What Thomas Nagel, among others, said about rights in general—namely that, regardless of whether there is, in reality, one correct understanding of them, rights are the subject of reasonable disagreement, due to a lack of methodological consensus

[116] See Alison L Young, *Democratic Dialogue and the Constitution* (OUP 2017) 129–130.

[117] James B Thayer, 'The Origin and Scope of the American Doctrine of Constitutional Law' (1893) 7(3) Harv L Rev 129, 144.

[118] See also 'Conference Report: High-Level Expert Conference "2019 and Beyond: Taking Stock and Moving Forward from the Interlaken Process"' (Kokkedal 22–24 November 2017).

about how to get at the truth about them[119]—also applies to the core, substance, or essence of the Convention's rights, including its non-derogable guarantees,[120] that is, to the question whether there are categorical limits to the (de)limitation of the Convention guarantees. Our approach does not allow us, therefore, to propose an equality-based conception of substantive limits to rights limitations, even though human rights are grounded in moral equality of all human beings. To be sure, like cases must be treated alike, but recall that, due to the normativity that inheres in claims of equality, these claims too are dependent on a—potentially controversial—conception of justice.[121] Granted, *some* principles of equality may enjoy the status of *ius cogens* and would therefore appear to be binding also for the entire Convention system. However, the emphasized substantive qualification already indicates the point that equality is multifaceted and partially controversial, such that it would be naive to believe that the principle according to which human rights are the equal rights of all could, in practice, operate in any meaningful way as a categorical limit on rights limitations.[122]

Note that if there is a high level of convergence concerning a certain right's specific (de)limitation, because of the widely shared view that the guarantee at stake is of particularly high importance, this is relevant for the procedural role of the international Strasbourg Court. However, it is relevant less for reasons pertaining to this substantive assessment of the guarantee's particular importance than for general procedural reasons pertaining to the Court's distinct institutional abilities and legitimacy. This is because the clearer and more widely shared a standard of Convention law, the more the Court, *qua* central judicial authority, will be in the best position to apply it vis-à-vis all decentral actors and the fewer problems of democratic legitimacy will arise from its doing so. As Jonas Christoffersen has observed, it is questionable whether the determination of an absolute essence of a right follows any other method than is applied otherwise to the case-based specification of rights. In his words: '[t]he absolute core of a right can be recognized only on the basis of general reasoning that will prevail in all circumstances'.[123] In short, the Court's role cannot depend on the particular importance of a right since this axiological issue may be just as controversial as any other interpretative question of Convention law.

Therefore, even when questions are at stake concerning what are arguably the most fundamental rights and the weight these should have, democratic legitimacy matters, as we argued already in Chapter 8. This means that truisms such as the

[119] Thomas Nagel, *The Last Word* (OUP 1997) 102.
[120] Article 15(2) ECHR.
[121] See Chapter 7.
[122] See Helen Keller and Reto Walther, 'Balancing Test: United Nations Human Rights Bodies' in Hélène Ruiz Fabri (ed), *Max Planck Encyclopedia of International Procedural Law* (April 2018, OUP) mn 27–31.
[123] Jonas Christoffersen, *Fair Balance* (Martinus Nijhoff 2009) 139.

'inalienability' of rights, the prohibition of measures that 'destroy' a right, and the absolute protection of core aspects of human dignity cannot specify the Court's subsidiary role, because they may be controversial not only per se but also as regards their content: they are difficult issues[124] that themselves raise the question of who decides on them.

This does not, of course, exclude the possibility of compelling arguments about the scope and content of a right's essence. A relatively easy and common example concerns the inviolability of the internal manifestation of the freedom of thought and religion (Article 9 of the Convention). Or, to give another example, it may indeed appear straightforward to argue, as the Strasbourg institutions did early on, that the procedural guarantees contained in Article 6 of the Convention includes a right to access the courts, because otherwise Article 6's more explicit content would risk being devoid of purpose.[125] Still, this abstract logic does not mean that the right to access the courts is, in practice, 'absolute' in one, and not another, specification.[126] Similarly, if one accepts the principle according to which Article 10 of the Convention absolutely protects any expression of criticism against government save for incitement to violence, this is not the end of the matter. An assessment of the impugned statement in its entire context, which the domestic authorities may better understand than the Court, remains indispensable to determining whether it crossed the threshold of incitement to violence.[127] The question of what response is proportionate to such incitement remains to be answered as well. Thus, the question of who decides is likely to remain relevant, even where there is, or seems to be, wide agreement on categorically protected rights.

What was just said can explain and justify why, over the past sixty years, the Court and its predecessor institutions have, at best, developed very vague, substantive 'red lines'—limits to rights limitations—in the form of notions, such as the 'core of a right' or the 'essence of a right',[128] meant to fix categorical prohibitions to rights limitations, no matter what values weigh in favour of a limitation.[129] Christoffersen opined that, in the Court's practice, instead of an absolutely inviolable core, a right's essence is what is left of it after it has undergone a proportionality analysis.[130] The merely semantic usage of the notion of a right's essence that is thus described can be read as the Court's attempt to leave even rights issues that arguably go to the heart of a Convention guarantee's protection subject to the Convention system's justificatory dialogue. This hesitation on the part of the

[124] See also Sébastien van Drooghenbroeck and Cecilia Rizcallah, 'The ECHR and the Essence of Fundamental Rights: Searching for Sugar in Hot Milk?' (2019) 20(6) Germ LJ 904, 912.
[125] *Golder v the United Kingdom*, 21 February 1975, Series A no 18.
[126] *Ashingdane v UK* (n 85) para 57.
[127] See eg *Sürek and Özdemir v Turkey* [GC], nos 23927/94 and 24277/94, paras 61–63, 8 July 1999.
[128] *Case 'relating to certain aspects of the laws on the use of languages in education in Belgium'* (merits), 23 July 1968, para 5 (p 28), Series A no 6.
[129] See van Drooghenbroeck and Rizcallah (n 124) 907.
[130] Christoffersen (n 123) 145, 163.

Court to clearly articulate rigid rules is in line with the more general observation of the Court's varied interpretative authority. Just as there is no clear jurisprudence concerning the issues of the Court's jurisprudential and precedential authority, the Court's jurisprudence too remains indeterminate about the essence, substance, or core of the guaranteed rights.

Indeed, given the Court's subsidiary role vis-à-vis the States sketched in Chapter 8, the Strasbourg judges can arguably better contribute to Europe's human rights protection by abstaining from the sort of categorical reasoning that a rigid doctrine of an essence of rights would demand: a flexible approach allows it to continuously fathom what level of rights protection is only just acceptable on the part of the States and to push this limit, whereas the rigid application of strict limits to rights limitations implied by a more categorical approach could force the Court to remain decidedly on the 'safe side'.

Lending support to this understanding of the Court's practice, Sébastien van Drooghenbroeck and Cecilia Rizcallah recently summarized their study of the Court's usage of limits on rights limitations with the observations that the Court has never 'explicitly defined and explained' the idea of the essence, core, or substance of rights and that it remains 'essentially pragmatic and unprincipled on this question'.[131] This approach may well be explained with, and justified by, understanding the Convention system as a collective endeavour to instigate a continuous process aimed at further developing Europe's human rights protections from the bottom up.

As the notion of the very essence of a right is conceptually controversial in legal theory and contestable as concerns its substantive content,[132] our account of the Convention's subsidiary principle would therefore reject as pretentious the Court judges' choice of a certain theory about the former, in order to determine the latter based on their own 'deep theory'. By contrast, nothing speaks against the gradual convergence of views on the general unjustifiability of certain rights-impinging measures. Arguably, this has already occurred with principles laid down in cases such as *Golder*, concerning access to courts, or *Soering*,[133] concerning the extradition of individuals who would be at risk of suffering ill-treatment contrary to Article 3 in the receiving state, and the respective follow-up jurisprudence.

The desirability of common standards of this kind notwithstanding, the point remains that they cannot emerge out of nothing and, in circumstances of reasonable disagreement, cannot derive their legitimacy from individual judges' pet theories of rights. Answers to the question of limits to rights limitations must be developed in the same way as answers to other rights issues, namely, through a discursive, justificatory dialogue. This implies that the meaning of the very essence

[131] van Drooghenbroeck and Rizcallah (n 124) 905.
[132] See ibid 911–912.
[133] *Soering v the United Kingdom*, 7 July 1989, Series A no 161.

of the Convention rights is developed incrementally and continuously. It appears misplaced, therefore, to use language such as 'always prohibited' and 'never justifiable'. Given the Convention system's premise that a fair balance must be struck in every individual case in light of all circumstances, this language does not fit well with established Convention law and practice. Furthermore, this parlance would appear to be hard to reconcile with the idea of human rights developed in Chapter 8. Therefore, as regards notions such as the core, substance, or essence of rights, the same thing holds as was said when discussing the notions of *res judicata* and *erga omnes inter partes* effect:[134] it appears better to avoid these terms since they cannot and should not operate according to the meanings that they convey. As a whole, the Convention law is continuously developing. It makes no sense to use language that points to a belief in rights determinations that are eternal or settled once and for all. All Convention standards, no matter how foundational they may appear to be, develop through the same infinite process of convergence, imposition, and adjustment that takes the form of a justificatory dialogue between all the participants in the Convention system.

G) The Court's subsidiary role explained and justified

It would appear that we have come full circle. The first part of this book linked the principle of subsidiarity to the ideas of plurality and self-government (Chapter 2), observed that the current emphasis on the Court's merely subsidiary role serves to highlight the States' democratic self-government (Chapters 3 and 4), expounded the difficult relationship between the liberal and democratic principles (Chapters 5–7), and explained why democratic politics are indispensable to a legitimate human rights system (Chapter 8): human rights are constitutive and expressive of the equal moral status of all human beings, which, however, requires not only equal rights but also an equal say in the specification of these rights, making the process of determining the scope and content of human rights an ongoing process that plays out among political equals. This crucial political dimension of human rights, we argued, explains and justifies why European-level actors must necessarily be subsidiary in Europe's human rights practice. If human rights must be specified mutually among political equals, this process must occur within a democratic polity, meaning that the Convention rights must primarily develop from the bottom up. As it is the undisputable purpose of the Court system to (re) impose human rights standards on the States, the Court plays a dual role, which forces it to continuously vacillate between exercising stronger and weaker, more legal and more moral, forms of authority—or so we have argued. This is also why

[134] See Chapter 9.

debating about the 'strength' of the Court's review and its possible 'supremacy' in categories known from constitutional law appears to be a rather futile exercise. The Court, although exercising constitutional functions, evades categorization along the lines commonly used to typify domestic apex courts.

We illustrated what this oscillation of the Court between its two roles implies in practice on the example of the interpretative praxis of the Convention system (Chapter 9). The Court's casuistry, including in its application of its European consensus method, and its abstention from taking strong, principled positions on its interpretative and precedential authority, and on the Convention law's status and effect in the domestic legal orders can, for many parts at least, be explained and justified by the need to keep the inter-institutional justificatory dialogue about the proper understanding of the Convention rights always going.

The present chapter aimed to do essentially the same with regard to the Court's review practice. It showed how the permissible limitation of rights links them to democracy and explained what this means for the Court's international judicial review of the State's domestic policies. In short, we suggested, on the one hand, that if the Court were to apply strict standards of review, it would seriously impede the democratic community's pursuit of its purposes and value choices and, on the other hand, that the attempt to derive certain categorical demands from the Convention's rights catalogue would fit poorly with the Court system's functioning as governed by the principle of subsidiarity.

Epilogue

A) Introduction: An Appeal to the States . . .

The European Court of Human Rights (the Court, ECtHR) must be (according to the law), should be (according to normative theory) and, all in all, is (according to legal practice) subsidiary—or so we argued in this book. Its member states (the States) have unmistakably expressed and regularly confirm their political will to have a *subsidiary* Court:[1] it is clear that there is robust political backing only for a Court that shows due respect to the States' democratic self-government. This demand is normatively justifiable, if not compelling. If Europe wants to uphold its democratic commitment to the political equality of all human beings, the Court cannot but play a subsidiary role. The primary locus of a liberal-democratic human rights practice must be democratic polities, and thus, in present times, the States. Fortunately, with regard to the Court's practice, the Court cannot be said to generally neglect or flout its subsidiarity: its practice abounds in accommodations of domestic views that ensure that the States have a proper say in the European Convention on Human Rights (the Convention, ECHR)[2] system.

There is no doubt that the Court's jurisprudence is far from perfect, sometimes in disrespect of its subsidiary role, and that its approach, as presented, discussed, and partly defended in the last two chapters, has clear downsides, which are partly mirrored in the criticisms that many politicians, scholars, and national judges have levelled against the Court, as we saw in Chapter 3. The most notable problem of the Court's practice is, from the present perspective, the Court's failure to provide the States with a reasonably clear proportionality framework, including consistent standards of review, within which to engage with the Court and its jurisprudence.[3]

Nevertheless, the Court has, on the whole, rightly refrained from distinguishing itself by establishing principled jurisprudence marked by doctrines that strongly predicate its further development of the Convention law. Thus, criticisms focussing on the Court's casuistry, which results not least from its efforts to account for national differences, as well as to respond and react to the States' views and practices, do not fit well with accusations of undue, democratically illegitimate judicial

[1] Recently, 'Reykjavík Declaration' (Summit of Heads of State and Government of the Council of Europe (Reykjavík, 16–17 May 2023)).

[2] Convention for the Protection of Human Rights and Fundamental Freedoms, as amended, of 4 November 1950, in force since 3 September 1953, 213 UNTS 221, CETS No 005.

[3] See Chapter 10.

Subsidiarity, Legitimacy, and the European Court of Human Rights. Reto Walther, Oxford University Press.
 DOI: 10.1093/9780198921455.003.0011

activism: the alternative to the Court's current casuistic judicial approach would be not a less activist Court but one that imposes much more rigid interpretations of the Convention rights—and perhaps also much stricter procedural standards—on the States.

The Court's critics should bear this in mind and reflect well about what their main concern is. Their criticism should not focus on the Court's variable, hence casuistic, case-law which, as explained, actually is a means of the Court to cater to their demand for a Convention law that develops in dialogue with the States. They should instead focus on judgments such as that in the recent *KlimaSeniorinnen* case where the Court significantly expanded its judicial domain through brash judicial activism as regards procedural and substantive Convention law, decided as a quasi-first-instance, as it did not take into account most recent legal developments within the respondent State's domestic order, and disrespected the legislative prerogative of the democratic political branches by venturing far into the making of general and prospective, viz political, choices, not least by disregarding explicit international law-making decisions. However, most problematic about this case perhaps is that a chamber relinquished its jurisdiction such that the case was directly decided by the Grand Chamber, despite its being the Court's first landmark climate-change judgment.[4] This problematically forestalls the judgment's referral to another, quasi-appellate, judicial formation and it deprives the respondent State as well as other States that disagree with the judgment to enter into a relatively soon, direct, and constructive dialogue with the Court about the proper reading of the Convention's substantive and procedural provisions. Thus, a reaction from the States' political branches is likely to occur at the implementation stage of the judgment and, at least in Switzerland, has already occurred in the form of a new wave of political backlash against the Court.[5] Both, political backlash such as a State's threat to leave the Convention system or to seek to curb the Court's powers, and a judgment's non- or minimalist implementation, generally are, to say the least, little constructive forms of inter-institutional dialogue and always come with the risk of severely undermining the authority of the Court and the Convention law—no matter how legitimate some response to activist judgments at the implementation stage may be in exceptional cases and under certain circumstances.[6]

This leads us to those who seek to defend a highly influential Court and welcome judgments such as that in the *KlimaSeniorinnen* case. They should be careful in their adoration of the Court, just like those who favour a markedly subsidiary Court should be careful in their criticism. Supporters of a strong Court should carefully think about how much judicial activism they welcome or even demand

[4] *Verein KlimaSeniorinnen Schweiz and Others v Switzerland* [GC], no 53600/20, 9 April 2024.

[5] See parliamentary declarations nos 24.053 (5 June 2024) and 24.054 (12 June 2024), as well as motion no 24.3485 (27 May 2024).

[6] See Chapter 8.

from the Court and how they portray the Court's practice, even if their desire for a Court that would be more principled, would apply stricter scrutiny, and would assert its judicial supremacy more forcefully is immense. Perhaps, it would be more effective to portray the Court in a way that emphasizes its attempts to live up to its subsidiarity—its relative, albeit with notable exceptions, modesty or 'unpretentiousness'—than to conjure up a fully-fledged (in the domain of human rights) *supra*-national European constitutional court following the logic 'for ... that which *must* not, *can* not be'.[7]

This is not to deny or devalue the reality of the Court system's tremendous impact on the States' treatment of individuals under their jurisdiction. Instead, our point is to emphasize, first, that the Court cannot just 'govern through' and, second, that it will only ever be as strong as the political backing it receives from the States. This also means, as we noted in Chapter 1, that less may sometimes be more. Those who really care about a Court that is viable and effective in the long run should thus think well about whether it is prudent to incite the Court to rulings such as that in the *KlimaSeniorinnen* case.

This implicit reminder of the power that the States ultimately yield about the Court and the entire Convention system shifts our focus on them and their 'primarity': the Court and the whole Convention system depend on their political commitment to Europe's central mechanism for the protection of human rights. Unfortunately, those who call the loudest for the Court's subsidiarity may sometimes and, assuming their commitment to human rights, somewhat paradoxically also be those who do the most to prevent the States from taking their primary role within the Convention system seriously. If their calls are to cohere credibly with a commitment to Europe's human rights system, any demands for subsidiarity on the part of the Court must go hand in hand with efforts to strengthen the States' contribution to the Convention system. These critics, too, should contribute to ensuring that their States assume their responsibility, sustain the Court's procedural legality, nurture substantive Convention law, and firmly back the Convention system and its value order on an ideological level. The States could and should reinforce subsidiary, European-level rights protection along these three overlapping dimensions—they bear the primary responsibility for a substantively convincing European human rights law, as well as for a procedurally sound and institutionally viable Convention system.

B) ... to sustain the Court's procedural legality

First, the States *qua* Convention-law-maker should assume more responsibility for the Convention system's procedure. The Convention system's procedural law

[7] Christian Morgenstern, 'Die unmögliche Tatsache'/'The Impossible Fact' in his *Gallows Songs* (Max Knight tr, University of California Press 1963) 34–35.

should be firmly rooted in political decisions taken by the States, since this is a central aspect of the separation of the political (law-making) and the legal (law-applying) powers and an important source of democratic legitimacy for the Court and its judgments and decisions. Seen from this perspective, the immense procedural discretion that the Court currently enjoys is a problem.

Indeed, the Court does both too little and too much as regards procedural Convention law. It does too little as regards certain difficulties concerning the procedure before the Court that observers have long criticized. First, the Court's Rule 47,[8] concerning the formal requirements of an individual application, is extremely strict. This may have the perverse effect of impeding access to the Court in a way that disadvantages, above all, those members of society who are already the worst off and the most silenced, and who would therefore most urgently need access to the Court. Second, the Court's practice of granting leave (or not) to civil society third-party interveners is problematic, since these procedural decisions of the Court are taken in an opaque and unreasoned manner. This is a problem for the legitimacy of the Court's judgments especially in important cases, viz in cases in which all the societal strata potentially affected by an outcome in the long term should be allowed to participate and be represented accordingly.[9] More broadly, increased transparency concerning the civil society actors working behind the scenes at the Court and their affiliations with Strasbourg judges would be desirable. The many connections between the Court's judges and non-governmental organizations pose a problem to the Court's independence and, hence, legitimacy.[10] Third, it is clear that the Court is never more effective *qua* forum for deliberation about important, but controversial, rights issues than when it adjudicates an issue in its Grand Chamber.[11] Therefore, its relatively discretionary, uneven (biased in favour of state requests for referral[12]), and opaque and unreasoned practice of referring (or not referring) cases to the Grand Chamber[13] appears problematic.[14] As illustrated above on the example of the *KlimaSeniorinnen* case, it is also problematic if the Court's chambers relinquish important cases to the Grand Chamber, since this means that the States are deprived of an important avenue of contestation of the

[8] Rules of Court of 28 March 2024, in force since 28 March 2024.

[9] See Nicole Bürli, *Third-Party Interventions Before the European Court of Human Rights* (Intersentia 2017) 115–116.

[10] See Chapter 4.

[11] See 'Copenhagen Declaration' (High Level Conference 'Continued Reform of the European Court of Human Rights Convention System—Better Balance, Improved Protection' (Copenhagen, 12–13 April 2018)) para 35.

[12] Alastair Mowbray, 'An Examination of the Work of the Grand Chamber of the European Court of Human Rights' [2007] PL 507, 513.

[13] See Article 43(2) ECHR; Rule 73(1)–(2) Rules of Court; European Court of Human Rights, 'Practice Followed by the Panel of the Grand Chamber when Deciding on Requests for Referral Under Article 43 of the Convention (Note Prepared by the Registry)' (2 June 2021).

[14] See *Ryser v Switzerland*, no 23040/13, paras 10–11, 12 January 2021 (dissenting opinion of Judge Keller).

Court's judgments. As regards these issues, the Court has done too little to bring about change to the better, presumably in an attempt to preserve its full discretion and perhaps also to avoid (even) more work: Grand Chamber judgments, in particular, are extremely resource-intensive.

On the other hand, the Court has done too much in terms of developing the Convention's procedural law in another sense: it is doubtful whether the Court should make watershed changes to its procedure without the States' prior, explicit, and formal approval. Seen through our lens, the Court is not the right authority for watershed procedural decisions. Examples include its introduction of standing of associations in climate-change litigation,[15] of the pilot judgment procedure,[16] and, its decision to select thematic focal points of its jurisprudence, such as climate cases,[17] as 'impact cases' that deserve prioritization,[18] which stands in a certain tension to the view of the States' experts about what discretion the Court should enjoy in the selection of cases it deems important.[19]

To some extent, we may excuse the Court for its habit of doing both too little and too much. If it seeks ways to reduce its—in reality, nearly unmanageable—workload, this problem is, in fact, due to the States' neglect of their primary responsibility not only to not give rise to applications to the Court in the first place, but also to fund and staff the Court appropriately. If the Court sometimes feels a strong need to take major decisions concerning its organization and procedures, this may, in part, simply be because the States do not do their share. For example, that the States never managed to agree in a formal, unequivocal, and legally binding manner on the pilot judgment procedure, but left it to the Court to introduce it through the backdoor, so to speak, although the problem of situations that cause innumerable near-identical justified applications to the Court is widely recognized.

So, the States as masters of the treaty and primary actors in the Convention system must assume their responsibility much more competently than they have done in the past. In cases where the Court appears to neglect problems in order to retain its full discretion and keep its workload 'low', the States' sense of responsibility should impel them to ensure change for the better, regardless of whether the Court displays reluctance. When the Court takes action in order to make up for the States' inaction, the pressure on the States to (finally) take responsibility is even stronger. The States are responsible for continuously doing their best to legitimize the Convention system, including by ensuring sound procedures that guarantee

[15] *KlimaSeniorinnen Schweiz v Switzerland* [GC] (n 4) para 502.

[16] Rule 61 Rules of Court; *Broniowski v Poland* [GC], no 31443/96, paras 190–191, ECHR 2004-V.

[17] See Robert Spano, 'Exchange of Views with the Committee of Ministers' (Strasbourg, 17 March 2021).

[18] European Court of Human Rights, '"A Court that Matters/Une Cour qui compte": A Strategy for More Targeted and Effective Case-Processing' (17 March 2021) 1.

[19] Steering Committee for Human Rights, 'Contribution of the CDDH to the Evaluation Provided for by the Interlaken Declaration' (11 December 2019, CM(2019)182-add) para 87.

against—even the appearance of—undue judicial discretionary powers within and over the Court's procedural order. The Court's independence must be respected, but the States should find ways to lend more democratic legitimacy to the procedural Convention law, adopt major procedural changes themselves, possibly on the Court's initiative,[20] and check the Court's procedural discretion when there are widely shared concerns about a lack of judicial accountability.

To do so, a Court statute containing the principal procedural rules and subject to the States' approval by (qualified) majority rule would be worthy of consideration[21]—all the more so if we bear in mind the Court's general support for this idea.[22] Such a statute would, for example, provide a way in which the States could, despite lack of unanimity, entrench the pilot judgment procedure, lay down a duty of the Court to give a reasoned decision on requests to refer a judgment to the Grand Chamber, or implement a procedure through which the States (and ideally other stakeholders too) could submit their views on whether a case should be referred to the Grand Chamber or not. The fact that the States have vainly voiced demands in relation to all these procedural amendments, makes them, *qua* composite principal of the Court, sometimes resemble a lame duck rather than the primary bearer of responsibility for the Convention system.

Beware, however, because what we just proposed is conditional on the State governments' having a thorough commitment, on an ideological level, to the Convention system and acting upon this commitment. It must not be that the State governments acting in the Committee of Ministers change the nature of the Convention system to an extent that appears incompatible with any reasonable interpretation of the Convention system as set up and endorsed by each State's domestic democratic ratification procedure. Most importantly, the Court must remain a thoroughly *judicial* authority: the States must respect—or better yet, enhance—its independence and impartiality, and they must not question its binding judgments. Yet, this does not contradict the demand that the Court be part of a system of institutional interdependence,[23] as is the case in domestic constitutional orders and without which the democratic legitimacy and social acceptance[24] of judicial powers would remain highly doubtful. This interdependence necessarily and rightly entails some degree of judicial accountability and 'merely' bounded judicial discretion[25] resulting, most significantly, from the States' ultimate

[20] cf Rule 116 Rules of Court.

[21] See also Steering Committee for Human Rights, 'Guaranteeing the Long-Term Effectiveness of the Control System of the European Convention on Human Rights: Addendum to the Final Report Containing CDDH Proposals (long version)' (14 April 2003, CM(2003)55-Add 2) Proposal B.8.

[22] European Court of Human Rights, 'Opinion of the Court on the Wise Persons' Report' (as adopted by the Plenary Court on 2 April 2007) 2.

[23] Aida Torres Pérez, 'In Nobody's Name: A Checks and Balances Approach to International Judicial Independence' in H Ruiz Fabri and others (eds), *International Judicial Legitimacy* (Nomos 2020) 60.

[24] See Jeffrey L Dunoff and Mark A Pollack, 'The Judicial Trilemma' (2017) 111(2) AJIL 225, 251.

[25] See Tom Ginsburg, 'Bounded Discretion in International Judicial Lawmaking' (2004) 45(3) Va J Intl L 631, 673.

retention of primary law-making powers in matters of procedural and substantive Convention law. Thus, it is crucial that the States assume their law-making responsibility within the Convention system. Otherwise the Court system will lack its most important source of democratic legitimacy.[26]

C) ... to nurture substantive Convention law

Second, as regards substantive Convention law, if it is to be nurtured and developed democratically, the States must politicize it. To be clear, this is not a call to politicize or democratize the Court and its jurisprudence, but rather it is a call to politicize Convention rights, that is, substantive Convention law, in the sense that the States' political actors—which we take to include not only government authorities, but also political parties, civil society and, ultimately, individual citizens—must engage with these rights. They must take them into account in their law-making, in their parliamentary debates, in committee hearings, in their lobbying and advocacy work, when casting their votes, and so on, and they must establish the necessary procedures and institutions to do so. Most obviously, an institutionalized form of thorough pre-enactment political rights review should be established in all States: the more developed and explicit the domestic rights practice is, the more there is that can feed into the Court's jurisprudence. Broadly in line with this, the Westminster Parliament's Joint Committee on Human Rights argued that 'parliamentary scrutiny facilitates democratic input into legal changes following court judgments and so helps to counter the perception that the legal protection of human rights tends to marginalise the role of democratic institutions'.[27] Indeed, 'enhancing the role of national parliaments in the ECHR system is the key to' ensuring the normative and sociological legitimacy that the Convention system needs to remain viable and effective.[28]

This means that the States should continuously reflect on the adequacy of the current catalogue of Convention rights and, more generally, of the Council of Europe's fundamental values in light of contemporary challenges. For example, the Court may well be right to emphasize climate-change-related human rights risks. However, compared to the Court's taking the lead in this issue area, it would not only be much more legitimate, but probably also much more effective if the States were to account for this through political action, even if 'merely' by coming together and agreeing on, say, an amendment to the Convention Preamble that underlines the need to make climate change part of Europe's human rights configuration.

[26] See Torres Pérez (n 23) 45.

[27] Joint Committee on Human Rights, 'Human Rights Judgments: Seventh Report of Session 2014–15' (HL Paper 130, HC 1088, 11 March 2015) para 1.1.

[28] ibid para 5.3.

A serious attempt to do so would be valuable in and of itself, regardless of its ultimate success, because it would spur much-needed debate on an issue that is urgent, but difficult, given its huge implications for virtually all aspects of human life, and controversial, given the uneasy relationship of this collective problem to individual rights.[29] In this sense, the recommendation to the Committee of Ministers adopted by the Parliamentary Assembly of the Council of Europe recommending the adoption of a new optional protocol to the Convention enshrining a 'right to a safe, clean, healthy and sustainable environment' is most welcome.[30] Similarly, it is laudable that the Committee of Ministers' considers new instruments in the field of human rights and the environment, and calls on the States to recognize this right at the national level.[31] This call on the States could, as discussed in Chapter 8, incite a process of bottom-up law development that might, at some point, legitimize the Court's recognition of a new right, for example, under Article 8 of the Convention, if the States did not choose to legislate on the international level.

However, sticking to our methodological approach of focussing on procedural and institutional questions, we shall not argue for or against the inclusion of one or more climate-related rights—or, for that matter, any other right—to the Convention's rights catalogue. Our point is merely that the States, including their delegations to the Parliamentary Assembly, should do their best to continuously engage in a democratic debate about the proper scope and content of the Convention's rights catalogue. As Michael Perry suggests, if a democratic polity aspires to progress—'to struggle incessantly to see beyond, and then to live beyond, the imperfections of whatever happens at the moment to be the established moral conventions'—it must always continue its 'vigorous revaluation' of its contemporary understanding of rights.[32]

Relatedly, the States should make sure to use the procedural options they have at their disposal to participate in the Court system, always respecting the principle of judicial independence. If they make no, or only sparing, use of the means they have available to communicate with the Court, they cannot plausibly complain that their views are not being given their due. In particular, the States could intervene as third parties before the Court far more often.[33] Note that not only State governments may submit their views: members of national and European parliaments have also occasionally done so in the past.[34] As Nicole Bürli suggests, as

[29] See eg Alan Boyle, 'Climate Change, the Paris Agreement and Human Rights' (2018) 67(4) ICLQ 759, 777; Benoit Mayer, 'Climate Change Mitigation as an Obligation Under Human Rights Treaties?' (2021) 115(3) AJIL 409, 418–419.

[30] Parliamentary Assembly, 'Recommendation "Anchoring the Right to a Healthy Environment: Need for Enhanced Action by the Council of Europe"' (29 September 2021, 27th Sitting, Rec 2211 (2021)).

[31] 'Reykjavík Declaration' (n 1) Appendix V.

[32] Micheal J Perry, *The Constitution, the Courts, and Human Rights* (Yale University Press 1984) 101.

[33] See 'Copenhagen Declaration' (n 11) para 34.

[34] See *Lautsi and Others v Italy* [GC], no 30814/06, 56, ECHR 2011 (extracts).

representatives of people under the Court's jurisdiction, their intervention is not objectionable per se.[35]

D) ... to cultivate the Convention system's moral foundations

It should be clear by now that, according to our argument, the democratic legitimacy of Convention law hinges on its bottom-up development.[36] That is, the initial impetus behind the Convention law must come from the States: the Court can only reap, process, and preserve what was sown and nurtured within flourishing democratic polities. This need for flourishing democratic polities leads to our last point, namely, the States' responsibility to cultivate their liberal-democratic convictions.

Since the Convention system, in line with the general ontology of the principle of subsidiarity, builds on the States, they bear what may be called a meta-responsibility for maintaining the Convention system, viz to cultivate its ideological foundations and to live up to the corresponding institutional- or operational-level commitments. Whoever has read this far will probably not be surprised to learn that this section, too, will refrain from distracting itself with the crucial, but utterly trite, issue of the implementation of the Court's judgments: the States are obliged to abide by those judgments to which they are a party, while *qua* members of the Committee of Ministers they are obliged to ensure that their peers adhere to this obligation.[37] No doubt, the Court system would be much better off if the States took both responsibilities much more seriously than they currently do in practice. In other words, although the implementation and execution of the Court's judgments is a huge problem in practice, there is nothing particularly interesting that we could contribute to this debate apart from a point made in Chapter 9, namely, that the critical engagement with the Court's rights interpretations *ex post* judgment may—under certain conditions—be a legitimate way to contribute to the development of the Convention law.

Similarly, it is abundantly clear that each State must adhere to what we called the *acquis conventionnel*. That is, where European human rights standards are clear, they should not be violated in the first place and, if this happens anyways, the violation should be remedied at the domestic level. Articles 1, 13, and 35 of the Convention, in particular, leave no doubt about this: although the Court may 'substitute' for failing State systems to some extent, a domestic practice of repetitive and systematic violations of well-established Convention standards without serious efforts on the part of the concerned State to put an end to this situation makes

[35] Bürli (n 9) 126.
[36] See Chapter 8.
[37] Article 46(1)–(2) ECHR.

a mockery of the Convention's procedural arrangement and subsidiary role. The Court system has not been set up to relieve the States of their human rights obligations, in the sense of assuming responsibility for them on behalf of the States, but rather to support the States in fulfilling their responsibility by complementing their domestic rights-protecting mechanisms.

Now to begin with what we may call the States' institutional- or operational-level commitment, the States should, first and foremost, fund the Convention system adequately. Or do we really want a Court that is so overburdened that it feels a need to 'outsource' its work to algorithms,[38] with all the ideological and practical risks this entails?[39] As the Parliamentary Assembly noted some years ago, the Court's authority is 'contingent on the political will and commitment of all member States of the Council of Europe ... to ensure that the Court is provided with the financial means to effectively implement its human rights mandate'.[40] Today, even the States' Heads of State and Government recognize that the Court's resources are 'are insufficient and unsustainable'.[41] Let us hope that they act on this insight of theirs.

To illustrate, even if only approximatively, how stretched the Court's budget is, suffice it to recall that the European Court of Justice's annual expenditure amounts to about six times the Strasbourg Court's budget, whereas the latter's annual case law is dozens of times larger than that of its counterpart in Luxembourg. Those who direct criticism against the Court concerning its backlog and/or its (alleged) jurisprudential weaknesses should do what they can to ensure that it is comfortably funded and to think well about whether their criticism is fair in light of the means they allow the Court—or would allow it, if they were in a position to decide.

Relatedly, the States should make sure that the Court has the opportunity to employ some of Europe's best lawyers as judges and registry staff. As regards the judges, this requires, among other things, adequate selection procedures where 'room for improvement' remains.[42] Each State bears its own responsibility, insofar as the nomination of the three candidates from among whom the Parliamentary Assembly elects a judge on behalf of the nominating State falls into the sphere of national competences.[43] Unfortunately, some States conspicuously fail to ensure proper nomination procedures, while the Parliamentary Assembly has—despite improvements and the assistance of an expert panel—sometimes failed to ensure that only candidates who meet the demanding criteria of Article 21 of the

[38] See Robert Spano, 'Human Rights and Democracy in the Age of Digital Transformation and COVID-19' (Speech to the German Marshall Fund, 16 March 2021) <https://www.youtube.com/watch?v=-6Kb5L2Kh3g> accessed 30 June 2024.

[39] See Veronika Fikfak, 'What Future for Human Rights? Decision-making by Algorithm' (*Strasbourg Observers*, 19 May 2021).

[40] Parliamentary Assembly, 'Resolution "Reinforcement of the Independence of the European Court of Human Rights"' (27 June 2014, 27th Sitting, Res 2009 (2014)) para 5.

[41] 'Reykjavík Declaration' (n 1) Appendix IV.

[42] Steering Committee for Human Rights, 'Evaluation' (n 19) para 133.

[43] Article 22 ECHR.

Convention are elected.[44] The national nomination and the subsequent European election processes are political to a considerable degree, and many of the most seriously deficient cases involve abuse of a political dimension, whether nepotism, outright politicking, lobbying with unfair advantages, or the like.[45]

The challenge is to strike the right balance between considerations of meritocracy and democratic legitimacy. The best possible middle way would probably be to guarantee that each State only nominates *highly qualified* candidates which would then allow the Parliamentary Assembly to proceed to its—by definition political—election.[46] This would require the domestic political actors ultimately in charge of the nomination procedure to be willing to give priority to meritocratic over political considerations—and place themselves, so to speak, at the service of the *demoi*-cratic Parliamentary Assembly. It would also require the States *qua* members of the Council of Europe to effectively police their peers in this regard, which is, once again, a political (ie diplomatic) responsibility.

One may also wonder how attractive it is to serve—together with, among others, not-up-to-par colleagues—on an underfunded and overburdened Court. Whatever the size of the Court's docket, the States should provide the resources necessary to cope with its caseload in a timely manner. As indicated, this would require more financial and human resources, but perhaps also institutional changes. Otherwise, it would hardly be possible for the Court to work off its huge list of long-pending cases without decreasing the quality of its jurisprudence. Angelika Nußberger, a former Vice-President of the Court, has thus recently contemplated the establishment of an entirely new Court unit responsible only for dealing with systemic and repetitive applications.[47] Regrettably, the States seem to prefer muddling through rather than implementing *reform* measures worthy of their name, viz measures that guarantee the Court system's effective and high-quality functioning in the long term.

The States operational- and institutional-level responsibility for the Convention system takes many other forms, of course. It must, for instance, find expression in the domestic authorities' practical cooperation with the Court, including full cooperation with the Court in the course of proceedings. This would, for example, include the invitation of judicial fact-finding missions (once again requiring resources), the granting of access to all evidence, and so on. It is a shame that, time and again, the Court finds violations of Article 38, according to which a respondent State must 'furnish all necessary facilities' for the investigations the Court needs to

[44] David Kosař, 'Selecting Strasbourg Judges: A Critique' in M Bobek (ed), *Selecting Europe's Judges* (OUP 2015) 158.

[45] See ibid 149–156; Koen Lemmens, '(S)electing Judges for Strasbourg: A (Dis)appointing Process?' in M Bobek (ed), *Selecting Europe's Judges* (OUP 2015) 108.

[46] See Lemmens (n 45) 117.

[47] Angelika Nußberger, '"To Be a Judge Means to be Criticized from All Sides" (Interview, Dana Schmalz and Raffaela Kunz)' (*Völkerrechtsblog*, 3 February 2020).

undertake in the course of its examination of a case,[48] as well as of Article 34, because a State disregards interim measures[49] ordered by the Court[50] or hinders an individual's right to apply to the Court.[51] Calls made by the States to their peers to respect and protect the right of individual application to the Court are laudable and important, but should not actually be necessary.[52]

Luckily, most of the States are relatively innocent when it comes to this fundamental issue. The sad truth is that almost all of the Court's violation judgments in these domains concern a very small group of States, raising strong doubts about the sincerity of their commitment to the overall Convention system.

This leads to our final point, the States' ideological support for the Convention system. Individually and collectively, the States, in particular insofar as they act as constituents of the Committee of Ministers, must act as staunch defenders of their liberal-democratic commitment and take action—politically persuasive efforts, diplomatic peer pressure, and the like—against peers who seriously call into question the fundamental values of the Council of Europe. If the States are committed to upholding the Convention system as a crucial part of a Council of Europe dedicated to liberal rights and democracy, they must do whatever is in their power to condemn and stop their peers from engaging in practices that are in blatant violation of any reasonable understanding of liberal democracy. Invading neighbouring states' territories, assassinating or otherwise eliminating political dissidents,[53] purging political opponents from all public offices and packing courts with loyal government supporters[54] are unequivocally incompatible with any plausible reading of equal individual and collective self-determination. If such government behaviour goes unpunished, especially when committed systematically and over extended periods of time, the risk of an erosion of the Council of Europe as a 'club' of liberal-democratic States[55] is imminent—as Edmund Burke supposedly said, 'all that is necessary for evil to triumph is for good men to do nothing'.[56]

The only viable Convention system—because it is accepted and acceptable—is a subsidiary one that 'merely' supports and complements the States in their domestic human rights practices. Yet, in order to be meaningful, the 'non-strong-form' Court system, in this sense, depends on States that are democratic or, at the

[48] See eg *Benzer and Others v Turkey*, no 23502/06, paras 154–161, 12 November 2013.

[49] Rule 39 Rules of Court.

[50] See eg *DA and Others v Poland*, no 51246/17, paras 96–101, 8 July 2021.

[51] See eg *Feilazoo v Malta*, no 6865/19, paras 117–133, 11 March 2021.

[52] Committee of Ministers, 'Resolution on Member States' Duty to Respect and Protect the Right of Individual Application to the European Court of Human Rights' (10 November 2010, 1097th mtg, Res(2010)25).

[53] See eg *Ilgar Mammadov v Azerbaijan*, no 15172/13, 22 May 2014; *Navalnyy v Russia (no 3)* no 36418/20, 6 June 2023.

[54] See eg *Reczkowicz v Poland*, no 43447/19, 22 July 2021.

[55] Armin von Bogdandy, 'In the Name of the European Club of Liberal Democracies: How to Evaluate the Strasbourg Jurisprudence' (*EJIL Talk!*, 20 December 2018).

[56] Vernon Bogdanor, *The New British Constitution* (Hart 2009) 87.

very least, credibly on the way of becoming proper democracies, that adhere to the rule of law, and are strongly and sincerely committed to liberal rights, even if they disagree about rights in many ways. Thus, the States that broadly satisfy these criteria and are sincerely committed to the (subsidiary) Court system—which is the majority of them—must defend this system against erosion from both within and without.

Unfortunately, there is more than enough for the committed liberal-democratic States to stand up against. Although it would be naive to believe that the Council of Europe alone could have stopped Vladimir Putin's Russia from extending its war of aggression from Crimea to the whole of Ukraine, how it dealt with Russia remains the best illustration of the States' failure to stand up against violations of the Council of Europe's core values. The annexation of Crimea by Russia, then and until mid-March 2022 still a member of the Council of Europe,[57] certainly represented the most blatant disregard of Europe's value order since Europe, as we know it today, rose from the ashes of the Second World War. It is highly problematic, therefore, that the States' delegates in the Parliamentary Assembly restored the Russian delegation's voting rights,[58] which were suspended in the wake of Russia's annexation of Crimea[59] without any significant concessions on Russia's part. Moreover, this occurred after the Russian delegation—instead of showing any readiness to participate in and cooperate with the Parliamentary Assembly[60]—withdrew completely from the Parliamentary Assembly and even withheld its mandatory financial contributions to the Council of Europe. Only after its rights were restored did Russia pay (although without the interests owed) and return to the table, without making any substantial concessions[61] or showing any will to do so.[62] In fact, the Council of Europe not only re-admitted Russia as a full member of its 'liberal-democratic club', but also changed its procedural rules, such that rogue States will have much less reason to fear sanctions in the future.[63] This episode and its aftermath left the strong impression that Russia not just blackmailed the

[57] See Committee of Ministers, 'Resolution on the Cessation of the Membership of the Russian Federation to the Council of Europe' (16 March 2022, 1428th mtg, Res (2022)2).

[58] Parliamentary Assembly, 'Resolution "Challenge, on Substantive Grounds, of the Still Unratified Credentials of the Parliamentary Delegation of the Russian Federation"' (26 June 2019, 24th Sitting, Res 2292 (2019)) para 10.

[59] Parliamentary Assembly, 'Resolution "Reconsideration on Substantive Grounds of the Previously Ratified Credentials of the Russian Delegation"' (10 April 2014, 16th Sitting, Res 1990 (2014)) para 15.

[60] See Kanstantsin Dzehtsiarou and Donal K Coffey, 'Suspension and Expulsion of Member of the Council of Europe: Difficult Decisions in Troubled Times' (2019) 68(2) ICLQ 443, 457–458.

[61] Parliamentary Assembly, 'Resolution "Challenge, on Substantive Grounds, of the Still Unratified Credentials of the Parliamentary Delegation of the Russian Federation"' (29 January 2020, 6th Sitting, Res 2320 (2020)) paras 2–5.

[62] See Parliamentary Assembly, Opening of the Sitting Num 7, Debate: Challenge, on Substantive Grounds, of the Still Unratified Credentials of the Parliamentary Delegation of the Russian Federation, 28 January 2021 (Verbatim).

[63] Parliamentary Assembly, 'Resolution "Strengthening the Decision-making Process of the Parliamentary Assembly Concerning Credentials and Voting"' (25 June 2019, 20th Sitting, Res 2287 (2019)) para 10.

Council of Europe into re-admitting it as a full member of its liberal-democratic club[64] and into changing its procedural rules, such that rogue States will have much less reason to fear sanctions in the future,[65] but outrightly fooled it, since Russia never ceased to exacerbate its disregard of the Council of Europe's foundational values, as everyone knew who was willing to know it.[66]

Since the Parliamentary Assembly's yielding to Russia was not only supported, but actually encouraged by the Committee of Ministers,[67] which has traditionally been even less strict on deviant States than the Parliamentary Assembly,[68] there is little hope for the future that either of the two bodies will take a decisive stance in relation to States that fundamentally deviate from the Council of Europe's values. It is thus even more important for individual States or groups of like-minded States to speak out and take appropriate action.

Without vigilance[69] and decisive action, no backsliding, no authoritarian turn can be prevented, especially if deviance is condoned or even abetted.[70] The Council of Europe, and with it the Convention system, risks undermining its own credibility and reputation as a community of liberal-democratic States, if the States individually and collectively, as the constituents of the Council of Europe's major political bodies, condone grave breaches of its foundational values. In the long run, this could be suicidal for the entire project.[71] That said, the possibility of excluding a State which shows 'persistent and clear disregard of the values and aims'[72] of the Council of Europe from the organization foreseen in Article 8 of its Statute[73] must not be ruled out as a measure of *ultima ratio* and, in exceptional circumstances, even deserves to be seriously contemplated.[74]

[64] Parliamentary Assembly, 'Resolution "Challenge, on Substantive Grounds, of the Still Unratified Credentials of the Parliamentary Delegation of the Russian Federation"' (28 January 2021, 7th Sitting, Res 2363 (2021)) para 2.

[65] Parliamentary Assembly, 'Res 2287 (2019)' (n 63) para 10.

[66] See Committee on the Honouring of Obligations and Commitments by Member States of the Council of Europe (Monitoring Committee) (Stefan Schennach, rapporteur), 'Challenge, on Substantive Grounds, of the Still Unratified Credentials of the Parliamentary Delegation of the Russian Federation' (26 January 2021, Doc 15216).

[67] See Committee of Ministers, 'Decision: A Shared Responsibility for Democratic Security in Europe—Ensuring Respect for Rights and Obligations, Principles, Standards and Values' (17 May 2019, 129th Sess, CM/Del/Dec(2019)129/2).

[68] Philip Leach, 'The Parliamentary Assembly of the Council of Europe' in M Breuer and S Schmahl (eds), *The Council of Europe* (OUP 2017) mn 7.56.

[69] See Donald Bello Hutt, 'The Deliberative Constitutionalism Debate and a Republican Way Forward' (2021) 12(1) Jurisprudence 69, 83.

[70] See Fabio Wolkenstein, 'European Political Parties' Complicity in Democratic Backsliding' (2022) 11(1) GlobCon 55, 57–70.

[71] Andrew Drzemczewski and Kanstantsin Dzehtsiarou, 'Painful Relations Between the Council of Europe and Russia' (*EJIL Talk!*, 28 September 2018).

[72] Dzehtsiarou and Coffey (n 60) 444.

[73] Statute of the Council of Europe of 5 May 1949, in force since 3 August 1949, 87 UNTS 103, CETS No 001.

[74] See also Dzehtsiarou and Coffey (n 60) 476.

In the absence of a minimum of ideological integrity and alignment, an organization, such as the Council of Europe, which is ultimately based on shared values much more than on economic and other such tangible interests will hardly be viable and effective in the long run. To be sure, excluding a State from the 'club' means that, six months later, it is no longer subject to the Court's jurisdiction, except for occurrences that happened before this date.[75] Potential applicants thus lose the chance to succeed in proceedings before the Strasbourg Court and gain some monetary just-satisfaction under Article 41 of the Convention, which the States, and even those among them that are more deviant, often pay. Yet, from a wider, but still State-oriented perspective, the impact that the Court has on States that strongly deviate from the Council of Europe's fundamental values may appear doubtful anyways:[76] a great many of the Court's judgments that require measures to be taken to address human rights problems more broadly have remained unimplemented in these States. Moreover, if one takes an even wider perspective, the risk that a deviant State knowingly and willingly destabilizes the system as a whole—or merely acts as a free-rider benefitting from the legitimacy gains stemming from its membership, while burdening the organization far more than it contributes to it[77]—and thus serves as an example for other States that are not so robustly committed to human rights and democracy is considerable and worrying.[78]

The inconvenient truth is that a State is likely to have much more effective means at its disposal to undermine the viability and legitimacy of the Convention system than the Court has to turn the State into a liberal democracy abiding by the rule of law. As the 'danger related to illiberal democracies and authoritarian regimes ... is one of a creeping decline', there is a real risk that it 'remains under the radar' for too long. The highest political bodies, namely, the Committee of Ministers, must thus take care to avoid excessive forbearance and to take those 'resolute political measures' that are needed in view of members that go astray.[79]

Thus, the Court's subsidiarity, and hence the States' 'primarity', may well be a timelier theme than ever before. When it comes to the authoritarian turns of some States and their flagrant and enduring disregard for the core principles of the Council of Europe, the Court may play an important role. It may, for example, fire warning shots or contribute to assessing the situation in a certain State in the course of infringement proceedings, wherein it assesses on request by the

[75] Article 58 ECHR; see also European Court of Human Rights, 'Resolution on the Consequences of the Cessation of Membership of the Russian Federation to the Council of Europe in light of Article 58 of the European Convention on Human Rights' (22 March 2022, plenary session).

[76] See also Dzehtsiarou and Coffey (n 60) 474.

[77] See Andreas Føllesdal, 'The Legitimate Authority of International Courts and Its Limits: A Challenge to Raz's Service Conception?' in P Capps and HP Olsen (eds), *Legal Authority Beyond the State* (CUP 2018) 200.

[78] Dzehtsiarou and Coffey (n 60) 457.

[79] See Wolfgang Benedek, 'Are the Tools of the Council of Europe Sufficient to Protect Human Rights, Democracy and the Rule of Law from Backsliding?' (2020) 1(2) ECHR L Rev 151, 157–158.

Committee of Ministers whether a State abided by a judgment,[80] or under Article 18, as we noted in Chapters 9 and 10—but the committed liberal-democratic States must, no doubt, play the decisive role: ultimately, human rights are a moral project borne by political will—the effectiveness of Convention rights is, in the final instance, grounded in nothing more than the conviction both of people and of peoples that they are worthy of protection. It is most welcome, therefore, that the States' Heads of State and Government 'firmly' recommitted to the Convention system, as well as to democratic governance.[81] They must now walk the talk and take political action to, most importantly, convince their citizens of the moral superiority of liberal-democratic constitutionalism over other forms of government.

The political-moral destination of Europe is a choice that must be made by society as a whole; the Court can only assist it in helping to stay on track.

[80] Article 46(4) ECHR.

[81] 'Reykjavík Declaration' (n 1) Appendices III and IV.

Bibliography

Allan James, 'Bills of Rights and Judicial Power—A Liberal's Quandary' (1996) 16(2) Oxford Journal of Legal Studies 337.

Alter Karen J, 'Agents or Trustees? International Courts in Their Political Context' (2008) 14(1) European Journal of International Relations 33.

Alter Karen J and Madsen Mikael R (eds), *The International Adjudication of Mega-Politics* (special issue) (2022) 84(4) Law and Contemporary Problems 1.

Alter Karen J and Madsen Mikael R, 'The International Adjudication of Mega-Politics' (2022) 84(4) LCP 1.

Anagnostou Dia, 'Law and Rights' Claiming on Behalf of Minorities in the Multi-Level European System' in Dia Anagnostou (ed), *Rights and Courts in Pursuit of Social Change: Legal Mobilisation in the Multi-Level European System* (Hart 2014).

Andersen Ellen A, *Out of the Closets and into the Courts: Legal Opportunity Structure and Gay Rights Litigation* (University of Michigan Press 2005).

Anderson Elizabeth S, 'What Is the Point of Equality?' (1999) 109(2) Ethics 287.

Aquinas Thomas, *Summa Theologiae, Part II (Second Part)* (Father of the English Dominican Province tr, first published 1265–1274, R & T Washbourne 1918).

Arai-Takahashi Yutaka, *The Margin of Appreciation Doctrine and the Principle of Proportionality in the Jurisprudence of the ECHR* (Intersentia 2002).

Arai-Takahashi Yutaka, 'The Margin of Appreciation Doctrine: A Theoretical Analysis of Strasbourg's Variable Geometry' in Andreas Føllesdal, Birgit Peters, and Geir Ulfstein (eds), *Constituting Europe: The European Court of Human Rights in a National, European and Global Context* (Cambridge University Press 2013).

Arendt Hannah, *The Origins of Totalitarianism* (2nd edn, Meridian Books 1958).

Arendt Hannah, 'Karl Jaspers: Citizen of the World?' in her *Men in Dark Times* (first published 1957, Harcourt, Brace & World 1968).

Aroney Nicholas, 'Subsidiarity in the Writings of Aristotle and Aquinas' in Michelle Evans and Augusto Zimmermann (eds), *Global Perspectives on Subsidiarity* (Springer 2014).

Arrow Kenneth J, 'A Difficulty in the Concept of Social Welfare' (1950) 58(4) Journal of Political Economy 328.

Barak Aharon, *Proportionality: Constitutional Rights and Their Limitations* (Doron Kalir tr, Cambridge University Press 2012).

Barber Benjamin R, *Strong Democracy: Participatory Politics for a New Age* (with a new preface, 20th anniversary edn, first published 1984, University of California Press 2003).

Barber Nicholas W, 'The Limited Modesty of Subsidiarity' (2005) 11(3) European Law Journal 308.

Bates Ed, 'Activism and Self-Restraint: the Margin of Appreciation's Strasbourg Career... Its "Coming of Age"?' (2016) 36(7–12) Human Rights Law Journal 261.

Bates Ed, *The Evolution of the European Convention on Human Rights: From Its Inception to the Creation of a Permanent Court of Human Rights* (Oxford University Press 2010).

Beitz Charles R, *Political Equality: An Essay in Democratic Theory* (Princeton University Press 1989).

Beitz Charles R, *The Idea of Human Rights* (Oxford University Press 2009).

Bellamy Richard, *Liberalism and Modern Society: An Historical Argument* (Polity 1992).

Bellamy Richard, *Liberalism and Pluralism: Towards a Politics of Compromise* (Routledge 1999).

Bellamy Richard, 'Introduction' in his *Rethinking Liberalism* (Pinter 2000).

Bellamy Richard, 'Schumpeter and the Transformation of Capitalism, Liberalism and Democracy' in his *Rethinking Liberalism* (first published 1991, Pinter 2000).

Bellamy Richard, *Political Constitutionalism: A Republican Defence of the Constitutionality of Democracy* (Cambridge University Press 2007).

Bellamy Richard, 'Political Constitutionalism and the Human Rights Act' (2011) 9(1) International Journal of Constitutional Law 86.

Bellamy Richard, 'Public Law as Democracy: The Case of Constitutional Rights' in Cormac Mac Amhlaigh, Claudio Michelon, and Neil Walker (eds), *After Public Law* (Oxford University Press 2013).

Bellamy Richard, 'Rights, Republicanism and Democracy' in Andreas Niederberger and Philipp Schink (eds), *Republican Democracy: Liberty, Law and Politics* (Edinburgh University Press 2013).

Bellamy Richard, 'The Democratic Legitimacy of International Human Rights Conventions: Political Constitutionalism and the European Convention on Human Rights' (2014) 25(4) European Journal of International Law 1019.

Bello Hutt Donald, 'The Deliberative Constitutionalism Debate and a Republican Way Forward' (2021) 12(1) Jurisprudence 69.

Benedek Wolfgang, 'Are the Tools of the Council of Europe Sufficient to Protect Human Rights, Democracy and the Rule of Law from Backsliding?' (2020) 1(2) European Convention on Human Rights Law Review 151.

Benhabib Seyla, 'The Legitimacy of Human Rights' (2008) 137(3) Daedalus 94.

Benvenisti Eyal, 'Margin of Appreciation, Consensus, and Universal Standards' (1999) 31 New York University Journal of International Law & Politics 843.

Besson Samantha, *The Morality of Conflict: Reasonable Disagreement and the Law* (Hart 2005).

Besson Samantha, 'The Reception Process in Ireland and the United Kingdom' in Helen Keller and Alec Stone Sweet (eds), *A Europe of Rights: The Impact of the ECHR on National Legal Systems* (Oxford University Press 2008).

Besson Samantha, 'The Authority of International Law—Lifting the State Veil' (2009) 31(3) Sydney Law Review 343.

Besson Samantha, 'The Erga Omnes Effect of Judgments of the European Court of Human Rights—What's in a Name?' in Samantha Besson (ed), *The European Court of Human Rights After Protocol 14: Preliminary Assessment and Perspectives* (Schulthess 2011).

Besson Samantha, 'European Human Rights, Supranational Judicial Review and Democracy: Thinking Outside the Judicial Box' in Patricia Popelier, Catherine van de Heyning, and Piet van Nuffel (eds), *Human Rights Protection in the European Legal Order: Interaction Between European Courts and National Courts* (Intersentia 2011).

Besson Samantha, 'Human Rights and Democracy in a Global Context: Decoupling and Recoupling' (2011) 4(1) Ethics & Global Politics 19.

Besson Samantha, 'International Judges as Dispute-Settlers and Law-Enforcers: From International Law Without Courts to International Courts Without Law' (2011) 34(1) Loyola of Los Angeles International and Comparative Law Review 33.

Besson Samantha, 'Sovereignty' in Rüdiger Wolfrum (ed), *Max Planck Encyclopedia of Public International Law* (April 2011, Oxford University Press) <https://opil.ouplaw.com> accessed 30 June 2024.

Besson Samantha, 'The Extraterritoriality of the European Convention on Human Rights: Why Human Rights Depend on Jurisdiction and What Jurisdiction Amounts to' (2012) 25(4) Leiden Journal of International Law 857.

Besson Samantha, 'Human Rights: Ethical, Political ... or Legal? First Steps in a Legal Theory of Human Rights' in Donald E Childress III (ed), *The Role of Ethics in International Law* (Cambridge University Press 2012).

Besson Samantha, 'The Egalitarian Dimension of Human Rights' (2013) 136 Archiv für Rechts- und Sozialphilosophie Beiheft [supplement] 19.

Besson Samantha, 'Human Rights and Constitutional Law: Patterns of Mutual Validation and Legitimation' in Rowan Cruft, S Matthew Liao, and Massimo Renzo (eds), *Philosophical Foundations of Human Rights* (Oxford University Press 2015).

Besson Samantha, 'Human Rights' Adjudication as Transnational Adjudication: A Peripheral Case of Domestic Courts as International Law Adjudicators' in August Reinisch, Mary

E Footer, and Christina Binder (eds), *International Law and ...: Select Proceedings of the European Society of International Law* (Hart 2016).
Besson Samantha, 'State Consent and Disagreement in International Law-Making. Dissolving the Paradox' (2016) 29(2) Leiden Journal of International Law 289.
Besson Samantha, 'Subsidiarity in International Human Rights Law—What Is Subsidiary About Human Rights?' (2016) 61(1) American Journal of Jurisprudence 69.
Bianku Ledi and Kempees Peter, 'The European Court of Human Rights' in Freya Baetens (ed), *Legitimacy of Unseen Actors in International Adjudication* (Cambridge University Press 2019).
Böckenförde Ernst-Wolfgang, 'The Rise of the State as a Process of Secularization' in Mirjam Künkler and Tine Stein (eds), *Religion, Law, and Democracy: Selected Writings, vol 2* (first published 1967, Oxford University Press 2020).
Bodnar Adam, 'Res Interpretata: Legal Effect of the European Court of Human Rights' Judgments for Other States Than Those Which Were Party to the Proceedings' in Yves Haeck and Eva Brems (eds), *Human Rights and Civil Liberties in the 21st Century* (Springer 2014).
Bogdanor Vernon, *The New British Constitution* (Hart 2009).
Bossuyt Marc, 'Judges on Thin Ice: The European Court of Human Rights and the Treatment of Asylum Seekers' (2010) 3(1) Inter-American and European Human Rights Journal 3.
Bossuyt Marc, 'The Court of Strasbourg Acting as an Asylum Court' (2012) 8(2) European Constitutional Law Review 203.
Boyle Alan, 'Climate Change, the Paris Agreement and Human Rights' (2018) 67(4) International and Comparative Law Quarterly 759.
Brems Eva, *Human Rights: Universality and Diversity* (Martinus Nijhoff 2001).
Brems Eva and Lavrysen Laurens, '"Don't Use a Sledgehammer to Crack a Nut": Less Restrictive Means in the Case Law of the European Court of Human Rights' (2015) 15(1) Human Rights Law Review 139.
Brennan Patrick M, 'Subsidiarity in the Tradition of Catholic Social Doctrine' in Michelle Evans and Augusto Zimmermann (eds), *Global Perspectives on Subsidiarity* (Springer 2014).
Breuer Marten (ed), *Principled Resistance Against ECtHR Judgments—A New Paradigm?* (Springer 2019).
Broude Tomer and Shany Yuval, 'Introduction' in Tomer Broude and Yuval Shany (eds), *The Shifting Allocation of Authority in International Law: Considering Sovereignty, Supremacy and Subsidiarity* (Hart 2008).
Buchanan Allen, *Justice, Legitimacy, and Self-Determination: Moral Foundations for International Law* (Oxford University Press 2004).
Buchanan Allen, 'The Egalitarianism of Human Rights' (2010) 120(4) Ethics 679.
Buchanan Allen, *The Heart of Human Rights* (Oxford University Press 2013).
Burbergs Maris, 'How the Right to Respect for Private and Family Life, Home and Correspondence Became the Nursery in Which New Rights Are Born: Article 8' in Eva Brems and Janneke Gerards (eds), *Shaping Rights in the ECHR: The Role of the European Court of Human Rights in Determining the Scope of Human Rights* (Cambridge University Press 2014).
Bürli Nicole, *Third-Party Interventions Before the European Court of Human Rights: Amicus Curiae, Member-State and Third-Party Interventions* (Intersentia 2017).
Butler Andrew S, 'Legal Aid Before Human Rights Treaty Monitoring Bodies' (2000) 49(2) International and Comparative Law Quarterly 360.
Calabresi Guido, 'Foreword: Antidiscrimination and Constitutional Accountability (What the Bork-Brennan Debate Ignores)' (1991) 105 Harvard Law Review 80.
Çali Başak, 'From Flexible to Variable Standards of Judicial Review: The Responsible Domestic Courts Doctrine at the European Court of Human Rights' in Oddný M Árnardóttir and Antoine Buyse (eds), *Shifting Centres of Gravity in Human Rights Protection: Rethinking Relations Between the ECHR, EU and National Legal Orders* (Routledge 2016).
Çali Başak, 'Coping with Crisis: Whither the Variable Geometry in the Jurisprudence of the European Court of Human Rights' (2018) 35(2) Wisconsin International Law Journal 237.
Çali Başak and Koch Anne, 'Foxes Guarding the Foxes? The Peer Review of Human Rights Judgments by the Committee of Ministers of the Council of Europe' (2014) 14(2) Human Rights Law Review 301.

Cameron David, 'Speech on the European Court of Human Rights' (Parliamentary Assembly of the Council of Europe, Strasbourg, 25 January 2012) <https://perma.cc/2N2S-2X2J> accessed 30 June 2024.

Cappelletti Mauro, 'Repudiating Montesquieu? The Expansion and Legitimacy of "Constitutional Justice"' (1985) 35(1) Catholic University Law Review 1.

Carozza Paolo G, 'Uses and Misuses of Comparative Law in International Human Rights: Some Reflections on the Jurisprudence of the European Court of Human Rights' (1997) 73(5) Notre Dame Law Review 1217.

Carozza Paolo G, 'Subsidiarity as a Structural Principle of International Human Rights Law' (2003) 97(1) American Journal of International Law 38.

Cass Deborah Z, 'The Word that Saves Maastricht? The Principle of Subsidiarity and the Division of Powers Within the European Community' (1992) 29(6) Common Market Law Review 1107.

Cassese Antonio, 'The Legitimacy of International Criminal Tribunals and the Current Prospects of International Criminal Justice' (2012) 25(2) Leiden Journal of International Law 491.

Chaplin Jonathan, 'Subsidiarity and Social Pluralism' in Michelle Evans and Augusto Zimmermann (eds), *Global Perspectives on Subsidiarity* (Springer 2014).

Christiano Thomas, *The Constitution of Equality: Democratic Authority and Its Limits* (Oxford University Press 2008).

Christoffersen Jonas, *Fair Balance: Proportionality, Subsidiarity and Primarity in the European Convention on Human Rights* (Martinus Nijhoff 2009).

Christoffersen Jonas and Madsen Mikael R, 'Postscript: Understanding the Past, Present, and Future of the European Court of Human Rights' in Jonas Christoffersen and Mikael R Madsen (eds), *The European Court of Human Rights Between Law and Politics* (paperback edn, Oxford University Press 2013).

Cliquennois Gaëtan, *European Human Rights Justice and Privatisation: The Growing Influence of Foreign Private Funds* (Cambridge University Press 2020).

Cohen Jean L, 'Rights and Citizenship, and the Modern Form of the Social: Dilemmas of Arendtian Republicanism' (1996) 3(2) Constellations 164.

Cohen Jean L, 'Rethinking Human Rights, Democracy, and Sovereignty in the Age of Globalization' (2008) 36(4) Political Theory 578.

Cohen Joshua, 'Minimalism About Human Rights: The Most We Can Hope For?' (2004) 12(2) Political Philosophy 190.

Cohen-Eliya Moshe and Porat Iddo, *Proportionality and Constitutional Culture* (Cambridge University Press 2013).

Colandrea Valerio, 'On the Power of the European Court of Human Rights to Order Specific Non-Monetary Measures: Some Remarks in Light of the Assanidze, Broniowski and Sejdovic Cases' (2007) 7(2) Human Rights Law Review 396.

Colb Sherry F, 'Why Is Torture "Different" and How "Different" Is It?' (2009) 30(4) Cardozo Law Review 1411.

Cover Robert M, 'The Uses of Jurisdictional Redundancy: Interest, Ideology, and Innovation' (1981) 22(4) William & Mary Law Review 639.

Craig Paul, 'Institutions, Power, and Institutional Balance' in Paul Craig and Gráinne de Búrca (eds), *The Evolution of EU Law* (2nd edn, Oxford University Press 2011).

Craig Paul, 'Subsidiarity: A Political and Legal Analysis' (2012) 50(S1) Journal of Common Market Studies 72.

Crick Bernard, *In Defence of Politics* (University of Chicago Press 1962).

Dagger Richard, *Civic Virtues: Rights, Citizenship, and Republican Liberalism* (Oxford University Press 1997).

Daly Eoin, 'Republicanizing Rights? Proportionality, Justification, and Non-Domination' in Ester Herlin-Karnell, Matthias Klatt, and Héctor A Morales Zúñiga (eds), *Constitutionalism Justified: Rainer Forst in Discourse* (Oxford University Press 2019).

Daly Tom G, *The Alchemists: Questioning Our Faith in Courts as Democracy-Builders* (Cambridge University Press 2017).

de Londras Fiona, 'International Human Rights Law and Constitutional Rights: In Favour of Synergy' (2009) 9(2) International Review of Constitutionalism 307.

Delmas-Marty Mireille, *Ordering Pluralism: A Conceptual Framework for Understanding the Transnational Legal World* (Naomi Norberg tr, first published 2006, Hart 2009).

Devins Neal and Fisher Louis, *The Democratic Constitution* (2nd edn, Oxford University Press 2015).

Djeffal Christian, 'Consensus, Stasis, Evolution: Reconstructing Argumentative Patterns in Evolutive ECHR Jurisprudence' in Panos Kapotas and Vassilis P Tzevelekos (eds), *Building Consensus on European Consensus: Judicial Interpretation of Human Rights in Europe and Beyond* (Cambridge University Press 2019).

Donald Alice, 'Book Review: Principled Resistance to ECtHR Judgments—A New Paradigm?' (2020) 1(2) European Convention on Human Rights Law Review 297.

Donald Alice and Leach Philip, *Parliaments and the European Court of Human Rights* (Oxford University Press 2016).

Dothan Shai, 'In Defence of Expansive Interpretation in the European Court of Human Rights' (2014) 3(2) Cambridge Journal of International and Comparative Law 508.

Dothan Shai, 'Judicial Deference Allows European Consensus to Emerge' (2018) 18(2) Chicago Journal of International Law 393.

Drzemczewski Andrew and Dzehtsiarou Kanstantsin, 'Painful Relations Between the Council of Europe and Russia' (*EJIL Talk!*, 28 September 2018) <https://www.ejiltalk.org> accessed 30 June 2024.

Duke George, 'Sovereignty and the Common Good' (2019) 17(1) International Journal of Constitutional Law 66.

Dunoff Jeffrey L and Pollack Mark A, 'The Judicial Trilemma' (2017) 111(2) American Journal of International Law 225.

Duranti Marco, *The Conservative Human Rights Revolution: European Identity, Transnational Politics, and the Origins of the European Convention* (Oxford University Press 2017).

Dworkin Ronald, *Taking Rights Seriously* (Harvard University Press 1977).

Dworkin Ronald, 'The Forum of Principle' (1981) 56(2–3) New York University Law Review 469.

Dworkin Ronald, 'Liberalism' in his *A Matter of Principle* (Harvard University Press 1985).

Dworkin Ronald, *Law's Empire* (Belknap Press 1986).

Dworkin Ronald, *Freedom's Law: The Moral Reading of the American Constitution* (Harvard University Press 1996).

Dworkin Ronald, *Justice for Hedgehogs* (Harvard University Press 2011).

Dzehtsiarou Kanstantsin, *European Consensus and the Legitimacy of the European Court of Human Rights* (Cambridge University Press 2015).

Dzehtsiarou Kanstantsin, 'The United Kingdom and the European Convention on Human Rights: Together Until the End?' (2024) 5(1) European Convention on Human Rights Law Review 1.

Dzehtsiarou Kanstantsin and Coffey Donal K, 'Suspension and Expulsion of Member of the Council of Europe: Difficult Decisions in Troubled Times' (2019) 68(2) International and Comparative Law Quarterly 443.

Endicott Timothy, 'The Logic of Freedom and Power' in Samantha Besson and John Tasioulas (eds), *The Philosophy of International Law* (Oxford University Press 2010).

Fabbrini Federico, 'The Margin of Appreciation and the Principle of Subsidiarity: A Comparison' (2015) iCourts Working Paper Series 15/2015 <https://papers.ssrn.com/abstract=2552542> accessed 30 June 2024.

Feichtner Isabel, 'Subsidiarity' in Rüdiger Wolfrum (ed), *Max Planck Encyclopedia of Public International Law* (October 2007, Oxford University Press) <https://opil.ouplaw.com> accessed 30 June 2024.

Fikfak Veronika, 'What Future for Human Rights? Decision-Making by Algorithm' (*Strasbourg Observers*, 19 May 2021) <https://strasbourgobservers.com> accessed 30 June 2024.

Finnis John, *Aquinas: Moral, Political, and Legal Theory* (Oxford University Press 1998).

Finnis John, *Natural Law and Natural Rights* (2nd edn, Oxford University Press 2011).

Fitzmaurice Gerald, 'The General Principles of International Law Considered from the Standpoint of the Rule of Law' (1957) 92 Recueil des cours 1.

Føllesdal Andreas, 'Survey Article: Subsidiarity' (1998) 6(2) Journal of Political Philosophy 190.

Føllesdal Andreas, 'Why the European Court of Human Rights Might Be Democratically Legitimate—A Modest Defense' (2009) 27(2) Nordic Journal of Human Rights 289.

Føllesdal Andreas, 'Much Ado About Nothing? International Judicial Review of Human Rights in Well-Functioning Democracies' in Andreas Føllesdal, Johan K Schaffer, and Geir Ulfstein (eds), *The Legitimacy of International Human Rights Regimes: Legal, Political and Philosophical Perspectives* (Cambridge University Press 2013).

Føllesdal Andreas, 'The Principle of Subsidiarity as a Constitutional Principle in International Law' (2013) 2(1) Global Constitutionalism 37.

Føllesdal Andreas, 'Competing Conceptions of Subsidiarity' in James E Fleming and Jacob T Levy (eds), *Federalism and Subsidiarity* (Nomos LV, NYU Press 2014).

Føllesdal Andreas, 'Tracking Justice Democratically' (2017) 31(3) Social Epistemology 324.

Føllesdal Andreas, 'Constitutionalization, Not Democratization: How to Assess the Legitimacy of International Courts' in Nienke Grossman and others (eds), *Legitimacy and International Courts* (Cambridge University Press 2018).

Føllesdal Andreas, 'The Legitimate Authority of International Courts and Its Limits: A Challenge to Raz's Service Conception?' in Patrick Capps and Henrik P Olsen (eds), *Legal Authority Beyond the State* (Cambridge University Press 2018).

Føllesdal Andreas, *Subsidiarity* (Cambridge University Press, 2025).

Føllesdal Andreas, Peters Birgit, and Ulfstein Geir, 'Introduction' in Andreas Føllesdal, Birgit Peters, and Geir Ulfstein (eds), *Constituting Europe: The European Court of Human Rights in a National, European and Global Context* (Cambridge University Press 2013).

Forst Rainer, 'The Basic Right to Justification: Toward a Constructivist Conception of Human Rights' (1999) 6(1) Constellations 35 (Jonathan M Caver, tr).

Fredman Sandra, *Human Rights Transformed: Positive Rights and Positive Duties* (Oxford University Press 2008).

Fredman Sandra, *Discrimination Law* (2nd edn, Oxford University Press 2011).

Fredman Sandra, 'From Dialogue to Deliberation: Human Rights Adjudication and Prisoners' Rights to Vote' in Murray Hunt, Hayley J Hooper, and Paul Yowell (eds), *Parliaments and Human Rights: Redressing the Democratic Deficit* (Hart 2015).

Freeman Samuel, 'Constitutional Democracy and the Legitimacy of Constitutional Review' (1990) 9(4) Law & Philosophy 327.

Fukuyama Francis, *The End of History and the Last Man* (Free Press 1992).

Fukuyama Francis, 'America: The Failed State' *Prospect* (London, 13 December 2016) <https://www.prospectmagazine.co.uk> accessed 30 June 2024.

Fuller Lon L, *The Morality of Law* (Storrs Lectures on Jurisprudence 1963, rev edn, Yale University Press 1969).

Fyrnys Markus, 'Expanding Competences by Judicial Lawmaking: The Pilot Judgment Procedure of the European Court of Human Rights' in Armin von Bogdandy and Ingo Venzke (eds), *International Judicial Lawmaking: On Public Authority and Democratic Legitimation in Global Governance* (Springer 2012).

Gardbaum Stephen, 'Limiting Constitutional Rights' (2007) 54(4) UCLA Law Review 789.

Gardbaum Stephen, *The New Commonwealth Model of Constitutionalism: Theory and Practice* (Cambridge University Press 2013).

Gardbaum Stephen, 'Proportionality and Democratic Constitutionalism' in Grant Huscroft, Bradley W Miller, and Grégoire CN Webber (eds), *Proportionality and the Rule of Law: Rights, Justification, Reasoning* (Cambridge University Press 2014).

Gardbaum Stephen, 'What Is Judicial Supremacy?' in Gary Jacobsohn and Miguel Schor (eds), *Comparative Constitutional Theory* (Edward Elgar 2018).

Gearty Conor, 'Building Consensus on European Consensus' in Panos Kapotas and Vassilis P Tzevelekos (eds), *Building Consensus on European Consensus: Judicial Interpretation of Human Rights in Europe and Beyond* (Cambridge University Press 2019).

Gee Graham and Webber Grégoire CN, 'What Is a Political Constitution?' (2010) 30(2) Oxford Journal of Legal Studies 273.

Gerards Janneke, 'How to Improve the Necessity Test of the European Court of Human Rights' (2013) 11(2) International Journal of Constitutional Law 466.

Gerards Janneke, 'The European Court of Human Rights and the National Courts: Giving Shape to the Notion of "Shared Responsibility"' in Janneke Gerards and Joseph Fleuren (eds), *Implementation of the European Convention on Human Rights and of the Judgments of the ECtHR in National Case-Law: A Comparative Analysis* (Intersentia 2014).

Gerards Janneke, 'Margin of Appreciation and Incrementalism in the Case Law of the European Court of Human Rights' (2018) 18(3) Human Rights Law Review 495.

Gerards Janneke, *General Principles of the European Convention on Human Rights* (Cambridge University Press 2019).

Gerstenberg Oliver, '(The Failure of) Public Law and the Deliberative Turn' in Cormac Mac Amhlaigh, Claudio Michelon, and Neil Walker (eds), *After Public Law* (Oxford University Press 2013).

Giannopoulos Christos, 'The Reception by Domestic Courts of the Res Interpretata Effect of Jurisprudence of the European Court of Human Rights' (2019) 19(3) Human Rights Law Review 537.

Ginsburg Tom, 'Bounded Discretion in International Judicial Lawmaking' (2004) 45(3) Virginia Journal of International Law 631.

Ginsburg Tom, 'Political Constraints on International Courts' in Cesare P Romano, Karen J Alter, and Yuval Shany (eds), *The Oxford Handbook of International Adjudication* (Oxford University Press 2013).

Grabenwarter Christoph and Pellonpää Matti, '"High Judicial Office" and "Jurisconsult of Recognised Competence": Reflections on the Qualifications for Becoming a Judge at the Strasbourg Court' (2020) 80(1) Zeitschrift für ausländisches öffentliches Recht und Völkerrecht 13.

Greer Steven, 'Should Police Threats to Torture Suspects Always Be Severely Punished? Reflections on the Gäfgen Case' (2011) 11(1) Human Rights Law Review 67.

Greer Steven and Wildhaber Luzius, 'Revisiting the Debate About "Constitutionalising" the European Court of Human Rights' (2012) 12(4) Human Rights Law Review 655.

Griffin James, *On Human Rights* (Oxford University Press 2008).

Griffith JAG, 'The Political Constitution' (1979) 42(1) Modern Law Review 1.

Groupe Plessis, 'Cour européenne des droits de l'homme: pourquoi en sortir est un impératif démocratique' *Le Figaro* (Paris, 21 June 2016).

Habermas Jürgen, 'Natural Law and Revolution' in his *Theory and Practice* (John Viertel tr, first published 1963, Beacon Press 1973).

Habermas Jürgen, *Between Facts and Norms: Contributions to a Discourse Theory of Law and Democracy* (William Rehg tr, first published 1992, MIT Press 1996).

Hanretty Christ, *A Court of Specialists: Judicial Behavior on the UK Supreme Court* (Oxford University Press 2020).

Harlow Carol, 'Public Law and Popular Justice' (2002) 65(1) Modern Law Review 1.

Hart HLA, 'Are There Any Natural Rights?' (1955) 64(2) Philosophical Review 175.

Harutyunyan Armen, 'The Future of the European Court of Human Rights in the Era of Radical Democracy' (2021) 2(1) European Convention on Human Rights Law Review 20.

Haslett DW, 'What Is Wrong with Reflective Equilibria?' (1987) 37(148) The Philosophical Quarterly 305.

Hayek Friedrich A, *Law, Legislation and Liberty, vol 3: The Political Order of a Free People: A New Statement of the Liberal Principles of Justice and Political Economy* (first published 1979, Routledge & Kegan Paul 1982).

Hayek Friedrich A, 'The Pretence of Knowledge: Nobel Memorial Lecture, December 11, 1974' (1989) 79(6) American Economic Review 3.

Heise Michael, 'Preliminary Thoughts on the Virtues of Passive Dialogue' (2001) 34(1) Akron Law Review 73.

Held David, *Models of Democracy* (3rd edn, Polity 2006).
Helfer Laurence R, 'Redesigning the European Court of Human Rights: Embeddedness as a Deep Structural Principle of the European Human Rights Regime' (2008) 19(1) European Journal of International Law 125.
Helfer Laurence R and Voeten Erik, 'International Courts as Agents of Legal Change: Evidence from LGBT Rights in Europe' (2014) 68(1) International Oganization 77.
Helfer Laurence R and Voeten Erik, 'Walking Back Human Rights in Europe?' (2020) 31(3) European Journal of International Law 797.
Hentrei Simon, 'Generalising the Principle of Complementarity: Framing International Judicial Authority' (2013) 4(3) Transnational Legal Theory 419.
Heri Corina, 'Loyalty, Subsidiarity, and Article 18 ECHR: How the ECtHR Deals with Mala Fide Limitations of Rights' (2020) 1(1) European Convention on Human Rights Law Review 25.
Hillebrecht Courtney, *Domestic Politics and International Human Rights Tribunals: The Problem of Compliance* (Cambridge University Press 2014).
Hirschl Ran, *Towards Juristocracy: The Origins and Consequences of the New Constitutionalism* (Harvard University Press 2004).
Hirschl Ran, 'The New Constitutionalism and the Judicialization of Pure Politics Worldwide' (2006) 75(2) Fordham Law Review 721.
Hittinger Russel, 'The Coherence of the Four Basic Principles of Catholic Social Doctrine: An Interpretation' in Margaret S Archer and Pierpaolo Donati (eds), *Pursuing the Common Good: How Solidarity and Subsidiarity Can Work Together* (Proceedings of the 14th Plenary Session, Pontifical Academy of the Social Sciences 2008).
Hodson Loveday, 'Activists and Lawyers in the ECtHR: The Struggle for Gay Rights' in Dia Anagnostou (ed), *Rights and Courts in Pursuit of Social Change: Legal Mobilisation in the Multi-Level European System* (Hart 2014).
Hogg Peter and Bushell Allison, 'The Charter Dialogue Between Courts and Legislatures (or Perhaps the Charter of Rights Isn't Such a Bad Thing After All)' (1997) 35(1) Osgoode Hall Law Journal 75.
Holmes John T, 'Complementarity: National Courts Versus the ICC' in Antonio Cassese, Paolo Gaeta, and John RWD Jones (eds), *The Rome Statute of the International Criminal Court* (Oxford University Press 2002) vol 1.
Holmes Oliver W, 'The Path of the Law' (1997) 110(5) Harvard Law Review 991.
Holmes Stephen, *Passions and Constraint: On the Theory of Liberal Democracy* (Chicago University Press 1995).
Howe Paul, 'Eroding Norms and Democratic Deconsolidation' (2017) 28(4) Journal of Democracy 15.
Huijbers Leonie M, *Process-Based Fundamental Rights Review: Practice, Concept, and Theory* (Intersentia 2019).
Inglehart Ronald and Norris Pipa, 'Trump and the Populist Authoritarian Parties: The Silent Revolution in Reverse' (2017) 15(2) Perspectives on Politics 443.
Jackson Vicki C, 'Constitutions as "Living Trees"? Comparative Constitutional Law and Interpretive Metaphors' (2006) 75(2) Fordham Law Review 921.
Jahn Jannika, 'Ruling (In)directly Through Individual Measures? Effect and Legitimacy of the ECtHR's New Remedial Power' (2014) 74(1) Zeitschrift für ausländisches öffentliches Recht und Völkerrecht 1.
Johnson Paul, 'Sociology and the European Court of Human Rights' (2014) 62(3) Sociological Review 547.
Kapotas Panos and Tzevelekos Vassilis P, 'How (Difficult Is It) to Build Consensus on (European) Consensus?' in Panos Kapotas and Vassilis P Tzevelekos (eds), *Building Consensus on European Consensus: Judicial Interpretation of Human Rights in Europe and Beyond* (Cambridge University Press 2019).
Keller Helen and Garin Aurore, 'Câmpeanu: quo vadis? Le recours individuel en péril' (2017) 28(111) Revue trimestrielle des droits de l'homme 485.

Keller Helen and Heri Corina, 'Selective Criminal Proceedings and Article 18 ECHR: The European Court of Human Rights' Untapped Potential to Protect Democracy' (2016) 36 Human Rights Law Journal 1.

Keller Helen and Marti Cedric, 'Reconceptualizing Implementation: The Judicialization of the Execution of the European Court of Human Rights' Judgments' (2016) 26(4) European Journal of International Law 829.

Keller Helen and Stone Sweet Alec (eds), *A Europe of Rights: The Impact of the ECHR on National Legal Systems* (Oxford University Press 2008).

Keller Helen and Walther Reto, 'Balancing Test: United Nations Human Rights Bodies' in Hélène Ruiz Fabri (ed), *Max Planck Encyclopedia of International Procedural Law* (April 2018, Oxford University Press) <https://opil.ouplaw.com> accessed 30 June 2024.

Keller Helen and Walther Reto, 'Resistance in Switzerland: Populist Rather than Principled' in Marten Breuer (ed), *Principled Resistance Against ECtHR Judgments—A New Paradigm?* (Springer 2019).

Keller Helen and Walther Reto, 'The Bell of Görgülü Can't Be Unrung—Can it?' (2020) 19 Global Community Yearbook of International Law and Jurisprudence 83.

Kelsen Hans, 'La garantie juridictionnelle de la Constitution (La Justice constitutionnelle)' (1928) 45 Revue du droit public et de la science politique en France et à l'étranger 197.

Kelsen Hans, *Introduction to the Problems of Legal Theory* (1st edn of the Reine Rechtslehre or Pure Theory of Law, with an Introduction by Stanley L Paulson, Bonnie Litschewski Paulson and Stanley L Paulson trs, first published 1934, Clarendon Press 1992).

Kleinlein Thomas, 'Consensus and Contestability: The ECtHR and the Combined Potential of European Consensus and Procedural Rationality Control' (2017) 28(3) European Journal of International Law 871.

Koch Ida E, *Human Rights as Indivisible Rights: The Protection of Socio-Economic Demands Under the European Convention on Human Rights* (Martinus Nijhoff 2009).

Koopmans Tim, 'Federalism: The Wrong Debate' (1992) 29(6) Common Market Law Review 1047.

Kosař David, 'Selecting Strasbourg Judges: A Critique' in Michal Bobek (ed), *Selecting Europe's Judges: A Critical Review of the Appointment Procedures to the European Courts* (Oxford University Press 2015).

Kosař David, 'Nudging Domestic Judicial Reforms from Strasbourg: How the European Court of Human Rights Shapes Domestic Judicial Design' (2017) 13 Utrecht Law Review 112.

Kosař David and Lixinski Lucas, 'Domestic Judicial Design by International Human Rights Courts' (2015) 109(4) American Journal of International Law 713.

Koskenniemi Martti, *From Apology to Utopia: The Structure of International Legal Argument* (first published 1989, Cambridge University Press 2006).

Kovler Anatoly and others, 'The Role of Consensus in the System of the European Convention on Human Rights' in European Court of Human Rights (ed), *Dialogue Between Judges* (Proceedings of the Seminar, Strasbourg, Council of Europe 2008).

Krotoszynski Ronald J, Jr, 'Constitutional Flares: On Judges, Legislatures, and Dialogue' (1998) 83(1) Minnesota Law Review 1.

Kumm Mattias, 'Who Is Afraid of the Total Constitution? Constitutional Rights as Principles and the Constitutionalization of Private Law' (2006) 7(4) German Law Journal 341.

Kumm Mattias, 'The Idea of Socratic Contestation and the Right to Justification: The Point of Rights-Based Proportionality Review' (2010) 4(2) Law & Ethics of Human Rights 140.

Lambert-Abdelgawad Elisabeth, 'The Court as a Part of the Council of Europe: The Parliamentary Assembly and the Committee of Ministers' in Andreas Føllesdal, Birgit Peters, and Geir Ulfstein (eds), *Constituting Europe: The European Court of Human Rights in a National, European and Global Context* (Cambridge University Press 2013).

Lambrecht Sarah, 'Assessing the Existence of Criticism of the European Court of Human Rights' in Patricia Popelier, Sarah Lambrecht, and Koen Lemmens (eds), *Criticism of the European Court of Human Rights: Shifting the Convention System: Counter-Dynamics at the National and EU Level* (Intersentia 2016).

Lautenbach Geranne, *The Concept of the Rule of Law and the European Court of Human Rights* (Oxford University Press 2013).
Laws John, *The Common Law Constitution* (Hamlyn Lectures 2013, Cambridge University Press 2014).
Leach Philip, 'The Parliamentary Assembly of the Council of Europe' in Marten Breuer and Stefanie Schmahl (eds), *The Council of Europe: Its Law and Policies* (Oxford University Press 2017).
Leach Philip, 'On Inter-State Litigation and Armed Conflict Cases in Strasbourg' (2021) 2(1) European Convention on Human Rights Law Review 27.
Lefort Claude, 'Politics and Human Rights' in his *The Political Forms of Modern Society: Bureaucracy, Democracy, Totalitarianism* (first published 1980, MIT Press 1986).
Leijten Ingrid, *Core Socio-Economic Rights and the European Court of Human Rights* (Cambridge University Press 2018).
Lemmens Koen, '(S)electing Judges for Strasbourg: A (Dis)appointing Process?' in Michal Bobek (ed), *Selecting Europe's Judges: A Critical Review of the Appointment Procedures to the European Courts* (Oxford University Press 2015).
Lepsius Oliver, 'The Standard-Setting Power' in M Jestaedt and others, *The German Federal Constitutional Court: The Court Without Limits* (Jeff Seitzer tr, Oxford University Press 2020).
Letsas George, *A Theory of Interpretation of the European Convention on Human Rights* (paperback edn, Oxford University Press 2009).
Letsas George, 'Strasbourg's Interpretive Ethic: Lessons for the International Lawyer' (2010) 21(3) European Journal of International Law 509.
Letsas George, 'The ECHR as a Living Instrument: Its Meaning and Legitimacy' in Andreas Føllesdal, Birgit Peters, and Geir Ulfstein (eds), *Constituting Europe: The European Court of Human Rights in a National, European and Global Context* (Cambridge University Press 2013).
Letsas George, 'Rescuing Proportionality' in Rowan Cruft, S Matthew Liao, and Massimo Renzo (eds), *Philosophical Foundations of Human Rights* (Oxford University Press 2015).
Letsas George, 'Proportionality as Fittingness: The Moral Dimension of Proportionality' (2018) 71(1) Current Legal Problems 53.
Levine Andrew, *Liberal Democracy: A Critique of Its Theory* (Columbia University Press 1981).
López Guerra Luis, 'The National Judge and Judicial Independence: The Case of the Strasbourg Court' (2017) 24(4) Maastricht Journal of European and Comparative Law 552.
Loughlin Martin, *Sword and Scales: An Examination of the Relationship Between Law and Politics* (Hart 2000).
Loughlin Martin, *The Idea of Public Law* (Oxford University Press 2004).
Loughlin Martin, 'What Is Constitutionalisation?' in Petra Dobner and Martin Loughlin (eds), *The Twilight of Constitutionalism?* (Oxford University Press 2010).
Loven Claire, '"Verticalised" Cases Before the European Court of Human Rights Unravelled: An Analysis of Their Characteristics and the Court's Approach to Them' (2020) 38(4) Netherlands Quarterly of Human Rights 246.
Madsen Mikael R, '"Legal Diplomacy"—Law, Politics and the Genesis of Postwar European Human Rights' in Stefan-Ludwig Hoffmann (ed), *Human Rights in the Twentieth Century* (Cambridge University Press 2011).
Madsen Mikael R, 'The International Judiciary as Transnational Power Elite' (2014) 8(3) International Political Sociology 332.
Madsen Mikael R, 'The Challenging Authority of the European Court of Human Rights: From Cold War Legal Diplomacy to the Brighton Declaration and Backlash' (2016) 79(1) Law and Contemporary Problems 141.
Madsen Mikael R, 'Rebalancing European Human Rights: Has the Brighton Declaration Engendered a New Deal on Human Rights in Europe?' (2018) 9(2) Journal of International Dispute Settlement 199.
Madsen Mikael R, '"Unity in Diversity" Reloaded: The European Court of Human Rights' Turn to Subsidiarity and Its Consequences' (2021) 15(1) Law & Ethics of Human Rights 93.

Mahoney Paul, 'Marvellous Richness of Diversity or Invidious Cultural Relativism?' (1998) 19(1) Human Rights Law Journal 1.

Mahoney Paul and Kondak Rachael, 'Common Ground: A Starting Point or Destination for Comparative-Law Analysis by the European Court of Human Rights?' in Mads Andenas and Duncan Fairgrieve (eds), *Courts and Comparative Law* (Oxford University Press 2015).

Mamolea Andrei, 'Good Faith Review' in Lukasz Gruszczynski and Wouter Werner (eds), *Deference in International Courts and Tribunals: Standard of Review and Margin of Appreciation* (Oxford University Press 2014).

Mann Roni, 'Non-Ideal Theory of Constitutional Adjudication' (2018) 7(1) Global Constitutionalism 14.

Marks Susan, 'Reservations Unhinged: The Belilos Case Before the European Court of Human Rights' (1990) 39(2) International and Comparative Law Quarterly 300.

Marquis de Condorcet, 'The Sketch', in Steven Lukes and Nadia Urbinati (eds), *Condorcet: Political Writings* (first published 1795 as Prospectus d'un tableau historique des progrès de l'esprit humain, Cambridge University Press 2012).

Marti Cedric, *Framing a Convention Community: Supranational Aspects of the European Convention on Human Rights* (Cambridge University Press 2021).

May Kenneth O, 'A Set of Independent Necessary and Sufficient Conditions for Simple Majority Decision' (1952) 20(4) Econometrica 680.

Mayer Benoit, 'Climate Change Mitigation as an Obligation Under Human Rights Treaties?' (2021) 115(3) American Journal of International Law 409.

McHarg Aileen, 'Reconciling Human Rights and the Public Interest: Conceptual Problems and Doctrinal Uncertainty in the Jurisprudence of the European Court of Human Rights' (1999) 62(5) Modern Law Review 671.

Mégret Frédéric, 'International Judges and Experts' Impartiality and the Problem of Past Declarations' (2011) 10(1) Law and Practice of International Courts and Tribunals 31.

Merrills John G, *The Development of International Law by the European Court of Human Rights* (Manchester University Press 1988).

Miller Bradley W, 'Majoritarianism and Pathologies of Judicial Review' in G Webber and others, *Legislated Rights: Securing Human Rights Through Legislation* (Cambridge University Press 2018).

Milner David, 'Protocols No. 15 and 16 to the European Convention on Human Rights in the Context of the Perennial Process of Reform: A Long and Winding Road' (2014) 17(1) Zeitschrift für Europarechtliche Studien 19.

Möllers Christoph, *The Three Branches: A Comparative Model of Separation of Powers* (Oxford University Press 2013).

Moravcsik Andrew, 'The Origins of Human Rights Regimes: Democratic Delegation in Postwar Europe' (2000) 54(2) International Oganization 217.

Mouffe Chantal, *The Democratic Paradox* (Verso 2000).

Mounk Yascha, *The People vs. Democracy: Why Our Freedom Is in Danger and How to Save It* (Harvard University Press 2018).

Mowbray Alastair, 'An Examination of the Work of the Grand Chamber of the European Court of Human Rights' [2007] Public Law 507.

Mowbray Alastair, 'A Study of the Principle of Fair Balance in the Jurisprudence of the European Court of Human Rights' (2010) 10(2) Human Rights Law Review 289.

Mowbray Alastair, 'An Examination of the European Court of Human Rights' Indication of Remedial Measures' (2017) 17(3) Human Rights Law Review 451.

Müller Amrei, 'Domestic Authorities' Obligations to Co-Develop the Rights of the European Convention on Human Rights' (2016) 20(8) International Journal of Human Rights 1058.

Mureinik Etienne, 'A Bridge to Where? Introducing the Interim Bill of Rights' (1994) 10(1) South African Journal on Human Rights 31.

Nagel Thomas, *The Last Word* (Oxford University Press 1997).

Nicol Danny, *The Constitutional Protection of Capitalism* (Hart 2010).

Nikolaidis Charilaos, *The Right to Equality in European Human Rights Law: The Quest for Substance in the Jurisprudence of the European Courts* (Routledge 2015).

Nußberger Angelika, 'Subsidiarity in the Control of Decisions Based on Proportionality: An Analysis of the Basis of the Implementation of ECtHR Judgments into German Law' in Anja Seibert-Fohr and Mark E Villiger (eds), *Judgments of the European Court of Human Rights: Effects and Implementation* (Nomos 2014).

Nußberger Angelika, *The European Court of Human Rights* (Oxford University Press 2020).

Nußberger Angelika, '"To Be a Judge Means to be Criticized from All Sides" (Interview, Dana Schmalz and Raffaela Kunz)' (*Völkerrechtsblog*, 3 February 2020) <https://voelkerrechtsblog.org> accessed 30 June 2024.

O'Connell Rory, *Law, Democracy and the European Court of Human Rights* (Cambridge University Press 2020).

O'Mahony Conor, 'If a Constitution Is Easy to Amend, Can Judges Be Less Restrained? Rights, Social Change, and Proposition 8' (2014) 27 Harvard Human Rights Journal 191.

Offe Claus, '"Homogeneity" and Constitutional Democracy: Coping with Identity Conflicts Through Group Rights' (1998) 6(2) Journal of Political Philosophy 113.

Ogus Anthony I, 'Law and Spontaneous Order: Hayek's Contribution to Legal Theory' (1989) 16(4) Journal of Law and Society 393.

Padmanabhan Vijay M, 'The Human Rights Justification for Consent' (2013) 35(1) University of Pennsylvania Journal of International Law 1.

Palmer Simon, 'The Committee of Ministers' in Marten Breuer and Stefanie Schmahl (eds), *The Council of Europe: Its Law and Policies* (Oxford University Press 2017).

Pape Poulsen Søren, 'Opening Speech', *Conference Report: High-Level Expert Conference "2019 and Beyond: Taking Stock and Moving Forward from the Interlaken Process"* (2017).

Pavel Carmen, *Law Beyond the State: Dynamic Coordination, State Consent, and Binding International Law* (Oxford University Press 2021).

Perry Micheal J, *The Constitution, the Courts, and Human Rights: An Inquiry into the Legitimacy of Constitutional Policymaking by the Judiciary* (Yale University Press 1984).

Pettit Philip, *Republicanism: A Theory of Freedom and Government* (Oxford University Press 1999).

Pius, XI, Pope, 'Quadragesimo Anno: Encyclical on Reconstruction of the Social Order' (15 May 1931).

Pogge Thomas W, 'Cosmopolitanism and Sovereignty' (1992) 103(1) Ethics 48.

Pollinico Oreste, 'Toward a Convergence Between the EU and ECHR Legal Systems? A Comparative Perspective' in Giorgio Repetto (ed), *The Constitutional Relevance of the ECHR in Domestic and Europen Law: An Italian Perspective* (Intersentia 2013).

Pontifical Council for Justice and Peace, *Compendium of the Social Doctrine of the Church* (Libreria Editrice Vaticana 2004).

Popelier Patricia, 'The Court as Regulatory Watchdog: The Procedural Approach in the Case Law of the European Court of Human Rights' in Patricia Popelier, Armen Mazmanyan, and Werner Vandenbruwaene (eds), *The Role of Constitutional Courts in Multilevel Governance* (Intersentia 2013).

Popper Karl, *The Open Society and Its Enemies* (first published 1945, Princeton University Press 2013).

Posner Eric A, 'Liberal Internationalism and the Populist Backlash' (2017) 49 (Special Issue) Arizona State Law Journal 795.

Posner Richard A, 'What Do Judges and Justices Maximize? (The Same Thing Everybody Else Does)' (1993) 3(1) Supreme Court Economic Review 1.

Poulsen Søren Pape, 'Opening Speech (abstract)' in Conference Report (High-Level Expert Conference '2019 and Beyond: Taking Stock and Moving Forward from the Interlaken Process', Kokkedal, 22–24 November 2017) <https://perma.cc/2WM6-356V> accessed 30 June 2024.

Ragnarrson Kári H, 'The Counter-Majoritarian Difficulty in a Neoliberal World: Socio-Economic Rights and Deference in post-2008 Austerity Cases' (2019) 8(3) Global Constitutionalism 605.

Rajamani Lavany, 'The 2015 Paris Agreement: Interplay Between Hard, Soft and Non-Obligations' (2016) 28(2) Journal of Environmental Law 337.
Rasulov Akbar, 'Review: From Apology to Utopia: The Structure of International Legal Argument' (2006) 18(8) Law & Political Book Review 583.
Rawls John, *Political Liberalism* (expanded edn, Columbia University Press 2005).
Raz Joseph, 'On the Nature of Rights' (1984) 93(730) Mind 194.
Raz Joseph, 'Rights and Politics' (1995) 71(1) Indiana Law Journal 27.
Raz Joseph, 'The Future of State Sovereignty' in Wojciech Sadurski, Michael Sevel, and Kevin Walton (eds), *Legitimacy: The State and Beyond* (Oxford University Press 2019).
Reich Johannes and Boss Nina, 'Switzerland' (2022) 33(1) Yearbook of International Environmental Law 149.
Resnik Judith, 'Courts and Economic and Social Rights/Courts as Economic and Social Rights' in Katharine G Young (ed), *The Future of Economic and Social Rights* (Cambridge University Press 2019).
Richardson Henry S, *Democratic Autonomy: Public Reasoning About the Ends of Policy* (Oxford University Press 2003).
Rivers Julian, 'Proportionality and Variable Intensity of Review' (2006) 65(1) Cambridge Law Journal 174.
Robertson Arthur H, 'The European Court of Human Rights' (1960) 9(1) American Journal of Comparative Law 1.
Robertson David, *The Judge as Political Theorist: Contemporary Constitutional Review* (Princeton University Press 2010).
Rosenfeld Michel, 'Is Global Constitutionalism Meaningful or Desirable?' (2014) 25(1) European Journal of International Law 177.
Rousseau Jean-Jacques, *The Social Contract* (Christopher Betts tr, first published 1762, Oxford University Press 1994).
Rui Jon P, 'The Interlaken, Izmir and Brighton Declarations: Towards a Paradigm Shift in the Strasbourg Court's Interpretation of the European Convention on Human Rights' (2013) 31 Nordic Journal of Human Rights 28.
Sadurski Wojciech, *Equality and Legitimacy* (Oxford University Press 2008).
Sadurski Wojciech, 'Partnering with Strasbourg: Constitutionalisation of the European Court of Human Rights, the Accession of Central and East European States to the Council of Europe, and the Idea of Pilot Judgments' (2009) 9(3) Human Rights Law Review 397.
Sadurski Wojciech, *Rights Before Courts: A Study of Constitutional Courts in Postcommunist States of Central and Eastern Europe* (2nd edn, Springer 2014).
Sajó András and Uitz Renáta, *The Constitution of Freedom: An Introduction to Legal Constitutionalism* (Oxford University Press 2017).
Sangiovanni Andrea, 'Justice and the Priority of Politics to Morality' (2008) 16(2) Journal of Political Philosophy 137.
Sartori Daria, 'End-of-Life Issues Under the European Convention on Human Rights: The Value of Personal Autonomy Within a "Proceduralized" Review' (2018) 52 Questions of International Law 23.
Saul Matthew, 'The European Court of Human Rights' Margin of Appreciation and the Processes of National Parliaments' (2015) 15(4) Human Rights Law Review 745.
Scelle George, *Précis de droit des gens: principes et systématique, vol 2* (Sirey 1934).
Schabas William A, *The European Convention on Human Rights: A Commentary* (Oxford University Press 2015).
Schlink Bernhard, 'Die Entthronung der Staatsrechtswissenschaft durch die Verfassungsgerichtsbarkeit' (1989) 28(2) Der Staat 161.
Schmahl Stefanie, 'Budget and Financing' in Marten Breuer and Stefanie Schmahl (eds), *The Council of Europe: Its Law and Policies* (Oxford University Press 2017).
Scholtes Julian, 'The Complacency of Legality: Constitutionalist Vulnerabilities to Populist Constituent Power' (2019) 20(3) German Law Journal 351.

Schumpeter Joseph A, *Capitalism, Socialism and Democracy* (with a new introduction by Richard Swedberg, 5th edn, first published 1976, Routledge 2003).

Schütze Robert, 'EU Competences: Existence and Exercise' in Damian Chalmers and Anthony Arnull (eds), *The Oxford Handbook of European Union Law* (Oxford University Press 2015).

Seiler Hansjörg, 'Menschenrechte—Das trojanische Pferd des demokratischen Rechtsstaats' in Jean-Baptiste Zufferey, Jacques Dubey, and Adriano Previtali (eds), *L'Homme et son droit* (Mélanges en l'honneur de Marco Borghi, Schulthess 2011).

Sen Amartya, 'The Impossibility of a Paretian Liberal' (1970) 78(1) Journal of Political Economy 152.

Shapiro Martin, 'The Success of Judicial Review' in Sally J Kenney, William M Reisinger, and John C Reitz (eds), *Constitutional Dialogues in Comparative Perspective* (Palgrave MacMillan 1999).

Shelton Dinah, 'Subsidiarity and Human Rights Law' (2006) 27(1–4) Human Rights Law Journal 4.

Shiffrin Steven, 'Liberalism, Radicalism, and Legal Scholarship' (6) 30(1983) UCLA Law Review 1104.

Simmons Beth, *Mobilizing for Human Rights: International Law in Domestic Politics* (Cambridge University Press 2009).

Skinner Quentin, *Liberty Before Liberalism* (Cambridge University Press 2012).

Skouteris Thomas, 'The Idea of Progress' in Anne Orford and Florian Hoffmann (eds), *The Oxford Handbook of the Theory of International Law* (Oxford University Press 2016).

Smet Stijn and Brems Eva (eds), *When Human Rights Clash at the European Court of Human Rights: Conflict or Harmony?* (Oxford University Press 2017).

Sottiaux Stefan, *Terrorism and the Limitation of Rights: The ECHR and the US Constitution* (Hart 2008).

Spano Robert, 'Universality or Diversity of Human Rights? Strasbourg in the Age of Subsidiarity' (2014) 14(3) Human Rights Law Review 487.

Spano Robert, 'The European Court of Human Rights and National Courts: A Constructive Conversation or a Dialogue of Disrespect?' (2015) 33(1) Nordic Journal of Human Rights 1.

Spano Robert, 'The Future of the European Court of Human Rights—Subsidiarity, Process-Based Review and the Rule of Law' (2018) 18(3) Human Rights Law Review 473.

Spano Robert, 'Exchange of Views with the Committee of Ministers' Speech' (Strasbourg, 17 March 2021) <https://perma.cc/N555-CCC8> accessed 22 January 2026.

Spano Robert, 'Human Rights and Democracy in the Age of Digital Transformation and COVID-19' (Speech to the German Marshall Fund, 16 March 2021) <https://www.youtube.com/watch?v=-6Kb5L2Kh3g> accessed 30 June 2024.

Spielmann Dean, 'Foreword' to George Letsas, *A Theory of Interpretation of the European Convention on Human Rights* (paperback edn, Oxford University Press 2009).

Stiansen Øyvind and Voeten Erik, 'Backlash and Judicial Restraint: Evidence from the European Court of Human Rights' (2020) 64(4) International Studies Quarterly 770.

Stone Sweet Alec, 'On the Constitutionalisation of the Convention: The European Court of Human Rights as a Constitutional Court' (2009) Yale Law School Faculty Scholarship Series no 71 <https://papers.ssrn.com/sol3/papers.cfm?abstract_id=1569359> accessed 30 June 2024.

Stone Sweet Alec, 'Sur la constitutionnalisation de la Convention européenne des droits de l'homme: Cinquante ans après son installation, la Cour européenne des droits de l'homme conçue comme une Cour constitutionnelle' (2009) 20(80) Revue trimestrielle des droits de l'homme 923 (Michel Puéchavy, tr).

Stone Sweet Alec, 'A Cosmopolitan Legal Order: Constitutional Pluralism and Rights Adjudication in Europe' (2012) 1(1) Global Constitutionalism 53.

Stone Sweet Alec and Brunell Thomas L, 'Trustee Courts and the Judicialization of International Regimes: The Politics of Majoritarian Activism in the European Convention on Human Rights, the European Union, and the World Trade Organization' (2013) 1(1) Journal of Law and Courts 61.

Stone Sweet Alec and Mathews Jud, *Proportionality Balancing and Constitutional Governance: A Comparative and Global Approach* (Oxford University Press 2019).

Strezhnev Anton, Simmons Beth A, and Kim Matthew D, 'Rulers or Rules? International Law, Elite Cues and Public Opinion' (2019) 30(4) European Journal of International Law 1281.

Sumption Lord, 'The Limits of Law' 27th Sultan Azlan Shah Lecture (Kuala Lumpur, 20 November 2013) <https://www.supremecourt.uk/docs/speech-131120.pdf> accessed 30 June 2024.

Sunstein Cass R, 'Interest Groups in American Public Law' (1985) 38(1) Stanford Law Review 29.

Sunstein Cass R, *The Partial Constitution* (Harvard University Press 1993).

Sunstein Cass R, *One Case at a Time: Judicial Minimalism on the Supreme Court* (Harvard University Press 1999).

Sunstein Cass R, 'Beyond Judicial Minimalism' (2008) 43 Tulsa Law Review 825.

Sunstein Cass R, *Legal Reasoning and Political Conflict* (2nd edn, Oxford University Press 2018).

Tan Floris, 'The Dawn of Article 18 ECHR: A Safeguard Against European Rule of Law Backsliding?' (2018) 9(1) Goettingen Journal of International Law 109.

Tasioulas John, 'Human Rights, Legitimacy, and International Law' (2001) 58(1) American Journal of Jurisprudence 1.

Thayer James B, 'The Origin and Scope of the American Doctrine of Constitutional Law' (1893) 7(3) Harvard Law Review 129.

Theilen Jens T, *European Consensus Between Strategy and Principle: The Uses of Vertically Comparative Legal Reasoning in Regional Human Rights Adjudication* (Nomos 2021).

Tomkins Adam, 'In Defence of the Political Constitution' (2002) 22(1) Oxford Journal of Legal Studies 157.

Tomkins Adam, 'The Role of the Courts in the Political Constitution' (2010) 60(1) University of Toronto Law Journal 1.

Torres Pérez Aida, 'In Nobody's Name: A Checks and Balances Approach to International Judicial Independence' in Hélène Ruiz Fabri and others (eds), *International Judicial Legitimacy: New Voices and Approaches* (Nomos 2020).

Touzé Sébastien, 'La complémentarité procédurale de la garantie conventionnelle' in Frédéric Sudre (ed), *Le principe de subsidiarité au sens du droit de la Convention européenne des droits de l'homme* (Anthemis 2014).

Trechsel Stefan, 'Preface' to Howard C Yourow, *The Margin of Appreciation Doctrine in the Dynamics of European Human Rights Jurisprudence* (Martinus Nijhoff 1996).

Tremblay Luc B, 'The Legitimacy of Judicial Review: The Limits of Dialogue Between Courts and Legislatures' (2005) 3(4) International Journal of Constitutional Law 617.

Tushnet Mark, *Taking the Constitution Away from the Courts* (Princeton University Press 1999).

Tushnet Mark, *Weak Courts, Strong Rights: Judicial Review and Social Welfare Rights in Comparative Constitutional Law* (Princeton University Press 2008).

Tzanakopoulos Antonios, 'Judicial Dialogue as a Means of Interpretation' in Helmut P Aust and Georg Nolte (eds), *The Interpretation of International Law by Domestic Courts: Uniformity, Diversity, Convergence* (Oxford University Press 2016).

Ulfstein Geir, 'The European Court of Human Rights and National Courts: A Constitutional Relationship?' in Oddný M Árnardóttir and Antoine Buyse (eds), *Shifting Centres of Gravity in Human Rights Protection: Rethinking Relations Between the ECHR, EU and National Legal Orders* (Routledge 2016).

Ulfstein Geir, 'Evolutive Interpretation in the Light of Other International Instruments: Law and Legitimacy' in Anne van Aaken and Iulia Motoc (eds), *The European Convention on Human Rights and General International Law* (Oxford University Press 2018).

Ulfstein Geir, 'Transnational Constitutional Aspects of the European Court of Human Rights' (2021) 10(1) Global Constitutionalism 151.

van den Eynde Laura, 'The Consensus Argument in NGOs' Amicus Curiae Briefs: Defending Minorities Through a Creatively Used Majoritarian Argument' in Panos Kapotas and Vassilis P Tzevelekos (eds), *Building Consensus on European Consensus: Judicial Interpretation of Human Rights in Europe and Beyond* (Cambridge University Press 2019).

van Dijk Pieter and van Hoof Fried, *Theory and Practice of the European Convention on Human Rights* (2nd edn, Kluwer 1990).
van Drooghenbroeck Sébastien, *La proportionnalité dans le droit de la Convention européenne des droits de l'homme: Prendre l'idée simple au serieux* (Bruylant 2001).
van Drooghenbroeck Sébastien and Rizcallah Cecilia, 'The ECHR and the Essence of Fundamental Rights: Searching for Sugar in Hot Milk?' (2019) 20(6) German Law Journal 904.
Voeten Erik, 'The Politics of International Judicial Appointments: Evidence from the European Court of Human Rights' (2007) 61(4) International Oganization 669.
von Bernstorff Jochen, 'Authority Monism in International Organisations: A Historical Sketch' in Joana Mendes and Ingo Venzke (eds), *Allocating Authority: Who Should Do What in European and International Law?* (Hart 2018).
von Bogdandy Armin, 'Pluralism, Direct Effect, and the Ultimate Say: On the Relationship Between International and Domestic Constitutional Law' (2008) 6(3–4) International Journal of Constitutional Law 397.
von Bogdandy Armin, 'In the Name of the European Club of Liberal Democracies: How to Evaluate the Strasbourg Jurisprudence' (*EJIL Talk!*, 20 December 2018) <https://www.ejiltalk.org> accessed 30 June 2024.
von Bogdandy Armin and Venzke Ingo, 'Beyond Dispute: International Judicial Institutions as Lawmakers' in Armin von Bogdandy and Ingo Venzke (eds), *International Judicial Lawmaking: On Public Authority and Democratic Legitimation in Global Governance* (Springer 2012).
von Bogdandy Armin and Venzke Ingo, 'In Whose Name? An Investigation of International Courts' Public Authority and Its Democratic Justification' (2012) 23(1) European Journal of International Law 7.
von Bogdandy Armin and Venzke Ingo, *In Whose Name? A Public Law Theory of International Adjudication* (Thomas Dunlap tr, Oxford University Press 2014).
von Staden Andreas, *Strategies of Compliance with the European Court of Human Rights: Rational Choice Within Normative Constraints* (University of Pennsylvania Press 2018).
Waldron Jeremy, 'Rights of Majorities and Minorities: Rousseau Revisited' in John W Chapman and Alan Wertheimer (eds), *Majorities and Minorities* (Nomos XXXII, NYU Press 1990).
Waldron Jeremy, 'A Right-Based Critique of Constitutional Rights' (1993) 13(1) Oxford Journal of Legal Studies 18.
Waldron Jeremy, 'Moral Truth and Judicial Review' (1998) 43(1) American Journal of Jurisprudence 75.
Waldron Jeremy, 'The Constitutional Conception of Democracy' in his *Law and Disagreement* (Oxford University Press 1999).
Waldron Jeremy, *The Dignity of Legislation* (Cambridge University Press 1999).
Waldron Jeremy, *Law and Disagreement* (Oxford University Press 1999).
Waldron Jeremy, 'The Core of the Case Against Judicial Review' (2006) 115(6) Yale Law Journal 1346.
Waldron Jeremy, 'Can There Be a Democratic Jurisprudence?' (2009) 58(3) Emory Law Journal 675.
Waldron Jeremy, 'Judicial Review and Judicial Supremacy' (November 2014) NYU School of Law Public Law & Legal Theory Research Paper Series No 14-57 <https://ssrn.com/abstract=2510550> accessed 30 June 2024.
Walen Alec, 'Judicial Review in Review: A Four-Part Defense of Legal Constitutionalism: A Review Essay on Political Constitutionalism, by Richard Bellamy' (2009) 7(2) International Journal of Constitutional Law 329.
Walen Alec, 'A Unified Theory of Detention, with Application to Preventive Detention for Suspected Terrorists' (2011) 70(4) Maryland Law Review 871.
Walker Neil, 'Constitutionalism and the Incompleteness of Democracy: An Iterative Relationship' (2010) 39(3) Rechtsfilosofie & Rechtstheorie 206.
Waluchow WJ, 'Constitutional Morality and Bills of Rights' in Grant Huscroft (ed), *Expounding the Constitution: Essays in Constitutional Theory* (Cambridge University Press 2008).

Walzer Michael, *Spheres of Justice: A Defense of Pluralism and Equality* (Basic Books 1983).
Weber Max, 'Die wirtschaftlichen Unternehmungen der Gemeinden' (Diskussionsbeitrag auf der Generalversammlung des Vereins für Sozialpolitik am 28. September 1909), in *Max Weber-Gesamtausgabe: Wirtschaft, Staat und Sozialpolitik: Schriften und Reden 1900–1912, Vol I/8* (Wolfgang Schluchter ed, Mohr Siebeck 1998).
White Robin CA and Boussiakou Iris, 'Separate Opinions in the European Court of Human Rights' (2009) 9(1) Human Rights Law Review 37.
Wildhaber Luzius, Hjartarson Arnaldur, and Donnelly Stephen, 'No Consensus on Consensus? The Practice of the European Court of Human Rights' (2013) 33(7–12) Human Rights Law Journal 248.
Wolkenstein Fabio, 'European Political Parties' Complicity in Democratic Backsliding' (2022) 11(1) Global Constitutionalism 55.
Wollheim Richard, 'A Paradox in the Theory of Democracy' in Peter Laslett and WG Runciman (eds), *Philosophy, Politics and Society, Second Series* (Blackwell 1964).
Woodhouse Diana, 'United Kingdom: The Constitutional Reform Act 2005—Defending Judicial Independence the English Way' (2007) 5(1) International Journal of Constitutional Law 153.
Xenofontos Stefanos, 'The End of the Interlaken Process: A (Yet Another) Missed Opportunity to Guarantee the Long-Term Future of the ECtHR' (*Strasbourg Observers*, 29 April 2020) <https://strasbourgobservers.com> accessed 30 June 2024.
Young Alison L, *Democratic Dialogue and the Constitution* (Oxford University Press 2017).
Zarbiyev Fuad, 'Judicial Activism in International Law—A Conceptual Framework for Analysis' (2012) 3(2) Journal of International Dispute Settlement 247.
Zglinski Jan, 'Doing Too Little or Too Much? Private Law Before the European Court of Human Rights' (2018) 37 Yearbook of European Law 98.

Index

For the benefit of digital users, indexed terms that span two pages (e.g., 52–53) may, on occasion, appear on only one of those pages.

D

F

G

H

T